The ULTIMATE ENCYCLOPEDIA OF MUSICAL INSTRUMENTS

THIS IS A CARLTON BOOK

Text and Design © 1996 Carlton Books Limited

First published in 1996 by Carlton Books Limited

10 9 8 7 6 5 4 3 2 1

A CIP catalogue for this book is available from the British Library

ISBN 1 85868 185 5

PROJECT EDITOR: Tessa Rose
ART DIRECTION: Zoë Maggs
DESIGN: Alyson Kyles and Zoë Maggs
PICTURE RESEARCH: Maja Mihajlovic
PRODUCTION: Garry Lewis

Printed and bound in Dubai

Carlton Books Limited
20 St Anne's Court, Wardour Street
London W1V 3AW

PICTURE CREDITS

The publisher would like to thank the following for their kind permission to reproduce the photographs and illustrations in this book:

Ancient Art and Architecture Collection 184(r); AKG London 15, 16, 17(t), 18, 25, 31, 35(t), 44(b), 48, 49, 50, 55(box), 56, 71, 73(t), 79, 86, 89(bl), 92(bl), 95(bl), 106(tr), 115(t), 128, 129, 130, 134, 161, 162, 163, 164, 168, 185, 186(tl & tr), 195(box), 198(tl), 199, 205, 206(tl), 217(t), 223(tl); Arbiter London/Fender, Scottsdale, Arizona 83; Bösendorfer/Stefan Jakubowski 120(b); Bridgeman Art Library 38(t), (Museo Dell'Opera Del Duomo, Florence) 88(bl), 158; Camera Press 152; Catgut Acoustical Society 87; Jean-Loup Charmet 5, 20(t), 74, 85, 186(br), 196(t), 210(t & b); Christies Images 24(r), 54(b), 57, 63, 60(bl); Bruce Coleman Picture Library 172, 177; Corbis/Bettmann 8(b), 11, 33, 45, 47, 60(tr), 72(bl), 75, 84, 124, 130(box), 133, 138, 144, 149, 175, 178, 179, 182, 184(l), 189(br), 191(br & tl), 217(b), 218, 221, 225, 226(t); Finchcocks Collection, Goudhurst, Kent 115(b), 116(b), 118, 120(t), 121, 123; Werner Forman Archive 214, 231; The Hanover Band 176; Michael Holford Photographs 12, 13, 230(br); Hulton Getty 10, 23, 44(tr), 52(box), 53, 77, 78(br), 92(cr), 96(tr), 98(cr), 101(tl), 103(tl), 106(bl), 110(bl), 116(t), 119, 125, 132, 139, 143(tr), 146(b), 155, 157, 169, 200, 202(l), 211(b), 215, 216, 220(tr), 226(b), (Auerbach) 64, 67, 81(t),166;

The Hutchison Library 193(tl); IMG artists 105(br); The Lebrecht Collection 14, 19(tr), 37, 58, 59(tl), 65, 66, 76, 105(tl), 135(box), 142, 145, 146(t), 147, 148(box), 150, 167, 174, 195(tl), (Betty Freeman) 108(cr), 151, (Nigel Luckhurst) 91(tl), 165, (Suzi Maeder) 34(b), 40, (W Suschitzky) 160; London Features International 98(bc), 107(bl), 154, 156; Mary Evans Picture Library 9, 17(box), 46, 54(l), 80(l), 100(bc); 170, 173, 111(br), 117(b), 140, 194, 228, 198(b), 202(r), 204, 207(b), 208(tr), 209, 212, 213(bl), 230(t); Maureen Gavin Picture Library 20(b), 51(tl), 229(tr & l); Mirror Syndication International 97(tl); National Trust Photographic Library 62, 112, 114; Performing Arts Library (Clive Barda) 30, 70, (Steve Gillett) 190, (J McCormick) 42; Pictorial Press 28; Popperfoto 82, 99(tc), 113, 136, 197, 201(tr), 218; Premier Percussion Ltd 94(bl), 104(br); Scala 6; Science & Society Picture Library 143(b); Steinway & Sons 126-127; University of Edinburgh, Collection of Historic Musical Instruments 36, 39(b), 78(l), 81(b), 96(bl), 108(bl), 189(c), 192; Yamaha 19(tl), 22, 27, 32, 41(b), 102(bl), 122, 126(tl), 127(b), 153.

All other images are from *Antique Musical Instruments & Their Players*, Bonanni (Dover), and *Music – A Pictorial Archive* (Dover)

The ULTIMATE

ENCYCLOPEDIA OF

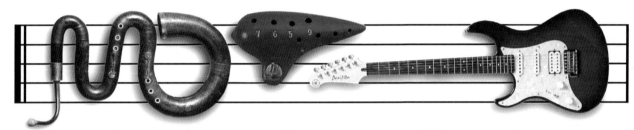

MUSICAL

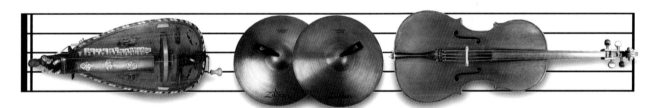

INSTRUMENTS

General Editor: ROBERT DEARLING

CARLTON

♪CONTENTS

Preface

BETWEEN 1953 AND 1957 the Swedish composer Lars-Erik Larsson wrote 12 *Concertini*, one for each orchestral instrument: flute, oboe, clarinet, bassoon, horn, trumpet, trombone, violin, viola, cello, double bass and piano. Charming works, they display the essential nature and capabilities of each instrument. What Larsson did in sound this encyclopedia tries to achieve in words.

Every instrument has its own special quality. Different makes or traditions, or indeed techniques of individual players, give instruments, whatever their type, a distinctive character or sound.

It is these similarities and differences that we have attempted to explain in clear, unambiguous language. However, we have gone further. Instruments have been set in their historical contexts, and have been fitted into that complicated jig-saw we call an orchestra.

In the largest orchestra ever assembled, 42 different types of modern instrument were required, plus four soloists and three choirs (see page 165). The composer of the work for which this orchestra was required, Havergal Brian, even introduced an African log drum to add an exotic touch. Completed in 1927, this 'Gothic' Symphony had to wait 34 years before its instrumental requirements could be met, but even then the impressive line-up represented a mere fraction of the different instruments the world has seen.

Many instruments are obsolete, such as the lute and the clavichord, though with the modern trend towards authenticity in performing early

music, 'obsolescent' should perhaps replace 'obsolete'. Others are folk instruments. Bagpipes and accordion are still with us, but would fit poorly into an orchestra. Others still, numbering possibly thousands, are heard only in remote areas or have been superseded by later and better models.

This encyclopedia suggests how music began and then takes each group of instruments, dissects it member by member, as did Benjamin Britten in *The Young Person's Guide to the Orchestra* (a superb guide for people of any age), and describes what makes that instrument sound the way it does. We begin with the familiar orchestral instruments, move on to keyboards and electronics and then, in the section entitled Ensembles, show the various ways in which instruments have been 'introduced' to one another. Authenticity, a buzz-word for the last two decades, ends our discussion of the instruments most closely associated with music making in the Western world. The book as a whole is rounded off by an exploration of the fascinating area inhabited by instruments of non-Western origin and ancient or obsolete Western types. The decision was taken not to call this section Ethnic Instruments – every instrument is ethnic in that it belongs to a distinct social or cultural group. Some duplication between sections has been introduced to make clear certain relationships that exist between types of instruments.

Many sources and individuals have contributed to the preparation of this encyclopedia and, where necessary, original and practical research has been undertaken. Tribute is due to my co-authors for their patience in assembling facts, their skill in setting them down, and their understanding when it was necessary to re-check certain details. Finally, a thank-you to all those at Carlton Books for their efforts in bringing this encyclopedia to publication, in particular to the ever-patient, wise and tactful Project Editor, Tessa Rose.

ROBERT DEARLING, JUNE 1996

THE Contributors

ROBERT DEARLING has been listening to music for 50 years, researching it for 40 and writing about it for 35. His books include *The Guinness Book of Music, The Guinness Book of Recorded Sound*, and *Mozart - The Symphonies*. He has also contributed to, among others, *The Ultimate Encyclopedia of Music* (Carlton Books). His special studies include the 18th-century symphony, authentic performance, and the history of musical instruments.

ATES ORGA is a writer and independent record producer and winner of a Royal Philharmonic Society Music Award for his 1993 Wigmore Hall concert series 'Piano Masterworks'. He was for 15 years a lecturer in music and concert director at the University of Surrey in Guildford. A regular contributor to the *BBC Music Magazine* and *Classic CD*, he is also author of biographies of Beethoven and Chopin.

PHILIP SLORICK studied piano from an early age, later switching to oboe and voice. Composition studies at Durham University with John Caskin and Roger Redgate were followed by oboe studies with Robin Canter and Jonathan Small, and woodwind chamber performance with Timothy Reynish and Nicolas Ingamells. In 1991 Philip joined the Royal Liverpool Philharmonic Orchestra as publications editor, which entailed writing and commissioning articles and programme notes. In addition to his current work for the Hallé Concerts Society, he remains active as an oboist and a freelance writer.

RODERICK SWANSTON is a Fellow and Principal Lecturer at the Royal College of Music in London where he teaches analysis, theory and the history of music. He is a regular broadcaster, principally on BBC Radio 3, and a contributor to major music magazines. Since 1993 he has been visiting professor at Dartmouth College, New Hampshire.

GEOFFREY THOMASON read music at Manchester University, graduating with degrees of Mus. B and Mus. M. He combines the roles of music librarian (Royal Northern College of Music) and freelance music journalist, having written copious amounts of programme notes and contributing articles to *The Musical Times, Early Music, Brio, Journal of British Music, Music Teacher* and, from 1989 to 1994, *The Guardian* newspaper as music critic. An occasional composer, his arrangements have been broadcast by BBC Radio.

BRIAN WRIGHT won second prize in the Guido Cantelli conducting competition at La Scala, Milan, was assistant to André Previn and the LSO and spent ten years with the BBC, conducting all the BBC orchestras. In addition, he has conducted the LSO, RPO, LPO, Philharmonia and ECO and has appeared as a guest conductor in Europe and North America. He has recorded for EMI in the UK, and for the Crystal label in America. He is a regular contributor to the major music magazines and a broadcaster on BBC Radio 3.

HOW
Music Began

THE EARLIEST MUSIC evaporated into the air, undocumented and unrecorded. Thousands of years of music is thus unknown to us. We cannot even say when it began, for music was in the world centuries before anyone invented writing; that was the Sumerians, in about 3600 BC. Neanderthal man, who disappeared from the Earth some 30,000 years before the Sumerians, may have played with noise-making instruments – it is difficult to imagine him not doing so. But homo sapiens, who replaced Neanderthal man, was superstitious. He had his deities, and would have danced round camp fires and worshipped en masse, probably to instrumental accompaniment. That he had the sensibility to appreciate some art forms is borne out by the figurines (dating from at least 30,000 BC) that have been discovered across Europe, and by the famous cave paintings in south-west France and north-east Spain which appeared by 16,000 BC. Even earlier, a pictorial representation of what might be a musician existed in the caves of Les Trois-Frères.

The first music was undoubtedly vocal. By shouting to one another, men would automatically alter the pitch of their tone to convey different meanings. This would not have been classed as 'music', but when this shouting occurred within the walls of a ravine or against the foot of cliffs, the echo it produced would have intrigued the shouters. They would have repeated their shouts just for the sake of hearing the mysterious answers, and different notes would have been invented for the fun of it. Shouting and chanting during festive dances to celebrate success in the hunt would inevitably have resulted in a predictable rhythm being created by clapping, stamping and slapping parts of the body. Obtuse would have been the man sitting by a log who could have resisted beating out an accompanying rhythm on the log with a stick. In turn, he would have been imitated by the clashing of spears and clubs. He, perhaps, was our first musician; the log, perhaps, our first musical instrument.

These men would have made their music out of everyday objects. Probably by accident, a rock would be hit by a club and produce an unexpected ringing tone which would then be used as a signal to warn of danger. Hollow tree trunks would fulfil the same requirement. In the hunt, men would need to keep account of the whereabouts of the rest of the tribe and would signal their positions by blowing on a conch shell, its sound carrying much further than would a shout. Perhaps a system of rhythmic signals was devised to indicate the location of prey or the direction the hunt was taking – two blasts for 'left', three for 'right', repeated notes for a kill, and so on. Such signals survive today, more reliant upon dif-

THE ANCIENT CONCH SHELL TRUMPET CONTINUES TO HAVE WIDE CEREMONIAL APPLICATIONS FROM MEXICO TO POLYNESIA.

sion of sounds – the first 'tune' – or grass might be used as a noise-maker when held rigid between the fingers and blown. The next step was to create instruments rather than just stumble across them. It is possible, though unprovable at this distance of time, that the step was taken when an anklet was fashioned from tiny rattles (nut shells, with the dried nuts still inside) to be worn during dance festivals. 𝄢

CAVEMEN CELEBRATING SUCCESS IN THE HUNT. THE HUNTER'S AND WARRIOR'S BOW STRING WOULD RESOUND AS THE ARROW WAS SENT ON ITS WAY.

ferent tones to convey greater subtleties perhaps, but still with origins in prehistory.

Music, if such it can be called, had a useful purpose and possibly even a warlike one, as when conch shells were blown to intimidate an enemy. Man was not always on the move, however. His prime concern, of course, was the desperate need to survive. He had to protect himself and his family from the climate, hunger,

predatory animals and marauding tribes, and what time was left in each day had to go towards improving his comfort. Even so, he found time for art. The figurines mentioned above may have fulfilled a ritual purpose, as the cave paintings probably related to the desire for successful hunting, but some have a grace and delicacy of line that suggest an appreciation of beauty.

In their primitive shelters, sometimes their movement restricted by weather conditions or long winter nights, they would amuse themselves by putting objects to a use for which they were not designed. Stones and rocks within a cave might be hit in a given order to make a succes-

THE EARLIEST *Instruments*

STONE GONG: a boulder or 'hanging stone' which, when struck, gives off a ringing sound. Oriental and African cultures still use stone as a sound-producer.

TREE STUMP: in certain conditions a hollow tree stump struck with a club would yield a tone.

BRANCHES: the branches of some trees, when flexed and released, will 'twang'. There is a report of a Siberian bear doing this for its own amusement.

GRASS: a blade of grass stretched between fingers or thumbs will emit a high-pitched squeal when blown. This is the origin of the reed principle in woodwind instruments.

CONCH SHELL: often empty when found on a beach, a shell with a broken tip would produce a loud sound when blown. The conch shell trumpet is still found in use today among some primitive peoples.

REEDS: in certain circumstances, reeds and grasses give off a hum when wind blows through them. This is the basis of the Aeolian harp.

BAMBOO: hollow or split bamboo canes will sometimes produce a series of tones in a breeze. The Aeolian organ was thus invented by nature.

THE MAKING OF
Instruments

LONG WINTER NIGHTS spent sitting round a fire in a cave would have been intolerably boring if men had not amused themselves by playing with the objects all about them. Survival may have been of prime interest to them, but with the security of the family and the tribe not in jeopardy there would have been time for experimentation. A cooking pot, gently tapped with a stick, would give off a pleasant sound, and much hilarity would be occasioned as the tone was changed by the addition, then subtraction, of liquid in the pot. Discarded animal skins lay all about. Some would be used as clothing but had to be dried out, a process aided by beating. If the skin was taut it would give a note when beaten. Our experimenting man would have fastened a fragment of skin across the top of the pot and hit it with a stick or drummed on it with his fingers. The first drum had been invented.

A hunting bow string would be plucked to yield a note, and if another string were attached at different points on the bow, a new note was created. The first bow harp had been made. Countless variations suggested themselves to those early experimenters: several strings to the

bow; a pot or gourd attached to the bow to amplify the sound, perhaps a modification accidentally discovered when the end of a bow was stood on a pot; the string struck with a stick to make a string drum; the joining of two bows with a transverse stick at the top, with strings running to the stick, making a lyre, and so on. One particularly sophisticated experiment involved application of a resin, exuded from a tree trunk, applied to a bow string, this string then rubbed crossways on another bow string. The scratchy sound would have needed much experimentation, but eventually a smooth vibrating sound would emerge from this earliest viol.

℅ Music and Magic

After a meal, a straight leg bone might be prepared as a flute. With marrow removed and holes cut at intervals along its length, sounds would emerge when the instrument was blown. This led to the recorder family. Later, one or two reeds were fitted into the recorder's mouthpiece, giving rise to the oboe family, the reeds perhaps being tough grass or slivers of wood found lying on the cave floor. Other experimentation led to the flute, played cross-ways rather than straight out from the mouth.

Gradually, these early musical instruments spread, and with their fame came a certain respect, even fear, for their makers. Magic powers were believed to reside in the instruments, for most members of the tribe, familiar only with thigh-slapping, stamping and log-banging as accompaniments to their dancing rituals, would find the creation of noises from devices they did not understand deeply disturbing. Players of

MAGIC AND SUPERSTITION WERE DECISIVE FACTORS IN THE DEVELOPMENT OF MUSIC AND IN TRIBAL DISCIPLINE. WITCH DOCTORS IN NEW GUINEA STILL FULFIL THESE FUNCTIONS.

instruments, too, became mysterious and objects of fear and veneration, and they would not have been human if they had not played on this fear to increase their personal power. Thus, music and magic became inextricably entangled.

Musician-magicians wearing hideous masks and head dresses, would shake gourd rattles, rub serrated wooden sticks together and, most frightening of all because inexplicably it produced a 'sound out of nothing', whirl bull-roarers round their heads to cow 'lower' members of the tribe. Witch-doctors and chiefs became the main disseminators of music, albeit music to be feared rather than enjoyed. All these instruments – gourd rattles, scrapers and bull-roarers – have been found in late Paleolithic deposits (made some 30,000 years ago) in Europe.

Later, voice-disguisers were used to scare the tribe. A wooden trumpet protruding from a mask and acting as a megaphone would give out orders and cast spells, the witch-doctor's voice grotesquely distorted into something regarded as supernatural. Sometimes a friction drum would be used, its harsh grating sound designed yet again to induce fear. But not all 'music' was fearful. The bow, much reduced in size and applied to the mouth, was more of a toy than a serious instrument, and from this came later developments during the Iron Age, such as the Jew's harp. The various early harps were also enjoyed as friendly family entertainment, and probably accompanied long verbal sagas of tribal historical events. ⑬

LEFT: A GOURD RATTLE, ITS HUMANOID MASK-LIKE FACE FASHIONED TO MAKE THE TRIBE BELIEVE IT POSSESSES A SOUL OF ITS OWN.

PRE-CHRISTIAN
Instruments

ONCE THE HABIT of making instruments, rather than finding them, became widespread there was an explosion of activity outwards from the centres in the Middle East and Europe. Again, firm dates cannot be established because records were not kept; neither can an exact chronology be suggested. But it is clear that experimentation became the order of the era.

Drummers, once satisfied with a single tone when stick hit log, sought to widen their repertoire. One way was to hollow out a log through a longitudinal slit and leave the two lips of the slit with different thicknesses of wood and different widths of inner overhang. Each lip would then give a distinct note. (Examples of the slit drum will be found under Non-Western Instruments: Banged.) By varying the thickness of each lip along the drum's length, several notes could be obtained. Because drums are relatively easy to make, dozens of different types soon emerged, some with membranes, some without. A few of the shapes are shown under Percussion (see pages 88–104), but primitive drums varied far more widely than these standard shapes.

Adventurous instrument makers would shun the lowly hunter's bow and make a purpose-built stringed instrument with a gourd resonator permanently attached. The spike fiddle is a fairly basic design (see page 199), as are early harps, but lyres and lutes soon reached improved levels of sophistication as man became aware of the importance of pitch. In singing, uncontrolled ululation had yielded to a vocalization in which rudimentary scales and the satisfying relation of one note to another were realized, so instruments had to play 'in tune' with the singers if they were to be accepted.

Similar rules applied to blown instruments. Random drilling of finger holes in a bone or wooden flute soon proved ineffective. They had to be drilled at certain points and of a certain diameter if the instrument were to be successful. It is possible that an important factor was the

A WALL PAINTING IN THE TOMB OF NEBAMUN, THEBES, SHOWING MUSICIANS WITH LUTES, 1400 BC.

need to imitate bird song correctly, for if a bird lure did not faithfully mimic the song of its intended victim it would fail. And it was all well and good to blow loud rasps through an animal horn, but by shaping the mouthpiece in a certain way to accommodate the lips effectively, more controlled sounds would result.

By 3000 BC at the latest instrument making had evolved from being a pastime into a disciplined craft. Soon it would be an art.

Having established a wide range of instruments it is only natural that man would wish to combine their sounds in some kind of group. Most obvious would have been a 'melody instrument' of some kind, probably a pipe, with a rhythmic accompaniment. As in much jazz, the

A LYRE PLAYER DEPICTED ON THE STANDARD OF UR (SUMERIA), C. 2600 BC: IN FRONT A ROYAL OFFICIAL, BEHIND A FEMALE SINGER.

lead would have been taken by the 'rhythm section' (a man hitting a log) and the piper would have adopted his rhythm. Simple enough, but each would have had to listen to the other.

Add more instruments and confusion threatened. Some control became vital. A leader would be elected, or elect himself, to direct the performance. He would have dictated rhythm and tempo (modern concepts yet to be fully comprehended) and suppressed an instrumentalist if he considered his playing too loud or otherwise unsatisfactory. How he did this is not clear, but stamping, arm waving, facial signals and threats were doubtless involved. Thus, these early leaders created order out of potential chaos, as do conductors today.

Concrete evidence of instruments of c.3000 BC comes from Sumerian drawings and remains. The Sumerians had bow harps, lyres, drums and clappers, and possibly flutes. Sophisticated lutes came later. Egypt knew the flute by that date and, shortly afterwards, *aulos*, harp, lyre, *sistrum* and other percussion. Tutankhamun's trumpets (one bronze, the other silver) date from c.1300 BC. 𝄢

OLD-WORLD (c.3000BC) *Instruments* ℅

BLOW: bone and wooden flutes (side-blown and end-blown), gourd flute (ancestor of the *ocarina*), recorder (end-blown), whistle, bird lure, panpipes, single- and double-reed pipes (ancestors of the clarinet and oboe families); animal-horn trumpet and horn, from about 20cm (8 inches) to the length of an elephant tusk; metal trumpet.

PLUCK: harp, lute, lyre; bamboo *zither* (formed by separating outer fibres and inserting bridges); mouth harp (many varieties, leading to the Jew's harp); string drum (might also be beaten); thumb piano (springy metal tongues in a resonator).

SCRAPE: friction drum (a pulled cord running from a membrane); wooden scraper with serrated edge; rattle (with wood or metal tongues flexed against a rotating cog); ?fiddle.

BANG: drums, with or without membranes; xylophone (wooden slats over a frame or pit); stamping tube (bamboo, or similar, bounced endways); ground 'harp' (wooden boards over a pit, struck with beaters or dancing feet; also beaten cords across a pit); mouth bow (a short bow, held endways in the mouth and struck with a stick); bells (wood, metal, with clapper or struck with beater); *maracas* (small wooden dish-shaped objects clashed together).

WHIRL: bull-roarer

SHAKE: rattles (open, with loose objects striking a frame or shaken freely; or closed, with hard objects inside a gourd, drum, pot, etc.); *sistrum* (early Egyptian 'Y'-shaped frame with captive metal or wood discs on wires).

Instruments AND Society

ACCORDING TO THE BIBLE (Daniel 3: 5, 7, 10, 15), Nebuchadnezzar owned an orchestra in Babylon in the 6th century BC. It consisted of "horn, pipe, lyre, trigon, harp, bagpipe, and every kind of music". The details of this ensemble, written down in Aramaic four centuries later and then translated into obsolete English, cannot be taken literally. However, this reference does illustrate two important points. First, the 18th-century custom of noble and royal courts supporting an orchestra has an ancient precedent; secondly, the existence of an orchestra so long ago was remarkable enough to be noted and the note handed down to a much later scribe.

Musicologist Curt Sachs gave a new interpretation of this Aramaic text in *The History of Musical Instruments* (1942). He suggested that, rather than enumerating the composition of an orchestra, the text gave a description of a performance: "a horn signal, followed by solos of oboe, lyre and harp, and a full ensemble of these and some rhythmical instruments." – see panel.

The Greek theorist Aristoxenus (fl 375–360 BC), working on Pythagoras's tuning system of two centuries earlier, helped to establish tuning principles. These encouraged makers to build better instruments. The bards, poets and singers found throughout Europe from before Christ were among the chief beneficiaries. Their favoured instrument, the lyre, was made versatile and melodic as a consequence of these sophisticated 'tuning systems', which enabled the instrument to be played at the same time as a spoken or sung narration.

In the Christian era advances in instrumental design continued to be made, and the use of instruments became more widespread. People became accustomed to them as part of their daily lives, for both pleasure and utilitarian purposes. Pipers, lute players and fiddlers would frequent taverns and inns in the hope of receiving a copper or two 'to wet the whistle' (though pedants may aver that 'whistle' in this context was Saxon *hwistle*, from Latin *fistula* = 'windpipe', the Latin word also means pipe in the wider, musical, sense). Pipers would busk in the streets for the same purpose.

A civic vacuum was created by the departure of the Romans from their European colonies during the fifth century. The realization that security was needed for their towns moved local committees of elders to set up a system of criers. The task of these men would be to warn of fire, flood or attack. Equipped with bells, horns and whistles they would patrol town streets at night, marking the time with the bell and sounding their wind instruments in the event of an impending threat. The use of sounds to warn of danger has been with us since time immemorial. Bells had been used by lepers to warn others of their approach. In our own century whistles have been used to raise the alarm or warn of attack, and church bells would have been rung in the event of a German invasion of Britain during World War II. In earlier centuries, posthorns sounded a happier arrival, that of the mail coach.

As civilization developed in post-Roman Europe, instruments accompanied civic occasions such as parades and proclamations. Street vendors would advertise their wares with shouts and also sometimes with instruments: in a busy market place the loudest noise secures the greatest attention. Military camps possibly used instrumental calls at reveille; this became a regular procedure after the return from the Crusades of soldiers who had encountered such practices in the Middle East. Marching to the sound of a drum to keep in step had been learnt from the Romans, however. Trumpets would announce officers' orders during battle; trumpets and drums remain the mainstay of military bands.

Some religions and cults forbade instrumental music in church, considering the playing of instruments a frivolous activity unsuited to sacred buildings. Others embraced it as a welcome enrichment to the singing of chants; sometimes also as contrast in the interludes between hymns and sermons. The deep, sonorous voice of the sackbut was particularly effective. The organ, too, still hand-pumped, was an almost inevitable fixture: it gave an even greater feeling of solemn splendour as well as reminding the choir of the opening phrase of the next hymn.

Domestic music-making was more common in the 8th century than it is today, for there were fewer distractions. Cheap or home-made stringed instruments, drums and pipes were found in the majority of homes. In the open air, pagan fertility festivals were danced to instrumental accompaniment, and at wild boar and wolf hunts the sound of primitive horns and trumpets would have been heard. 𝄡

Nebuchadnezzar's Orchestra

6TH CENTURY BC

℁

ORIGINAL NAME (PHONETIC)	ACCEPTED TRANSLATION (RV)	CURT SACHS' INTERPRETATION
quarna	horn	horn or trumpet (cf Latin cornu= horn
masroquita	pipe	pipe (from verb sriquá=to whistle; cf Middle English scritch= screech, shriek
qatros	lyre	lyre (cf Greek kithara)
sabka	trigon	horizontal angle harp. The word sabka also meant a naval war machine, a boat with a vertical ladder at one end. The instrument's tuning pegs would have suggested ladder rungs, and strings stretching from 'mast' to 'deck' would have completed the triangle suggested in trigon.
psantrin	harp	vertical angle harp (cf Greek psalterion).
sumponiah	bagpipe	a 'sounding together' (Greek symphonia). The word symphonia meaning bagpipe, arose much later, and the same word meaning hurdy-gurdy comes from 12th-century France.
zmara	every kind of music	ensemble, plus rhythm and percussion music.

𝄞 A TEUTONIC WARRIOR WITH A *LUR* (WAR TRUMPET); FROM THE SARCOPHAGUS OF EMPEROR HOSTILIANUS, DIED 251 AD.

DISSEMINATION AND
Experimentation

BY THE 11TH CENTURY instrumental developments in China, India and probably the yet to be explored continent of Africa, were more varied than those in the West. The Americas were limited to wind and percussion until the Iberians introduced the guitar family there. Europe was emerging from the Dark Ages and experiencing a flowering of vocal music. In France, Germany, England and northern Italy from around 1100, the Goliards travelled from town to town, court to court, singing to their own accompaniment on harps and veilles, transportable instruments of light tone against which they sang their poems of secular delights. Carl Orff raided these poems, which he dressed in his own brilliant orchestral colours, for his *Carmina Burana* (1937).

In southern France from c.1100 to c.1300 the troubadours (from *trouver*, to find or invent, because they travelled the land finding folk tales and melodies and inventing their own brands of both) also played such instruments, plus pipes, hurdy-gurdys and drums. The *trouvères* (from c.1137 to c.1400) were, like the troubadours, high-born and well-educated – some, indeed, were reigning princes. They ranged more widely over France and other areas of north-west Europe.

German poets also took up the life of wandering minstrels, singing to their own accompaniment. The Minnesingers (from c.1180 to c.1500), and the Mastersingers (from 1311 to the 17th century), all spread jollity with their bawdy and witty songs, carrying with them every portable instrument available. At the courts they would have met up with resident musicians who would have joined in the merry-making. Many of the poems survive; rather fewer of the melodies. No instrumental directions were written down, so we have to rely upon clues as to what music accompanied the voices. A great deal may be gleaned from the types of instruments available in those days, and modern revivers of such music would do well to study these and include as many of them as possible. The medieval spirit was predominantly robust and it is a fair assumption that instruments would have been played with more enthusiasm than subtlety.

Although purveying primarily a vocal art,

MINNESINGERS AT THE WARTBURG SINGING CONTEST C. 1206. PRESENT WERE HEINRICH VON OFTERDINGEN, WOLFRAM VON ESCHENBACH AND WALTER VON DER VOGELWEIDE.

BERNARD DE VENTADORN, POSSIBLY THE FINEST TROUBADOUR. HE SERVED ELEANOR OF AQUITAINE, WIFE OF HENRY PLANTAGENET, AND BECAME A MONK LATE IN LIFE.

these itinerant poets were vitally important in the dissemination and popularization of instruments. By introducing them to outlying areas as well as palaces, they familiarized countless communities with their qualities and encouraged others to play and to make instruments. They also brought about far-reaching improvements in instrumental construction and design. The hard life of travelling on rough tracks would have made these poets find ways of strengthening delicate lutes; varying weather conditions would have suggested better and quicker ways of tuning; and the different moods and circumstances found at successive courts would have demanded versatility, resulting in cross-fertilization of playing techniques between different types of instrument.

With our instrumental history poised at the threshold of further important developments we may take stock. Lute, lyre, hurdy-gurdy, fife, cornett and many others were becoming obsolete. The violin family was set to displace the viols, and great improvements in wind instruments were soon to appear. The modern orchestra was being conceived. 𝄡

TRAVELLING POETS OF THE *Middle Ages*

GOLIARDS, c.1100–c.1250
HUGH PRIMAS (c.1095–1160+), whose reported deformed features may account for the mordant nature of his poems.
SERLO OF WILTON (c.1110–c.1181), an Englishman teaching in Paris who became so sickened with his own erotic poems that he became a monk.
ARCHIPOETA (c.1130–1165+), a pseudonym of a punning *goliard* from Cologne.

TROUBADOURS, c.1100–c.1300
DUKE GUILHEM IX OF AQUITAINE (1071–1127), who "was much addicted to jesting, and surpassed the innumerable pranks of the greatest clowns. He knew well how to sing and make verses and ... deceive the ladies."
BERNART DE VENTADORN (1125–1195), probably the finest poet of the troubadours. Some of his poems were adopted by Minnesingers.
GUIRAUT DE BORNEIL(L) (c.1140–c.1200), called *maistre dels trobadors*.
COUNT RAIMBAUT III OF ORANGE (c.1144–1173), consort of Countess Beatriz.
COUNTESS BEATRIZ OF DIA (late 12th century), the only woman troubadour to have a complete song preserved.
GUIRAUT RIQUIER (c.1230–c.1294), a morose character whose playing and singing gave a deceptively joyful impression.

TROUVERES, c.1137– c.1400
BLONDEL DE NESLE (c.1155/60– ?), from northern France, whose melodies show the influence of Gregorian chant.
COLIN MUSET (fl. 1200–1250), a *jongleur*, or juggler, whose manual dexterity doubtless extended to the playing of instruments.
ADAM DE LA HALE (c.1250–c.1288?), 'The Hunchback of Arras', composer of the dramatic pastoral *Le jeu de Robin et Marion*.

Despite this, and the similarity of name, there is no evidence to link him with Alan a'Dale, minstrel of the Robin Hood stories first noted in c.1377.

MINNESINGERS, c.1180–c.1500+
DER VON KÜRENBERG (c.1160– ?), an Austrian nobleman.
WALTER VON DER VOGELWEIDE (c1170–c1230), regarded as the most outstanding and influential of the Minnesingers.
GOTTFRIED VON STRASSBURG (fl. 1200–1210), whose epics *Tristan* and *Parzifal* provided Wagner with operatic subjects.
DER TANNHÄUSER (c.1200–c.1270), whose songs tell of his (probably imaginary) exploits as a soldier and crusader. Wagner borrowed him, too.
HEINRICH VON MEISSEN (1250–1318), a clever and virtuosic artist who is regarded by some as the first Mastersinger.

MASTERSINGERS, 1311–17th century
HEINRICH VON MÜGELN (died c.1369+), a poet active in Prague, Buda (Hungary) and Vienna.
HANS FOLZ (c.1435–1513), a barber and surgeon whose poetry was admired by Hans Sachs.
HANS SACHS (1494–1578), a shoemaker who composed over 6000 poems. Richard Wagner immortalized him in the opera *Die Meistersinger von Nürnberg*.

A MEDIEVAL DEPICTION OF A POET-MINSTREL. MORE POEMS THAN MELODIES COMPOSED BY THESE WANDERING ARTISTS SURVIVE.

CHAPTER 1

Woodwind and Brass Instruments

THE WOODWIND AND brass are among the oldest families of instruments in the history of music, probably because of the very simple principle on which they work. In a nutshell, the player blows through a hole in the end of a tube to make the column of air inside vibrate. The actual or effective length of that vibrating column determines the pitch of the sound produced. The name 'woodwind' applies, not surprisingly, to those instruments originally and mostly still made of wood (the flute and saxophone are the obvious exceptions). Similarly, brass instruments were originally made of that material, though these days they are often made of other metals. The other principal difference between the two groups is the means used to set the column of air vibrating. In all woodwind instruments (again, except the flute) a vibrating reed is used, whereas brass players press their lips against a funnel-shaped mouthpiece and blow something akin to a raspberry down it. The usual orchestral woodwind grouping consists of flutes, oboes, clarinets and bassoons, often joined by a piccolo, cor anglais, bass clarinet and contrabassoon, and occasionally a saxophone. A typical brass section consists of French horns, trumpets, tenor and bass trombones and a tuba.

WIND INSTRUMENTS WERE AMONG THE FIRST TO BE GROUPED TOGETHER TO FORM ENSEMBLES. THIS 17TH-CENTURY PROCESSIONAL GROUP INCLUDES FORERUNNERS OF THE BASSOON, OBOE, CLARINET, TRUMPET AND TROMBONE.

FLUTE

THE EARLIEST FLUTE capable of playing a melody of more than two or three notes was discovered recently in a Slovenian cave and dates no less than 45,000 years ago. It was fashioned by a Neanderthal man from the leg bone of a young bear. Although damaged, its four finger-holes show that it was made deliberately for the purpose of making music. The musicologist Curt Sachs claimed that a 9th-century Chinese instrument called the *chi'ih* was actually the oldest transverse flute in history, and there are early depictions from the 2nd and 3rd centuries AD showing 'side-blown' instruments. But this evidence is not conclusive, and not until the 1100s was the instrument regularly illustrated in works of art.

The earliest Western European representations come from Germany, giving rise to the popular term 'German flute'. From here use of the instrument spread throughout Europe. Its common use in England is demonstrated by Henry VIII's famous inventory of instruments. In France the flute was held in very high regard. However, the flute's place among the world's most popular and accessible instruments

was not assured until the 18th century. This stabilizing of the instrument's fortunes was due to the work of the composer and flautist Johann Joachim Quantz, his pupil Frederick the Great of Prussia, himself a distinguished flautist, and later the efforts of instrument-maker Theobald Boehm.

Construction

The modern orchestral flute is made in three sections with some sixteen padded keys. Some players still prefer wooden instruments, but it is more common to see metal flutes, usually of silver or a metal alloy, but sometimes of gold and

ORIGINALLY MADE OF WOOD, THE FLUTE IS MORE FAMILIAR AS A METAL INSTRUMENT TODAY.

TYPES OF Flute

PICCOLO Half the size of the standard flute, and pitched one octave higher (though it is a transposing instrument, its music being written an octave lower than it sounds). It is fingered the same as the concert flute, with almost the same compass, though its lowest note is usually d". The piccolo came into orchestral use about 1800. Beethoven, in his Fifth Symphony, was one of the first composer's to use it.

TREBLE FLUTE IN G Pitched a 5th above the concert flute, this fills the gap between that and the piccolo. It was introduced in about 1950 to replace the obsolete band flute in B flat.

CONCERT FLUTE IN C The standard modern orchestral flute.

ALTO FLUTE IN G Simply a larger version of the concert flute (but pitched a 4th lower, in G), and with a compass from g to c'''. It has sometimes also been called the 'bass' flute, and has been used in music by Stravinsky (*The Rite of Spring*) and Ravel (*Daphnis and Chloe*).

BASS FLUTE Pitched in C, sounding an octave lower than the concert flute. It is characterized by a double-U head joint, and is held like an ordinary flute but often with a support that allows the player to carry most of the instrument's weight on the right leg.

JACQUES HOTTETERRE, SON OF JEAN, WAS A FLAUTIST AT THE COURT OF LOUIS XIV AND LOUIS XV OF FRANCE.

𝄞 IN ITS TRANSITION FROM A SIMPLE WOODEN INSTRUMENT, THE TRANSVERSE FLUTE SOON ACQUIRED SOME QUITE COMPLEX KEYWORK.

occasionally even platinum. Though the form of the modern flute is developed from Boehm's design of around 1847, the instrument as we know it had its beginnings before 1500 when it was a simple cylindrical tube with six finger-holes and a blow-hole or 'embouchure'. The three members of the flute family from this time (bass, alto or tenor and descant sizes have been identifed) had wider bores than the narrow contemporary fifes, giving a mellow tone well suited to consort music. By about 1650 the skilled hands of the celebrated French instrument maker Jean Hotteterre had begun to transform the flute. Intonation had always been a problem, to the extent that composers such as Martin Agricola recommended buying sets of instruments together to avoid too many discrepancies in tuning. Hotteterre's conically-bored instruments began to address that problem with the first real measure of success. His flutes were constructed in three sections, allowing small adjustments to the length to be made where the sections met. During the 18th cen-

tury experimentation continued with instruments in four sections, three-joint examples with a tuning slide, and new finger-holes and keywork, so that by 1800 there was an abundance of different models of flute available.

℁ *The Boehm Flute*

In 1831 the German goldsmith, jeweller and flautist Theobald Boehm was visiting London where he heard the playing of one Charles

Nicholson junior. The design of Nicholson's flute, a father and son collaboration, featured larger finger-holes than Boehm had seen before, affording a stronger and more stable sound. Recognizing the advantages of the design, Boehm began work straight away and by 1843 his new flute, complete with a largely cylindrical bore and more elaborate keywork, was in production in Paris and London. The definitive Boehm flute appeared in 1847. Its larger finger-holes were placed according to best acoustical principles and did not sit comfortably under the player's fingers, so Boehm developed a new system of keys and levers to aid performance. Many players were deterred by the fact that this mechanism demanded a new system of fingering, and some tried to develop their own flutes based on earlier instruments. However, it is the Boehm flute that enjoys almost universal favour today.

℁ *In Performance*

It was not until the late 17th and early 18th centuries that composers began to respond seriously to the flute's popularity, though some early music does exist, including two sets of

𝄞 THEOBALD BOEHM. THE FLUTE HE PRODUCED IN 1847 INCORPORATED PRINCIPLES THAT HAVE CONTINUED TO INFLUENCE DESIGN TO THIS DAY.

chansons issued by the French publisher Pierre Attaignant in 1533. The tendency of composers before 1600 not to write with specific instruments in mind and the overwhelming popularity of stringed instruments, especially the violin, during the rise of the Baroque style in the 17th century, meant that it was not until Lully first called for the transverse flute in his ballet *The Triumph of Love* in 1681 that the instrument began to find favour. Bach and Handel frequently used the flute as an *obbligato* instrument, but the first published music of any sort for solo flute was Michel de la Barre's collection of 1702, predictably titled *Pieces for Transverse Flute with Basso Continuo*. Spurred on by the sudden vogue for the flute, several virtuoso players began to make a name for themselves. These included Johann Christoph Denner (also an instrument maker who laid the foundations for the clarinet), Quantz and Mozart's favourite flautist Johann Wendling, the principal player in the Mannheim Court Orchestra during the 1770s.

During the 19th century the flute fell out of fashion. Beethoven and Schubert contributed minor works, including the Serenade, Op. 25 (1801), and the Introduction and Variations, D802 (1824), respectively, but otherwise the flute repertory consisted of lightweight salon or chamber music. It was the French who came to the flute's rescue around the turn of the 20th century when composers like Debussy and Ravel moved away from the grand late Romantic style in favour of more delicate tonal colourings. Debussy included an important flute melody in his orchestral *Prélude à l'après-midi d'un faune* (1892–4) and in 1912 wrote his famous *Syrinx* for solo flute. Many 20th-century composers have since written for the flute, including Luciano Berio, John Cage and Pierre Boulez who have written for some of the century's many virtuoso performers. Among them, of course, is the man almost universally credited with the flute's popularity today, the Irish virtuoso James Galway.

Flute Concertos

VIVALDI Antonio Vivaldi played a seminal part in the development of the concerto, establishing both the prominence of the solo part and a standard three-movement construction. He composed about eighteen flute concertos, though the true designation of some of them has caused debate, for his early publishers tended not to discriminate between those written for flute and those for recorder. Two of the most popular of the eighteen number among those works to which Vivaldi gave a descriptive title: *Il Gardellino* ('The Goldfinch') in D, RV428, and *La tempesta di mare* ('The Stormy Sea') in F, RV433. Both are, in fact, arrangements of earlier works and were probably performed at the Venetian orphanage for girls where Vivaldi worked for much of his career.

QUANTZ The contribution of Quantz to the flute repertory is made remarkable by the sheer volume of his output. Of over 300 concertos, some 277 are known to have been written for Quantz's most celebrated employer and pupil, Frederick the Great. The concertos commonly adhere to the standard three-movement fast-slow-fast form established by Vivaldi and were performed by Frederick, in strict numerical order, at daily court concerts conducted by the composer. Particularly noteworthy are Quantz's delightful long-breathed slow melodies, in which Frederick took special pleasure.

MOZART Mozart's two concertos for flute (K313 and K314) and that for flute and harp (K299), all dating from 1778, are among the most popular in the repertory. Whatever the truth of rumours that Mozart disliked the flute and avoided writing for it, he certainly admired fine playing. In a letter to his father in 1778, Mozart praised the Duc de Guines as one who "plays the flute incomparably". Duc de Guines, for whom Mozart wrote the Concerto for Flute and Harp, was one of two amateur flautists on whose patronage depended the very existence of the composer's major works for flute. The other was Dejean, for whom Mozart wrote the concertos K313 and 314, of which the latter (in D) is the more famous. Ironically, K314 is actually an adaptation of the Oboe Concerto in C, written a year earlier and hurriedly modified to help satisfy Dejean's commission.

IBERT Of the more recent concertos for flute, that by Jacques Ibert is often counted among the masterpieces. Dedicated to the French flautist Marcel Moyse, the work draws on the flute's most expressive qualities. It is an elegant and gracious but impassioned piece that has found a central place in today's repertory. In fact, so quickly was the concerto's value recognized that the third movement was adopted as one of the Paris Conservatoire's infamous *pièces de concours* in 1934, the same year that it was written.

𝄞OBOE

WHILE THE FLUTE and its predecessors are known to number among the world's oldest instruments, a pair of Ancient Greek silver pipes, or *auloi*, dating from around 2800 BC (see page 184), lend reed instruments respectable antiquity. The label 'reed instrument' seems only to have been coined during the Middle Ages, when conical wind instruments using a reed were given the Latin name *calamellus* from *calamus* ('a reed'). Later came the 'shawm' and eventually the French *hoboy* from *hautbois* ('high-', 'strong-' or 'loud-wood'). But the changes in name belie the fact that these were all in essence the same instrument, that which later formed the foundation of the orchestral woodwind section – the oboe. In fact, such were the geographical variations in the use of the instrument's name in the early to mid-1600s that *hautbois* variously described the smaller members of the shawm family as well as the newer instrument, even though the two existed alongside one another for some time, each with a distinct musical purpose.

It is Jean Hotteterre who is commonly credited with the invention, in the mid-1600s, of the oboe proper. Previously the player had little control over the tone of the sound produced, its harsh and rather strident quality making it ideal for outdoor ceremonies and pageants. With the refinements made by Hotteterre and others in France, the sound lost much of its coarseness, and during the 18th century the oboe gradually became fully accepted into the developing mixed ensembles for indoor performances. Into the 19th century the oboe's development became divided between makers in Germany and France, though it was in the latter of these two countries that it underwent its most radical modifications, with makers taking advantage of the rods, axles and key-rings invented by Theobald Boehm.

✻ Construction

Although a number of different models of oboe exist today, the overriding influence of the French makers remains in evidence. Constructed in three sections or 'joints' from grenadilla, rose or cocus wood, the modern oboe has the same narrow bore opening out into a slight bell at the end. It is the highest-pitched member of the double-reed family, which includes the bassoon and which is distinguished from the clarinets and saxophones by, as the name suggests, a double rather than single reed which is held in the player's mouth. Aside from slightly varying characteristics in the bodies of individual oboes, it is the reed which plays the most crucial part in determining the instrument's sound quality or *timbre*. The reed consists of a thin piece of split cane which is folded and shaped and tightly bound to a small tube or 'staple', then inserted into the top of the instrument. While the reed allows the player a great deal of control over the sound produced, that control is one of the most difficult things to master when learning to play the oboe. The reed has only the tiniest of openings at its tip, through which must be forced air at considerable pressure. Oboe players quickly develop strong stomach and cheek muscles!

In medieval instruments the reed and staple were completely enclosed within a shaped wooden block known as a pirouette. This disappeared with Jean Hotteterre's attempts to civilize the shawm during the 1650s, at which time also the instrument's bore became considerably narrower and a thumb-hole was added to the existing six finger-holes. As with the early flutes, players of the first oboes had great difficulty controlling intonation. Perhaps not surprisingly, some of the techniques for improving intonation that were tried for the flute also found their way onto the oboe, notably the supply of upper joints in different lengths, known as *corps de réchange*. Towards the end of the 18th century keywork was designed and added to the oboe by makers such as Jakob Grundmann and Carl Grenser of Dresden. In the first twenty years of the 19th century the number of keys increased to eight, providing alternative fingerings and further improvements in intonation. Then around 1825 the instruments designed by the Viennese player Josef Sellner marked a turning point by increasing the number of keys to thirteen. Sellner's oboe formed the basis of the instrument used throughout Germany during the 19th century, where it continued with very little modification.

𝄞 THE MODERN OBOE FEATURES ONE OF THE MOST COMPLEX SYSTEMS OF KEYWORK OF ANY WOODWIND INSTRUMENT.

𝄞 ONE OF THIS CENTURY'S MOST CELEBRATED OBOISTS, LEON GOOSSENS (PICTURED HERE WITH HIS SISTERS SIDONIE AND MARIE) SHOWS OFF HIS PROWESS WITH AN OBOE IN HIS RIGHT HAND AND A COR ANGLAIS IN HIS LEFT.

TYPES OF
Oboe
℅

TREBLE OR SOPRANO OBOE The
principal member of the family, pitched
in C with a compass of three octaves
from *b flat to a'''*.

OBOE D'AMORE Pitched in A, this is
the alto member of the family. It originated in Germany, and is known to have
been in existence by 1719. Bach used it in
some 60 works, beginning with the *St
John Passion*. It was obsolete for over 100
years from about 1770, until it was
revived in a modern form by Charles
Mahillon for 'authentic' Bach performances. The type has found occasional
use in 20th-century scores, including
Richard Strauss's *Sinfonia domestica*,
Debussy's *Images* and Ravel's *Boléro*. John
McCabe wrote a Concerto for Oboe
d'amore in 1972.

COR ANGLAIS ('ENGLISH HORN')
Invented in 1760 by Ferlandis of
Bergamo, this is neither English nor a
horn but the tenor member of the oboe
family. It is a transposing instrument
pitched in F, with a compass of about two
and a half octaves from e. Not much used
before the Romantic period, a number of
well-known solos have been written for it
since, including Sibelius's *The Swan of
Tuonela* and the slow movement of
Dvořák's *New World* Symphony.

BARITONE OBOE
Originated possibly in the 17th or early
18th century, this is pitched in C, sound-
ing an octave below the soprano oboe.
Today its place is often taken by the
German heckelphone for use in scores by
Richard Strauss (*Elektra* and *Salome*) and
Delius (including *Fennimore and Gerda*
and *Songs of Sunset*).

✄ The Modern Oboe

In France, meanwhile, at the crafts-men Henri Brod and Guillaume Triébert the oboe was undergoing fundamental change. Every part of the instrument was redesigned in a succession of different systems, the work of Triébert and his two sons being continued by their company foreman, François Lorée. Despite the attempts of Louis-Auguste Buffet to develop an oboe based on Boehm's revolutionary modifications to the flute, including an enlarged bore and key-holes, it is Lorée's work in developing the 'Conservatoire' model that has remained the key influence in the modern oboe. François' work was continued by his son, Adolphe, in the 20th century.

Ciufolo del Villano

XXXIX

✄ In Performance

After the early instrument's exclusive use for outdoor performances, the shawm, with its rougher tone, continued in this role, playing folk music in particular. The oboe, however, quickly found its way into the recently developed genre of opera, first appearing in Cambert's *Pomone* in 1671 (though it is sometimes claimed that Lully's ballet *L'amour malade* of 1657 marked its first appearance). It seems to have made its first public appearance in England in a masque called *Calisto* by John Crowne and Nicholas Staggins in 1675, and its first inclusion in a score by Henry Purcell was in the ode *Swifter Isis, swifter flow* in 1681. Purcell's use of the instrument until his death in 1695 is often held up as an example unmatched by his contemporaries. The composer included oboes in all his larger works and wrote at least three major *obbligato* solos for oboe, including a particularly lyrical example in his large-scale ode for the birthday of Queen Mary in 1694, *Come ye sons of art*.

Over the course of the 18th century, as the oboe gradually came to be accepted into the mixed orchestra, its role moved from simply doubling string parts to establishing an expressive and individual solo voice of its own. That very individuality has since

𝄞 EARLY KEYWORK, AS ON THIS THREE-KEYED OBOE, OFTEN ALLOWED FOR FINGERINGS USING 'FISHTAIL' KEYS.

𝄞 THE CHARACTERISTIC STRIDENCY OF THE SHAWM MADE IT PARTICULARLY WELL SUITED TO OUTDOOR PERFORMANCE AND PAGAENTRY.

𝄞 HENRY PURCELL'S REGULAR USE OF
THE OBOE OVER THE LAST 15 YEARS
OF HIS LIFE MADE HIM AN UNRIVALLED
CHAMPION OF THE INSTRUMENT.

attracted many composers to write fine solo works for the oboe, exploiting both its melancholy and lyrical qualities and its sprightly agility. There are sonatas and concertos by Handel, Vivaldi, Telemann, Giuseppe Sammartini and Bach. Later Mozart wrote his famous Concerto K314 and, probably the highlight of the Classical oboe repertory, the Quartet K370 for oboe and strings (1781) which was exceptional at the time for demanding a top *f′″* from the soloist. Today the oboist's solo repertory is extensive, including well-loved concertos by Richard Strauss, Vaughan Williams and Martinů, and works for unaccompanied oboe, such as Britten's *Six Metamorphoses after Ovid* (1951) and Berio's *Sequenza VII*, an avant-garde *tour de force* from 1969 which demands an extensive range of advanced technical skills. 𝄢

THE OBOE'S USES IN
The Orchestra
⁂

The oboe's bright, penetrating sound lends itself to successful characterization in the middle of an orchestral score. Composers have exploited its timbre for everything from evoking pastoral serenity to sheer sound effect.

BEETHOVEN: SYMPHONY NO. 6
On the first page of his manuscript for the Sixth Symphony, Beethoven noted down some observations about programmatic music (music that paints a picture): "The listener should be able to discover the situations for himself", he said, adding the cautionary note, "every kind of painting loses by being carried too far in instrumental music." Nonetheless, the 'Pastoral' Symphony, each of whose five movements bears a descriptive title, is quite explicit in transferring its pictures to music. The second movement Andante, headed 'Scene by the brook', ends with a coda which includes bird calls notated in the score as a nightingale, a quail and a cuckoo, with the part of the quail being taken very effectively by the oboe. This is followed in the third movement, 'A merry gathering of country folk', by a jaunty pastoral theme for solo oboe, accompanied by bassoon and violins, in a passage that clearly sets the scene for the peasants' merrymaking. Incidentally, Beethoven's quail is not the first use of the oboe to represent a bird. Haydn, for example, uses the instrument to represent a hen in the symphony of that name (No. 83, 1785) and the crowing cock in his oratorio *The Seasons* (1801).

BERLIOZ: *SYMPHONIE FANTASTIQUE*
Once again, it is the oboe's lyrical pastoral qualities that are exploited by the composer. Written quickly during the early months of 1830, Berlioz's 'Episode in an Artist's Life' (*Symphonie fantastique* is actually only the work's subtitle) evokes many favourite Romantic themes, including a high-society ballroom, shepherds in the fields and bachanalian devilry. The slow movement, entitled 'Scène aux champs' ('In the meadows') explores the artist's melancholy and uses a cor anglais and an off-stage oboe to represent the piping of the shepherds.

PROKOFIEV: *PETER AND THE WOLF*
Written in 1936, Prokofiev's musical entertainment for children is one of the most often-quoted examples of instruments being used directly to represent characters in a story. In this case some of those characters are animals from the forest (the bird and the wolf, for example) and some are human (including Grandfather, the hunters and, of course, Peter). Prokofiev even represents the sounds of the hunters' guns using timpani. By featuring different instruments for each character, each with its own identifiable theme, the music even educates while it entertains. In the story the duck is represented by an oboe with a rather lugubrious theme (at first in any case), which makes the most of the oboe's lyrical qualities, particularly in its lower register, while remaining tonally close to the distinctive squawk of a duck.

CLARINET

IN A WORLD OF musical instruments dominated by double reeds, the arrival of the single-reeded *chalumeau* in the late 17th century caused something of a stir. The instrument was far from flexible, having a compass of less than an octave and a half and no capacity to overblow. It did, however, precipitate the invention of the clarinet in the early 1700s.

There is some confusion as to who was responsible for 'inventing' the clarinet, largely due to uncertainty over what actually distinguishes a clarinet from a *chalumeau*. It may be that each was designed to operate in its namesake register (see below), though the instruments were such close cousins at their time of origin that attempts to draw any distinction between them are barely useful. The invention of the clarinet is commonly attributed to one Johann Christoph Denner of Nuremberg, though instruments by his son Jacob were the first to use the name 'clarinet'. It is not even clear if either of the Denners was responsible for the one innovation that could be said to constitute the 'invention' of the clarinet, namely the addition of the 'speaker key' which opens a small hole and allows the instrument to overblow at the 12th (other woodwinds overblow at the octave). The clarinet's early history certainly seems to be cursed by a dearth of reliable information which leaves theories about its birth largely unsubstantiated.

The separate registers that characterized the clarinet during the early years of its development remain a vital part of the instrument's personality today. Constructed in five parts of mouthpiece, barrel, upper joint, lower joint and bell, the modern clarinet's compass is divided into almost as many more or less distinct registers. The *chalumeau* and clarinet registers (the latter has also been labelled *clarion* or *clarino*) constitute the heart of the instrument, with the notorious break or throat register between them, and at the upper end of the compass the extreme or acute register.

✄ Improvements

As the *chalumeau* was gradually superseded by the clarinet, technical improvement became vital. The clarinet did not achieve popular appeal until the last quarter of the 18th century, by which time J. C. Denner's original two-keyed instrument had become decidedly more sophisticated. In England five-keyed clarinets made more primitive models obsolete by 1770, and on the Continent the introduction of larger tone-holes helped to create a more satisfactory *chalumeau* register. Difficulties of fingering meant that the clarinet appeared in several transposing versions, most commonly C and B flat. However, these fully-chromatic instruments still suffered shortcomings in terms of intonation and sound quality, despite attempts around 1785 to provide a more efficient tuning mechanism by separating the mouthpiece and the barrel. The problems persisted until Iwan Müller, one of the most influential German players of his day, developed his thirteen-keyed instrument in about 1812. The new clarinet's tone-holes were positioned with greater acoustical accuracy, achieving much improved intonation, and a new fingering system allowed performance in any key. Indeed, such was Müller's confidence in his clarinet that he grandly claimed it was no longer necessary to use different instruments. The player's enormous influence encouraged the widespread adoption of his clarinet, and it remained very popular until the late years of the 19th century.

ABOVE: UNUSUAL MEMBERS OF THE CLARINET FAMILY: (FROM LEFT TO RIGHT) BASS CLARINET, BASSETT HORN AND ALTO CLARINET.

 TODAY'S STANDARD ORCHESTRAL
CLARINET IN **B** FLAT DATES FROM THE
EARLY 1700s.

TYPES OF
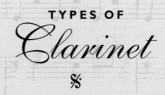
Clarinet
𝄐

OCTAVE CLARINETS in C, B flat and A Early to mid-19th century. High-pitched 'piccolo' clarinets often employed in military or folk contexts and now obsolete. Italy was their probable country of origin.

CLARINETTO SESTINO IN A FLAT c. 1839. A very shrill-toned instrument designed for military use and often played with conspicuous virtuosity in Balkan folk-bands. 'Sestino', diminutive of Italian sesto ('sixth'), refers to its pitch of a sixth higher than, presumably, the sopranino clarinet in E flat.

SOPRANINO CLARINET IN G Late 18th century. An obsolete instrument pitched a semi-tone below the clarinetto sestino. Once heard in Viennese Schrammel Quartets (two violins, bass guitar, clarinet), but an accordion has replaced the clarinet since c. 1895.

SOPRANINO CLARINETS in F, E, E flat and D. 18th century. Now obsolete or very rare, these instruments had mainly military use and occasional use in the orchestra for special effect. The sopranino in D was also once used as a concerto instrument.

SOPRANO CLARINET IN C Early 18th century. A standard orchestral instrument until the end of the 19th century.

SOPRANO CLARINET IN B Late 18th century. A rare instrument, virtually unknown today.

SOPRANO CLARINET IN B FLAT Early 18th century. Today's standard orchestral clarinet.

SOPRANO CLARINET IN A 18th century. A standard orchestral clarinet, now yielding to the B flat instrument (entry immediately above).

BASSET HORN IN G c.1770. Semi-circular in shape, later angled. This, or a near relative, may be the instrument now called 'basset clarinet' (see below).

BASSET HORN IN F Late 18th century. A slightly later development of the above, its pitch standardized at F. The circular or angled body enters a box containing three folds of the tube which then gives into the metal bell. This produces a fuller sound than that of the standard clarinets. The weight of the instrument is supported by a sling or spike.

BASSET HORN IN D Late 18th century. A rare local example, mainly in Bohemia.

CLARINETTE D'AMOUR IN D 1772. Called for by J. C. Bach in his opera *Temistocle* but otherwise undocumented. It has been suggested that he meant the basset horn in D (immediately above).

CLARINETTE D'AMOUR IN A FLAT c.1760. Similar to the G instrument below (next entry), but much rarer.

CLARINETTE D'AMOUR IN G c. 1760. A straight clarinet with a bent brass crook at the top, three keys and a pear-shaped bell to give a soft, velvety tone. Still current in the Middle East but obsolete in the West.

'BASSET CLARINET' IN G c. 1789. A mysterious instrument developed by Anton Stadler with a range extending four semi-tones below the standard clarinet. It may equate with the basset horn in G, though Stadler probably introduced modifications.

CLARINETTE D'AMOUR IN F Early 19th century. Also called 'tenor clarinet', a version of the G instrument (entry immediately above).

Perhaps, inevitably, it was the influence of Theobald Boehm's ground-breaking work with the flute that ultimately dimmed the music world's enthusiasm for Müller's innovations. Boehm himself was not involved in work on the clarinet system that by the 1860s carried his name. Rather, it was the result of a collaboration between the clarinettist Hyacinthe Eleanore Klosé and instrument maker Louis-Auguste Buffet between 1839 and 1843. Buffet was familar with Boehm's work on the flute and, applying some of the same principles, he and Klosé almost completely redesigned the system of tone-holes and keywork. The result was the instrument that is in most use today.

The modern clarinet has a similar, if more refined, quality of sound to that of 1716 when Vivaldi first used it in his oratorio *Juditha triumphans*. Quite different, however, was the piercing tone of the clarinets pitched in D, G and A (as opposed to Vivaldi's in C and D) used by Johann Melchior Molter, a prolific court composer in Karlsruhe, who composed the first six concertos for a solo clarinet around 1745, although one source reports a performance of a clarinet concerto played by a Mr Charles in Dublin three years earlier. It is possible that what Mr Charles played was a concerto for flute or oboe arranged for clarinet.

When Mozart came to London as an eight-year-old in 1764, he was lent a symphony by the German composer Karl Friedrich Abel and was given the exercise of adapting the oboe parts for clarinets. Because the work was now in Mozart's handwriting, it was for nearly two centuries regarded as authentic, given the Köchel number 18 and titled Mozart's Symphony No. 3. Later,

Mozart wrote two major works for clarinet: a Quintet in A, K581 (1789) and a Concerto, K622, both for his friend Anton Stadler. Stadler favoured a now obsolete clarinet in G, a lower-pitched instrument recently dubbed 'basset clarinet', but Mozart's Concerto, originally in G (1789, but re-written by him in A in 1791), was arranged for the standard A clarinet before its first publication in 1801.

℘ *Today's Clarinet*

The clarinet has appeared in many varieties during its short history. The standard instruments today are in A and B flat. In the 19th century the clarinet was a permanent member of the orchestra as well as an effective concerto and chamber instrument. Weber wrote two concertos for it in 1811, and Louis Spohr contributed four between 1808 and 1828. Brahms's Clarinet Quintet (1891) and Nielsen's Concerto (1928) are among many works to display the standard clarinet's capabilities.

The unusual, stark high-pitched sound of the E flat clarinet has also been used to good effect. Berlioz included one in his *Symphonie fantastique* (1830) as did Richard Strauss in *Till Eulenspiegel* (1895). More recently, Messiaen's *Quartet for the End of Time* (1940) contains an affecting clarinet solo and Stockhausen explored in depth its exotic and virtuosos possibilities in five pieces entitled *Amour* (1974–6). These call for extreme ranges of pitch and dynamic, rasping tone, flutter-tonguing and, in *The Butterflies are Playing*, an amazing effect in which the key 'plops' represent insects' flapping wings. ℬ

𝄞 THE CLARINET AND SAXOPHONE ARE TWO OF THE MOST POPULAR JAZZ INSTRUMENTS. DUETTING HERE ARE A CLARINET AND (RIGHT), IN THE HANDS OF VIRTUOSO SIDNEY BECHET, A SOPRANO SAX

THE CLARINET IN *Jazz* ℅

When the American bandmaster Patrick Sarsfield Gilmore put together his band in 1878, he established an instrumental line-up that remains typical, including the ubiquitous clarinet. Even before a true jazz idiom emerged, the clarinet featured in cakewalk and ragtime in American minstrel shows of the late 19th and early 20th centuries. Similarly, in the traditional and Dixieland jazz 'combos' of New Orleans, a clarinet could usually be found in the front line alongside cornet and trombone.

In the 1920s the 'blues' of players like Johnny Dodds kept the clarinet in the limelight, but it was during the revolutionary 'swing era' from the mid-1930s to mid-1940s that the jazz clarinet made its mark; never before, or since, was the clarinet so at home in popular music. The swing years were ruled by an undisputed 'King of Swing', clarinettist Benny Goodman. "Goodman is now making jazz history in Chicago," ran one 1936 review. Goodman did more than most to establish the style and popularity of swing jazz. His numbers were often better suited to the concert hall than the ballroom. They featured clarinet playing of show-stopping virtuosity and imagination (his intimate quartet version of the Lockhart/Seitz tune *The World is Waiting for the Sunrise* is a notable example), and some of them, like *Clarinet à la King* and *Scarecrow*, have become timeless jazz anthems.

During the 1940s jazz underwent a stylistic transition from swing to be-bop, later to become 'modern jazz'. With the change, the clarinet lost some prominence in favour of the saxophone in the hands of Coleman Hawkins, Charlie Parker, Stan Getz and others. Today, however, alongside the saxophone, the clarinet still forms an important part of the reed player's armoury.

♪ BASSOON

KNOWN VARIOUSLY AS the 'gentleman' and the 'clown' of the woodwinds, the bassoon is an instrument whose compass and range of tonal colour make it one of the most versatile members of the orchestra. Oddly, even the most exhaustive of studies seems to have failed in pinpointing the origin of the bassoon. This may well be due to the inconsistent and often ambiguous naming of the instrument, though the bassoon's immediate ancestor was almost certainly the *dulcian* or *curtal*. The 17th-century English musicologist James Talbot was among the first, in about 1695, to identify a 'basson in four joynts' and the anglicized version 'bassoon' came into use after it appeared in Purcell's 1691 score *The History of Dioclesian*. However, the one-piece *curtal* seems only to have been finally displaced by the bassoon proper, with its four-joint construction, in the 18th century.

Early bassoons were developed by makers such as the Denners in Nuremberg, who built the first three-key model and later one with four keys which remained standard for most of the 18th century. This instrument also displayed advances in terms of tone colour, becoming more mellow and expressive. It was more capable technically and allowed composers like Telemann in his early Sonata (1728) and Mozart in his Concerto (1774) to write characterful and demanding music. The bassoon had always played an important role as a continuo instrument at the bass of ensemble music (indeed, the original French form of its name, *basson*, indicated simply the bass-register version of any instrument, for example *basson de hautbois* or *basson flûte*). With the rise of the 19th-century solo virtuoso-composer, demands for the bassoon's range to be extended upwards increased, as did the need for louder-toned instruments with more reliable intonation. The problems were not successfully tackled until Carl Almenräder (hailed by Curt Sachs as the 'Boehm of the bassoon') developed his fifteen-key instrument around 1820. From 1831 onwards Almenräder collaborated with Johann Adam Heckel in developing the bassoon further. The Heckel family have since continued the work and today produce one of the two versions of bassoon in common use, the other being a French model by the Parisian firm Buffet-Crampon.

❅ *In Performance*

The bassoon's career as a solo and chamber instrument began very early in its life. By the early 1600s the bassoon was beginning to find its feet in an independent role outside the *basso continuo*. The first composition for solo bassoon was a Fantasia by the Venetian Salaverde which appeared around 1638, followed some years later by Bertoli's set of nine sonatas, the first such set for any one instrument. The bassoon was also quickly accepted as an integral part of the developing orchestra and its value as the bass part of wind chamber groups was beginning to figure in composers' thinking.

The arrival of the new jointed bassoon, with its greater possibilities for expressive playing, gave considerable impetus to writing for the instrument. During the 18th and 19th centuries music for the bassoon as a solo and ensemble instrument appeared in abundance. It featured as a key *obbligato* instrument in several of J. S. Bach's cantatas. There were sonatas, concertos and *concertante* symphonies by composers such as Haydn, Paganini and Weber, to name just a few. Chamber music featuring the bassoon was also

♪ THE MODERN ORCHESTRAL BASSOON SECTION, USUALLY CONSISTING OF AT LEAST ONE PAIR OF STANDARD BASSOONS, SITS AT THE BACK OF THE WOODWIND, NEXT TO THE CLARINETS.

on the increase, large numbers of works for bassoon and strings appearing around the turn of the 19th century by Karl Stamitz, Krommer, Danzi and many of their contemporaries. Neither has the bassoon's popularity waned during the 20th century. There are notable solo, *concertante* and chamber works by Elgar, Villa-Lobos, Strauss, Hindemith, Prokofiev and Dutilleux. Even the avant-garde sound world of Stockhausen has exploited the bassoon's versatility in works such as the wind quintet *Adieu* (1966). 𝄡

RIGHT: CLEAR SIMI-
LARITIES IN DESIGN
AND USE SUGGEST THE
CURTAL OR *DULCIAN* WAS
THE TRUE FORERUNNER
OF THE BASSOON.

A CLOWN AND A
Gentleman

Both the bassoon's comic reputation and its capacity for a more lyrical mode of expression have proved sources of inspiration for composers since the instrument's early days.

VIVALDI: If any composer has managed to combine both characteristics of the bassoon successfully it is Vivaldi, who completed no less than 37 concertos for the instrument. That he wrote so many is curious, for there was no recent tradition of solo bassoon writing in Venice. They were probably composed for the orphanage where he taught, though two (RV502 and 496) appear to be dedicated to local musicians. Along with agile material that skips between the bassoon's bass and tenor registers, Vivaldi includes lyrical passages that belie the instrument's reputation for jocularity.

DUKAS: Of all the works that introduce the bassoon as the clown among instruments, Dukas' famous depiction of a bewitched mop lumbering off to fetch its own bucket of water, in *The Sorcerer's Apprentice* (1897), must be the favourite. As the young, disastrously inexperienced sorcerer casts his spell, Dukas introduces the theme of the work in a phrase that exposes the clowning bassoons at their pompous best.

STRAVINSKY: Further use of the bassoon to comic effect can be found towards the end of Stravinsky's ballet *Pulcinella* (1920). At the other end of the spectrum, though, is his ballet *The Rite of Spring* (1913), depicting a solemn pagan rite associated with the violent eruption of spring in Russia. The ballet opens with an extremely demanding and exposed bassoon solo derived from a Lithuanian folk tune and pitched high in the instrument's top register. Its peculiar and remote sound, about as far as it is possible to be from most people's perception of the 'clowning' bassoon, provides an appropriately mystical opening to this raw and passionate music. Stravinsky used the same effect later in his *Symphonies of Wind Instruments* (1920, revised 1945–7).

BARTOK: The second movement of this composer's Concerto for Orchestra (1943) is another example of the bassoon as 'gentleman' to listen for.

♪ SAXOPHONE

OF ALL THE MEMBERS of the woodwind family, the saxophone is the most modern and probably the most familiar among non-musicians. The instrument's role in popular music idioms, particularly jazz, has afforded it the sort of exposure that is not typical among other woodwinds. It is also the one instrument whose genesis can be quite clearly identified, though the reasons for its taking the shape it did remain rather more of a grey area.

♪ Construction

Antoine Joseph or Adolphe Sax was a Belgian instrument-maker who had long sought a solution to the weak link in contemporary military bands – the lack of an instrument that satisfactorily filled the tonal gap between the clarinets and the tenor brass. Combine this with the suggestion that Sax also dreamed of inventing a clarinet that would overblow at the octave (instead of the 12th), as well as replacing all the woodwinds in a military band with a more powerful group of instruments, and it becomes clear that Sax was an inventive musician with no mean amount of vision. Sax had found what he believed to be the answer by about 1845, though the idea was not an entirely original one. By falling back on the first principles of acoustics he realized that he was looking for a single-reed instrument with a conical bore, rather than the cylindrical bore of the clarinet. A Scot named William Meikle had come to the same conclusion some time earlier and had experimented along these lines with his alto bassoon of 1830. Earlier still, the French instrument-maker Desfontenelles had produced a wooden instrument with a mainly conical bore,

though this was subsequently found to overblow at the 12th.

Sax almost certainly drew inspiration from these crude efforts. He applied the same principles to an instrument that could also carry the new, more sophisticated keywork developed for other woodwinds and produced the first saxophone. By the mid-1840s he had established a successful workshop in Paris and French military bands began using his instruments in preference to clarinets and bassoons. Thanks to the bands' willing adoption of the saxophone, except in Germany, the instrument rapidly found its primary function in popular music. This was particularly so in America where from 1890 onwards John Philip Sousa and his peers intro-

♪ THE TENOR SAXO-PHONE IN B FLAT IS PERHAPS THE MOST EASILY RECOG-NIZABLE MEMBER OF THE FAMILY.

duced the saxophone to their wind bands. It is believed to have made its first appearance in England at a concert promoted by the ill-fated French impresario Louis Jullien in about 1850.

♪ In Performance

Conversely, the instrument was slow to find its way into symphonic music, with at first only French composers like Delibes, Saint-Saëns and Bizet using it. In fact, such was the dearth of specialist saxophonists that Richard Strauss had great difficulty finding four for the premiere of his *Symphonia domestica* in New York in 1904. Happily, the mellow and peculiarly 'vocal' tone of the saxophone has since found a more regular place in the orchestra. Perhaps the best-known example is its role of the troubadour singing at the gate of 'The Old Castle' in Ravel's orchestration (1922) of Mussorgsky's *Pictures at an Exhibition*. Other composers have exploited its sound, including Vaughan Williams in *Job* (1930) and his Sixth Symphony (1947), Prokofiev in *Romeo and Juliet* (1936) and Britten in *Billy Budd* (1951).

At the hands of modern virtuosos like John Harle the saxophone has found its place in the 'art music' of the late 20th century. Harle's popular persona and performances of music by composers such as Dominic Muldowney and Sir Harrison Birtwistle have helped blur the distinction between classical and jazz saxophone. However, it is in the world of jazz that many people believe the saxophone belongs. The saxophone has a noble heritage as a jazz instrument, thanks to gifted exponents like Charlie Parker and, more recently, Courtney Pine and Andy Sheppard. ♭

♪ AMERICAN SAXOPHONIST CHARLIE PARKER, PICTURED IN 1949, BECAME SYNONYMOUS WITH THE POST-'SWING' ERA OF MODERN JAZZ.

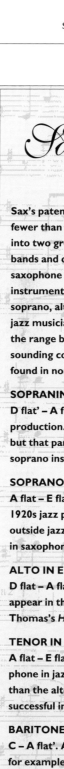

TYPES OF
Saxophone
※

Sax's patent granted in 1846 covered no fewer than fourteen instruments divided into two groups of seven, one for miltary bands and one for the orchestra. The saxophone family today consists of seven instruments, the most common being soprano, alto, tenor and baritone. Some jazz musicians have extended the top of the range by up to an octave, but the sounding compasses indicated are those found in normal use.

SOPRANINO IN E FLAT

D flat' – A flat'''. Rarely heard but still in production. Ravel used one in his *Boléro*, but that part is now usually taken by a soprano instrument.

SOPRANO IN B FLAT

A flat – E flat''. Made famous by the 1920s jazz player Sidney Bechet, but outside jazz it is only usually heard today in saxophone quartets.

ALTO IN E FLAT

D flat – A flat''. First saxophone to appear in the symphony orchestra, in Thomas's *Hamlet* (1868).

TENOR IN B FLAT

A flat – E flat''. The most popular saxophone in jazz, used in the orchestra later than the alto. An earlier model in C was successful in the United States.

BARITONE IN E FLAT

C – A flat'. A popular jazz instrument; for example, through Gerry Mulligan in the 1950s. Also used by Stockhausen in *Carré* (1960).

BASS IN B FLAT

A flat' – E flat'. Rarely heard outside full saxophone ensembles.

CONTRABASS IN E FLAT

D flat' – A flat. Very rare, only made to order today.

♪ HORN

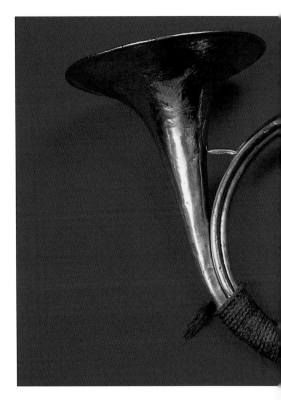

SINCE ANTIQUITY, WHEN simple animal horns were used for sending signals, the horn has been a symbol of power and strength. Whether in Europe, Africa or Asia, horns have served similar purposes, and though individual instruments may have been distinguishable through their sound or appearance, the horn's rural beginnings still find themselves reflected in the instrument's association with things pastoral.

The horn we are concerned with is the European orchestral horn, more commonly called the French horn, due to the supposed origins in France of an instrument close in principle to the one we know today. Of all the winds, the French horn has undergone some of the most interesting technological modifications during its history. From the early simple hoop-like instrument to today's sophisticated 'double' horn, makers have been faced with severe acoustical obstacles in the quest for a fully chromatic instrument that is both reliable and convenient to use. Though it remains one of the most taxing instruments to play well, the mellow tone produced by its small funnel-shaped mouthpiece makes it an enduring favourite. Not only can it stand out in a large modern orchestra, where four or more may be found, but it mixes well with woodwind in the more intimate setting of a wind quintet. It has a fine reputation, too, as an effective soloist in both sonata and concerto.

♪ BELOW: BARRY TUCKWELL HAS INSPIRED WORKS FOR SOLO HORN BY SEVERAL MODERN COMPOSERS, INCLUDING THEA MUSGRAVE'S CONCERTO.

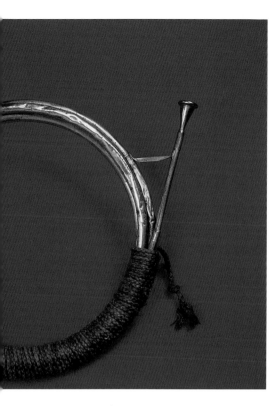

FAR LEFT: THE SINGLE-LOOP BUGLE, DEVELOPED IN THE 18TH CENTURY FOR MILITARY USE.

LEFT: FOR ALL THE COMPLEXITY OF THE MODERN ORCHESTRAL HORN, ITS 17TH-CENTURY ANCESTOR WAS A SIMPLE TRIPLE-COILED INSTRUMENT.

the name 'French horn' by the early 1600s and this corresponds with the date of the Grand Tour of Count von Sporck from Bohemia who encountered the horn in Paris. The instrument was quite a novelty to him, suggesting that it was unknown outside France. It was not until about 1717 that French horns were heard in an English orchestra, when Handel included them in his *Water Music*. These early horns were constructed in a single piece, so players had to use instruments of different lengths with each key change.

℀ Early Construction

If there is one property that gives the French horn a tone quite distinct from other brass instruments, it is the conical shape of its bore, though the development of playing techniques such as 'hand-stopping' have also helped define this instrument's very individual character. Originally the European horn came from the fields, where hunting and military horns were in widespread use by the late 14th century. Huntsmen and militia remained the horn's principal users almost until the end of the 17th century, although by this time two more advanced horns were in use. Of these the close-coiled *trompe Maricourt* represented an early stage in the development of the hoop-like orchestral horn, the instrument thought to have been used in Lully's comedy ballet *La princesse d'Elide* (1664). From this time on horns became increasingly popular for providing fanfare effects in musical dramas.

Although there is no proof that the horn originated in France there are clear indications that support the theory. The English were using

℀ Crooks & Hands

In Vienna Michael Leichnamschneider developed a means of addressing this problem. He introduced a system of 'crooks' (separate rings of

TYPES OF *Horn* ℀

HUNTING HORN A high, lively sounding instrument used for important signals during fox or stag hunts. It is known to have existed as early as the 14th century, and later in three versions: English, German and French. The English hunting horn is a short, straight instrument dating from the time of Charles II, while the German circular version was introduced in late 19th century. The French *trompe de chasse* is a large, circular instrument and a direct antecedent of the orchestral horn. Haydn quotes one of the common French hunting horn calls in *The Seasons* (1801). Their typical 6/8 rhythm influenced Mozart in the rondo finales of his horn concertos.

POSTHORN Originally used to signal the arrival and departure of postboys on horseback and later by guards on mail coaches. The Continental version dates from the early 17th century and is typically made in a circle of tightly wound coils. Much imitated in music of early 1700s, it later developed into a semi-orchestral instrument. A valved version is said to have been the origin of the cornet in Paris in the 1820s. The English posthorn is long and straight and pitched in A flat. Koenig's famous *Posthorn Galop* (1844) is based on genuine posthorn calls.

SIGNAL HORN Also known as the bugle, it dates back to the Seven Years' War (1756–63) since when it has had mostly military use in both Europe and America. Originally a large semicircular horn, it was developed into single-loop form around 1700. The present two-loop form was adopted after the Crimean War (1853–6), although the one-loop version is still sometimes preferred on the Continent. It is rarely seen outside military use: Suppé quotes a bugle call at the opening of *Light Cavalry* (1866) and Britten's *Noye's Fludde* (1957) uses an actual bugle.

ORCHESTRAL HORN Operates on the same acoustical principle as other brass instruments, but physical differences determine its distinctive tonal character. The modern horn is an intricately coiled tube nearly 3.5 metres (c. 11 feet) long with a narrow, funnel-shaped mouthpiece. Its conical bore ends with a large bell 28–35cm (c. 11–14 inches) in diameter. The horn was once described as "the most refined and poetical voice in the symphony orchestra", but the technique it requires is the most difficult of all the orchestral instruments to master, which may explain why concertos for it are rare and of short duration.

tubing in different lengths) which allowed the horn to be put into any key required. By now composers like Bach and Handel were writing quite high and florid horn parts, probably the best known Baroque concerto with horns being Bach's First 'Brandenburg' Concerto. Although it was becoming apparent that the clumsiness of instruments with loose crooks was far from ideal, no alternative appeared until the early 19th century.

Meanwhile, makers and players continued to experiment. The Dresden player Anton Joseph Hampl, for example, developed the hand-horn method. This method of performing with the natural horn, first developed by Bohemian players, was refined by Hampl around the mid-1700s. By placing the right hand in the bell and fully or partially stopping the tube, the player could raise or lower notes and fill the gaps in the horn's natural harmonic series. Hampl also invented a new instrument, the *Inventionshorn*, to complement his method of playing (see panel feature) and trained many fellow horn players in its use, including the celebrated Bohemian Giovanni Punto for whom Beethoven composed his Sonata in F, Op.17 (1800).

✄ *The Valve Horn*

The first moves towards the valve horn we know today came with the development of the 'omnitonic' horn around 1815 (see panel feature). In fact, the first valve horns were patented around the same time but they suffered from deficient valves, particularly in terms of intonation, for at this stage the extra lengths of tubing brought into play by the valves did not include any tuning mechanism. Although the valve horn was not readily accepted in official circles (it did not become the recognized instrument at the Paris Conservatoire until 1903), composers began to include it in their scores. It made its orchestral debut in Jacques Halévy's opera *La juive* (1835), the work that brought the composer fame. Schumann, too, was among the first to write for the valve horn with his Adagio and Allegro in A flat, Op. 70, for horn and piano, and the *Concertstück* in F, Op. 86, for four horns and orchestra, both dating from 1849. The Adagio and Allegro was the first significant solo work for the new valve instrument. The earliest version of the instrument commonly used today, the 'double' horn in F and B flat, first appeared in Germany towards the end of the 19th century.

This was the instrument to benefit from the introduction of a refined piston-valve system patented in 1912, though by the mid-20th century rotary valves had rendered piston valves all but obsolete for the horn.

Against the backdrop of these considerable technical advances, Richard Strauss wrote his demanding Second Horn Concerto in 1942. The circumstances of Strauss's composition of his First Concerto (1882–3) were curiously similar. It came at a time when composers were beginning to write music for the valve horn that extended its range of tonal colour (though interestingly, Brahms persisted in scoring for the hand horn – his Piano Concerto No. 2 in B flat of 1881 opens with a famous passage for hand horns in that same key, B flat). *Glissandos* and 'flutter tonguing' became popular devices, and Debussy made particularly effective use of the horn's adaptable timbre in his *Prélude à l'après-midi d'un faune* (1892–4). However, the concerto

RIGHT: EARLY DEPICTIONS OF THE HORN – THIS ONE DATES FROM THE MIDDLE AGES – CONFIRM ITS BEGINNINGS IN THE HUNTING FIELD.

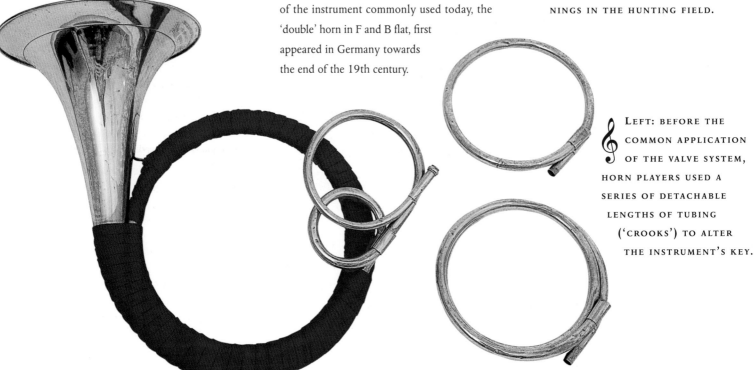

LEFT: BEFORE THE COMMON APPLICATION OF THE VALVE SYSTEM, HORN PLAYERS USED A SERIES OF DETACHABLE LENGTHS OF TUBING ('CROOKS') TO ALTER THE INSTRUMENT'S KEY.

NATURAL HORN Developed from the looped hunting horn of the 15th to 17th centuries. Its first known purely musical use is believed to be an anonymous Czech sonata for strings and *corno da caccia* (1670s). Natural horns in F were known in Germany by 1700 – the earliest example is by the Leichnamschneider brothers of Vienna, dated 1710.

NATURAL HORN WITH CROOKS Invented by the Leichnamschneiders in the early 18th century. The horn was made shorter and a socket incorporated to take additional loops of tubing called 'crooks'. In combination, 'master crooks' and 'couplers' allowed the player to change the instrument's key. This system was superseded after 1750 by a set of up to nine separate crooks, one for each different key.

INVENTIONSHORN Devised by Hampl in about 1750, this allowed crooks to be fitted into the body of the horn (usually onto the inner coil of a two-coil instrument). A similar instrument in France was known as the *cor solo*.

'OMNITONIC' HORN An attempt by Dupont around 1815 to produce a fully chromatic horn without crooks. It included enough built-in tubing to allow the instrument to play in any key and used plungers and sliding shutters, etc., to bring different lengths of tubing into play.

VALVE HORN The earliest example developed by Stölzel and Blühmel in 1818. The most successful were Blühmel's rotary variety, and these are usual today. Modern horns normally have three or four valves – on 'double' instruments in B flat and F, the fourth valve controls about one metre (3 feet) of tubing, modifying a medium-length F horn into a short B flat horn.

had not been seen as an ideal vehicle for the horn due to the strenuous demands of the now highly-developed genre. Indeed, between a minor *concertino* by Weber (1815) and Strauss's First Concerto, very little of consequence was written for solo horn.

The story has been rather different since, with virtuoso players like Aubrey and Dennis Brain,

Barry Tuckwell and, recently, Michael Thompson, encouraging leading composers to write for the horn. Both Hindemith and Tippett have written sonatas for four horns; in 1943 Britten composed the Serenade for tenor, horn and strings; and more recently Thea Musgrave and Anthony Powers have written concertos for horn and orchestra (1971 and 1991 respectively).

♪ TRUMPET

AMONG ALL THE INSTRUMENTS of the woodwind and brass families, the trumpet enjoyed the unique, if dubious, distinction of suffering a fall from grace when it joined the orchestra. "Notwithstanding the real loftiness and distinguished nature of its quality of tone," said Berlioz in his *Treatise on Modern Instrumentation and Orchestration* (1843), "there are few instruments that have been more degraded than the trumpet." This 'degradation' concerns the instrument's descent from its highly regarded social function in the 1500s to its often meagre subordinate role in the late-Classical symphony orchestra. In fact, during the trumpet's early history its players were among the first to form a trade union of sorts. From the mid-16th century trumpeters were prized court employees (many Renaissance sovereigns measured their own importance in terms of the number of trumpet ensembles at their disposal). The social distinction between trumpet players and other musicians broadened gradually but noticeably (with kettle drummers, they were often set on raised platforms), and in 1623 an Imperial Guild of Trumpeters was established in the Holy Roman Empire, its function being to control who played the trumpet and where. The trumpeter's protected position served his profession well until around the time of Bach when the trumpet began to be absorbed into the orchestra as a purely *tutti* instrument. From the early 1800s the only relatively secure livelihood for a trumpeter was to be found in the ranks of an orchestra. Notwithstanding the later success of some jazz trumpeters and cornet soloists, it was not until after World War II that the trumpet once again emerged as a solo instrument in orchestral music, in the hands of players like George Eskdale and Helmut Wobisch.

✄ Early History

Just as the horn is distinguished by its conical bore, so the trumpet's bright, perky character is determined to an extent by its cylindrical bore, which has been a constant in the instrument's design since the Middle Ages. The bright sound has always been well suited to military and \ceremonial roles and even in Ancient Egypt trumpets served just this purpose. Two well-known extant examples are the straight silver and bronze instruments rescued from the tomb of Tutankhamun. Curt Sachs claimed that the trumpet disappeared from Europe with the fall of the Roman Empire and did not reappear until around the turn of the second millennium. Even then the trumpeter's social position was far from stable. It was not until the 14th and 15th centuries that players started to find regular employment, typically as tower watchmen, coinciding with early technical development of the instrument itself.

About 1400 the previously straight instrument took on an 'S' shape, shortly afterwards becoming a loop. The use of crooks to change an instrument's key became common, and the slide trumpet was also beginning to appear. Commonly used in church music, this instrument featured telescopic tubing behind the mouthpiece, allowing the player to alter the length of the instrument mid-performance. By the 16th century the trumpet's compass had been extended upwards, and players now began to specialize in performance in specific registers. Of the two main registers, the *principale* (medium) and *clarino* (upper), it was the latter that became the realm of the virtuoso. The label *clarino* proba-

ala ghcoa de nuß s
como a ñoli dela far

♪ EVEN AS EARLY AS THIS 12TH CENTURY ILLUMINATION THE TRUMPET'S IMPORTANCE AS A COURT INSTRUMENT, PARTICULARLY ON CEREMONIAL OCCASIONS, WAS CLEAR.

bly came from 'clarion', the name originally used to distinguish the short ceremonial trumpet from the larger *trumpe* and quoted by Chaucer as early as 1375 in *The House of Fame*. *Clarino* playing was used in Monteverdi's 'musical fable' *Orfeo* (1607), but its most celebrated adoption was by Bach, particularly in the first and third movements of the 'Brandenburg' Concerto No. 2 (c.1721).

TYPES OF
Trumpet

℅·

TRUMPET IN B FLAT The most common modern instrument used in orchestras, bands and jazz, with a compass of nearly three octaves from e. Its total length of 130cm (over 4 feet) consists of a tapered mouthpipe, holding the mouthpiece, the central section of cylindrical tubing including the tuning-slide, valves and their associated tubing, and a conical bell section ending in a flare about 12cm (5 inches) in diameter. For the valves to give accurate intonation on some notes, particularly in the low register, slides are included to be activated by the player as necessary.

TRUMPET IN D/E FLAT Introduced after the B flat trumpet, probably for performances of music by Bach at the time of his bicentenary in 1885. The Baroque trumpet's principal key was D, but the new model used half the length of tubing. It was pitched in E flat and had alternative tuning slides to lower the pitch to D. The penetrating tone of the D trumpet has been used by some more recent composers including Ravel in *Boléro*, Stravinsky in *The Rite of Spring* and Britten in *Peter Grimes* (1945). These parts are now often played on the piccolo trumpet.

PICCOLO TRUMPET IN B FLAT This was used for the first time around 1906 for a performance of Bach's Brandenburg Concerto No. 2. Pitched an octave above the standard B flat instrument, it has now superseded the trumpet in D/E flat. In principle it is built in the same form as the normal B flat instrument, though it has appeared in a wide variety of shapes. It may also be pitched in A, using alternative slides, and it usually has a fourth valve to allow performance of notes below concert e'.

BASS TRUMPET Specially designed to specifications from Wagner for use in his *Ring* cycle. Wagner originally imagined a huge instrument pitched an octave below the valve trumpet in F with which he was familiar. The actual instrument is only slightly longer than the standard F trumpet, and is pitched in C, sounding an octave below the normal B flat trumpet, with crooks for B flat and A. It has a more mellow tone than other trumpets and has an impressive compass of three octaves from G flat. Some commentators maintain this instrument is more properly a valved trombone than a trumpet; it is certainly usually played by a trombonist.

THIS MID-19TH CENTURY ENGLISH SLIDE TRUMPET IN F BY LONDON MAKERS KÖHLER & SON DEMONSTRATES THAT EVEN AFTER THE INTRODUCTION OF VALVES OTHER EXPERIMENTS CONTINUED.

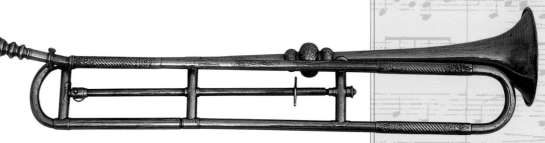

✵ Valve Trumpet

By now new musical styles were emerging which favoured the oboe, flute and violin, so trumpet writing fell into decline. Ironically, at the same time the instrument began to undergo some of its most radical and successful technical develop-ment. There were several attempts at producing a fully chromatic trumpet, including the 'key trumpet' for which both Haydn and Hummel wrote their popular concertos. More successful was the 'stop trumpet', an instrument made short enough to allow the player to stop the bell with his hand. This principle was first introduced on the trumpet by Michael Wöggel in 1777, some 20 years after A.J. Hampl used the same technique for the horn (see page 36). A later improvement came with A.F. Krause's *Inventionstrompeten* in the 1790s which incorporated a tuning slide in the body of the instrument. However, as with the horn, it was the successful development of valves, attributed to Stölzel and Blühmel of Berlin, that made truly chromatic trumpets possible. The

CONCERTOS FOR THE
Trumpet

VIVALDI: CONCERTO FOR TWO TRUMPETS IN C, RV537

Vivaldi contributed only this virtuoso work to the trumpet repertoire. Why he did not write more solo material for the instrument is not entirely clear. It may have been that trumpets were not often played by the girls in the orphanage for whom he wrote most of his concertos. Instruments were probably brought in from outside to perform works like the Concerto. Vivaldi certainly recognized the value of the trumpet to the developing orchestra, and when trumpets were not available he used oboes and even violins to simulate them.

GEORG PHILIPP TELEMANN

In 1718 Telemann said about his concertos, "I must own that since the concerto form was never close to my heart it was indifferent to me whether I wrote a great many or not." So it is perhaps surprising to realize that he contributed in excess of 100 fine examples to the genre. These include six for trumpet which, though not too demanding on the whole, allow the player great scope for spirited playing.

HAYDN: CONCERTO IN E FLAT

This was among the works to figure in the trumpet's resurgence as a solo instrument, after a lengthy fallow period lasting from the early 19th century to around 1945. The last of the composer's purely orchestral music, it was written in 1796 after Haydn had returned to Vienna from London to retire. The solo part was written for a rudimentary keyed *clarino* in E flat, designed and played by Anton Weidinger, a trumpeter in the Viennese Court Opera Orchestra. It was for this same instrument that Hummel later wrote his concerto.

HUMMEL CONCERTO IN E FLAT

The Trumpet Concerto in E flat is probably one of the most popular and regularly heard constituents of the trumpeter's repertoire. However, so swamped is it by the volume of the rest of Hummel's output that little is known about the circumstances of this charming work's creation. It probably dates from the end of 1803, shortly before Hummel was appointed as *Konzertmeister* to Prince Nikolaus Esterházy, where Haydn was the (ostensibly retired) *Kapellmeister*.

❧ In Performance

Remarkably little music has been composed for the solo trumpet since Haydn and Hummel. Among the most recent pieces are Poulenc's Triple Sonata for trumpet, horn and trombone (1922) and Hindemith's Sonata (1939). During the 20th century it is in the jazz world that the trumpet has made its mark, thanks largely to Louis Armstrong, whose importance is difficult to overstate. Armstrong set the standard for jazz trumpet playing in many ways: he was the first trumpeter, for example, to extend the instrument's range up to f''' (concert pitch $e\ flat''$). He actually started out playing the cornet and only came to the trumpet later. His contemporary Bix Beiderbecke followed the same route, and Beiderbecke's so-called 'Chicago style' of lyrical improvisation became a model still taken up by jazz trumpeters today. Other important players have included Dizzy Gillespie in the 'be-bop' era and Miles Davis who played 'cool jazz'. Between them, these two demonstrated the enormous tonal range of the trumpet. Gillespie was an extrovert showman known for his nonchalant bravado and breathtaking virtuosity. By contrast, Davis played very few notes to Gillespie's many per second but their *vibrato*-less emotion and colour were unequalled. The current generation of jazz trumpeters includes Winton Marsalis who, in 1993, became the first jazz trumpeter to perform with his own ensemble at the BBC Henry Wood Promenade Concerts in London. 𝄢

'stop trumpet' continued to be used until well into the 19th century, but it was for the valve instrument that Berlioz and Rossini wrote parts in *Les francs-juges* (1826) and *William Tell* (1829) respectively. Towards the end of the 19th century trumpet parts in music by Wagner, Mahler and Richard Strauss made such demands on the typical F trumpet that players began to change to shorter, and therefore higher, instruments in B flat and C. It is the B flat valve trumpet that has endured to become the most commonly used today.

𝄞 RIGHT: THE B FLAT TRUMPET IS THE STANDARD INSTRUMENT IN USE TODAY.

𝄞 LEFT: WINTON MARSALIS REPRESENTS FOR MANY THE BENCHMARK AGAINST WHICH MODERN JAZZ PLAYING SHOULD BE MEASURED.

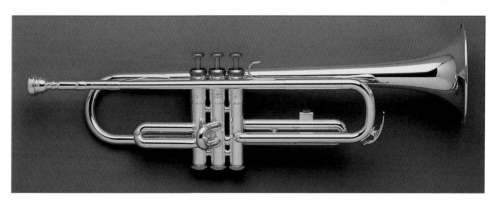

TROMBONE

ONCE DESCRIBED BY the sharp-witted conductor Sir Thomas Beecham as a "quaint and antique drainage system", the trombone occupies a special place in the woodwind and brass families. It is unique in being the one naturally chromatic wind instrument. This is due to the slide which corresponds to the valves used by other brass instruments, but which antedates valves by some four centuries.

The trombone, or 'sackbut' as the English then preferred to call it, originated in the 15th century, apparently as a modified version of the slide trumpet. The principles of design established for the instrument then have largely held good until the present day. The most noticeable physical difference between the early instrument and its successors was the almost complete lack of a flaring bell, which did not appear until around 1740 when players and composers began to demand a stronger sound.

In Performance

The trombone was used extensively for royal ceremonies and feasts, often paired with the cornett, a small, curved, wooden horn. The same combination of trombones and cornetts was also common in churches. The trombone began to find a place in ensembles accompanying opera, a notable example being Monteverdi's *Orfeo* (1607). Both Giovanni Gabrieli and Heinrich Schütz made good use of the instrument as did Matthew Locke in *Music for His Majesty's Sagbutts and Cornetts* (1661). The trombone was not adopted as an orchestral instrument until the late-18th century. The wind music fashions of that century were led by the French, who avoided using the trombone after Lully abolished it from court ensembles in the 1660s. Consequently, little of significance was written for the trombone for much of the 18th century.

With the adoption of the trombone into military bands and as a bass strengthener in the orchestra around the turn of the 19th century, the instrument could at last be said to have come of age. It was probably inevitable that the experimentation with valves on brass instruments around 1820 would include the trombone. Happily, their limited success meant a quick return to the slide, and the instrument was none the worse for diversion. By the Romantic period of the mid- to late-18th century the trombone had developed a reputation as a highly expressive instrument, yet the development around 1850 of trombones with wider bores seemed only to encourage composers to use the instrument as much for its loudness as its capacity for subtler emotional colouring. It is the brazen side of the trombone's character with which audiences remain most familiar, for little has been done during the 20th century to redress the balance. Having inspired only a handful of solo works, including a delightful concerto (1952) by Gordon Jacob and Sandström's remarkable *Motorbike* Concerto of 1969, the trombone remains a relative stranger to the solo platform.

In common with other instruments of the Renaissance and Baroque periods the trombone was produced in several sizes in its early days. Michael Praetorius identified four varieties of trombone: alto, tenor, bass and contrabass. In addition the recent trombone family has included soprano and tenor-bass models. It is the tenor instrument in B flat that finds most common use today. The seven positions of the slide, each lowering the fundamental note by one semitone, and the associated harmonic series give the instrument a compass of about two and a half octaves from *E*. Pitched in B flat an octave above the tenor, the soprano probably appeared in the late 17th century and was called for in scores by Purcell and Bach. Alto trombones, commonly in E flat or F, were used extensively from the 16th to 18th centuries but were often replaced by the tenor thereafter so use of them declined. More recent scores to use the alto trombone include Berg's *Three Orchestral Pieces* (1914) and Britten's church parable *The Burning Fiery Furnace* (1966). The contrabass trombone in B flat or C, an octave below the tenor, has appeared in many variations, usually with a 'double slide', affording extra length without the need for slide positions beyond that of a tenor instrument. The tenor-bass trombone in B flat/F and bass trombone in F are in fairly common use today. Both use one or, in the case of the bass, two valves to bring extra lengths of tubing into play without requiring the player to stretch an unreasonable distance with the slide.

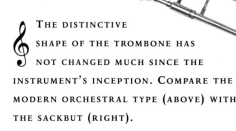

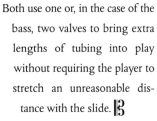

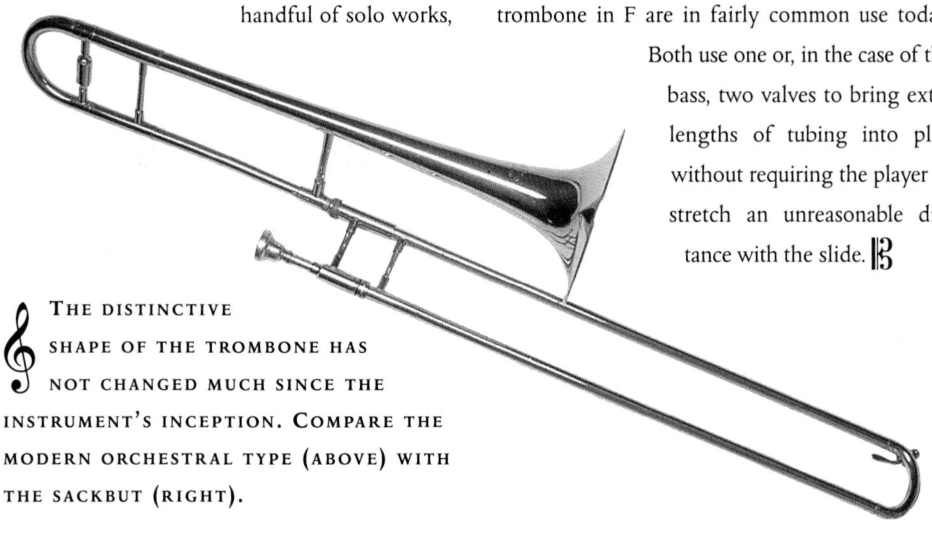

THE DISTINCTIVE SHAPE OF THE TROMBONE HAS NOT CHANGED MUCH SINCE THE INSTRUMENT'S INCEPTION. COMPARE THE MODERN ORCHESTRAL TYPE (ABOVE) WITH THE SACKBUT (RIGHT).

THE TROMBONE'S USE IN THE
Orchestra

※

BEETHOVEN The first important use of the trombone in a symphony was by Beethoven in his *Fifth Symphony* (1804-8), which uses normal Classical forces until the finale. After the hushed transition from the C minor third movement to the finale, the trombones make an impressive first appearance as the daylight of C major bursts forward.

SCHUBERT AND WAGNER By the end of the 19th century the trombone was part of the standard resources of an orchestra. It had regained what Berlioz described as its 'epic' character. In 1825 Schubert had used three trombones throughout his 'Great' C major symphony and Wagner composed one of the best known orchestral trombone themes in his *Tannhäuser* overture of 1845.

STRAVINSKY The most famous property of the trombone is its capacity to produce comic *glissandos*. Stravinsky used this to great effect, though more in the style of grotesque parody than comedy. Good examples can be found in his ballets *The Firebird* and *Pulcinella*, both dating from around 1919.

♪ TUBA

ALTHOUGH THE NAME 'tuba' was originally coined by the Romans for their forerunner of the trumpet, the word is now universally associated with that large, fun-loving brass instrument that rumbles away beside the trombones in an orchestra. In fact, the tuba is a remarkably versatile and agile instrument, as solo works by Vaughan Williams, Gordon Jacob, Edward Gregson and Derek Bourgeois demonstrate.

℘ *Bass Tuba*

The modern tuba has a wide conical bore and between three and six valves, depending on the instrument's size. The tuba family includes some instruments usually known by other names, such as the euphonium and sousaphone – these and other unusual brass instruments are discussed separately (see pages 46–7). Like the saxophone in the woodwinds, the tuba is a relatively recent addition to the brass section, though of course the principles of its design had been established and developed for the trumpet for some considerable time. It was the arrival of Stölzel and Blühmel's piston valve around the 1820s that first prompted the production of brass instruments to operate in the bass register. Wilhelm Wieprecht, bandmaster of Prussian Dragoon Guards and a trombonist by training, produced a 'bass tuba' in collaboration with the Berlin instrument-maker Johann Gottfried Monitz in 1835. The 'bass tuba' may have grown from the seed of the 'Berlin piston valve' also developed by the two men. It was a short valve of unusually large diameter which seemed to Wieprecht and Moritz most suitable for use on a brass instrument with a wide bore. In true chicken and egg style, however, it has already been suggested that the genesis of the 'Berlin valve' actually lay in work already done on the wide-bored 'bass tuba', rather than the other way round.

Whatever the truth of the matter, the first 'bass tubas' laid important groundwork for the instrument familiar today. There were differences in physical appearance, but many of the technical

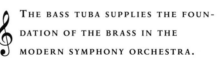

♪ THE BASS TUBA SUPPLIES THE FOUN-
DATION OF THE BRASS IN THE
MODERN SYMPHONY ORCHESTRA.

characteristics, including being pitched in F, were the same as they are now. Soon after 1835 other makers began to adapt the original 'bass tuba' design to their own purposes, producing tubas in a wide variety of shapes and sizes, some using rotary valves in preference to the Wieprecht/ Monitz *Berliner-Pumpen*.

℘ *Wagner Tuba*

Berlioz became the first major composer to use the tuba in his works, shortly followed by Wagner who included it in his orchestration for *Der fliegende Holländer*, first performed in 1843. About ten years later, while writing *Das Rheingold*, part one of the *Ring* cycle, Wagner came across the saxhorns being produced by Adolphe Sax in Paris, and he determined to include similar bass instruments in his works

VAUGHAN WILLIAMS'
Tuba Concerto

In describing the music of his Tuba Concerto, Vaughan Williams said it is "fairly simple and obvious and can probably be listened to without much previous explanation". When it was first performed it was probably the light-hearted image of the tuba, rather than the music, that resulted in the piece not being taken terribly seriously. Instead, it was regarded as something of a romp. This attitude fails to do justice to the work's achievement, particularly in the central Romanza movement, where the composer's efforts to discover all the instrument's capabilities come to light in some beautifully lyrical writing. If the work does have a lighter side, it is in the Finale which has been likened in spirit to an instrumental version of *Falstaff* and the fairies of Shakespearean fame. The Tuba Concerto was premiered in June 1954 by Philip Catelinet and the London Symphony Orchestra (to whom it is dedicated) under the direction of Sir John Barbirolli.

♪ RALPH VAUGHAN WILLIAMS (LEFT) PICTURED WITH SIR JOHN BARBIROLLI WHO CONDUCTED THE FIRST PERFORMANCE OF THE COMPOSER'S TUBA CONCERTO.

(saxhorns actually ranged in size from sopranino to contrabass). The result of this encounter is the so-called 'Wagner tuba', a hybrid of tuba and French horn with a distinctive oval shape and a wide bore that tapers rapidly towards the mouthpipe so that a horn mouthpiece can be used. Also in common with the horn, it uses rotary valves positioned under the fingers of the left hand rather than the right as in a normal tuba. The similarities mean that in performances of Wagner's *Ring* cycle, four of the eight horn players can double on Wagner tubas, two of them playing tenor instruments in B flat and two bass models in F (the same keys as standard orchestral horns). Wagner's instrument was later also used by Bruckner in his last three symphonies, Nos 7, 8 and 9, by Richard Strauss and by Schoenberg in *Gurrelieder* (1900–3).

♪ The Tuba Range

To this day the proliferation of different sized tubas has persisted, with instruments used in Britain, on the Continent and in America all differing in key. In Britain the E flat tuba is now most common, though in the late 19th century F instruments were typical. American orchestras, meanwhile, used contrabass B flat or E flat instruments. Later, tubas in low C were adopted to replace those in E flat and the F tuba came to be used as necessary to play parts at the upper end of the range. Different again were the French players who typically used 'tenor' tubas in C, and it was probably this instrument that Ravel had in mind when he used a high, muted tuba in *Bydlo*, part of his 1922 orchestration of Mussorgsky's *Pictures at an Exhibition*. Since 1945, the tuba has undergone something of a renaissance, with jazz and avant-garde musicians demonstrating that there is considerably more to this instrument than the 'Tubby' persona typically associated with it. ♪

♪ A SUB-CONTRA BASS TUBA WITH 34 FEET (10.5 METRES) WHICH CAME TO LIGHT IN 1957 IN THE BASEMENT SHOP OF SOHO (LONDON) INSTRUMENT MAKERS, PAXMAN BROTHERS.

♪ RARE BRASS

Although the instruments discussed here are being treated as distinct from the other members of the brass family, and by rights they are, several of them are closely associated with the standard brass through the tuba. Indeed, the euphonium and sousaphone are usually included as members of the modern tuba family.

℅ *Serpent*

Of these 'rare brass' the serpent is the most singular in appearance, with its characteristic undulating shape. However, it is unclear whether it should properly be treated as a brass instrument at all; really, it lies squarely in the no-man's land of plain 'wind'. The serpent's deep sound is half-way between a tuba and a bassoon. It is played like a brass instrument, with a cup-shaped mouthpiece, but its body is wooden and has keyed fingerholes. The instrument is said to have originated in France in the late 1500s to accompany plainchant in church. Towards the end of its life, in the late 19th century, it was used in military bands to support the bassoons' bass part.

The serpent rarely appeared outside church music and military bands, but Handel did include one in his celebratory *Music for the Royal Fireworks*

(1749). There are also reports of a player in the Prince Regent's private band commissioning an arrangement for serpent of a violin concerto by Corelli. What the instrument lacked in accuracy of intonation it must have made up for in agility! (See also page 193)

℅ *Ophicleide*

The ophicleide forms a useful link between the serpent and the euphonium. It is pitched in B flat, the same key as the euphonium, and it shares the same mouthpiece, but in appearance it is closer to an upright serpent (sometimes called 'Russian bassoon'), and it uses keys rather than valves. Though the ophicleide is now obsolete, it was used extensively during the 19th century to provide a bass part in brass and military bands as well as in the orchestra's brass section. When

played at its loudest the tone can be powerfully coarse, but the instrument is equally capable of a subtler 'vocal' quality of tone. The adaptable sound made the ophicleide a popular addition to the orchestrator's palette. (See also page 189)

℘ Saxhorn

Not satisfied with these other instruments, or with sticking to the saxophone for that matter, the ever-inventive Parisian Adolphe Sax produced, in 1845, the saxhorns. (Incidentally, we might conjecture that this over-expanded his business, for by 1852 Sax was bankrupt.) The saxhorns are closer still to the tubas, with bells pointing upwards (except in the smallest sizes) and *Berliner-pumpen* valves, patented in Germany for the first tubas. In actual fact, instrument-makers across Europe were all developing new brass instruments in different sizes, but Sax was the first to produce a complete family. It is believed to be the larger saxhorns that first prompted Wagner to come up with his own special tubas for the *Ring* (see page 45). The complete saxhorn family comprised nine sizes, from sopranino in B flat (the pitch of the present piccolo trumpet) to a 'sub-bass' model in E flat. The E flat alto remains in use as the tenor horn and the B flat bass is now the euphonium.

Berlioz is probably the best-known user of the saxhorn, having used two in his epic opera *Les Troyens* (1858), one sopranino in B flat and in 'The Royal Hunt and Storm' an E flat alto, though he later rescored the latter part for horn. The tenor horn is closely related to the *flügelhorn* (see below), and the name *flügelhorn* is sometimes mistakenly applied to the sopranino and soprano saxhorns.

℘ Euphonium

It is with the euphonium that we come closest to the modern tuba family. The instrument is usually referred to as the tenor tuba when it is used as an orchestral instrument. Its immediate predecessor is accepted as the bass saxhorn, although its name seems to have been adopted from an 1840s German design, suggesting the influence of the earlier *bombardon* bass tuba from that country. Pitched in B flat, the euphonium has a compass of about three octaves and is most commonly encountered in British brass bands where its velvety tone has an important solo role.

The euphonium has always had a special place as a solo instrument in British brass bands, so players of it are often capable of considerable virtuosity. Many of the 20th century's most important British composers have exploited this, using the euphonium to great effect in their music. They include Elgar, Vaughan Williams, Walton, Tippett and particularly Holst in *The Planets* (1916). Other notable users of the instrument have included Richard Strauss in *Don Quixote* (1897) and Stravinsky in *The Rite of Spring* (1913).

℘ Sousaphone

John Philip Sousa's bass tuba or sousaphone, designed for use in marching bands, was developed from the helicon introduced in Vienna in 1849. The helicon's name came from its 'helical' or spiral design which had tubing encircling the player's body with the instrument's weight carried on his left shoulder. Sousa's very similar version was topped by an enormous bell pointing straight up (a design irreverently dubbed 'the rain catcher'), though after modifications in 1908 it pointed forward to give the now-distinctive shape. This large bell actually serves no special purpose; rather its role is simply to pro-

vide a spectacle at the rear of the band. The sousaphone has also occasionally found its way into jazz ensembles.

℘ Flügelhorn and Mellophone

Of the multitude of other ancient and modern brass rarities, two are particularly worth mentioning. The first is the *flügelhorn*, a cornet-like instrument found in British brass bands and used by British composer Ralph Vaughan Williams in his Ninth Symphony (1956–8). The second is the mellophone, or tenor cor, which, although now very rare indeed, has found use as a jazz instrument and, on occasion, as a replacement for the French horn.

CHAPTER 2

Stringed Instruments

STRINGED INSTRUMENTS ARE those which produce their sound from a vibrating string set in motion by bowing, plucking or striking it. The first category includes not just the violin family, which has become the foundation of the modern orchestra, but also the viols which developed alongside them, plus a whole range of instruments whose existence has been more transitory. All of these rely on the player's non-bowing hand to stop the vibrating string at different points in order to raise its pitch. This is also a feature of many plucked instruments such as the guitar, although the harp provides the most notable exception. Most of the commoner struck stringed instruments really belong to the category of either keyboard or non-Western instruments.

THE ASSUMPTION OF THE VIRGIN (C. 1500), BY PIETRO DI CRISTOFERO VANUCCI, SHOWING ANGELS PLAYING HARP AND VIOLA DA BRACCIO.

VIOL

It is a common misconception that the viols preceded and evolved into the modern string family. Both can trace their ancestry back at least as far as the closing years of the 15th century and earlier paintings reveal evidence that in the Middle Ages two distinct types of bowed instruments were recognized, those played on the arm or shoulder (*da braccio*) and those held between the legs (*da gamba*). Nevertheless, it was the viol which first emerged as a distinct instrumental type and which remained the most important of the bowed strings throughout the Renaissance period.

Construction

The structure and design of the viol continued to evolve well into the Baroque, all the while retaining a number of features which distinguished the instrument from the upstart violin, principally the flat back and sloping shoulders. Its fingerboard was fretted like that of a guitar and its bow held with an underhand grip, not overhand as with the violin, viola or cello, thus enabling the player to control the tension of the hair with the middle finger. Moreover, it had between five and seven strings, with six being by far the commonest number. Another characteristic shared with the guitar is its tuning in fourths with the interval of a third between the third and fourth strings of six-stringed instruments.

A VIOL BY THE VENETIAN MAKER ANTONIO CICILIANO, DATED c. 1600.

Both viols and violins are already mentioned in the very first printed treatise on musical instruments, Sebastian Virdung's *Musica getutscht* (1511), in which a nine-string instrument is described. Eighteen years later five- and six-string viols are described in Martin Agricola's *Musica instrumentalis deudsch*. But the most important 16th-century document to discuss the instrument is the *Regolo Rubertina*, published by Silvestro Ganassi in 1542. This is the first treatise not only to describe and illustrate the viol but to provide instruction in how it was to be played. Both Agricola and Ganassi refer to the treble (its bass closer in tuning to what we would recognize as the tenor), tenor and bass as being the most important sizes. Ganassi, however, gives for these three instruments the tuning that was to become standard in the later Renaissance and Baroque: the bass pitched an octave lower than the treble and the tenor a fourth higher than the bass (see panel feature).

In Performance

The viol quickly established itself as a gregarious instrument, well suited to domestic music making. Affluent households would possess a 'chest' of viols as we might today have a piano, and it was considered part of a sound education to be able to take

---

TYPES OF *Viol*

PARDESSUS DE VIOLE Pitched a fourth above the treble but often lacks the lowest string, although seven-string instruments tuned like the treble but with an extra top g" string are known. A latecomer to the family, it developed in France in the early 18th century and was a popular amateur instrument.

TREBLE VIOL The smallest of the commonly used viols, this generally takes the top line in consort music. The six strings of the Baroque instrument are usually tuned *d, g, c', e', a', d"*.

ALTO VIOL Developed alongside its better known companions but was largely restricted to the occasional appearance in consort music, particularly in England. Ganassi describes it as a small tenor with identical tuning, but by the 17th century it was commonly pitched a whole tone lower than the treble, with some five-stringed examples lacking a top *c"*.

TENOR VIOL Provides the middle voices in consort music but has little solo repertoire. Its commonest tuning is *G, c, f, a, d', g'*; an instrument pitched a tone higher is occasionally found.

LYRA VIOL Can refer to an instrument midway in size between the tenor and bass, but equally used to describe a richly chordal style of solo playing popular in the 17th century.

BASS VIOL Often referred to simply as the viola da gamba. The foundation of the consort, it emerged in the Baroque era as a solo instrument in its own right. Its six strings are generally tuned *D, G, c, e, a, d*, but seven-string instruments with a low *A'* are not uncommon.

GREAT BASS VIOL Can be tuned like the seven-string bass without the top *d*, or with the *c* tuned to *B*.

VIOLONE Pitched an octave below the bass viol and the ancestor of the modern double bass.

one's part in a piece for a group, or consort, of viols. This was particularly true in England which, like France, was slower to succumb to the charms of the violin, which was then gaining ground in Italy. In the Elizabethan and Jacobean periods particularly, pieces in several parts were often deemed 'apt for voices or viols', while a great heritage of purely instrumental music has been bequeathed to us by composers such as William Byrd and Orlando Gibbons.

In England chamber music with viols, or for the 'broken consort' of mixed instruments, remained popular well into the 17th century. Charles I learnt the viol from the younger Alfonso Ferrabosco and maintained his own consort, as did Oliver Cromwell, despite his strict views on public music. Chamber music actually flourished during the Protectorate, with

composers like John Jenkins and William Lawes contributing significantly to the viol's repertoire. It also witnessed the increasing emergence of the bass viol as a solo instrument. In 1659 Christopher Simpson published his enormously successful *The division violist*, giving instruction in the playing of 'divisions' or variations as well as the technique of the viol. Although the Restoration saw the beginning of the decline in the viol's fortunes, it did produce, in Purcell's *Fantasias*, a worthy swansong to a noble tradition. At the same time France was enjoying a golden age of viol playing; the solo music of Marin Marais, Caix d'Hervelois and Antoine Forqueray is central to the player's art. In Germany, too, the late Baroque produced some fine music for the bass viol. Bach wrote three sonatas for the instrument and included it in the sixth

'Brandenburg' concerto as well as numerous choral works. Carl Friedrich Abel, the last of the great viola da gamba virtuosi, was the business partner of Bach's youngest son, Johann Christian, in London.

Although the bass viol probably never became totally obsolete as an amateur instrument, the viols disappeared from concert life during the Classical and Romantic periods. Their modern revival began in the 1890s when the pioneering early music specialist Arnold Dolmetsch gave his first concerts on surviving viols and began to make modern copies. A century later we take it for granted that we can hear the huge viol repertoire played on the instruments for which it was intended. Many fine instruments are also being made or copied from originals. 𝄢

Viol
CONFUSION
※

The fact that the word viol translates into Italian as viola sometimes causes confusion. True viols are always played between the knees, hence the name viola da gamba ('leg viol'). This can refer to instruments of any size within the family, but is usually reserved for the bass viol (see illustration left). The commonest types of viol are the treble, tenor and bass; see page 49.

A GROUP OF MUSICIANS DEPICTED BY LOUIS LE NAIN (C. 1593–1648). THE PLAYER ON THE LEFT HOLDS A BASS VIOL.

♪VIOLIN

♪ AN EXAMPLE OF A
VIOLIN FROM THE
WORKSHOP OF ONE OF
THE GREATEST MAKERS OF
STRINGED INSTRUMENTS,
NICOLO AMATI –
SEE FEATURE

IF YOU STAND beneath the dome of Saronno Cathedral in Italy and look upwards, your eye will be caught by the splendid frescoes painted by Gaudenzio Ferrari. They date from around 1535 and show angels playing instruments, among them the earliest known collective representation of the modern string family of violin, viola and cello. They appear to have three strings, but by the mid-century four-stringed instruments were already known, as both written and pictorial evidence shows. Much of this evidence confirms that, although the violin family soon found its way across Europe, it was in Italy that it could claim to have been born. Some of the earliest true violins to survive come from northern Italy, chiefly the Milanese areas of Brescia and Cremona, and Venice, a part of the world which was to maintain pre-eminence in violin making for the next two centuries. The first known maker was Andreas Amati, the founder of the celebrated Cremona school, who was born there some time at the beginning of the 16th century.

The Italian *violino* simply means 'little viola', but there is no evidence to support the notion that the viola predates its smaller sibling. Confusion is apt to arise because *viola* is the Italian for 'viol'. Early references to both viola and violin often specify that they are *da braccio*, probably to differentiate them from the viols, which were never played 'on the arm'.

✳ Construction

Although the violin has undergone several modifications since the 16th century, its structure has remained essentially the same. The front (or belly), the back and the middle section (or ribs) are made as separate pieces from a soft wood, such as spruce. The bottom, top and corners of the rib section are reinforced by blocks. The belly is pierced by two sound holes shaped like a cursive 'f', and a bass bar is attached to its underside, running parallel to the lower strings, its position determined by one foot of the bridge which supports the strings. Underneath the opposite foot of the bridge is the soundpost, which runs vertically towards the back of the instrument. At one end of the neck, which is made separately of a harder wood, is the scroll, containing the tuning pegs. The strings run from these across the fingerboard, placed on top of the neck, over the bridge to the tail piece which is looped around the end button. The start of the fingerboard is marked by the nut. The inlaid decoration around the edges of the belly and back is known as 'purfling'.

The earliest bows of the violin family seem to have been modelled on those of the viol. The wood was convex and the frog which held the horsehair at the end nearest the player was fixed, leaving the fingers of the right hand to vary the tension. Violin bows of the 16th and early 17th centuries could be as short as 35cm (14 inches), particularly those used in dance music, one area where the violin quickly found a niche.

For four-stringed instruments the modern *g, d', a', e"* tuning had been established by the late

♪ AS THIS ILLUSTRATION SHOWS, THE
EARLIEST VIOLINS WERE NOT HELD
ON THE SHOULDER AS THEY ARE
NOWADAYS. NOTE ALSO THE BOW, WHICH
IS SHORT AND CONVEX.

Famous Violin Makers

THE AMATIS

Italy's early predominance in the making of string instruments lasted for well over two centuries. The earliest recorded name is that of Andrea Amati (c.1505–80), the Cremonese founder of a whole dynasty of makers, or *luthiers*. He was followed by his two sons, Antonio (c.1538–95) and Girolamo (c.1561–1630). The latter's son Nicolo (1596–1684) was the most illustrious of the Amatis. Some of his violins are characterized by their large size compared to those of his father and uncle and by their correspondingly more powerful tone. Instruments by Nicolo Amati can be recognized from their label signed *Nicolaus Amati Cremonens, Hieronimi filius Antonii nepos* ('Nicolo Amati of Cremona, son of Girolamo and nephew of Antonio'). Nicolo was also the teacher of Guarneri and Stradivari. His son Girolamo II (1649–1740) was the last of the dynasty. Although influenced by Stradivari, his workmanship rarely equalled that of his mentor or his father.

THE GUARNERIS

The head of Cremona's second great violin-making dynasty, Andreas Guarneri (c.1625–98), trained under Nicolo Amati and lived in his house as an apprentice. Instruments from this period are labelled *alumnus* ('pupil'); from 1655 this changes to *ex alumnis* ('from the school of'). His son Pietro (1655–1720) worked first at Cremona and thereafter at Mantua. Like his father, he often designated himself *sub titolo Sanctae Theresiae* ('under the label of St. Teresa'). His brother Giuseppe (1666–c.1740) remained in and eventually inherited his father's workshop; his own son Pietro II (1695–1762) moved to Venice and is distinguished from his uncle by the epithet *Pietro di Venezia*. The most celebrated Guarneri violins are those of Giuseppe's son, Giuseppe Antonio (1698–1744), known as *Giuseppe del Gesù* from the *IHS* (*Iesus hominum salvator* or 'Jesus, saviour of mankind') which distinguishes his labels. He sought constantly to improve the violin through experimenting with different materials and designs; as a result, his instruments are held by many to be second only to those of Stradivari.

STRADIVARI

Antonio Stradivari (1644–1737) claimed to have been Nicolo Amati's pupil from 1667 to 1679, although his earliest known instrument is dated 1666. He may have begun as a wood carver under Amati and possibly worked for others in this capacity, since otherwise few instruments survive from these years. His earlier violins reveal Amati's influence and his most highly prized ones date from the first two decades of the 18th century. Several of them are highly ornate, especially in such details as the purfling or tailpiece. The best of these instruments fetch very high prices; Stradivari's cellos and violas, being rarer, higher still. A genuine 'Strad' bears the label *Antonius Stradivarius Cremonensis fecit anno* ('made by Anthony of Cremona in the year'), followed by the year of manufacture. Two of Stradivari's sons, Francesco (1671–1743) and Omobono (1679–1742), were also active as makers under his tutelage.

Renaissance. The strings at this stage were of gut, and would remain so until the 19th century, although a wire-bound *g* string was increasingly common from the start of the 18th. The practice of *scordatura* (that is, tuning the strings to other than their normal pitches) was already known in the 17th century, as witnessed by the *Rosary* sonatas (c.1676) of the Austrian Heinrich Biber.

❧ The Violin in Music

The violin was naturally first used consistently in Italy, but its description as a familiar instrument in Michael Praetorius's *Syntagma musicum* (1618) shows that it must have been established in Germany by this time. Its profile in France was boosted by the establishment in 1626 of Louis XIII's *24 violons du Roi* (actually a string orchestra rather than a collection of violins), which was continued by his successor, Louis XIV, and imitated at the English court of Charles II. It was already accepted practice to divide the violins proper into first and second players; a distinction maintained, with few exceptions, in the modern orchestra. The orchestra would be directed either from the keyboard or by the principal first violin, hence the tradition of regarding this player as the leader of an orchestra. In large-scale 19th- or 20th-century works he or she may be called upon to play major orchestral solos, such as those in Richard Strauss's *Ein Heldenleben* or Rimsky-Korsakov's *Scheherazade*.

The violin's good fortune was to be recognized for its versatility and wide expressive range at a time when instrumental music was in the ascendant. The early Baroque composers had not been slow to employ it in their vocal music, but it was in the expanding field of chamber and later orchestral music that the violin was to achieve a position of dominance, and once again it was Italy which took the lead. Arcangelo Corelli, a gifted violinist himself, developed the three main instrumental forms of the late Baroque. These were the solo sonata for treble instrument and continuo, the trio sonata for two treble instruments and continuo, and the *concerto grosso*. The last-mentioned contrasted a solo group or *concertino*, usually of two violins and cello, with a fuller body, or *ripieno*, of strings and continuo. With the concurrent rise of the solo concerto under composers such as Antonio Vivaldi, the violin emerged as the virtuoso's instrument *par excellence*.

ONE OF LOUIS XIII'S FAMED 'VIOLONS DU ROI', A STRING ORCHESTRA COMPRISING 24 PLAYERS RESIDENT AT THE FRENCH COURT.

Violin Concertos

ANTONIO VIVALDI wrote more than 300 concertos for one or more violins, including the well known 'Four Seasons' which appeared as part of his Op.8 collection *Il cimento dell'armonia e dell'invenzione*.

WOLFGANG AMADEUS MOZART was only seventeen years old when he composed his first violin concerto, in 1773. Two years later, he produced another four, all in the space of six months. The last of them is sometimes called the 'Turkish' Concerto on account of an episode in its rondo which reflects the contemporary fashion for Turkish culture.

LUDWIG VAN BEETHOVEN'S violin concerto is one of the finest works of his middle period and the first of the great 19th-century concertos. When the dedicatee, Clement, complained of its difficulty, the composer is reputed to have replied, "What do I care for your miserable fiddle when I am talking to my God?"

FELIX MENDELSSOHN wrote a concerto for violin and strings while still in his teens, but the work for which he is remembered is the Op. 64 Concerto in E minor (1845). This was written towards the end of his short life, for Ferdinand David, then leader of the Leipzig Gewandhaus orchestra.

JOHANNES BRAHMS wrote his concerto for the famous Hungarian violinist Joseph Joachim. It was for Joachim and the cellist Robert Hausmann that he also wrote the Double Concerto, Op. 102 (1887) – his last orchestral work.

PYOTR IL'YCH TCHAIKOVSKY wrote a concerto for Leopold Auer which the player initially refused to perform on the grounds that it was too difficult. Only after reading a review did the composer become aware that the first performance had been given in Vienna by Adolph Brodsky, to whom he re-dedicated the work in gratitude.

JEAN SIBELIUS, himself a violinist, wrote his only violin concerto in 1903. The version usually heard nowadays is a revision of 1905.

EDWARD ELGAR Many would claim the finest English violin concerto to be that written by Elgar. Completed in 1910, the work was premiered that year by Fritz Kreisler.

ALBAN BERG wrote his hauntingly lyrical violin concerto (1935), originally a commission from the American violinist Louis Krasner, in memory of Alma Mahler's daughter, Manon Gropius, who had died in her teens. The closing pages of the concerto, which was Berg's last completed work, quote the Bach chorale *Es ist genug*.

SERGEI PROKOFIEV's first violin concerto (Op. 19 in D major) is a youthfully energetic work, composed between 1916 and 1917 when the composer was working on his well known *Classical Symphony*. Its darker-hued companion, Op.63 in G minor, dates from 1935 – the same period as *Peter and the Wolf*.

DMITRI SHOSTAKOVICH, Prokofiev's Russian compatriot, also wrote two violin concertos, both for David Oistrakh. The first was completed in 1948 as Op. 77, but not premiered until 1955 and then in a revised version as Opus 99. The second, one of its composer's last orchestral works (Op. 129), followed in 1967.

ALFRED SCHNITTKE, the contemporary Russian composer, has consistently championed the concerto. The first of his four works in the medium was written in 1957 and revised six years later; the others date from between 1966 and 1984. Schnittke has also written concertos for viola and cello and his six *Concerti grossi* have significant parts for one or more violins.

✄ The Violin and the Bow

The instrument itself was adapted to meet the new demands being made on it. The string player's left hand alters the pitch by stopping the string with the fingers to shorten it. Placing the index finger at differing places on the string is known as 'changing position'. The increasing

PAGANINI, THE MOST CELEBRATED OF ALL VIOLIN VIRTUOSOS AND ONE OF THE MOST ACCOMPLISHED.

use of higher positions led to a lengthening of the neck. The bow, too, changed, losing some of its convexity and becoming standardized in length at around 75cm (30 inches), giving a playing length of some 65cm (26 inches). The bridge would have been flatter than a modern one, facilitating the performance of multiple stops (playing on more than one string at a time), which were now part of the instrument's vocabulary. Composers openly exploited such colouristic devices as *pizzicato*, or plucking the string, and the rapidly reiterated bow-stroke known as *tremolando*. Much of what we know about 18th-century tech-

nique is found in important treatises, such as Leopold Mozart's *Versuch einer gründlichen Violinschule* (1756) or Francesco Geminiani's *The art of playing on the violin* (1751).

A major breakthrough in the development of the modern bow came in the 1780s with a new design by François Tourte. His bow was concave, with an adjustable frog at the heel and a broader hair-width. The hair was prevented from bunching at the frog by means of a ferrule. At the opposite end from the heel, the point assumed its current upward, curving profile to compensate for the maximum concavity at the centre. South American pernambuco was the favoured wood.

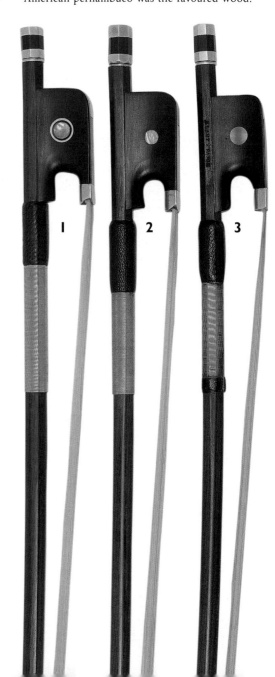

1   2   3

Tourte's design combined lightness – the whole bow weighed around 56 grammes – with power and strength. These innovations played their part in establishing a French school of violin technique equal to that of the hitherto dominant Italians. By the 19th century, and despite the emergence of players like Nicolo Paganini, the Italian school had been virtually overtaken.

♪ BOWS BY FAMOUS MAKERS DISPLAY EXQUISITE CRAFTSMANSHIP AND THE USE OF FINE MATERIALS SUCH AS EBONY, SILVER AND PEARL. BELOW ARE BOWS FOR VIOLIN (1), VIOLA (2) AND CELLO (3–6).

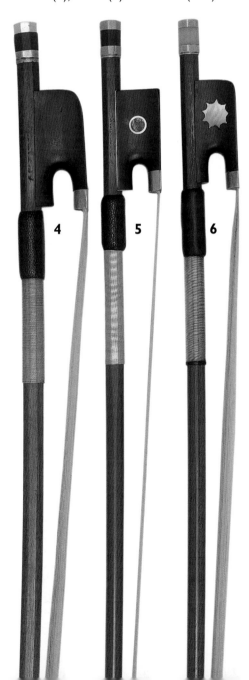

4   5   6

Past Masters

NICOLA MATTEIS was one of the many musicians drawn to the artistic climate of Restoration London, the Neapolitan Matteis is among the earliest recorded violin virtuosos. In London he published a theoretical tutor, *The false consonances of musick* (1682), and four volumes of pieces for violin. Writers including John Evelyn, Roger North and Charles Burney testify to the part he played in introducing the Italian style to England. His son, also called Nicola, taught Burney.

ARCANGELO CORELLI's legacy includes four sets of trio sonatas for two violins and continuo, Op.1–4, the Op.5 solo sonatas and the Op.6 *concerti grossi*. Born in Bologna, he went to Rome in 1671 as a professional violinist. He was the creator of modern violin technique; among his innovations was the exploitation of double and triple-stopping. (Corelli's portrait above right)

FRANCESCO GEMINIANI was a pupil of Corelli who paid his master the compliment of publishing several arrangements of his music. In 1731 he settled in London where he published numerous treatises, of which the most important is *The art of playing on the violin* (1751), credited with being the first comprehensive tutor for the instrument. Geminiani inherited his teacher's interest in technical development and was a pioneer in demanding frequent changes of position.

GIUSEPPE TARTINI was not originally intended for a musical career. He became director of music at the church of St. Antonio in Padua, where he was also active as a violinist and teacher. His interest in acoustics led, in 1714, to his discovery of resultant tones (formed by the difference between two frequencies). Of Tartini's 191 violin sonatas, the most famous is the so-called *Devil's Trill*. His influential treatise *L'arte dell'arco* contains 50 variations on a gavotte from one of Corelli's Op.5 sonatas.

NICOLO PAGANINI was the last and greatest of the Italian virtuosi; some would say the greatest violinist ever. Of humble Genoese origins, he initially studied the mandolin with his father. He was also an expert guitarist and left many compositions for that instrument as well as for violin. The latter include concertos, chamber music and works for solo violin, all of which testify to his extraordinary technical skill. The last of his 24 *Caprices* for solo violin is the source of the theme used for variations by Rachmaninov, Brahms, Lutoslawski and others.

HENRI VIEUXTEMPS This Belgian-born violinist was a child prodigy who gave his first recital at the age of six. His many violin works include seven concertos, highly thought of in their day, and a number of salon pieces. Vieuxtemps eventually became Professor of Violin at the Brussels Conservatoire, where his pupils included Eugène Ysaÿe.

HENRYK WIENIAWSKI succeeded Vieuxtemps at the Conservatoire. Polish-born, he studied in Paris and toured widely as a virtuoso. He is one of the few composer-virtuosos whose output was not wholly dominated by music for his own instrument.

JOSEPH JOACHIM's compositions may not be as popular now as during his lifetime, but the Hungarian violinist is remembered as a friend of Brahms and the dedicatee of his violin concerto.

PABLO DE SARASATE, a Spanish contemporary of Brahms, wrote a series of *Spanish dances* which retain their popularity as showpieces.

℘ *The Violin as Performer*

The violin of the early 19th century is essentially the instrument as it appears today. The neck is somewhat longer than in the violin of the preceding century, because playing up to the seventh position was now taken for granted. To facilitate this, the angle of the neck was made more pronounced and a sturdier bass-bar and soundpost incorporated to withstand higher

string tension and to give more power to the sound. Many older violins were adapted to accommodate these changes. Strings were still of gut and the *d'* and *a* strings were now sometimes wound with wire as the *g* had been for several decades, although the all-metal *e'* string was still unknown. The bridge supporting the strings was generally more arched. One important addition of the period was the introduction of the chin-rest, an invention attributed to the composer and violin virtuoso, Louis Spohr. This freed the left hand from any role in supporting the instrument

YEHUDI MENUHIN BEGAN HIS CAREER AS A CHILD PRODIGY AND DEVELOPED INTO ONE OF THE WORLD'S MOST RENOWNED PLAYERS.

and allowed for a greater use of *vibrato*, the conscious oscillation in the sound effected by the fingers of the left hand; this had previously been used more sparingly as an expressive device.

Numerous other techniques had become accepted by the 19th century, although used with varying frequency. They include playing *col legno* (that is, with the wood of the bow), first required by Haydn in his Symphony No. 67 (c.1778); and *sul ponticello* (on the bridge), which gives a particularly eerie, nasal sound. Harmonics are produced by touching, rather than pressing, an open or stopped string at specific points. They are a great feature of certain virtuoso showpieces, as is left-hand *pizzicato* used in conjunction with bowed notes. Older recordings also show how much the tradition of sliding between notes, or *portamento*, survived into the early decades of the present century. To these colouristic effects the 20th century has added the so-called 'Bartók pizzicato', where the string is plucked with sufficient force for it to rebound on the fingerboard. Electronic amplification has also been tried, especially where the violin is employed in jazz or folk music. 𝄢

THE 'DORIA' VIOLIN BY OMOBONO STRADIVARI, YOUNGER SON, AND PUPIL, OF THE RENOWNED CREMONESE MAKER ANTONIO STRADIVARI.

Violin Virtuosos
OF THE 20TH CENTURY

FRITZ KREISLER Many of the great players of the Romantic era were still active when Kreisler was born. He died in an age which deemed technical wizardry alone insufficient qualification for immortality and where recorded sound could broadcast the artistry of the few to an audience of millions. Born in Vienna, where he studied with Hellmesberger and Dont, Kreisler eventually settled in the United States and took US citizenship. Unlike his predecessors, whose chief vehicle for display was their own music, Kreisler was renowned as a great interpreter and advocated re-evaluation of the violin's early repertoire. To this end he even promoted pieces of his own composition, which he ascribed to older masters. His lighter pieces are the staple of the recitalist's encore repertoire. He gave the first performance of the Elgar concerto.

JASCHA HEIFETZ, whom many would put on a par with Kreisler, was born in Vilna, Lithuania. He, too, became an American citizen. Heifetz made his recital debut at the age of five and a year later performed the Mendelssohn Concerto. He was only eleven when he tackled the Tchaikovsky Concerto in public, in Berlin under Artur Nikisch. His technique was flawless and always placed at the service of the music. Among the numerous concertos written for him is that by Walton. He retired from solo playing around 1970, but continued to teach.

JOSEF SZIGETI, a Hungarian and yet another adoptive American, was the co-dedicatee (with the clarinettist Benny Goodman) of Bartók's *Contrasts*. He epitomized the notion that musicianship is ultimately more important than mere technical brilliance.

GINETTE NEVEU would undoubtedly be recognized as one of the finest players of her generation if she had she not died in a plane crash at the age of 30. A child prodigy who studied with Menuhin's teacher, George Enescu, and Carl Flesch, she beat David Oistrakh into second place at the 1935 International Wieniawski Competition. Poulenc dedicated his Sonata to her.

DAVID OISTRAKH went on to become the most famous Russian violinist of the post-war period, premiering major works by, among others, Shostakovich and Prokofiev. His son and most illustrious pupil, Igor Oistrakh, now wears his father's crown.

YEHUDI MENUHIN is honoured as much for his skills as an educationalist and conductor as for his violin playing. Another child prodigy, he made a memorable recording of Elgar's concerto under the composer. The Menuhin School, which he founded in Surrey in 1963, is an important training ground for young musicians. His enquiring mind has led him in the direction of Indian music and, in 1973, he recorded an album with the jazz violinist Stephane Grappelli. Among the many works written for him is Bartók's unaccompanied Sonata.

ISAAC STERN, an American violinist of Russian origin, is a grand-pupil of Adolph Brodsky, having studied with his protégé, Naoum Blinder. Open-minded in his approach to new repertoire, he premiered the Concerto (1985) by Peter Maxwell Davies. A noted chamber musician, he founded a successful piano trio with Eugene Istomin and Leonard Rose in 1961.

ITZHAK PERLMAN, the child of Israeli parents, is equally at home in chamber music as in the concerto repertoire, like his compatriot, Stern. After studying at the Juilliard School he launched a brilliant career with a Carnegie Hall debut in 1963.

VIOLA

IT IS IRONIC THAT the instrument regarded for much of its history as the Cinderella of the string family should bear the name from which those of its members are derived. *Viola* is simply the Italian word for 'viol'. Throughout the 16th and early 17th century it is usually found with the designation *da gamba* or *da braccio* to indicate the family of instruments to which it belonged. The viola, like the violin, appears in the Saronno Cathedral frescoes of c.1535. By the end of the 16th century it had established itself as the alto or tenor instrument of the violin family.

THIS CLOSE-UP SHOWS THE METICU-
LOUS FINISH ENJOYED BY THE BEST
STRINGED INSTRUMENTS. NOTE THE
FINE GRAIN AND THE DECORATED EDGE
TO THE BODY, KNOWN AS 'PURFLING'.

❧ Construction

The existence of numerous violas from the late Renaissance and early Baroque periods shows that it was frequently made in different sizes, with the smaller instruments used for the higher middle parts in ensemble playing and larger ones for the lower parts. The *c, g, d', a'* tuning, a fifth below the violin, was the same for each. Even today the viola remains the most variable in size of the string family. In order for it to be as acoustically perfect as the violin, it needs to be half as long again, rendering it unplayable on the shoulder. The resultant compromise, giving an instrument of anywhere between 38 and 45 centimetres (15–18 inches) in length, has played its part in the viola's slow emergence as a solo instrument compared with the violin and cello.

❧ In Performance

Nevertheless, the survival of numerous instruments from the 16th and 17th centuries shows that the viola's role as a harmonic filler, if humble, was deemed essential. Five-part string textures, with two violas, are not uncommon in 17th-century French music, for example; Jean-Baptiste Lully for one was especially fond of them. Yet the viola could never compete in brilliance with the violin, nor could it share the cello's usefulness in providing a continuo bass. Viola players, who were rarely, if ever, specialists, were not expected to possess the same level of proficiency as violinists. They were the beginners, the also-rans or, in contemporary parlance, "horn players who had lost their teeth".

Besides, the musical language of the high Baroque was conceived essentially in three parts. The viola had no place in the trio sonata for two treble instruments and continuo, or its orchestral counterpart, the *concerto grosso*'s preferred *concertino* group of two violins and cello. Only at the very end of the period do we find composers, such as Francesco Geminiani, expanding the *concertino* to include a solo viola.

In the orchestral music of the late Baroque and early Classical era the viola, where it was not omitted entirely, was frequently called upon to double the second violins at the unison or, more commonly, the bass line an octave higher. This latter practice died hard, so that even in early 19th century scores such doubling is extremely

THE GERMAN COMPOSER PAUL HINDEMITH, HIMSELF A VIOLA PLAYER OF GREAT DISTINCTION, CONTRIBUTED MAJOR WORKS TO THE INSTRUMENT'S REPERTOIRE, INCLUDING A NUMBER OF SONATAS AND *CONCERTANTE* PIECES WITH ORCHESTRA.

common in orchestral *tuttis*. Composers were, moreover, reluctant to entrust any important thematic material to the violas. For example, as late as his Ninth Symphony (1824) we find Beethoven, in the slow movement, doubling the violas with the second violins as a safety measure. Imagine the surprise, perhaps even shock, experienced by the viola players at the first rehearsals for Tchaikovsky's Symphony No. 6 in B minor, the *Pathétique* (1893), who found themselves expected to play the main theme of the first movement *on their own*.

Viola Concertos

J.S. BACH The viola's long neglect as a solo instrument has left it with only a minimal number of concertos from the Baroque era. By far the most important is Bach's sixth 'Brandenburg' Concerto (c. 1718), a chamber concerto in which the two upper parts are taken by a pair of violas, accompanied by two viole da gamba with cello and bass. The violas and cello alone play in the trio-sonata style slow movement.

GEORG PHILIPP TELEMANN Bach's contemporary was reputedly the most prolific composer in Western music, so it is not surprising that he wrote the first concerto for solo viola to survive in the repertoire. This is the concerto in G major; there is also a concerto for two *violetti*, also in G major.

WOLFGANG AMADEUS MOZART A violist himself, Mozart gave the instrument a prominent role in many of his chamber works but left no solo concerto. What we do have is the magnificent *Sinfonia concertante* (K364) for violin, viola and orchestra, written in 1779. Mozart's intention, rarely observed these days, was that the solo viola should be tuned a semitone higher so as to balance the violin in brilliance; since the work is in E flat, the viola would thus have to play in the brighter key of D major, allowing for more use of open strings. In all three movements the orchestral violas, like the violins, are divided into firsts and seconds. Mozart sketched but never completed a similar work for violin, viola, cello and orchestra.

HECTOR BERLIOZ The two finest *concertante* works from the 19th century are not concertos at all. When Paganini approached Berlioz for a solo work to show off a Stradivari viola he had acquired, the response was *Harold in Italy*, a symphony with viola *obbligato* which Paganini dismissed as insufficiently virtuosic. Inspired by Byron's *Childe Harold*, this programmatic work of 1834 casts the soloist as the eponymous hero.

RICHARD STRAUSS adopted a similar technique to Berlioz in his tone-poem *Don Quixote* of 1897, personifying Quixote and Sancho Panza as, respectively, solo cello and viola.

WILLIAM WALTON Completed in 1929 and revised in 1961, the concerto by Walton established him as a major young force in English music. Despite being one of the composer's earliest and most lyrical scores, it was rejected as too modern by its intended executant, Lionel Tertis, and the premiere was given by Hindemith.

PAUL HINDEMITH did more than any other composer to enrich the 20th-century repertoire with works for an instrument he played himself. As well as several sonatas for viola, he composed four *concertante* works with orchestra: *Kammermusik No. 5* (1927), *Konzertmusik* (1930), a concerto (*Der Schwanendreher*), based on folk material (1935), and the *Trauermusik* (1936), written at short notice in memory of King George V.

BELA BARTOK The virtuoso player William Primrose commissioned a concerto from Bartók in 1945. Left incomplete at the composer's death, the piece was reconstructed from Bartók's sketches by Tibor Serly and in this form is accepted as a core work in the violist's repertoire.

ABOVE: LIONEL TERTIS, A GREAT 20TH CENTURY ENGLISH PIONEER OF THE VIOLA. HE FAVOURED A LARGE INSTRUMENT.

LEFT: AN ITALIAN VIOLA FROM THE SCHOOL OF GASPARO DA SALÒ, C. 1600.

℣ The Viola Comes of Age

Real liberation for the viola came through the medium of chamber music, and most of all through the emergence of the string quartet, yet even here the path to equality was by no means smooth. In several early quartets by Joseph Haydn, the composer who did more than any other to develop the genre, the viola is still to be seen chasing the cello in octaves or at the unison. It is only with the ground-breaking Op. 33 quartets of 1781 that the egalitarian ideal is truly achieved.

A further step forward is taken in the string quintets of Wolfgang Amadeus Mozart. These use two violas, with the first player, along with the violinist, often enjoying a *concertante* role, as in the slow movement of the C major quintet (K515). However, even Mozart's quintets found few immediate imitators and his piano quartets, which added a viola to the more familiar three-some of piano, violin and cello, were regarded as a commercial risk. Ironically, the most familiar Mozart's trios is the so-called *Kegelstadt* ('Skittle-ground') Trio for clarinet, viola and piano (K498), which Mozart is said to have composed while playing skittles.

To play an effective part in chamber music the violist would require more technical facility than his or her orchestral counterpart. Taking a role equal to that of the violin or cello demanded a greater proficiency in the higher positions, for example. By the 19th century this was taken for granted. Violists would have a rewarding time in works such as the youthful Octet of Mendelssohn or the two string sextets by Brahms. Unlike their predecessors, who scorned the viola's lack of brilliance, the Romantic composers valued the viola precisely because of its darker, rather veiled sound, thereby opening up a whole new world of possibilities for the orchestral player. At the same time the solo repertoire remained small. There are no major concertos and precious few sonatas, although examples exist by Mendelssohn and Glinka, and Brahms' two sonatas for clarinet prescribe the viola as an alternative. The charming *Märchenbilder* of Robert Schumann should not be forgotten, either. Nor were there any important tutors; viola technique was still held to be little different from the violin's.

A change of attitude has finally come about in the present century, principally through the pioneering efforts of players such as Lionel Tertis and William Primrose and of the composer and violist Paul Hindemith. No longer seen as the preserve of second-rate violinists, the viola now enjoys parity with its smaller and larger companions. The result has been a larger solo repertoire than at any other time in its history, and a growing one at that. With this resurgence in the viola's popularity, the instrument preferred by Bach, Mozart and Schubert has finally taken its rightful place on the concert platform. 𝄡

Famous Violists

THE SPECIALIST VIOLA PLAYER IS A RECENT PHENOMENON, A REFLECTION OF THE INSTRUMENT'S HISTORICAL LACK OF STATUS. MANY PLAYERS OF THE PAST, PARTICULARLY ORCHESTRAL MUSICIANS, WOULD HAVE BEEN PRIMARILY VIOLINISTS. NEVERTHELESS, SEVERAL COMPOSERS OF THE 18TH AND 19TH CENTURIES ARE KNOWN TO HAVE PREFERRED TO PLAY THE VIOLA, NOTABLY J. S. BACH, MOZART AND SCHUBERT. THE FIRST GREAT VIRTUOSO WHOSE NAME IS LINKED WITH THE INSTRUMENT IS ALSO BETTER REMEMBERED AS A VIOLINIST.

NICOLO PAGANINI not only played but wrote for the viola, even though his compositions for it are far less numerous than those for the violin. The most important are a *Terzetto concertante* for viola, cello and guitar (1833) – Paganini was also a noted guitarist – and the intriguingly entitled *Sonata per gran viola* (1834) with orchestra, the 'large viola' of the title being a five-stringed instrument. Paganini's rejection of what would have become the finest work in his viola repertoire is discussed in the feature Viola Concertos on page 59 (see under Berlioz).

LIONEL TERTIS was the pioneer of the viola's rehabilitation as a solo instrument. Initially a violin student at the Leipzig Conservatoire, the English-born Tertis was prompted to devote himself to the viola by his experience in playing quartets. In his long career he toured as a virtuoso and recounted his experiences in three books, *Beauty of tone in string playing* (1938) and two autobiographical works, the appropriately named *Cinderella no more* (1953) and *My viola and I* (1974). Tertis was the inspiration for several 20th-century viola works, including Walton's Concerto; his main shortcoming as far as the history of the viola is concerned was a lack of sympathy with contemporary music. Only belatedly did he warm to the Walton and he never played any of Hindemith's viola works.

WILLIAM PRIMROSE also began as a violinist and took up the viola at the suggestion of his teacher, Ysaÿe. Much of the Scotsman's career was in the United States; he led the violas in Toscanini's NBC Symphony Orchestra from 1937 to 1942 and later taught at the universities of Southern California and Indiana. He founded his own quartet in 1937, published *A method for violin and viola players* in 1960 and is best known for having commissioned Bartók's unfinished concerto.

FREDERICK RIDDLE, at one time principal viola with the London Philharmonic and Royal Philharmonic, was an enthusiastic champion of contemporary music. He made the first recording of Walton's concerto in 1937 and is the dedicatee of concertos by Martin Dalby and Justin Connolly.

YURI BASHMET is considered by many to be the finest violist of his generation – and certainly the only one to cite playing guitar in a rock band as a formative influence. He switched to viola only in his teens after starting his musical education as a violinist. Thereafter he studied with Vadim Borisovsky at the Moscow Conservatoire. Bashmet won the prestigious Munich Competition in 1976. He is the founder of the Moscow Soloists, with whom he premiered Schnittke's Concerto, and has appeared with leading orchestras worldwide.

CELLO

THE FULL NAME of the cello is violoncello, which literally means 'little violone' – the violone being the double bass. Paradoxically, although the cello was fairly quick to achieve a recognizably modern form, its name emerged only in the 17th century, some century or so after the instrument itself. One of its earliest designations was, confusingly, *basso di viola da braccio*, a correct if clumsy attempt to indicate that it was the bass of the family of 'arm viols' – the violins – as opposed to the viols which were held, like the cello, between the knees. In England the simple name bass violin persisted for much of the 17th century, paralleled in France by the equivalent *basse de violon*, although both were eventually to take on a distinct meaning of their own.

✻ Tuning

Once again it is Agricola's *Musica instrumentalis deudsch* which provides us with our first description of the cello, in this case a three-stringed instrument tuned *F, c, g*, giving the instrument the same pitch relationship to the viola as that instrument has to the violin. Consequently, when a fourth string was added, it was the *B flat* below the bottom *F*. Several 16th-century theorists refer to such a tuning, but as early as 1532 the modern tuning *C, G, d, a* is mentioned in Gerle's *Musica teusch*. The second part of Michael Praetorius *Syntagma musicum* (1619) describes both the modern tuning and one a fourth higher (*F, c, g, d*) and illustrates a five-stringed cello, tuned *F', C, G, d, a*. This instrument, which goes almost as low as the modern double bass, was obviously too large to be held between the knees, because it is shown with a tail-pin.

The higher pitched modern tuning certainly appears to have been commoner in Italy by the beginning of the 17th century. The lower tuning seems to have been indicated for the English bass violin and the French *basse de violon*, and this was retained in both countries into the early 18th century.

✻ Fingering and Bowing

Although the cello is tuned in fifths like the violin and viola, its larger size precludes the adoption of their pattern of fingering. In first position on the cello the index finger will give a tone above the open string, but two fingers are

'A MUSIC PARTY' (1733), BY PHILIP MERCIER, SHOWING THE CELLO-PLAYING FREDERICK, PRINCE OF WALES, AND HIS SISTERS.

necessary for a further tone and the fourth finger provides the next semitone or tone. The implications of this for changes of position, coupled with the somewhat more arched left-hand technique which the early cello inherited from the violin, may account for experiments with smaller or five-stringed instruments as a means of extending the compass upwards. Not until the 1720s, when the modern, flatter left-hand position gained ground, did players realize the potential of the left thumb in acting as a bar across the string, like the guitar's *capo dastro*. At the same time the length of the instrument was standardized at around 75cm (30 inches), a development credited to Antonio Stradivari.

Bowing technique also underwent change in the 18th century. Before this time pictures show either an underhand grip, as on the viol, or an overhand one further away from the heel than is common today, limiting movement. Freeing the whole of the bow went hand-in-hand with the developments in fingering technique. The bow itself became more curved as the century progressed. All in all the player gained more control over the bow, with a concomitant potential not just for producing a bigger sound but a broader range of articulation and expression.

The dawn of the 19th century saw a drawing together of the various approaches which had hitherto characterized cello playing. Before Jean-Louis Duport's *Essai sur le doigté du violoncelle et sur la conduite de l'archet* (c.1813) there had been no major tutor and significant variations existed between largely nationalist schools. Thanks to Duport's development of a workable system of fingering, use of the thumb in the higher positions, where the shorter vibrating string allowed for fingering as on the violin, was now taken for granted. So, too, were other techniques pioneered by the violin, such as multiple-stopping and harmonics. The instrument itself was little changed except in two significant respects. It was no longer gripped between the knees but supported on a tail-pin resting on the floor. As players closer to the present day have shown, the longer the tail-pin, the less vertical the playing position and therefore the greater freedom enjoyed by the left hand. The bow had by this time also acquired the concave profile developed in the late 18th century and was shorter and thicker than that of the violin and viola.

AN ENGLISH CELLO MADE AROUND 1830–40 BY ARTHUR AND JOHN BETTS.

Cello
VIRTUOSOS OF THE PAST

THE DUPORTS Like his Italian contemporary Luigi Boccherini, Jean-Louis Duport served as a cellist to both the Spanish and Prussian courts. Despite writing the first major tutor for the cello and being a brilliant player, he is possibly less well-remembered than his brother Jean-Pierre, also a cellist at the Prussian court, for whom Beethoven intended his Op. 5 sonatas, despite dedicating them to Duport's cello-playing employer, Friedrich Wilhelm II. Both brothers also composed for the instrument. Mozart's visit to the court at Potsdam in 1789 resulted in the three Prussian String Quartets, parts of which give prominence to the cello, and the piano variations, K573, based on a minuet from one of Jean-Pierre's sonatas.

BERNHARD ROMBERG The most famous player of the generation succeeding the Duports was the German Romberg, author of a *Méthode de violoncelle* (1840) and several solo works.

DAVID POPPER The Czech-born Popper gave the classic encore piece *Elfentanz* to the cello repertoire. His Op. 66 of 1892 for three cellos and orchestra is unique in being a Requiem entirely devoid of voices.

Other distinguished cellists of the 19th century include the Italian Alfredo Piatti and the German Julius Klengel, both of whom wrote minor works for their instrument.

✄ *In Performance*

One obvious result of these developments was the cello's increasing appeal as a solo instrument. Although its solo repertoire in the Baroque period was not negligible, it had been valued more as a useful continuo bass, a role it had fulfilled since the rise of the continuo principle in the early 17th century. By the middle of the 18th century the popularity of the bass viol was also in decline, even in France where it had held its own against the cello for longest. Ironically, the ascendancy of the piano had only a minimal effect in releasing the cello from its assumed place in chamber music. Whereas the keyboard moved from subservience to dominance, the cello often clung to its old role. Mozart's piano trios may occasionally allow the cello to step into the limelight, but Haydn's tie it down to doubling the piano's bass line. Only where the piano was absent, as in the string quartet, was the cello offered a real chance of coming to the fore.

In the orchestra, too, the cello had established itself as the natural bass (as opposed to

𝄞 THE RUSSIAN-BORN CELLIST MSTISLAV ROSTROPOVICH, SEEN HERE REHEARSING WITH BENJAMIN BRITTEN IN 1961.

PABLO CASALS, ONE OF THE CELLO'S GREATEST CHAMPIONS IN THE 20TH CENTURY, DID MUCH TO REHABILITATE BACH'S SUITES AS CORE REPERTORY.

contrabass) of the string group which formed its core. Nevertheless, it was a rare composer of the Classical period who treated the orchestral cello section in anything like a soloistic capacity. Solos for the principal player, such as are found in some of Haydn's symphonies (for example, No. 13 of 1763 and No. 95 of 1791) or Zerlina's *Batti, batti* aria in Mozart's *Don Giovanni* are exceptions to a norm. In the opera house, the continuo remained for dry recitative. Beethoven's fourth piano concerto (1806–7) contains a late example of the cello providing a quasi-continuo function in an orchestral work.

The cello now developed two distinct personalities. It could still be called upon to fulfil its traditional function as the bass line in orchestral or chamber music, but expansion of its range released a melodic capacity which the Romantic composers were not slow to exploit. A good

Cello Concertos

BAROQUE

Outside the *concerto grosso*, where the cello provided the bass to the *concertino* group, the composers of the Baroque did not automatically think of the cello as a solo instrument. The first concertos are those by Giuseppe Jaccini, in 1701, and Antonio Vivaldi, who wrote a small number of concertos for one or two cellos as well as six sonatas with continuo. A compatriot of Jaccini and Vivaldi, Leonardo Leo published six concertos in the 1730s.

CLASSICAL

BOCCHERINI Not until the Classical period, with the liberation of the cello from its duty as continuo provider, was the instrument's increasingly important role in chamber music paralleled by an expanded concerto repertoire. Among the earliest Classical concertos of note are those by Luigi Boccherini. One of these, a concerto in B flat major (c. 1770), achieved later popularity in an edition by the cellist Leopold Grützmacher; in this the scoring was expanded, the solo line re-written and the slow movement from a different work substituted.

HAYDN Boccherini's contemporary produced two fine concertos. The one in D major was for a long time ascribed to his pupil Anton Kraft until the reappearance of the manuscript established Haydn's authorship. The C major concerto was known only from an entry in its composer's own catalogue of works until its rediscovery in Prague in 1961. Up to three other cello concertos allegedly by Haydn remain lost.

BEETHOVEN wrote, in addition to five sonatas for cello and piano, the so-called 'Triple Concerto', Op. 56, which calls for a solo group consisting of piano, violin and cello. Completed in 1804, it is one of the most expansive works of his middle period and frequently gives the cello the lion's share of the solo material.

ROMANTIC

SCHUMANN Among the earliest concertos of the Romantic period is Schumann's Op. 129, written in 1850. Like the near-contemporaneous violin concerto by Mendelssohn, this dispenses with the opening orchestral *tutti* of Classical precedent and plays without a break between movements. Schumann uses material freely between movements, even to the extent of beginning the last of the three with a resumé of what has gone before, as in the last movement of Beethoven's Ninth Symphony.

SAINT-SAENS wrote two cello concertos; the second (Op. 119 in D minor), of 1902, remains little known but the first, Op. 33, has always been a favourite with cellists, as has the concerto by his fellow Frenchman, Edouard Lalo.

BRAHMS On the evidence of his chamber music, in which the darker-toned lower strings are often singled out for favourable treatment, Brahms might have written a splendid cello concerto. Instead, we have the Double Concerto, Op. 102, for violin, cello and orchestra. His last orchestral work, written for Joseph Joachim and Robert Hausmann, as in Beethoven's Triple Concerto it affords the cello most opportunities to shine. Brahms also included a long solo for the principal cello in the slow movement of his Second Piano Concerto.

DVORAK arguably wrote the finest 19th-century concerto. Brahms is alleged to have said that, had he known it was possible to write such a work, he would have done so. The B minor Concerto, Op. 104, is actually Dvořák's second; an early essay in A major, dating from 1865, survives in piano score. A late work, Op. 104 was begun in 1894, while the composer was in the United States, and finished the following year in Prague. Dvořák intended it for the Czech cellist Hanuš Wihan, but the first performance was given by Leo Stern in London in 1896.

example of the coexistence of both elements can be seen in a work such as Schubert's late String Quintet with two cellos. The second cello can maintain the bass of the ensemble, leaving the first to soar into its high register. The two Sextets by Brahms also revel in this duality. In the orchestral repertoire the 19th century yields such celebrated passages as the opening of Rossini's *William Tell* overture (with five solo parts), the overture to Glinka's *Ruslan and Lyudmila*, the third movement of Brahms' Third Symphony and the Offertorium of Verdi's *Requiem*. From there it was but a short step to composers expecting orchestral cellists to cope easily with passages like the opening of Stravinsky's *Petrushka* or the slow movement of Elgar's First Symphony.

LUIGI BOCCHERINI. HIS CONCERTOS ARE AMONG THE EARLIEST STILL TO HAVE A REGULAR PLACE IN THE CELLO REPERTOIRE.

Chamber Works

❦

BAROQUE TO ROMANTIC

BACH The six suites for solo cello by J. S. Bach are important, not just as the first works we have for unaccompanied cello but as the first significant contribution to the repertoire by a non-cellist. Their chief glory lies in the skill with which Bach's melodic lines suggest a rich harmonic texture. They date from the 1720s when Bach was Kapellmeister at Cöthen and may have been intended for the court cellist Christian Linike. The fifth suite uses *scordatura*. The sixth was written for viola pomposa; see under Violino Piccolo, page 86.

Sonatas with continuo become more numerous towards the end of the Baroque period and survive in those written later by Boccherini.

BEETHOVEN Otherwise the emergent duo sonata of the Classical era rarely favoured the cello. This has left the Op. 5 sonatas (1796) of Beethoven in a pioneering position. They were commissioned by Friedrich Wilhelm II of Prussia. Beethoven produced three more sonatas; the isolated Op. 69 in A major (1808) and the two sonatas Op. 102 (1815), in C major and D major, which stand at the threshold of his final period.

MENDELSSOHN's two sonatas are often overlooked. The first, Op. 45 (1838), was written, like the earlier *Variations concertantes* (1829), for the composer's brother, Paul. The second, Op. 58 (1843), is a splendid work which was praised by Schumann; it was intended for the Polish Count Mateusz Wielhorski, a pupil of Romberg.

SCHUMANN himself composed a set of *Five pieces in folk style* for cello and piano and sanctioned the use of the cello in the Op. 70 *Adagio and allegro* and the Op. 73 *Fantasiestücke*, intended for horn and clarinet respectively. All were composed in 1849.

CHOPIN and **RACHMANINOV** were pianist/composers whose rare forays into the field of chamber music yielded a sonata for cello and piano apiece.

BRAHMS More frequently heard are the two sonatas by Brahms, Op. 38 in E minor (1865) and Op. 99 in F major (1886).

There is also a sonata, Op. 6 in F major, by the young Richard Strauss (1883), and two sonatas by Fauré (1917 and 1921).

MODERN CHAMBER REPERTOIRE
Many composers have enriched the cello's chamber repertoire in the 20th-century.

The Hungarian Zoltan Kodály's contribution includes an unaccompanied sonata (1915), a sonata with piano (1909–10) and a *Duo* for violin and cello (1914). The last genre was also represented by Ravel in his Sonata (1920–2). The Czech Martinů produced three sonatas and two sets of variations with piano. Shostakovich and Prokofiev each wrote a single sonata with piano and there is a fine one by their compatriot, Schnittke. Benjamin Britten wrote a sonata with piano and three solo suites for Mstislav Rostropovich.

Unaccompanied works, exploiting the cello's wide range and expressive potential, have proliferated in the post-war period. In addition to the Britten suites can be cited the *Serenade* by Henze, the Sonata by the American George Crumb and the *Trois strophes sur le nom de Sacher* by Henri Dutilleux, one of many such works commissioned for the conductor Paul Sacher's seventieth birthday in 1976 and based on his name. The biennial Manchester Cello Festival has become established as a showcase for the performance of new works and attracts the participation of leading players from all over the world.

Cello Virtuosos
OF THE MODERN ERA

❧

No-one did more than Pablo Casals to promote the cello in the 20th century. His career was already established by 1900, partly due to support from the Spanish royal family. He died in 1973, aged 97. One of the many debts owed to him is for the rehabilitation of the Bach suites as core repertoire. Casals was also a composer of some ability, and not merely for his instrument. His first wife was Klengel's pupil, Guilhermina Suggia.

Great cellists from the mid-century include Gregor Piatigorsky, the Russian who inspired works by Martinů and Hindemith; the Frenchman Pierre Fournier, for whom Albert Roussel and Frank Martin wrote concertos; and his compatriot Paul Tortelier, whose art is distilled in his book *How I play, how I teach* (1975). Among their successors the leading name is that of the Russian Mstislav Rostropovich, dedicatee of Shostakovich's two concertos and Britten's Cello Symphony, Sonata and three suites. The career of the late Jacqueline du Pré was cut short by multiple sclerosis, but she remained a valued teacher and her incandescent playing on record has provided inspiration to many.

From the many outstanding players of the present generation mention should be made of the Americans Ralph Kirshbaum, Lynn Harrell and Yo Yo Ma, the Englishmen Steven Isserlis and Raphael Wallfisch, the Armenian Karine Georgian and the Scandinavians Frans Helmerson and Truls Mørk.

❧ *Versatility and Virtuosity*

For the various virtuosos produced by the 19th century, technical brilliance could often become an end in itself. As with the violin, emphasis in the present century has shifted towards exploration and interpretation of a wider repertoire. The remarkably high number of first-rate cellists which the 20th century has produced, and continues to produce, testifies to the versatility which is today one of the instrument's most prized assets. There are now probably more major 20th-century works for solo cello than for solo violin. The 20th century has produced several concertos of the first rank, not least that by Edward Elgar, a late work (1919), full of autumnal beauty and post-war melancholy. Dmitri Shostakovich wrote two concertos; the first, Op. 107 (1959), has to date proved more popular than its successor, Op. 126, of 1966. The Polish composers Krzystof Penderecki and Witold Lutoslawski have both written concertos, the latter's being one of the best from recent decades.

At the same time it has become apparent that our knowledge of the cello's early repertoire is far from exhaustive. Fortunately, there are now a number of makers producing excellent copies of 17th- and 18th-century orchestral stringed instruments. 𝄡

DOUBLE BASS

OF ALL THE MEMBERS of the modern string family the double bass is the only one which can claim real kinship with the viols (see pages 48–9). It is a direct descendant of the *violone* – the 'big viol', which played at 16-foot pitch (that is, sounding an octave lower than written) and which, unlike the smaller viols, succeeded in finding a place in the modern orchestra.

References to double bass viols exist from the early 16th century, and some instruments themselves have survived from only slightly later. Generally with six strings, they display a variety of shapes and tunings, and may or may not have the viols' characteristic fretted neck. The neck itself appears to have been more vertical at this stage and the bridge positioned lower down the belly. Contemporary iconography shows an underhand bow grip.

Six-stringed *violoni* continued to be used throughout the 17th century, taking their place alongside a five-stringed model which was commoner in the German-speaking countries. Such instruments were obviously familiar to several theorists of the following century. Leopold Mozart, in his *Versuch einer gründlichen Violinschule*, criticized the weakness of the sound resulting from the thinness of the strings and noted the danger of hitting the wrong string by mistake, but remarked that "on such a bass one can play difficult passages more easily, and I have heard concerti, trios, solos and such like performed on one of these with great beauty". Johann Albrechtsberger's *Gründliche Anweisung zur Compositionen* (1790) refers to an instrument tuned *F', A', D, F sharp, B* which was fretted, and Joseph Quantz's seminal *Versuch einer Anweisung die Flöte traversiere zu spielen* (1752) supports the retention of frets but prefers the more modern three- or four-string basses which lacked them. Both instruments lived quite happily alongside each other in early 18th-century Germany and Austria, the four-stringed model sometimes tuned in fifths an octave below the cello. This was favoured in France as well. Common tunings for the three-stringed instrument were *G', D, G,* or *A', D, G,* but huge variations still occurred.

Although the fretted *violone* was still around at the beginning of the 19th century, its place in the orchestra had now been taken by its unfretted counterpart. It is in the orchestra that we must trace the instrument's development, since solo repertoire is virtually non-existent before the mid-18th century. Even after the establishment of the string family as the core of the orchestra, instruments of 16-foot pitch could not always be taken for granted. They were unknown in England, for instance, until the 1690s. One of the earliest tutors, Michel Corrette's *Méthodes pour apprendre à jouer de la Contre-basse à 3, à 4 et à 5 cordes* (1773) mentions that a lot of the time, the basses, where they were present, "unfortunately stayed silent".

The Double Bass Finds its Voice

The double bass was rarely treated as an independent voice until well into the 19th century. Four-part harmony was complete in the string group of two violins, viola and cello, a distribution which the rise of the string quartet served only to reinforce. The double bass, when it was used, invariably doubled the cello's bass line at the lower octave. This practice, moreover, took little heed of whether the instrument was tuned

THE MODERN DOUBLE BASS RETAINS THE SLOPING SHOULDERS OF THE *VIOLONE* OR DOUBLE BASS VIOL.

in such a way as to make this genuinely achievable. In the Classical and early Romantic periods some concessions were made in that composers might indicate where the basses were to drop out altogether or provide simplified parts where the bass line was deemed too challenging for them to play the notes as written. Not until the 19th century discovered the melodic potential of the cello was the double bass allowed to provide the true bass to the orchestral strings. Even then it was common for composers to show caution and

♪ A MEDIEVAL WOODCUT SHOWING A GROUP OF DOUBLE BASSISTS. THESE EARLY INSTRUMENTS OFTEN HAD ONLY THREE STRINGS.

retain some cellos to play along with the basses. Berlioz was one who advocated this compromise, but then it was usual for French orchestras of the period to have far more cellos than basses, whereas in some countries, notably Italy, the basses often outnumbered the cellos.

THE DOUBLE BASS AS
Soloist
%

From Haydn to Peter Maxwell Davies, more composers have taken the double bass seriously as a solo instrument than is popularly imagined. It is a pity that no concerto by Joseph Haydn has survived, but we do have the solos in the trios of his symphonies Nos. 6–8, *Le matin* (c. 1761), *Le midi* (1761), and *Le soir* (c. 1761), and the variation finales of symphonies Nos. 31 (1765) and 72 (1763). Mozart included a bass *obbligato* in his concert aria *Per questa bella mano*, K612 and there exist concertos by his contemporaries Karl Ditters von Dittersdorf, Johann Baptist Vanhal and Giovanni Battista Cimadoro.

Solos within the orchestral repertoire often exploit the bass's capacity for grotesqueness. A famous example is 'The Elephant' in Saint-Saëns' *Carnival of the Animals* (1886). Others feature in the First Symphony (1886) of Gustav Mahler and the ballet *Pulcinella* (1920) by Stravinsky. The solo in Prokofiev's *Lieutenant Kijé* (1934) shows the bass in lyrical rather than comic mode.

Meanwhile, the instrument did enjoy some measure of independence in certain types of chamber music. Before the general availability of the contrabassoon, for example, it could be called upon to add weight to the bass in wind ensembles. Mozart's *Serenade for 13 wind instruments* (K361) is really misnamed, since the *Contra Basso* is clearly marked *pizzicato* at one point. Mozart also wrote several *divertimenti* for 2 horns, 2 violins, viola and *basso*, including the well-known *Musical joke* (1787). The illustration in

SOME NOTABLE
Double
Bassists

℁

DOMENICO DRAGONETTI A good deal of the bass's concert solo repertoire is the product of composers who were players themselves. In the 19th century two names stand out. One was the Italian Dragonetti, hailed as the 'Paganini of the double bass'. He was born in Venice in 1763 but settled eventually in London, where he was still appearing in public in the 1840s. His concertos, written for a three-stringed instrument, are fiendishly difficult even by modern standards.

GIOVANNI BOTTESINI The second great name is that of Bottesini, a native of Crema and a graduate of the Milan Conservatoire. He travelled extensively as a virtuoso in Europe, Russia and the United States and at Verdi's request conducted the premiere of *Aida* in Cairo in 1871. Bottesini was a prolific composer, writing operas, symphonies and chamber music as well as several concertos and show pieces for his own instrument. As a teacher he published, in the 1860s, a *Metodo completo per contrabbasso*, one of the first tutors seriously to discuss the instrument's solo and orchestral repertoire.

SERGE KOUSSEVITZKY is best remembered as a conductor of the Boston Symphony Orchestra, but he studied the double bass at the Moscow Conservatoire and during his early career as a soloist was known as 'the Russian Bottesini'. He wrote several works for bass, of which the most substantial is the Op. 3 Concerto, first performed by him in 1905.

Other players who have done much to promote the instrument include the Englishmen Eugene Cruft, Rodney Slatford and Duncan McTier (dedicatee of a concerto by Peter Maxwell Davies).

the first edition of that work, plus the analogous example of the solo group in his *Serenata notturna* (1776), indicates that *basso* here means just the double bass and not the usual cello *and* bass. The double bass also features in various works for mixed ensemble by Haydn. Important works from the next generation to call for the double bass include Beethoven's Septet (1800) and Schubert's Octet (1823) and Trout Quintet (1819). As late as Dvořák's Op. 77 Quintet of 1875, the inclusion of the double bass in chamber music for strings alone was still a rarity.

𝄋 *The Modern Instrument*

The modern double bass retains the viol's preference for tuning in fourths, rather than fifths. This is to some extent necessitated by the large span required of the left hand. The four strings are now tuned *E′, A′, D, G*. Modern instruments often have a fifth string tuned to *C′* or *B′*. The low *C′* has been taken for granted by many composers from the turn of the century onwards, and an extra string has proved more satisfactory than simply tuning the *e* string down. For solo work it has been common since the late 18th century to tune the strings up a tone, making the bass a transposing instrument twice over. Conventional parts are written an octave higher than they sound, solo parts a ninth higher. Early double basses were tuned by means of wooden pegs, like the rest of the violin family. These were replaced in the 17th century by wooden cogs; these days the cogs are of metal.

Even today the design of instruments can differ quite significantly, and there is a marked variation in size, with the largest instruments standing nearly a metre and a half tall (5 feet) and the smallest 25–30cm (10–12 inches) or so less. Most instruments have the viol's flat back. This is usual in instruments which keep the characteristic sloping-shouldered shape of the viol, but can also be found in those basses which resemble a large violin. Some schools of playing retain the underhand bowing technique as well.

The publication of Franz Simandl's *Neueste Methode des Contrabass-Spiels* (1874) had been a milestone in the development of bass playing. From the late Romantic period onwards composers felt no compunction in expecting as much from the bottom end of the string section as from the rest of it. One result has been a latter-day preference for the sloping-shouldered design, which facilitates playing in the higher positions. Players of our own day have shown the double bass to be as versatile an instrument as its smaller brethren, not least in the one area where their presence is minimal – jazz.

FAR LEFT: A LINE-UP OF DOUBLE BASSES IN A MODERN SYMPHONY ORCHESTRA.

A DOUBLE BASS OF AROUND 1840. BY THIS TIME IN THE INSTRUMENT'S EVOLUTION, THE FOUR-STRING MODEL HAD BECOME COMMON.

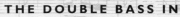

THE DOUBLE BASS IN *Jazz*

The double bass was often used as a 16-foot instrument in the 18th-century wind band. In our own time it is an established member of the wind orchestra and jazz band. A typical 17-piece jazz band of the 1930s or 1940s would contain, in addition to saxes, trumpets and trombones, piano, guitar, bass and drums. Nowadays the bass is invariably played *pizzicato*, sometimes employing *slap* technique, where the string is allowed to bounce off the fingerboard. It has also moved from being a purely rhythmic instrument to a jazz soloist in its own right.

Earlier jazz bassists include John Lindsay and 'Pops' Foster (real name George Murphy Foster), both of whom played in Louis Armstrong's band in the 1930s. Walter Page and Charles Mingus are prominent names from the 1940s. More recently, Ron Carter has successfully used a smaller piccolo bass and published a tutor in jazz playing.

The American Gary Karr, who was born into a family of bass players, has successfully bridged the gap between the worlds of classical music and jazz. As an orchestral player he has appeared with many world-class ensembles, and his interest in expanding the bass's contemporary repertoire has led him to commission several compositions.

♪ HARP

THE HARP IS ONE of the oldest musical instruments we possess. "David took an harp, and played with his hand: so Saul was refreshed" the first book of Samuel tells us, in one of the many biblical references to the instrument. There is every reason to suppose that even then it was an established instrument. In what must be one of the oldest pictorial representations of any instrument, a fragment of Mesopotamian pottery from around 3300 BC shows the harp in its earliest known form. A piece of wood is carved into an arc, between the ends of which are stretched strings of differing lengths giving different pitches. Its origins are likely to be the hunter's bow, whose single, tensed string would resonate at a recognizable pitch when plucked; the shorter the string, the higher the pitch. The addition of some means of amplifying the resonance was all that was needed to turn an everyday weapon into a true musical instrument.

♪ Angle Harp

Arch harps such as this are also known from Egyptian paintings of the 3rd century BC. The first actual instrument to survive, also Egyptian, dates from around a thousand years later. The Louvre in Paris possesses a so-called angle harp or *trigonon*. Standing just over 1.05 metres (40 inches) high, it has 21 strings stretched at an angle between a vertical neck which is itself attached to a horizontal soundboard. Pictorial evidence suggests that such instruments were also common in Greece; indeed, its name is merely the Greek word for 'triangle'. Plato alludes to it in his *Republic*, claiming it inferior to the lyre, or *kithara* , which had fewer strings. There also existed by then a type of angle harp in which the vertical member forms the soundboard with the strings strung from a horizontal pegboard.

♪ Frame Harp

During the last centuries BC and the early Christian era, various sizes of arch and angle harp spread first to eastern Asia and later to northern Europe. An important step forward was marked by the emergence of the frame harp. This was an angle harp in which the third side of the

♪ TOP: AN EARLY REPRESENTATION, REPUTED TO BE KING DAVID, PLAYING A SIMPLE BOW HARP.

♪ LEFT: A CELTIC HARP (IRISH *CLÁIRSEACH*, MEANING 'LITTLE FLAT THING' ALTHOUGH, PERVERSELY, IT WAS BIG AND VERTICAL), WHOSE BASS STRINGS AND HEAVY BODY PRODUCED A STRONG TONE WHEN PLUCKED.

decachordum. From this period also come the first English occurrences of the word 'harp'. The Anglo-Saxon *hearpen*, meaning to play a string instrument, is derived from the Nordic *harpa*.

Although actual instruments from this period are rare, a fairly clear picture emerges of the early medieval European harp as a small, framed instrument with few strings. That this remained a standard design is corroborated by those instruments which have come down to us from the later Middle Ages. The soundboard, with or without soundholes, is towards the player, opposite a (usually curved) forepillar. The strings may have been of metal, perhaps of brass as on the Irish harp, and would have been plucked with the fingernails. The Irish harp itself was larger, with a soundboard made in one piece and between 30 and 36 strings. A famous example from the 14th century, now the Irish national symbol, survives without its strings in Trinity College, Dublin.

By the 16th century the European harp had grown larger than its medieval prototype but remained a diatonic instrument. Its two dozen or so strings, by now often of gut, were tuned to specific notes, making chromatic alteration impossible. Martin Agricola, for example, in his *Musica instrumentalis deudsch* (1529), refers to a three and a half octave instrument, *F* to *c'''*, where the relevant strings could be tuned to *b sharp* or *b flat* as necessary.

✄ Double and Triple Harps

A solution was sought in the double harp. This had a second row of strings tuned in such a way as to provide those notes lacking in the first row. The Italian theorist Vincenzo Galilei describes such a harp, with 58 strings, in his *Dialogo della musica antica e della moderna* (1581). This is the *arpa doppia* scored for in Monteverdi's *Orfeo* (1607). Praetorius illustrates one in the second

An Egyptian wall painting of c. 1500 BC, showing (from left) angle harp, long lute and lyre.

triangle was closed, so that all the strings were enclosed in a wooden frame of which one side acted as a resonator. (This enclosing side is usually referred to as a forepillar.) The modern harp is a frame harp, but the earliest evidence of such instruments, which are depicted in Europe from about the 8th century, shows that they were nothing like the size of their later counterparts. Illuminated manuscripts show a portable instrument, often with ten or sometimes twelve strings. Appropriately enough, many such illustrations are found in psalters, since King David was the alleged author of the psalms. The ten-string instrument he is frequently shown with may represent an attempt to show the Jewish

part of his *Syntagma musicum* (1619), together with a triple harp. This had three rows of strings; the outer ones have an identical tuning, while between them runs a row tuned to those chromatic notes otherwise missing from them. The triple harp was known in England by the middle of the 17th century and proved even more popular in Wales, where it became the standard instrument for virtuosos until well into the 19th century and was often referred to simply as the Welsh harp. This is the instrument associated with the tradition of *penillion*, where a melody is improvised as a counterpoint to an existing one played on the harp. Several fine Welsh-made triple harps survive from the 18th and 19th centuries.

℅ *Pedal Harp*

Attempts at improvement were made as early as the 17th century. Some German single harps of this period have hooks placed at the neck end of certain strings which, when turned by the fingers, raise the pitch by a semitone. This had the double disadvantage of being manually controlled and applicable to only one string at a time. A major breakthrough came with the development of pedal-operated mechanisms to alter the pitch. The first such pedal harp is usually attributed to the Bavarian Jakob Hochbrucker around 1720 (some sources say earlier). Bavaria might have become the European centre for harp making had its thunder not been stolen by Paris, allegedly spurred on by the fact that Marie-Antoinette, like a good many aristocratic women, was a harpist.

A typical French pedal harp of the later 18th century had around 40 strings. The pedal

THIS BEAUTIFULLY CRAFTED 18TH-CENTURY FRENCH HARP BELONGED TO LOUIS XVI'S QUEEN, MARIE-ANTOINETTE.

brought into play a hook, or crochet, which pressed the string against a fixed point, thereby sharpening it. This system was improved by the family firm of Cousineau, who replaced the hook with a pair of levers which turned in opposite directions, gripping the string in the process. The pedals could either be set beforehand to give a basic tuning most amenable to the key of a piece or changed during its course. Sébastien Erard's revolutionary patent harp of 1792 refined this by substituting for the levers two brass forks mounted on a small movable wheel. The pedal action turns the wheel, again in opposite directions, so that the string is gripped by the forks.

All of these systems raise the pitch of a string by half a tone. Cousineau experimented with a second set of pedals which extended the harp's tonal possibilities, albeit in a cumbersome way. But it was Erard, again, who developed the double-action harp which is essentially the instrument of today. His instrument, patented in 1810, tuned its 43 open strings to a scale of *C flat*, with a range of *F flat'* to *f flat''''*. It used the same fork system as his single-action harp. The seven pedals could each be used in two positions, raising the pitch by a half or whole tone respectively. Erard's nephew, Pierre, extended the number of strings to 46, as in the modern concert instrument. Further improvements were made around the turn of the 20th century by the American firm of Lyon-Healy, mainly by enclosing the mechanism (which had been on the outside of the neck in the Erard model) within the neck.

The double harp, in particular, held its own throughout the 19th century and was still favoured in some circles in the early 20th century. Its effective swansong is Debussy's *Danse sacrée et danse profane*, commissioned by the firm of Pleyel in 1904 to show off its double harp. Not to be outdone, the firm of Erard responded by commissioning Ravel's *Introduction et Allegro* (1905) to show off its pedal harp.

MATERIALS USED IN THE MAKING OF

Harps

It is likely that various materials were used to make early harps. Irish harps were often strung with brass. Willow was used for their soundboard. English harps before the Norman Conquest of 1066 had strings of twisted horsehair. By the 16th century, these were usually made of gut.

The soundboard of Erard's patent harp of 1792 was made of pine. The neck was made separately of laminated wood and the metal parts of brass. Gut was still used for most of the strings, with the lowest ones of silk wound with wire. Modern developments of this design include the replacement of silk with steel for the lower strings and the strengthening of the soundboard with a layer of veneer.

THE HARP MADE ITS FIRST APPEARANCE IN A SYMPHONY IN 1830. MANY LARGE WORKS FOR ORCHESTRA REQUIRE MORE THAN ONE HARP.

℅ The Harp in the Orchestra

The harp's appearances in the orchestra were few in the 18th century and restricted to providing special effects. Handel used the instrument, appropriately, in the oratorio *Saul* (1738) and both Gluck and Haydn call for it in their operas on the Orpheus legend – *Orfeo ed Euridice* (1762) and *L'anima del filosofo* (1791) respectively. Elsewhere Handel scored for the harp in a small number of operas and as an alternative to the organ in the concerto Op. 4 No. 6 (1736). Mozart used it once, in his Concerto for flute and harp, K299, as did Beethoven in his ballet music for *Die Geschöpfe des Prometheus* (1801). Bach's son Carl Philipp Emanuel wrote a sonata, and minor pieces were produced by such composers as Johann-Baptiste Krumpholtz, himself a harpist, Mozart's friend Jan Ladislav Dušek, who was married to one, and François Boieldieu. The first appearance of the harp in a symphony is in Berlioz's *Symphonie fantastique* (1830) where, as if to make up for lost time, Berlioz asks for six instruments – but writes only two parts. ⑬

 GUITAR

THE GUITAR HAS a venerable ancestry and can claim to be one of the few stringed instruments to have bridged the divide between classical and popular music with any great success. Yet the fact that it has rarely been used as an orchestral instrument has led many to underestimate its importance and the size of the solo repertoire which it commands.

✤ Origins

The very early history of the guitar remains to some extent unclear. If the distinguishing feature of the instrument is taken to be the manner in which it is held, then plucked instruments of the guitar type, as opposed to harps, existed in the pre-Christian era. A Babylonian clay relief of around 1900 BC shows various instruments which appear to have two or more strings. All have the typical neck of the guitar family and are plucked with the right hand. A Hittite carving of some six hundred years later appears to have a neck with an early form of frets. An actual instrument found in an Egyptian grave of c.1500 BC has a rounded body, rather like the resonators of contemporary harps, but a perfectly straight, elongated neck. Similar instruments were in use in Egypt until the early centuries AD. One important survival, found in a Coptic tomb and now in the Oriental Institute in Heidelberg, is dated to between 400 and 600 AD. It has a flat back and a resonator made in two distinct pieces connected by a ribbed section to form a hollow box with inward curving sides – in short the prototype of the modern guitar.

If, as some authorities claim, such instruments were introduced into Europe by invading

Arabs, then we have strong grounds for associating the guitar with the European country where Arab influence was strongest – Spain. The first identifiable depiction of a guitar to come from that country is in an illustrated commentary on the New Testament *Book of Revelations* known to have originated in the monastery of San Miguel de Escalada near Leon in the year 926. One illustration shows four individuals playing long, plucked instruments held either upright or across the knee. Each of these instruments has a pear-shaped body and a neck which diminishes towards a large scroll containing tuning pegs. Although one of them is being played with a bow, the remaining three are being plucked, one with a plectrum. Another illustration from the same source shows a larger number of people with plucked instruments which this time are held across the body and have narrower, parallel necks and three strings. Again, some of the instruments appear to be being played with plectra.

However, this should not be taken as conclusive evidence that the guitar came to Europe via Spain. A German psalter from the same period, for instance, depicts a different kind of instrument, held in most cases almost at right-angles to the player, with an almost square body and parallel neck ending in a disc-shaped scroll into which are inserted tuning pegs. The fact that representations of similar instruments are found in both manuscript and sculptural sources well into the Middle Ages would argue for the existence of an indigenous European tradition co-existing with an imported one.

Another theory postulates that the guitar might have entered Europe via southern France, because Provence was the centre for the medieval troubadour tradition which spread to a number

THE ENTRY OF THE GUITARISTS AT THE GRAND BAL DE LA DOUAIRIERE DE BILLEBAHAUT GIVEN IN 1629.

of other countries, Spain included. Some of the most important evidence is to be found in the highly developed examples of figurative sculpture adorning the large churches of the early Gothic period in England and France – such as the angelic musicians in the Angel Choir at Lincoln Cathedral, the magnificent series in Beverley Minster or at the cathedrals of Chartres and Rheims.

℅ Construction and Tuning

As with the harp, the dawn of the Renaissance marks an important watershed in that from this period onwards we have examples of the instruments themselves to set beside documentary or illustrative evidence. One feature of the contemporary instrument is that its strings were commonly arranged in courses: pairs of strings tuned either to the same pitch or in octaves. Six-course guitars are known from the 15th century.

This arrangement, with the courses tuned in unison, is a feature of the Spanish *vihuela*, a flat-backed plucked instrument popular in the later 15th and 16th centuries. With its barely waisted body and narrow neck it proclaims a link with the proto-guitars of the Middle Ages. Guitars of the 16th century usually had four or five courses and were smaller than their modern counterparts. Tuning might vary, but appears to have displayed a consistent preference for a third between the middle courses and a fourth between them and the highest and lowest ones. The model here is obviously contemporary viol tuning. This pattern of fourths with an interpolated third is reflected in the tuning of the single strings of the modern guitar: *E, A, D, g, b, e'*.

It seems that, while the five-course guitar was preferred as an accompanying instrument, the four-course variety was deemed, like the lute, more suited to polyphonic music. This is confirmed by the first music to be printed for it, in the *Tres libros de musica en cifras para vihuela* prepared in 1546 by the Spaniard Alonso Mudarra. The music is written in tablature, giving, not the

actual notes to be played, but a system of symbols indicating the position of the fingers on each string with symbols indicative of note lengths. Such music would be played, in the terminology still in use, not *rasgueado* (strummed) but *punteado* (plucked). Thus it presupposes the plucking of the strings with the fingers themselves, as in the case of the lute, rather than with a plectrum. Mudarra's publication was followed by a number of others, not least in France where the guitar became enormously popular. The first English tutor, James Rowbotham's *The breffe and plaine instruction for to learne the gitterne*, is a translation of a French publication of 1551. It is unfortunately lost.

In addition to being smaller than the modern guitar, the instrument for which such publications were intended would have had a less pronounced waist (although more pronounced than that of the *vihuela*) and often an intricately carved rose in place of the latter day open sound-hole. The back would have been flat. A rounded back is commoner in the five-course instrument known as the *chitarra battente*, used, as mentioned

Guitar Virtuosos

%

NICOLO PAGANINI played the guitar as well as the violin and left a substantial amount of music for it, including pieces for guitar and violin duo.

FERNANDO SOR, Paganini's Spanish contemporary, was a native of Barcelona who spent the later part of his life mostly in Paris. Encouraged by several composers, he was able to establish himself as a virtuoso guitarist as well as a minor composer of stage works. His large output for the guitar includes a *Méthode pour la guitare*, published in Paris in 1830.

NAPOLEON COSTE had earned a reputation as the finest French guitarist of his time and a worthy rival to Sor (whose *Méthode* he re-edited) by the time an accident ended his playing career in 1863. Coste left numerous guitar works, some of them intended for the large, lower-pitch instrument he favoured. The guitar was the main instrument of Coste's countryman, Hector Berlioz, although he never composed for it.

FRANCISCO TARREGA was the first Spanish guitarist to exploit the innovations of Antonio de Torres Jurado. As important as his own small-scale compositions are the many transcriptions he made of music by other composers, some of which remain in the recitalist's repertoire.

AGUSTIN BARRIOS MANGORE, a Paraguayan, was the first significant Latin American guitarist. A cultured man, he was acutely conscious of the guitar's European roots and the debt it owed to players like Sor. Many of his compositions remain unpublished, but the excellence of his technique has been captured in a number of recordings.

ANDRES SEGOVIA is for many synonymous with the guitar. This remarkable Spanish musician gave his first recital at the age of 14 and was still appearing in public in his eighties. No one did more than he to establish the guitar as a concert instrument, through playing, composing, editing and commissioning music for it. Composers who dedicated works to him include Turina, Roussel, Ponce, Castelnuovo-Tedesco and, most notably, Rodrigo.

DJANGO REINHARDT, the Belgian jazz guitarist, was forced to develop a technique using only two fingers after damaging his left hand in a fire in 1928. In the 1930s he was a founder, with the violinist Stephane Grappelli, of the celebrated Quintette du Hot Club de France. He later worked with Duke Ellington. His playing had a profound influence on many younger jazz players.

JULIAN BREAM and **JOHN WILLIAMS** are two of the most well known guitarists of today. Bream, who is also a lutenist, has had works written for him by, among others, Britten, Tippett, Walton, Henze and Malcolm Arnold. The Australian-born Williams, a pupil of Segovia, has premiered pieces by Takemitsu, André Previn and Stephen Dodgson. His interest in the guitar extends beyond the classical repertoire and into the fields of popular and folk music, where he has made several recordings.

LEFT: AN EXAMPLE OF AN EARLY VENETIAN GUITAR BY MATTEO SELLAS. NOTE THE INTRICATE ORNAMENTATION OF THE TABLE AND SOUNDHOLE.

above, largely to accompany. It was played with a plectrum and had metal rather than gut strings. Its frets, too, were of metal like those of the modern guitar; elsewhere they tended to be of gut and tied around the fingerboard. Sometimes it had courses of three strings.

⅋ Notation Systems The Alfabeto

As the Renaissance gave way to the early Baroque, so the four-course guitar yielded increasingly to the conventional five-course type. The first printed music for it had been published in 1554, in Spain, in Miguel Fuenllana's *Orphenica lyra*. It assumes an instrument tuned like the modern guitar but without its lowest string. A year later another Spaniard, Juan Bermudo, mentions a variety of tunings, but Fuenllana's reappears in the *Guitarra española* of Juan Carlos Amat, published in Barcelona in 1596. Here the *A* and *D* courses are tuned in octaves, the rest in unison. This was to remain, with little variation, a standard tuning throughout the Baroque period. To yet another Spanish theorist we owe the system of tablature known as *alfabeto*, which appears in the first manuscript source of music for the five-course guitar compiled by Francisco Palumbi in the 1590s. In this, chords are identified by letters of the alphabet. Of great significance is the fact that the system employs a series of vertical lines to indicate either an upward or downward stroke of

LEFT: GUITARIST AND LUTENIST JULIAN BREAM HAS BEEN THE DEDICATEE OF A NUMBER OF WORKS BY SOME OF THE LATE 20TH CENTURY'S MOST EMINENT COMPOSERS.

RIGHT: AN EARLY 18TH CENTURY GUITARIST AS DEPICTED BY THE ARTIST ANTOINE WATTEAU.

♭ THE HARP-GUITAR WAS A CURIOUS
HYBRID POPULAR IN ENGLAND IN
THE EARLY 19TH CENTURY. IT
WAS DEVELOPED BY EDWARD LIGHT
IN 1798 AND IMPROVED BY HIM
AS THE HARP-LUTE IN 1811
(ALSO SEE PAGE 83).

♭ THE GREAT SPANISH VIRTUOSO
GUITARIST ANDRES SEGOVIA
HAD A PHENOMENALLY
LENGTHY CAREER BEFORE THE
PUBLIC, MAKING HIS DEBUT AT THE
AGE OF 14 AND STILL PERFORMING
INTO HIS EIGHTIES.

the right hand across the strings. With certain refinements, such as greater detail in notating rhythmic groupings, the *alfabeto* became the commonest way of notating guitar music through the 17th century.

By the mid-century, the five-course guitar was in general use in Italy, England and France as well as Spain. In Italy, music for it using *alfabeto* notation had been published as early as 1606 and found its first important native exponent in the person of Giovanni Foscarini, who worked in Italy and the Netherlands and published several books of *Intavolatura di chitarra spagnola*, not all of which have survived. The most renowned Italian guitarist of the succeeding generation is Francesco Corbetta, who published his first guitar music in 1639 and later settled in Restoration London as court guitarist to King Charles II. It was through Corbetta that the guitar in England achieved enormous popularity which played its

own part in the decline of the lute. Corbetta had also been active in France, where the first tutor for the guitar was actually the work of a Spaniard – Luis de Briceño's *Metodo mui facilissimo para aprender tañer la guitarra a lo Español* (1626). The French Baroque school was brought to a peak of excellence in the music of Corbetta's pupil, Robert de Visée.

USUALLY PLAYED BY A STANDING MUSICIAN, THE FLAMENCO GUITAR IS LIGHTER THAN ITS STANDARD CLASSICAL COUNTERPART.

THE Guitar Repertoire
§

APART FROM THE THREE CONCERTOS BY THE ITALIAN MAURO GIULIANI (1808–20), THE MAJOR WORKS IN THE REPERTOIRE REFLECT OUR OWN CENTURY'S ACCEPTANCE OF THE GUITAR AS A CONCERT INSTRUMENT.

RODRIGO By far the most popular work – the *Concierto de Aranjuez* – is, fittingly, by a Spaniard: the Valencian Joaquin Rodrigo. It was first performed in 1940 and was followed by the *Fantasia para un gentilhombre* (1955) for guitar and orchestra, written for Segovia; the *Concierto Andaluz* (1967) for four guitars and orchestra; and the *Concierto-madrigal* (1968) for two guitars and orchestra. Rodrigo himself is not a guitarist, but writes idiomatic music imbued with the essence of his native country.

CASTELNUOVO-TEDESCO The Italian-American Mario Castelnuovo-Tedesco wrote two concertos (1939 and 1953) and a concerto for two guitars and orchestra (1962). He also wrote a series of 24 preludes and fugues in all keys for two guitars, *Les guitares bien temperées* (1962), modelled on Bach's *Well-tempered Clavier*. His Serenade for guitar and orchestra (1943) was another piece inspired by Segovia.

PONCE The Mexican Manuel Ponce, whose output consisted mostly of songs and works for piano and guitar, made a notable contribution to the guitar repertoire with the *Concierto del Sur* (1941), also written for Segovia.

BRITTEN Several leading British composers have been attracted by the guitar, mostly through the artistry of particular players. Benjamin Britten wrote his *Nocturnal*, based on a theme by Dowland, for Julian Bream in 1963. Six years earlier he wrote a cycle of *Songs from the Chinese* for voice and guitar.

WALTON The song cycle *Anon in love* by William Walton was written for Bream and Peter Pears in 1959. In 1971 Walton completed a set of *Bagatelles* for solo guitar, also for Bream.

TIPPETT In 1983 Bream gave the first performance of *The blue guitar* by Michael Tippett.

MALCOLM ARNOLD and **LENNOX BERKELEY** have written concertos for guitar; Arnold's dates from 1959, Berkeley's from 1974.

STEPHEN DODGSON has written several *concertante* works, most recently the *Duo concerto* for violin, guitar and orchestra of 1991. Although not a guitarist himself, he has produced a substantial number of chamber works featuring the instrument, some of the more recent for Nicola Hall.

℅ *The Making of the Modern Guitar*

It was in France that the guitar was to metamorphose into the instrument we know today. Where courses were tuned in octaves, the lower note was known as a *bourdon* (*bordón* in Spanish). Around 1750 bourdons on the two lowest courses began to be accepted as the norm. At the same time it abandoned vestiges of so-called re-entrant tuning, where the pitches of the courses did not necessarily ascend or descend in sequence. The distinction between *punteado* and *rasgueado* lost some of its earlier significance as both styles were by now well and truly merged in guitar music. At this point tablature started to give way to staff notation, which established the modern practice of treating the guitar as a transposing instrument, its music written in the treble clef an octave higher than it sounds. The guitar, in fact, was losing its image as a specifically treble instrument, especially when a sixth course was added, tuned a fourth below the previous lowest.

Progressively the idea of courses was abandoned, leaving an instrument with six single strings such as we have today. Resistance to this survived until the early 19th century in Spain, no doubt as a reaction to the ultimate irony that a country to which the instrument had been 'imported' was now keen to sell back the improved model. Some of the principal tutors of the period are also by Spaniards; for example, the *Escuela de guitarra* by Dionysio Aguado (1825). By the second half of the century several modifications had taken place to produce what is essentially the modern guitar. These include the replacement of gut frets by fixed metal ones, the raising of the older,

𝄞 THE FENDER STRATOCASTER ELECTRIC GUITAR IS REGARDED AS THE STRADIVARIUS OF ITS TYPE AND IS FAVOURED BY MANY TOP ROCK MUSICIANS, INCLUDING ERIC CLAPTON.

♭ STEEL OR HAWAIIAN GUITARS. UNLIKE
STANDARD ELECTRIC GUITARS THEY ARE
NOT HELD BY THE PLAYER.

lower bridge and the introduction of internal strutting in a radial or fan-shaped pattern instead of the former cross-struts. Credit for some of these innovations must go to Spain, notably to the father of the modern guitar, Antonio de Torres Jurado to whom a host of subsequent Spanish makers owe a debt of gratitude. Torres increased the size of the guitar, standardizing the vibrating string length at 65cm (26 inches) and facilitating the modern playing position in which the instrument is supported on the player's left knee. With this playing position the *apoyando*, or sweep of the hand across the strings, was free to emerge as a characteristic of guitar technique.

The renewed interest in the guitar from the late 19th century onwards has taken the Torres developments as its starting point. Chief innovations since 1945 have included a preference for nylon strings and an increasing interest in electronic amplification. The bass guitar which is commonly met with these days may seem like a new idea, but in its acoustic form dates back to experiments made in late 16th Italy in fitting the five-course guitar with a second neck carrying seven bass strings. Other bass instruments, with a single neck, were made in the 18th century. The modern bass guitar, invariably an electric bass, is tuned like the double bass (see page 68).

The electric guitar is not solely the preserve of the rock band. Several classical composers have exploited its sonorities, among them Michael Tippett in his opera *New Year* (1988). 𝄡

Related
INSTRUMENTS
℘

STEEL OR HAWAIIAN GUITAR
An electrically amplified instrument which stands horizontally on a tripod in front of the player. The sound is produced by means of a slide, operated by the left hand, to alter the sounding lengths of the strings. The instrument became popular in the 1930s when its characteristic *glissando* tones gave spurious ethnic flavour to Western dance music.

HARP-GUITAR/LUTE The first had eight gut strings running over a neck slightly shorter than that of the conventional guitar; a later model had 11 strings with the lowest four unfretted. The special feature of the harp-lute was its second neck, connected by a forepillar similar to a harp's. Most of the strings have only one fret, raising the pitch by a tone; a key at the back of the instrument raises it a semitone. The back was usually flat, enabling the instrument to be placed on a table to be played (see illustration on page 80).

UKELELE Developed from the *machete*, a small guitar introduced into Polynesia by the Portuguese. The word is Polynesian for 'jumping flea'. A *ukelele* usually has four strings, and tuning can vary. Its music is normally written in tablature.

BANJO Possibly originating in Africa, this round-bodied instrument consists of a skin or vellum resonator and has five strings. Early types are unfretted. Like the *ukelele*, the *banjo* is primarily an accompanying instrument. Hybrid *ukelele-banjos*, strung like the former but shaped like the latter, also exist.

𝄞 RARE STRINGS

THE GROWING INTEREST in period performance has brought about a situation in which virtually no instrument can be said to be obsolete. Nevertheless, a number of instruments now revived to serve the music originally written for them remain infrequent visitors to the concert hall, among them both bowed and plucked strings. There also exists a distinct group of instruments which attempt to combine the characteristics of both.

𝄋 *Viola d'Amore*

Pride of place in the first category goes to the viola d'amore, an instrument which owes allegiance to both the violin and viol families. When it was first reintroduced to the public in the 1950s the contention was that its name should be 'viola d'amor' ('viola of the Moors'), indicating that it had entered Europe via the Moorish invasions of Spain. This suggestion was supported by the shape of the soundholes in the face of the instrument: 'flaming swords', an Islamic emblem. But the date of the end of the Moorish occupation of the Iberian peninsula, 1492, gives too great a hiatus before the earliest known reference to the instrument. This is dated 1679 and appears in John Evelyn's Diary which, written in London, puts the presumed Spanish invention of the instrument at some time in the mid-17th century. In fact, there is no evidence for the instrument's Spanish origin. Its invention further north, perhaps in Germany, is indicated.

The viola d'amore retains the flat back and sloping shoulders of the viol, but is played on the shoulder like a conventional viola and lacks frets. Early models sometimes had only five strings, later ones seven, although tuning was by no means standardized, with players adopting a *scordatura* appropriate to the key of a piece. Nevertheless, a common later tuning is *A, d, a, d', f sharp, a', d"*. Its chief attraction, however, is the presence of so-called sympathetic strings. These are not bowed but, tuned an octave higher than the main strings, resonate 'in sympathy' with them, giving a sweet and rather delicate sound.

As the name, which means 'love viola', suggests, the viola d'amore is one of several d'amore instruments. Another of this type is the oboe d'amore, which was prized in the late Baroque period for its special tonal quality as a solo rather than an orchestral instrument, not least as an *obbligato* instrument in vocal works. As such it features in several cantatas by J. S. Bach as well as in his *St. John Passion*, where two viole d'amore are deliciously paired with a lute. Its popularity

𝄞 A RARE CONCERT APPEARANCE BY THE BARYTON, IN THE HANDS OF JANOS LIEBNER, ONE OF A TINY BAND OF PROFESSIONAL BARYTON PLAYERS.

appears to have been highest in the German-speaking countries. Georg Philipp Telemann used it together with oboe d'amore and flute in a concerto, and parts for it are found in operas by his North German contemporaries Reinhard Keiser and Johann Mattheson.

The repertoire greatly diminishes after the mid-18th century, although there survive concertos by Karl Stamitz, a talented viola and viola d'amore player, and chamber works by him and his contemporaries. Thereafter its use in the 19th and early 20th centuries was as an isolated special effect, again more often than not in the opera house. Giacomo Meyerbeer wrote for it in *Les Huguenots* (1836), as did Puccini in *Madama Butterfly* (1904) and Janáček in *Katya Kabanova* (1921) and *The Makropulos Case* (1925). Taking the instrument's name literally, Janáček even considered using the viola d'amore instead of the viola in his second string quartet *Intimate letters* (1928), which was inspired by his unrequited passion for Kamila Stösslová.

By the beginning of the 20th century the viola d'amore had joined the growing ranks of older instruments then enjoying revival. One notable outcome of revival rather than survival is the *Kammermusik No. 6* (1927) of Hindemith, for viola d'amore and chamber orchestra. Hindemith also wrote a sonata for viola d'amore and piano, Op. 29/2, in 1929.

𝄋 *Baryton*

The baryton is really a larger version of the viola d'amore, held between the knees like a true viol, which enjoyed some popularity in the later 18th century. It has six bowed strings and up to 40 sympathetic strings. Joseph Haydn's patron Prince Nikolaus Esterházy was a gifted executant, and Haydn himself is known to have played the instrument. Haydn left several *divertimenti* which use the instrument.

℅ *Viola Bastarda*

This is a true viol, identical with the instrument known in England as the 'division viol'. It developed in Italy in the late 16th century as a smaller version of the bass viol and, as its English name suggests, was used for playing elaborate *divisions*, or variations, on existing melodies. Another name for it is the lyra viol, so called because it is played 'lyra-way'; ie, from tablature rather than from staff notation. This cross-fertilization between viol and lyra may account for the somewhat insulting name which this innocent instrument is given here.

℅ *Pochette*

Another group of bowed instruments is more directly related to the violin family. The pochette or kit violin is, as its name implies, a portable 'pocket-sized' instrument, particularly favoured by dancing-masters, and by street musicians, shepherds and others for whom the slim shape and diminutive size of the instrument proved handy. Although some specimens resemble genuinely small violins, the pochette is generally boat-shaped and has only three strings. These are the instruments designated as *violini piccoli alla francese* in the opera *Orfeo* (1607) by Monteverdi. Stradivari made a *kit* in 1717 which resembles a grotesquely stretched violin. Others were straight-sided from base to tuning pegs.

THE DIMINUTIVE POCHETTE OR 'POCKET FIDDLE', THE HANDIEST RELATIVE OF THE VIOLIN FAMILY.

✤ *Violino Piccolo*

The true violino piccolo is pitched a minor third higher than the violin. Its most celebrated use is in the first 'Brandenburg' concerto by J. S. Bach. Bach also wrote for a violoncello piccolo in some of his cantatas; there is a concerto in C for it by Giuseppe Sammartini. This instrument may be identical with the viola pomposa required for the sixth of his suites for solo cello. This is tuned like an ordinary cello but has a fifth string, sounding the *e'* above the *a* string. Some authorities, though, have claimed that the viola pomposa was an instrument played, like the viola proper, on the shoulder, whereas the violoncello piccolo was held like an ordinary cello but was of a smaller size.

✤ *Mandolin*

Of those instruments which are plucked, the mandolin is the best known and, at least as an amateur's instrument, has never really fallen into disuse. It takes its name from its shape; the Italian *mandolino* means 'little almond'. The mandolin's fingerboard is fretted like a guitar's and its tuning is identical to the violin's. The strings, however, are of wire and arranged in four pairs, each pair being tuned to the same note. This allows for one of the most characteristic features of mandolin playing, and the instrument's most effective way of sustaining a sound, the rapid *tremolando* between two notes of the same pitch.

From time to time the mandolin has attracted the attention of serious composers. Vivaldi wrote a concerto for two mandolins and another for one. Mozart used it in two songs of 1781: *Die Zufriedenheit* (K349) and *Komm, liebe Zither* (K351). His best known use of the mandolin is to accompany Don Giovanni's serenade *Deh, vieni alla finestra* in the opera of the same name (1787), a picturesque piece of scoring duplicated in the operatic repertoire's other *Barber of Seville* (1782), the one by Giovanni Paisiello. Even Beethoven, as a young man, produced two small-scale sonatas for the instrument. The mandolin was also the instrument taught to the young Paganini by his father.

✤ *Arpeggione*

The arpeggione was the invention of Georg Staufer of Vienna in 1823. This violoncello-guitar, as he called it, sought to combine the characteristics of the two instruments. Resembling a small cello, it possessed the six strings and fretted fingerboard of the guitar but was held between the knees and bowed. Its chief virtue lay in its extended compass and facility in playing full chords, together with the guitar-like effect of its *pizzicati*. It did not prove popular. Although the cellist Vincenz Schüster published a tutor for the instrument, it might have died virtually at birth had not Schüster prevailed upon Schubert to write a sonata for it. This work, D821, written in November 1824, has passed into the repertoire of cellists and violists. Arpeggiones have survived, though, to enable us to fulfil Schubert's – and Schüster's – original intentions. 𝄡

𝄞 THE MANDOLIN, NAMED FOR ITS SHAPE, AFTER THE ITALIAN FOR 'LITTLE ALMOND'.

THE NEW *String Family* ✤

Except in the case of the double bass, changes to the modern string family have been relatively few since the 18th century. This is not to deny that occasional attempts have been made to take a completely fresh approach, as in the case of the acoustically rational instruments produced in France by François Chanot and Félix Savart in the 1820s. The former proposed a violin of almost guitar-like shape, completely curved and with long, narrow soundholes, while Savart's instrument was near triangular and not unlike the modern balalaika in appearance.

More conventional in design is the New Violin Family developed in recent years by the American Catgut Acoustical Society. This comprises eight instruments, the smallest being pitched an octave higher than the violin and the largest (shaped like a large cello) of the same pitch as the double bass. The standard violin is retained as, after a fashion, are the viola and cello, but these last two are of a size which complements their pitch relationship to the violin and to each other. Consequently the viola, known as the alto violin, is larger than its orthodox counterpart and has to be played between the knees like a cello. The cello itself, again larger, is called the baritone violin.

In addition, there is a soprano violin, pitched an octave higher than the alto; a tenor violin tuned an octave lower than the violin proper; and a bass violin with tuning a third lower than that of the baritone.

𝄞 RIGHT: THE VIOLIN OCTET OR NEW VIOLIN FAMILY, ACOUSTICALLY MATCHED VIOLINS CHARACTERIZED BY THEIR TONAL HOMOGENEITY.

CHAPTER 3

Percussion Instruments

YOUTHFUL CONCERTGOERS often find the percussion section of the orchestra immediately attractive. Strings, woodwind and brass offer mysteries yet to be solved, but with percussion you can instantly see what is happening. Furthermore, percussion makes fine sounds. The timpanist crouches over his drums, tapping them lightly and listening (making sure they are in tune, see page 92), then hitting them with exciting thwacks at the appointed times. The bass drummer will set pulses throbbing with the deep thud of his enormous drum, and in really colourful music the side drum, cymbals, triangle and perhaps even more exotic instruments, such as Chinese block, tom-tom, wind machine, castanets and whip, will add their stimulating sounds. With the crashing of metal on metal, metal on wood and wood on wood (and the presence of kettle drums), it was inevitable that the percussion instruments came to be known irreverently as 'the kitchen department'.

LEFT: MARBLE RELIEF FROM THE CANTORIA BY LUCA DELLA ROBBIA, DATED C. 1435, SHOWING CHERUBS DANCING TO ANGELS PLAYING PIPE AND DRUMS.

Percussion is probably the oldest of all the instrumental groups. It has been used to accompany dancing, ceremonies and battle since prehistoric days, whether it be wooden bowls or frames with membranes attached, bells, or blocks of wood or stone which ring when hit. Percussion actually means two bodies coming together forcibly. However, that is not the end of it. The two bodies might meet gently or be slid against one another, as is sometimes required of cymbals, and subtle effects can be created with light touches on tubular bells, tam–tam, triangle – in fact, almost any of the percussion instruments.

By convention, percussionists are also called upon to operate other instruments which fail to qualify as woodwind, brass or strings. While the xylophone is undoubtedly a struck instrument, the glockenspiel is less obviously so since one version of it has a keyboard and resembles a miniature piano – but then, the piano, for all its strings, is a percussion instrument itself, for its strings are hit by hammers.

With the wind machine (not a wind instrument!) the player turns a handle, which shows how versatile percussionists have to be. This is not meant slightingly. For all the apparent expenditure of muscle that it takes to play the drums, percussionists are a well-trained, disciplined and skilful group of performers. Without their skill the carefully written requirements of composers, who spend a great deal of thought upon obtaining the percussive sounds they want in their music, would descend to mere meaningless noise. 𝄡

WORKS FOR
Percussion Alone
§

Only in the 1930s was it realized that diverse and entertaining sounds could be coaxed from a, by then, large range of percussion.

GEORGE ANTHEIL *Ballet Méchanique* (1924, revised 1954), for four pianolas, two xylophones, glockenspiel, timpani, tenor and bass drums, military drum, triangle, gong, cymbals, woodblock, aeroplane propellers (ie, recordings of aeroplane engines), and two electric bells. Originally written for an abstract film, and re-composed for concert performance, it represents, according to Antheil, "the barbaric and mystic splendour of modern civilization – mathematics of the universe in which the abstraction of the human soul lives."

BELA BARTOK Sonata for two pianos and percussion (1937). A fully–fledged recital work of amazing originality and imagination.

CARLOS CHAVEZ *Toccata* (1942), for xylophone, side drum, Indian drums, tenor and bass drums, bells, cymbals (suspended), large and small gongs, chimes, claves and maracas. A work of mesmeric rhythms, constantly changing in detail but maintaining a fascinating momentum.

HENRY COWELL *Ostinato Pianissimo* (1934), for four percussionists, who maintain, as the work's title suggests, a quiet rhythm throughout. *Pulse* (1939), for brake drums, pipe lengths, dubaci, rice bowls, woodblocks, dragons' mouths, tom-toms, drums, cymbals and gongs. An extraordinary rhythmic exercise in constantly varying timbres.

SIEGFRIED FINK *Beat the Beat*, for bass drum, two tom-toms, snare drum, hi-hat, cymbals and cow bells. Intended for a solo beat drummer, but written out rather than left to imagination.

ALAN HOVHANESS *October Mountain* (1942), for marimba, glockenspiel, timpani, tenor and bass drums, gong and tam–tam.

Marimba and glockenspiel provide the melodies, the rest create a mysterious atmosphere.

OSVALDO LACERDA *Three Brazilian Miniatures*, for vibraphone, timpani, side drum, xylophone and native Brazilian instruments.

RONALD LOPRESTI *Sketch* (1956), for xylophone, marimba, celeste, timpani, side drum, bass drum, gong, piano, triangle and cymbal (suspended), winner in 1956 of the first prize at the Eastman School of Music annual contest.

TORBJORN IWAN LUNDQUIST *Sisu* (1976), for xylophone, crotales, vibraphone, cymbals, marimba, tom-toms, xylorimba, tam-tam, timpani, Thai and Chinese gongs and tubular bells. This Swedish composer has a superbly subtle sense of rhythm and outstanding control of large forces.

ISTVAN MARTA *Doll's House Story* (1985), for percussion and synthesizer. A work of considerable length which tellingly blends natural drum sounds with synthetic gong chimes, marimbas, Chinese cymbals and bells.

LASZLO SARY *Pebble Playing in a Pot* (1978), in which marimbas somewhat over–insistently imitate the scene suggested in the title.

YOSHIHISA TAIRA *Hiérophonie V* (1974), for four timpani, six bongos, a small snare drum, eight gongs, two bass drums, two side drums, eight tom-toms, 16 woodblocks, eight claves, 15 Chinese woodblocks, whip, wood chimes, maracas, log drum, nine dubaci, five tam-tams, eight Thai gongs, four anvils, Chinese cymbal, eight Philippine gongs, three cow bells, flexatone, two glass chimes, six Turkish cymbals, two metal sheets, saw and Chinese gong. This Japanese composer draws on his nation's drumming tradition by encouraging his players to utter cries as they attack their instruments.

𝄞 TIMPANI

TIMPANI, ALSO CALLED kettledrums because of the cauldron-like hemispherical shape of their bowls, are the kernel of the percussion group. Today, it is rare to encounter an orchestral work lacking timpani.

While 'kettle', from Latin *catillus* = small bowl, refers to the body of the instrument, the modern name, 'timpani' (singular: timpano), describes the head; this relates to tympanum, after the membrane in the eardrum. Orchestral

timpani are tuned to definite pitches. At one time their heads were laboriously tensioned by laces, and later screws were used to apply tension where the outer rim of the skin is connected to the body. In practice, this meant that once the drum had been tuned it could sound only that note until it was re-tuned. An alternative method of tuning in some drums is by rotating the bowls. Modern timpani are tuned by means of pedals, allowing instantaneous re-tuning and even the possibility of *glissandi*. Pedal timpani are called 'machine' drums.

✺ Early History

Once Stone Age man had learnt to carve wood and cure animal skins, drums could be made. Hollowed-out logs, ceramic pots, perhaps even tortoise or turtle shells, were turned into drums with a calf-skin or other animal hide stretched across the top and fastened with a cord or a strip of leather. So ancient are these experiments that it is impossible to state categorically where timpani originated. The Middle East has given us the earliest representation of one, in a Babylonian plaque of about 700 BC. Thereafter, drawings and paintings including them are quite common. They show kettledrums ranging from very small to very large, and from shallow to deep, with the bowl shape varying from conical to rotund. These instruments were used in court for ceremonial purposes, less formally for danc-

𝄞 THERE ARE FEW MORE MENIAL TASKS FOR A SERVANT THAN TO ACT AS A HUMAN DRUM SUPPORT, AS IN THIS EARLY 18TH-CENTURY TURKISH SCENE.

A TIMPANIST WITH A RANGE OF 'MACHINE' DRUMS (IE, WITH PEDALS FOR TUNING), AND AN EVEN LARGER RANGE OF STICKS FOR PERCUSSIVE EFFECTS.

ing, and belligerently in war. By the 13th century in the Middle East mounted drummers came to be associated with mounted trumpeters, as indeed they did later in Europe where it became standard practice in concert halls, though by then the steeds had been dispensed with. Trumpets had been used occasionally without drums, especially in virtuoso roles, since the early 18th century, but in orchestral music trumpets and timpani were considered inseparable by composers, who often failed to indicate that the latter were required; it was 'understood'. Many drummers employed primarily for the court militia could not read music, and took their cues from the trumpeters.

If timpani became established first in the Middle East, they soon spread to India and Europe, where new varieties arose. Small hand-drum pairs, *tabla* and *bayan*, are now familiar in India: they are miniature kettledrums much more deserving of that name than the 'cauldron' drums of elsewhere. In Arabia, the *naqqara* were small kettledrums up to 25cm (10 inches) in skin diameter. They spread west and north; in England they are the ancestors of orchestral timpani and were called *nakers* (to rhyme with 'crackers'). Pronounced 'nackers' (not related to a knacker, a person who deals in old horses), this slang word has a musical, not a vulgar, origin. A player of two *nakers* would suspend them against his upper thighs from a waist belt. *Nakers* were useful for small parties of instrumentalists at court or in taverns; because they were portable they could be heard in almost any situation which demanded rhythm. They were of less use for formal gatherings.

By the time orchestras were first assembled (about 1600) to provide support for the singers in opera and oratorio, kettledrums had grown and developed a stronger voice. From there they moved with the rest of the orchestra into the concert hall and by 1800 had become a permanent part of the orchestra. Of course, not all operas or concert works called for drums, though opera generally gained from their presence because they could reinforce dramatic moments, imitate thunder in wild weather scenes, herald the entrance of ominous characters, announce the arrival of important personages and so on. The demands on timpani increased. No longer were they required purely as 'noise-makers', so the problem of tuning had to be addressed.

TIMPANI
EXPERIMENTS

ONE CAN IMAGINE the difficulties players encountered in the early days in trying to tune their kettledrums, and keep them in tune. Laces attached to the skins had to be tensioned with wooden chocks and brute force. Animal skins, perhaps inefficiently cured and dried, would slacken if hit too hard, and atmospheric humidity, or lack of it, made tuning to the correct pitch haphazard.

On the battlefield, if a soldier noticed that one of the cavalry's drums had gone out of tune he is likely to have had too many other things on his mind to let it worry him. There were two drums somewhere in the mêlée, one high pitched, the other low, and when they sounded a certain rhythm it would indicate 'advance', 'stand' or 'retreat', while a continuous high-pitched rattle would order 'left wheel', a

low-pitched one the opposite. That was all a soldier needed to know. Tone-deaf soldiers had to take their lead from comrades.

The situation was more critical in opera and concert performances. Laces were still in use in the 1730s, although by this time German drum makers had introduced screw tensioning. With this method, tuning is effected by turning screws at the rim of the skin: tightening the skin raised pitch, loosening it lowered pitch. Turning was achieved by means of a key or by a stick through loops or rings. Much trial and error was needed to obtain the right pitch and a great deal of care to avoid tearing the delicate vellum skin. Screw-

A 'MACHINE' TIMPANO, THIS ONE PART OF THE BERLIN PHILHARMONIC ORCHESTRA'S 'KITCHEN DEPARTMENT', OFFERS QUICK, ACCURATE TUNING.

A TIMPANIST REHEARSING UNDER HERMANN SCHERCHEN TESTS HIS INSTRUMENT'S TUNING BY TAPPING THE SKIN WITH THE FINGERTIPS.

tensioned timpani are still occasionally seen, mainly for historical accuracy in 'authentic performance' ensembles.

Some composers circumvented the problem of the time needed to change the note by the simple expedient of requiring more than the standard pair of timpani. Johann Melchior Molter wrote a Symphony in F (rather, a suite) about the middle of the 18th century which called for timpani tuned to five different notes, the effect in performance being almost that of a timpani continuo. Haydn dared not rely upon the availability of more than two timpani for his London concerts at the Hanover Square Rooms in 1791. The first movement of Symphony No. 94 in G, 'Surprise', requires timpani tuned to G and D with the G instrument having to retune to A. The composer neatly got round the problem by allowing the timpanist a full 19 bars to make the change from G to A – and a further 17 to retune back to G. His oratorio *The Creation* (1799) calls for seven re-tuning operations.

Clearly, drum makers were falling behind the requirements of composers. They responded with various inventions. In 1821 a rotating bowl was introduced in Amsterdam. A cable arrangement by a London maker included a pitch indicator which, so a famous timpanist recently remarked, "is less reliable than my ears". An early pedal timpano (1855) by saxophone-inventor Adolphe Sax proved to be a remarkable affair. The skin was extended taut over a cone-shaped resonator and pedals operated a series of shutters which blocked off certain lengths of the resonating tube, according to the note required. Rods, rings, cams, pedals and handles were all brought to bear on the problem, but none of these experiments found total success.

PROMINENT
Timpani
IN THE ORCHESTRA

One of the most startling timpani solos opens Bach's *Christmas Oratorio* (1734), answered immediately by flutes to create a pompous introduction to the chorus *Jauchet, frohlocket* ('Rejoice, exult').

JOSEPH HAYDN sometimes wrote adventurously for timpani, notably when it, and the rest of the orchestra, provides the surprise chord "to startle the ladies" in the Andante of the eponymous Symphony No. 94. However, a greater surprise comes in the finale, when a *forte* timpani entry abruptly follows eight quiet bars.

BEETHOVEN virtually liberated the timpani from its predominantly subordinate role, most dramatically in the Symphony No. 9, 'Choral' (1823). No less than 41 continuous bars of ferocious drumming mark the climax of the first movement's development, and solo timpani octaves, highly unusual in themselves at that date, answer the opening string phrases of the Scherzo.

Thereafter, timpani were used with increasing freedom and increasing dramatic effect, as in Tchaikovsky's *Romeo and Juliet Overture* (1880), a doom-laden crescendo near the end, and in the first movement of Dvořák's Symphony No. 9, *From the New World* (1893), where they decisively confirm the first *tutti* in the first movement and make exciting contributions later in the work.

Paralleling Beethoven a century later, Stravinsky set percussion totally free. His *Rite of Spring* (1913) requires incredible virtuosity from the timpanists as well as from the rest of the large orchestra. Three years later Carl Nielsen's Symphony No. 4, 'The Inextinguishable', placed a timpanist on either side of the orchestra and in conflict with it, maintaining, according to the composer's instructions, a menacing tone throughout.

Since then, Holst, Bartók, Britten, Tubin and many others have utilized the wide possibilities offered by modern pedal timpani. Some, such as the Belgian Victor Legley and the New Zealander Lyell Cresswell, have provided concertos for timpani and orchestra.

Finally, during the early years of the 20th century, a wholly satisfactory pedal system was introduced whereby, with the player seated, foot pressure controlled the pitch of the drum. Sophisticated models gave the timpanist the facility of a tuning gauge. But even with this refinement, in passages where different timpani notes occur in quick succession, one drum is still required for each note.

A TURKISH KETTLE-DRUM PLAYER OF THE EARLY 18TH CENTURY.

MULTIPLE TIMPANI

A PAIR OF TIMPANI were required by most composers until about 1800. Various tunings were called for but things settled down to one drum tuned to the tonic (the key the work was 'in') and another tuned a fourth below. Therefore, in a work in C major, one drum would be tuned to C,

A SELECTION OF DRUM STICKS WITH HEADS RANGING FROM SPONGE AND WOOD TO IVORY AND WIRE.

the other to the G below. This meant that, in sonata-form movements in C major, when the second theme arrived in the dominant, five steps up the scale (ie, G major), the lower drum was now in the new 'tonic'. However, when the slow movement arrived, usually in the subdominant (F major in our C major example) either the timpani had to be retuned or stay silent. Mostly, they stayed silent.

As we have seen, some composers introduced additional timpani to deal with such tonal problems, but this did not become acceptable practice until the middle of the 19th century. Before then, Antonín Reicha, an experimenter with many musical

novelties to his credit, required eight timpani in *Abschied der Johanna d'Arc* (1806), a score which, incidentally, also includes musical glasses (see Scraped Instruments, page 197). The rest of the 19th century saw a gradual and spasmodic use of multiple timpani, usually for special effects, but the bulk of standard works – Schumann, Brahms, even Nielsen (only later would he fully exploit the possibilities of percussion) – use the traditional pair. In *The Planets* suite (1914–6) Gustav Holst wrote for two timpanists at six drums; almost a century earlier Berlioz had required 16 in his *Requiem* (1837).

Numerical superiority is not the only way to ensure percussive novelties in timpani writing. In 1794 the German composer Johann Paul Aegidius Martini, called Martini il Tedesco (Martini the German) – to distinguish him from several Italian Martinis around at the time, just in case his given names failed to do so – conceived the idea of striking two timpani of different pitches simultaneously in his opera *Sappho*. This idea appealed also to Stravinsky: he required five differently tuned timpani to be struck together in his *Rite of Spring* (1913). A variation of this, the hitting of one drum with two sticks, was adopted by Mahler in his Symphony No. 8 (1906).

Heads and Sticks

As indicated earlier, timpani skins were made of vellum (that is, calf skin) or sometimes skins of other bovines, such as ox. After World War II, however, the increasing availability of synthetic materials invaded the musical instrument business and plastic drum heads were introduced. Drummers still disagree as to whether this move resulted in a genuine advance in tonal quality. Drumsticks are made of wood but the ends, the part that makes contact with the skin, might be fashioned from a wide selection of materials and also vary greatly in shape.

Until recently, the sound of drums in performances of orchestral music was regarded as almost obscene. This attitude was partly a by-product of the 19th-century audience's insistence upon a 'heavy' wash of orchestral sound. A Bruckner pedal point on timpani had to be a distant murmur, and on no account should a single stroke be allowed to disturb the enveloping cloak of the rest of the orchestra. Anything as coarse as an identifiable drum stroke was frowned upon. It was almost as if drummers were present in the orchestra merely to be seen at their acrobatic antics, and not heard. This situation

was exacerbated by the inadequacies of early recording techniques. The grooves of 78rpm and LP discs were too violently distorted to enable accurate tracking of the pick-up by the abrupt impact of a drum attack. Drum noise had to be damped down almost to inaudibility, lest it upset the balance or the comfort of armchair listening.

Fortunately, tastes change and recording technology has come on apace. Listeners now like to hear the voices of the drums. Drumsticks might be made of two layers of felt over a hard core, giving a smooth, rounded tone, or hard felt or wood, which produce a sharp and incisive sound. There are grades between these extremes, and the shape of the head also varies from spherical to wheel-shaped, via oval and pear-shaped. The correct stick is now chosen to suit the music being played. Sticks are held between thumbs and the first two fingers, and there is usually a ferrule of wood, plastic or metal to aid grip. ⑬

UNUSUAL USES OF *Timpani* ※

Apart from unusual tunings, which were adopted by many composers for specific effects or purposes, imaginative deployment of orchestral timpani began, possibly, in 1781, when Mozart called for them to be muted (ie, covered with a cloth) in the opera *Idomeneo*. Haydn required the same in Symphony No. 102 in B flat (1794). Berlioz, in his *Symphonie fantastique* (1830), marked his timpani part *baguettes d'eponge* ('with sponge-headed sticks') to create approaching thunder in the third movement and a feeling of dread in the following 'March to the Guillotine'. Later in that fourth movement, a fearsome rattle is created at the direction *baguette de bois* ('with wooden sticks').

In 1899 Elgar directed that a timpani roll in the *Enigma* Variations should be executed with side drum sticks to suggest the engine of an ocean liner, but he later agreed that two coins tapping the skins would equal the effect. Charles Villiers Stanford asked for timpani to be played with fingertips in *Song of the Fleet* (1910), and both Nielsen in Symphony No. 2, *The Four Temperaments* (1902), and Britten, in the opera *Death in Venice* (1973), instructed that drumsticks be laid aside and the timpani played with birch twigs.

HECTOR BERLIOZ IN 1846, THE YEAR HE COMPLETED *THE DAMNATION OF FAUST*. HIS PREDILECTION FOR LARGE FORCES EXTENDED TO A GENEROUS PERCUSSION CONTINGENT.

♪ SIDE·DRUM

SIDE DRUMS ARE frame drums, with a circular wood or metal frame and two heads of parchment. Usually the frame is shallower than the diameter of the heads (an exception is the long drum), and a snare is fitted against the outside of the lower (or upper) head. This snare, which gives the instrument its alternative name of snare drum (one preferred in jazz and popular music circles), consists of wires of gut in older models or, lately, nylon. When the upper head of the drum is struck with hard sticks the vibration within the drum is carried to the lower head where the snares react by rattling against the skin, producing a sharp hissing sound. This, combined with the instrument's naturally high tone, results in a distinctive noise that can cut through the heaviest orchestration. In certain circumstances the snares can be released from the head to give a tone not unlike that of a tom-tom.

In older models of side drum the skins were tensioned by ropes in a 'V' configuration with thongs which, when slid upwards, converted the 'V' into a 'Y', thereby increasing the tension. In modern orchestral side drums the tension is achieved by metal rods. Side drums are not tuned to a specific pitch: it is up to the player and/or conductor to decide what is the most effective tensioning for the work to be played.

Sticks are made of wood, with a plastic or ivory striking head in the form of a slim acorn. Typically, sticks measure about 40cm (16 inches). The drum bodies reach a maximum of 30cm (12 inches) deep, and the parchment (or plastic) heads a maximum of 40cm in diameter. Older models of both drums and drum sticks vary widely. Some drums resembled large barrels, which must have been tiring to carry if suspended round the neck or from a belt, and drumsticks ranged in shape from small clubs to unadorned wooden sticks.

❧ *Early History*

As with all drums, the side drum's origin is lost in antiquity. Small drums of all shapes and sizes existed thousands of years ago, many of them shallow framed such as are encountered even now in non-orchestral environments in many countries. One of the earliest representations of snares is to be found on a relief dated about 1454

♪ A PROVENÇAL LONG SIDE DRUM WITH SNARES AGAINST THE UPPER FACE. THE DRUMMER ALSO OPERATES A RECORDER.

♪ A MID-18TH CENTURY SIDE DRUM AND DRUM STICKS. AGAIN, THE SNARE OF THE DRUM LIES ACROSS THE UPPER SKIN.

in the church of St. Francis at Rimini. The drum is held perpendicularly from its frame by a cord in the left hand. A snare lies against the head, which is being beaten.

The side drum was originally used in military establishments, and that is where it got its name. Slung by a cord round the soldier's neck, the instrument hung against his side with the head at an angle. Its distinctive voice could be heard at considerable distances by marching men and in the heat of battle. The tradition, now he struck with a stick in the right hand.

Side drums play a vital part in military ceremonies of the British Army. In Scottish Highland regiments, for example, the drummers are tasked with setting up rhythmic patterns for the bagpipes. This requires immense skill and discipline. The drums set the tempo of the march at the start and maintain the pace when the pipers pause for breath or between tunes. As with military timpani, the side drum was also once used to pass messages and give instructions in the battlefield and in camp. It once served to accompany ceremonial floggings in the navy, adding a spurious solemnity to a barbarous act.

🎼 DRUMMERS OF THE ARGYLE AND SUTHERLAND HIGHLANDERS, COMPLETE IN THEIR FULL CEREMONIAL REGALIA WITH LEOPARD SKINS.

dying out, of military drummers donning leopard skins over their uniforms began in the late 18th century, when a fashion for black drummers arose. Military bands for long maintained this exotic symbol as a reminder of the past.

🎵 In Performance

Side drums, it was once maintained, are most effective when performing rolls or repeated quasi-military rhythms. This may have been true in the days of luxurious orchestrations, but now, with leaner sounds and the increasing incidence of chamber sonorities even in works for full orchestra, composers are quite happy to write single notes and intricate rhythms, knowing that the drums will make their due effect.

Side drums have been put to a number of musical purposes. In Elizabethan England and elsewhere the combination of pipe and tabor, to accompany dancing or marching, was common among travelling musicians. The tabor needed only to have one or more snares – as on occasion they did – to qualify as a snare drum. The musician would have a flageolet in the left hand and a small tabor hung from the neck or waist which

Side Drum
TERMINOLOGY
🎵

BATTER HEAD The upper playing skin; that which is 'battered'.

DRAG A roll.

FLAM A two-note figure.

MAMMY-DADDY The technique of producing a roll on the side drum, each stick alternately striking twice in quick succession to make a seamless roll.

PARRADIDDLE A descriptive way of indicating a succession of strokes: single, flam, drag.

RIM SHOT The laying of one stick on the drum head and rim simultaneously while this stick is struck with the other to make a very loud *staccato* sound, similar to a pistol shot.

RUFF A short series of quick notes terminating in a *forte* stroke.

SNARE The wires running under the lower head which vibrate against the head when the upper skin is struck.

SNARE HEAD The lower head, against which the snares lie.

SIDE DRUMS IN PERFORMANCE

MOST OF US ARE used to seeing the side drum as a member of the orchestral percussion. The French composer Marin Marais was apparently the first to use it in this role, possibly in his opera *Alcione* (1706). Far easier to verify is Handel's call for side drums in his *Musick for the Royal Fireworks* (1749). André-Ernest-Modeste Grétry was the first to use a side drum in a symphony: his multi-movement overture (a symphony in all but name) to the opera *Le Magnifique* (1773). The instrument's first appearance in a true symphony is courtesy of the little-known Bohemian composer František Krystof Neubauer, who includes *tamburo*, by which is meant side drum, in his highly descriptive 'Battle' Symphony, Op. 11. This work commemorates the so-called 'Siege of Helden Coburg', when Field Marshal Prince Coburg-Saalfeld led his Austrian army to victory over the Turks at Martinesti, Romania, on 22 September 1789. Mozart marked the same event that year with a lightweight country dance notable for

RIGHT: CLASSICAL PERCUSSIONIST JAMES BLADES IN ACTION.
BELOW: A MODERN SET OF 'TRAPS' FOR JAZZ AND ROCK USE. THE HI-HAT CYMBALS AND BASS DRUM ARE FOOT-OPERATED.

its exclusion of all military instruments.

Neubauer's remarkable work predates Beethoven's notorious 'Battle' Symphony by 24 years. Beethoven gave the opposing French and English armies their own side drum signals in his 'recreation' of the Battle of Vitoria, but sadly omitted the ingredient of genius. Rossini gave side drums unusual solo status at the start of his *Thieving Magpie* Overture (1817). Most famous of all in the side drum's repertoire is the gruelling slow crescendo of Ravel's *Boléro* in which, for over 300 bars, side drummers have to repeat the same rhythm while gradually increasing the power of the tone. Shostakovich combined Ravel's idea with vivid images of war in his 'Leningrad' Symphony (1941). In the first movement the approaching German army is represented by a two-bar pattern played no fewer than 176 times by side drum, rising from *ppp* to *fff*, and later a further ten times, fading to silence. Even if shared between players, this slow build-up of tension must rank as one of the most arduous of all side drum parts for the endurance, concentration and sheer physical strength required for its performance.

Various methods of making the side drum 'speak' in unusual ways have been devised by composers. The American Aaron Copland, in his Symphony No. 3 (1946), employs a most telling example of rim shot (see page 97). His compatriot William Russell's *Fugue for Eight Percussion Instruments* shows even greater imagination: at one point a piece of paper is placed over the drum head; at another, a handkerchief; and a resined glove or cloth is to be rubbed over the drum stick. Incidentally, Russell extended his oblique requirements to the piano, whose strings have to be played *pizzicato* with fingertips and fingernails, and scratched lengthways with a coin. Conventional use of the side drum in an unconventional setting is met in a Piano Sonata (1927) by the Russo-American composer Nikolai Lopatnikov, wherein it is awarded an important part.

Nielsen
AND THE SIDE DRUM

Early audiences at performances of Carl Nielsen's Symphony No. 5 (1922) were at first puzzled, then alarmed and finally driven in terror from the hall by the anarchic behaviour of the side drummer. It was indeed an extraordinary scene. The man seemed to go crazy. He stood near the back of the orchestra and created such a frenzy of noise that the orchestra, playing at full blast, was almost overwhelmed. What did it mean?

It was Nielsen's instruction to him that had caused him to display this behaviour. He must "improvise as if at all costs to stop the progress of the orchestra". This was not some modern gimmick to create headlines but a scrupulously planned strategy to convey the message of Nielsen's latest work. In his depiction of good versus evil, the composer divided his instrumental forces into two opposing camps, with the side drum (together with the clarinet, cymbals, triangle, etc.) given the role of an evil 'character'. The majority of the orchestra represented 'good'. A well-worn cliché, perhaps, but superbly carried out.

The symphony opens negatively, then disruptive figures are quietly introduced. These coalesce into a frightening march led by a repetitive side drum rhythm. Eventually this episode fades and yields to a noble Adagio ('the forces of good') which

DANISH COMPOSER CARL NIELSEN'S IMAGINATIVE EMPLOYMENT OF PERCUSSION SENT AUDIENCES HURRYING TO THE EXIT.

also fades, only to return. At this return it is attacked by the disruptive elements and a battle ensues. At its height, the side drum re-enters and launches upon its 'death or glory' assault. No two side drummers play the same music here, this being an improvisation. Some are not equal to being 'evil'; others let go with enormous vehemence, introducing every kind of alien rhythm and letting off 'rim shots' as the crisis approaches. Side drummers can show distinct signs of fatigue after their ordeal, even expressing regret at their failure to stop the orchestra.

Six years later Nielsen returned to the side drum, in his Clarinet Concerto. Written with the clarinettist of the Copenhagen Wind Quintet, Aage Oxenvad, in mind, this work reflects Nielsen's interest in the make-up of his fellow men. Oxenvad is characterized (accurately) as a sharp-tempered, choleric but humorous and at base kindly man. Nielsen adds a biting edge to the character in a carefully written and elaborate part for the side drum, which at times 'argues', at others 'agrees', with the clarinet. Unlike the symphony, open conflict is avoided, but familiarity with both works points up the strong link between them. Furthermore, both works allow the side drum more freedom and prominence than others in the repertoire.

𝄞 BASS DRUM

VISUALLY, THE BASS DRUM is an imposing instrument. It cannot be overlooked as it stands vertically in the percussion section (see pages 98 and 103). Some models are mounted on a stand (see page 102) to enable alteration of the head angle, especially for works that demand that the percussionists move quickly from instrument to instrument. Like the side drum, the bass drum is an instrument of indefinite pitch, which means it does not need to be tuned to a definite note. Its voice can change according to what the composer requires of it, from the slightest mutter to an elemental thundercrack. The instrument is equally effective at producing single notes or rolls.

The modern bass drum has two plastic heads, each with a skin diameter of approximately one metre; the depth of the wooden frame is about half this. A single-headed variety, of vellum, with a shallower frame was once quite common. This type was called the gong drum, due to its appearance not its material. Since their invention almost 6000 years ago, large drums have tended to reduce in size for standard usage, though there are exceptions (see below). Early versions stood nearly 2m (7 feet) high and were installed in permanent positions in court or palace, probably as a rallying point or time signal. Bass drums were known in Asia by at least 3500BC, and some thousand years later they were part of Sumerian culture. They have since appeared in many different forms.

𝄞 MINSTRELS AT VAUXHALL GARDENS, IN 1806, WITH TURKISH PERCUSSION (CYMBALS, TRIANGLE, BASS DRUM, TURKISH CRESCENT, TAMBOURINE) AND PANPIPES.

✳ The Bass Drum and Janissary Music

The modern orchestral bass drum is clearly descended from a Turkish military model, the 14th century *davul*, which is approximately the same size and in the same proportions. The *davul* has two heads, but is laced as opposed to being screw-tensioned, and struck with a heavy wooden beater rather than the large felt-headed drumsticks commonly used by orchestral drummers. During the heyday of the Ottoman empire in the late 14th century the peoples of the Balkans came to fear the sounds associated with the Turkish armies. Principal among these was the noise created by the *davul*, together with shawms, jingles and cymbals, which signalled the

The description 'Janissary music' indicates exotic music, often in A minor, which is intended to convey the flavour of Turkish military bands with cymbals, triangle (substituting for Turkish crescent, see page 229) and bass drum. The following works may all be described as 'Janissary music':

GIOVANNI DOMENICO FRESCHI *Berenice vendicativa*, opera (1680).

GOTTFRIED FINGER *Concerto alla turchesa* (c. 1725).

CHRISTOPH WILLIBALD GLUCK *Le cadi dupé*, opera (1761); *La rencontre imprévue*, opera (1764); *The Pilgrims of Mecca*, opera (1764).

GEORG GLANTZ 'Turkish' Symphony (1774).

JOHANN MICHAEL HAYDN 'Turkish' Suite from music to Voltaire's *Zaire* (1777); Turkish March in C (1795).

WOLFGANG AMADEUS MOZART *Die Entführung aus dem Serail* (opera) (1782).

FRANZ JOSEPH HAYDN Symphony No 100 in G, 'Military' (1794).

LUDWIG VAN BEETHOVEN 'The Ruins of Athens' (incidental music) (1812), 'Battle' Symphony (1813'), Symphony No 9 in D minor, 'Choral', (1823).

approach of the invaders. The Sultan's guard was made up of 'new troops' (*yeni çeri*), or Janissaries (war captives who were trained into an elite fighting corps). Their war-like sound was thus termed 'Janissary music'. Although other instruments were included, the combination of cymbals, jingles and bass drum came to be so closely identified with this music that 18th-century composers, wishing to add exotic Eastern colour to their Turkish opera plots or concert pieces, invariably scored for them, replacing the jingles with a triangle.

In a military band the soldier playing the big drum has it strapped vertically in front of him, striking it with the drumstick held in the left hand while the right hand damps the reverberation of the skin on the opposite side. To the bystanders' amusement, the drummer's right hand jumps away from the skin and back again at every blow. Unlike the orchestral bass drum, which is rod-tensioned, military models still adhere to rope-tensioning, in which ropes are attached criss-cross between the heads and tightened by sliding braces.

An interesting variation arose in the military use of the bass drum and came about in imitation of Janissary music. In cases where the drum pos-

Bass drummers using headless sticks and leading a somewhat depleted procession; North of England, 1930s.

sesses two heads, one would sometimes be played with a cane or birch twig, and these might even be used on the drum casing. In his 'Military' Symphony, No. 100, Haydn faithfully reflected this practice (which is more than most performances manage) by writing the bass drum part on one line with the note tails descending for normal strokes and ascending for the birch twig strikes. The downbeats are accented by the drumstick strikes. Birch twigs on the skin produce a dry, flat sound with a faint resonance, but when beaten on the drum casing this resonance is further reduced and the result merely provides rhythmic pulse.

So pervasive did this Turkish craze become in the 18th century that it even entered music whose scoring is totally devoid of percussion. Mozart, in the finale of his Violin Concerto No. 5 in A, K219 (1775), known as the 'Turkish', switched to A minor for an extended episode strongly redolent of folk music of that culture. About eight years later another A major work

put the whole of the finale into A minor. This is the Piano Sonata in A, K331, where the finale is marked *Allegretto alla turka* and popularly called the 'Turkish rondo'. Some pianos of the time were equipped with percussive attachments that not only rang little bells to imitate the Turkish crescent but also damped the lower strings to create the impression of a bass drum.

BASS DRUM IN THE ORCHESTRA

IN THE 17TH CENTURY the bass drum was waiting to be introduced into the orchestra. People were already familiar with big drums in the spheres of folk and ethnic music. As so often, it was via the opera house that this novelty came to be accepted in a serious work, in 1680 (see panel). Its acceptance grew quite gradually during the next century and a half, being carried by the Janissary connection (see page 100–1). Then came Berlioz.

If Haydn, followed by Beethoven, liberated the timpani, Berlioz released the bass drum from its association with Turkey. Within three years of Beethoven's 'Choral' Symphony, Berlioz had scored for bass drum in his very first orchestral work, the Overture *Les francs juges*, omitting cymbals and triangle. Part of the drum's function was to reinforce the cross-rhythm of the timpani in the central section. Later, in his *Grande messe des morts*, Berlioz required the drum's two skins to be struck alternately with padded sticks.

Thereafter, the bass drum was used frequently by many composers and with increasing imagination, its Turkish adjuncts rarely if ever in attendance. Liszt is credited as the first to require a bass drum roll, in his first symphonic poem, *Ce qu'on entend sur la montagne*, though the idea may have come from Joachim Raff who assisted Liszt with orchestration in his early works. An effective roll in Dukas's *Sorcerer's Apprentice* is created by twisting a double-headed stick to produce rapid strokes, an effect taken up by Stravinsky in *The Firebird*.

But a problem remained: audibility. Heavy orchestration can smother the bass drum's natural tone unless some means can be found to accentuate it. Composers have found different solutions to this shortcoming. In his *Missa da Requiem* Verdi called for a 'very large bass drum'; in *En Saga* Sibelius required the extra clarity imparted by the use of timpani sticks; and in *Madama Butterfly* Puccini instructed that the instrument be attacked with an iron rod. In Britten's opera *Peter Grimes* the bass drum is struck with side drum sticks. And, in a revision to his original score to *The Rite of Spring*, Stravinsky asked for wooden sticks to be played near the edge of the skin.

Owing to its spare and cunning orchestration, Prokofiev's score for *Lieutenant Kijé* requires no such 'extras' to allow the bass drum to be heard. Shostakovich, too, realized the importance of lean scoring if the bass drum's voice is to be heard with clarity. He went to the extreme in his Cello Concerto No. 2, first movement, giving the bass drum eight *ff secco* ('very loud and dry') and five *mf* (medium loud) strokes, its only competition being from the cadenza of the soloist. In his Symphony No. 12, 'dedicated to the memory of Lenin', Shostakovich called for a strange percussive effect at the end of the first movement and leading into the second. Over the space of 95 bars he has the bass drum, side drum and timpani in unison, intermittently contributing to a vast *diminuendo*, opening at a violently hammering *fff* (extremely loud), dropping quickly and eventually reaching a whispered *morendo* (dying away). The effect of all three drum timbres together is both ominous and mysterious.

✗ Sizes

There is little doubt that drums, and particularly big drums, hold a fascination for audiences, whether at a concert or anywhere else. Showmen will attract a fairground or circus crowd to their displays by banging a drum (if, that is, they have resisted the temptation to modernize the process by deafening their prospective clients with a

A MODERN BASS DRUM BY YAMAHA, MOUNTED ON A SWIVELLING FRAME FOR 'FACE TO FACE' PLAYING.

BERLIOZ *Les francs juges*, Op. 3, overture (1826), the first orchestral work to use the bass drum independently of other Turkish percussion.

BRITTEN *Peter Grimes* (opera) (1945), uses side drum sticks; *Young Person's Guide to the Orchestra* (1946), a short solo with two drum rolls.

DUKAS *The Sorcerer's Apprentice*, scherzo (1897), includes rapid beats created with a double-headed drumstick.

LISZT *Ce qu'on entend sur la montagne*, symphonic poem (1849), believed to be the first use of the bass drum roll.

PROKOFIEV *Lieutenant Kijé*, suite from an aborted film (1934), gives prominent bass drum solo against light scoring.

PUCCINI *Madama Butterfly* (opera) (1904), requires an iron bar to replace the usual drumstick.

SHOSTAKOVICH Symphony No 12, Op. 112, 'The Year 1917' (1961), uses bass drum in unison with side drum and timpani; Cello Concerto No. 2, Op. 126 (1966), has bass drum strokes to accompany the cello cadenza.

SIBELIUS *En Saga*, symphonic poem (1892), uses timpani sticks.

STRAVINSKY *The Firebird* (ballet) (1910), as Dukas, above; *The Rite of Spring* (ballet) (revised version, 1947), calls for wooden sticks to be used near the edge of the skin.

VERDI *Missa da Requiem* (1874), requires the largest big drum available.

THE PERCUSSION SECTION OF THE HALLÉ ORCHESTRA AT THE ROYAL FESTIVAL HALL, LONDON, IN 1952, A YEAR AFTER THE HALL OPENED TO THE PUBLIC.

ghetto-blaster), and the bigger the drum the better. Theoretically.

In practice there is a size at which a drum becomes dangerous because the vibrations within could cause it to explode if struck too enthusiastically. This size may almost have been reached by the Remo company of North Hollywood, California when, in 1961, they built a huge drum for Disneyland. Its head measures almost 3.7m (10.5 feet) in diameter and the instrument weighs 204kg (93lb). Such an instrument might have indulged the craze for large-scale effect displayed by Verdi, but practicalities preclude its use even for 'authentic' performance.

A-Z OF OTHER PERCUSSION

Tenor Drum

Most familiar of the rest of the percussion section is the tenor drum, also called the long drum. This type has a dry, commanding tone of no definite pitch, like that of a deep side drum without snares, although of decisive effect. Its use in the military in Europe was, and is, widespread, and it was from the military that it first ventured into the orchestra, where it has been employed by many 20th-century composers. Like so many other 'exotic' instruments, the tenor drum was given its first opportunity in 'serious' music by opera. Meyerbeer's grand opera *Robert le Diable* was a great success in Paris in 1831; its use of tenor drum probably suggested to Berlioz that the hollow voice of the instrument was appropriate for solemn, sacred music (two tenor drums occur in the *Grande Messe des morts* of 1837) and in a hymn of praise (his *Te Deum* of 1849 requires six tenor drums). At that time the instrument was tensioned by ropes. Modern examples use rods, as does the side drum. It may be struck with hard or soft sticks, depending upon the musical circumstances.

AFTER THE DRUMS, the percussion group boasts a whole host of varied instruments, some tuned to specific scales or notes, others not. The instruments listed below are of indefinite pitch (ie, they are untuned) unless otherwise noted.

Castanets

A name taken from the Spanish for 'chestnuts' and the instrument itself taken from Spanish folk culture and chestnut wood. Castanets were in existence in Roman times and probably long before. Each castanet is a disc-shaped piece of wood, hollowed on one side and with flanges extended from the edge to hold the cord by which it and its fellow are held by the fingers. Traditionally the two discs are brought together rhythmically by manual manipulation, but this Spanish folk skill is rarely shared by orchestral musicians. They cheat by fastening the instruments to a piece of wood, upon which they are held apart by elastic until fingers play upon them. Naturally, non-Spanish composers wishing to evoke a Spanish atmosphere will employ castanets. The first to do so was Bizet in *Carmen* (1875), to be followed by Chabrier in *España* (1883) and Massenet in his opera *Le Cid* (1885). In 1877 Saint-Saëns extended the geographical possibility of castanets by including them in *Samson and Delilah*, set in Gaza.

Celeste

A 'heavenly' sounding instrument of definite pitch, invented in 1880 in Paris. Tchaikovsky, amid great secrecy, endeavoured to be the first to use this instrument of hammered metal plates in his *Nutcracker* ballet (1892), but he was thwarted by Charles Widor, who introduced it in his ballet *La Korrigane* (1880).

Claves

Simply two sticks up to 25cm (10 inches) in length, struck together to provide a rhythmic accompaniment. Edgard Varèse was the first to use claves in his *Ionisation* (1931), and others have followed. Elisabeth Lutyens, the English composer, brought them into her curiously titled charade in four scenes and three interruptions, *Time off? – Not a Ghost of a Chance!*.

TENOR DRUMS BY PREMIER – HIGH-PITCHED AND SPECIALLY STRENGTHENED INSTRUMENTS FOR MARCHING.

104

ABOVE: EVELYN GLENNIE PLAYING
HAND DRUMS. THIS BRILLIANT
SCOTTISH PERCUSSIONIST COMPOSES
AS WELL AS PLAYS.
BELOW RIGHT: THE SAFRI DUO.

℅ Cymbals

Of great antiquity, these are part of the Janissary music we met with under Bass Drum. China, so obviously the land of clashing metal, is probably innocent of cymbals; their place of origin may be Turkey or India. The design of these two plates banged together has undergone many detail changes. In shape they vary from slightly dished to cup-shaped; in size they can reach 65cm (26 inches) in diameter or be tiny enough to be held by threads to the finger and thumb of a dancer, to be sounded during the dance. The first use in serious music seems to have been in 1680, when Adam Strungk included them in his opera *Esther*. Since then they have done prominent service in many a 19th-century overture, and more recently have been sounded with a violin bow when suspended, and struck with beaters. ℬ

Percussion

PERFORMERS

℅

AMADINDA PERCUSSION GROUP, a Hungarian ensemble formed in 1984 by Károly Bojtos, Zoltán Rácz, Zsolt Sárkány and Zoltán Váczi.

JAMES BLADES, though not a regular recitalist, is a world-renowned player with the London Symphony Orchestra (since 1940) and many other organizations. He is an unequalled percussion authority, giving lectures and broadcasts as well as making an illustrated recording about percussion in 1973 (see page 98).

ENSEMBLE BASH, formed in 1990 by Richard Benjafield, Stephen Hiscock, Chris Brannick and Andrew Martin. It is currently Britain's only professional percussion group.

EVELYN GLENNIE (left), Scottish percussion virtuoso and composer who, despite being deaf, recognizes the musical sounds through vibrations in her body and through her acute visual sense.

KODO, a Japanese group whose name means 'heart beat', founded in 1971 by Den Tagayasu. Originally called Ondekoza ('demon drum group'), the ensemble now consists of ten members who value, and maintain, traditional Japanese music.

KROUMATA PERCUSSION ENSEMBLE, formed in Stockholm by Ingvar Hallgren, Jan Hellgren, Anders Holdar, Anders Loguin and Martin Steisner. *Kroumata* is the ancient Greek generic term for percussion.

NEXUS, a Canadian ensemble formed in 1970 by Russell Hartenberger, John Wyre, Robin Engelman, Bob Becker and William Cahn. The group's repertoire ranges from ragtime to classical.

SAFRI DUO (shown below) Danish percussionists Uffo Savery and Martin Friis have played percussion together since, as children in the early 1970s, they joined the Tivoli Boys' Guard in Copenhagen. They arrange old music for percussion and work with contemporary composers during the writing of new works.

STRASBOURG PERCUSSION ENSEMBLE (Les Percussions de Strasbourg) was founded in that city in 1961 and has been conducted by, among others, Pierre Boulez.

JAMES WOOD, English composer and percussionist, and authority on percussion.

⅋ *Flexatone*

Once described as the instrument with the least attractive sound of all (by a critic evidently unfamiliar with the serpent), the flexatone was invented in England in 1922. Two wooden knobs on wires flank a metal strip and when the instrument is shaken the knobs hit the strip to produce a rapid rattling sound. Meanwhile, the strip is capable of being flexed to change its note, and while this is happening a weird *glissando* effect is punctuated by the rattle. Honegger gave the flexatone its first chance in *Antigone* (1927), Khachaturian risked a solo for it in his Piano Concerto (1946), and the Finnish composer Lief Segerstam created symphonic history by putting one in his Symphony No. 11 (1986).

⅋ *Glockenspiel*

(German for 'bell-play') An instrument of definite pitch, being a series of metal bars struck either directly with beaters or via a keyboard. Handel's call for 'carillon' in his oratorio *Saul*

(1738) has been put forward as the earliest use of a *glockenspiel*, but as he is more likely to have used a frame of bells, the *glockenspiel* in Mozart's *The Magic Flute* (1791) is probably its earliest appearance. The Austrian-born Finnish composer Herman Rechberger 'prepared' ten of the instruments (by placing foreign objects on the bars) in his children's piece *Mobile 4* (1977).

⅋ *Gong*

In orchestral parlance the 'tam-tam', this is a circular metal plate at least 80cm (32 inches) in diameter which is suspended from a frame and struck with a soft-headed stick. François-Joseph

𝄞 A PORTABLE *GLOCKENSPIEL* MOUNTED UPON A LYRE-SHAPED STAND AND PLAYED BY A BANDSMAN OF THE US ARMY AIR FORCE.

Gossec, the Belgian composer, was the first to put it in the orchestra, in his *Funeral Music for Mirabeau* (1791).

⅋ *Marimba or Marimbaphone*

A pitched invention of the early 20th century. Its shape resembles a xylophone but with resonating tubes hanging below the keys to give a soft sonority. The American composer Paul Creston wrote a concerto for it in 1940, and the Japanese composer Teruyaki Noda included one in his Quintet for three flutes and bass (1968).

✇ Tambourine

A round, frame drum with metal discs inserted loosely in the frame. These jingle when the skin is hit or rubbed, or the whole instrument shaken. The earliest tambourines of prehistoric times differ little from the modern instrument, which entered the orchestra only in 1779, with Gluck's opera *Echo et Narcisse*. A craze for accompanying the piano with tambourine in dances and sonatas was short-lived around 1800, but modern composers use the instrument regularly. A long tambourine roll accompanies a cadenza in Shostakovich's Cello Concerto No. 2 (1966).

✇ Triangle

A companion of cymbals and bass drum in European 'Turkish' music, the triangle is the orchestral instrument with the least mass but the most penetrating voice. A triangular rod of steel hit with a steel beater, it once bore metal rings to still further intensify the sound. Again, opera, ever watchful for telling effects, was responsible for bringing it into the orchestra, but what work

♪ ROY AYERS PLAYS THE VIBRAPHONE, WHICH FOUND ITS PLACE IN JAZZ THROUGH MILT JACKSON.

John Cage
INVENTOR AND COMPOSER
✇

One Tuesday in Seattle in 1938 John Cage was asked by the dancer Syvilla Fort to write a Baccanale for the following Friday. A percussion group was indicated, but none was available at such notice. Cage improvised by means of applying kitchen utensils (cutlery, crockery, metal dishes, for example) to the strings of a piano to modify its tone. Unfortunately, they slid about when the strings vibrated. Undeterred, he turned to woodscrews, erasers, mutes and bolts, fixing each type to a specified string at a precise distance from damper or bridge.

This experiment proved to be the first in a long line of works by Cage for 'prepared' piano. In addition he experimented with electronics, in one instance applying contact microphones to a glass of water containing dissolving aspirins). In 1952 he 'composed' the notorious 4' 33" in which, for that length of time, any instrumentalists present (and any may be) must not play.

CAGE ALSO WROTE A LARGE QUANTITY OF MUSIC FOR PERCUSSION ALONE:

- ↝ Quartet (1935)
- ↝ Trio (1936)
- ↝ First Construction (in Metal), for six percussion (1939)
- ↝ Second Construction, for four percussion (1941)
- ↝ Credo in Us, for four percussion (1942)
- ↝ Imaginary Landscape 2, for five percussion (1942)
- ↝ Imaginary Landscape 3, for six percussion (1942)
- ↝ The Wonderful Widow of 18 Springs, for one voice and piano (1942), the piano to remain closed while its case is played
- ↝ A Flower, for voice and closed piano (1950)
- ↝ Music for Carillon 1 (1952), for bells
- ↝ Music for Carillon 23 (1954), for bells
- ↝ 7' 10.554", for percussion (1956)
- ↝ Music for Carillon 4 (1966), for bells

it graced at the Hamburg Opera in 1710 is not known. It invariably accompanied cymbals in 'Turkish' music during the 18th century but assumed more independent roles in Paganini's Violin Concertos No. 2 (1821) and No. 4 (1830).

✇ Tubular Bells

In an orchestral environment tubular bells are considerably more convenient than real bells, the main advantage being that of portability. Tuned lengths of narrow metal tubing are hung from a frame and struck with hard mallets at the top edge to create a convincing bell like tone. Their invention during the 1880s by a Coventry manufacturer, John Hampton, was quickly followed

by their first concert appearance: in Arthur Sullivan's *Golden Legend* (1886).

✇ Vibraphone

Called vibraharp when it was invented in 1910, this instrument has been known by its current name since 1927. It is happier in a jazz setting than in the orchestra. Like the marimba, it resembles a xylophone with two ranges of tuned metal keys, and with vertical resonators underneath. Darius Milhaud appears to have been the first to use it 'seriously', in his incidental music for Claudel's play *L'annonce faite à Marie* (1932). The Japanese composer Akira Miyoshi has awarded the vibraphone a concerto (1969). 𝄢

✧ Whip

A name which reflects this instrument's sound. Its alternative name, 'slapstick', betrays its construction. It is difficult to imagine a musical use for a whip in ancient times, unless a real whip was cracked as an audible guide should the rhythm flag. A third name for the instrument, 'jazz stick', suggests that it is a fairly recent phenomenon. In the early days of jazz, with bandleaders competing for the latest gimmick to surprise the crowds, whips were only one of the devices to see service, but more formal uses demanded a specially designed noise-maker. Modern orchestral whips consist of two pieces of wood hinged near the end and kept apart at an angle by a weak spring. When required, the woods are brought together with a sharp crack. Probably the best known example of the use of the whip occurs at the opening of Ravel's Piano Concerto in G (1931). It is also heard, punctually and in its place, in the galaxy of instruments paraded in Britten's *Young Person's Guide to the Orchestra* (1946).

✧ Wind Machine

This noise maker for special effects might be expected in the opera house, the usual spawning ground for such things, but it seems, as far as its

well known appearances are concerned, to be more welcome in the concert hall. As its name suggests, it creates artificial wind sounds by mechanical means. When Ralph Vaughan Williams used it in his *Sinfonia Antartica* (1952), written originally for the film *Scott of the Antarctic*, he requested that the wind machine should be played out of sight of the audience, so that the chilling effect of the sound comes as a complete surprise. There are two models of wind machine. The less frequently encountered is an electric fan to the blades of which have been fitted slats of wood. More familiar is the rotating drum version, the drum covered by canvas or silk which rubs against wood laths or cardboard tongues when a handle is turned. The faster the rotation of either model, the higher the pitch. However, with such an instrument precise pitch is neither possible nor desirable.

♪ A DRUM-TYPE WIND MACHINE. WHEN THE HANDLE IS TURNED A CONTINUOUS BUT VARIABLE SWISHING SOUND IS CREATED TO REPRESENT A HIGH WIND.

℀ *Woodblocks*

A catch-all name for Chinese blocks, temple blocks and Korean temple blocks. Each type is different, their only point of similarity being that each is constructed from a round or rounded block of wood. The original Oriental blocks sometimes exceeded 60cm (24 inches) in diameter, their resonant tones being used in religious ceremonies. Orchestral blocks are about a maximum of 15cm (6 inches) in diameter and have a slit in the lower face. They are ranged before the player who hits them with a knobbed, wooden stick. An obvious use is in imitation of horses' or other quadrupeds' hooves, but in rapid action they have been used to imitate the chattering of apes. The first composer to use woodblocks was Sir William Walton, in *Façade* (1923). They also appear in two piano concertos: by George Gershwin (1925) and Constant Lambert (1931).

Confusion surrounds the terminology applied to these instruments. Sometimes the term 'woodblock' is used for a modern adaptation of the ancient design, made from a hollow piece of rectangular wood and played with side drum sticks. A further development of this type can sound two different notes. This has slits and wooden tongues on its upper surface and relates to the larger African message drum (see page 215).

℀ *Xylophone*

Slats of tuned wood ranged according to size and pitch are common in ethnic communities, a pointer to the concept's considerable antiquity. Hans Christian Lumbye was the first to score it, in his *Traumbilder* (1873); Saint-Saëns's *Danse Macabre*, a vivid portrayal of a dance of death in which the Devil plays the violin, followed a year later. István Lang wrote a concerto for xylophone (1961), and the Japanese composer Toshiro Mayuzumi composed a *concertino* for it in 1965.

HARRY PARTCH (CENTRE) WITH INSTRUMENTS INVENTED BY HIMSELF. EACH REQUIRES SPECIAL PLAYING SKILLS. ON THE RIGHT STANDS THE FAMOUS GOURD TREE.

Richard Strauss used a species of wind machine in his tone-poem *Don Quixote* in 1897 (where, in the English translation of the score, it is described as a 'ventilator'), and – to add meteorological and atmospheric verisimilitude – in his highly descriptive 'Alpine' Symphony (1915).

THE *Partch* PHENOMENON ℀

In addition to inventing a number of stringed instruments and his own tuning system, the American experimentalist Harry Partch built many novel percussion instruments. He developed his own scale of 43 notes to the octave and composed music for the strange instruments he invented. Among the percussion were:

CONE GONGS Cone-shaped metal structures about one metre (3 feet) high and 35cm (14 inches) in diameter round the base, supported on a wooden structure;

GOURD TREE Literally a tree branch supported on a wooden stand and hung with gourds which are struck with sticks.

In addition, the following percussion were invented by Partch. Their names and materials give a hint as to their sound quality:

Bass marimba (wood)
Boo(bam) (bamboo)
Cloud chamber bowls (glass)
Diamond marimba (wood)
Marimba eroica (wood)
Mazda marimba (glass)
Quadrangularis roverscum, spoils of war (glass, wood, metal)
Zymo-xyl (glass, wood, metal)

℀ *Xylorimba*

This early 20th-century development of the xylophone has a much extended range. After its initial trial runs in music halls, Alban Berg included it in his *Three Pieces for Orchestra* (1915). In his Hymnody (1963) for chamber ensemble, the Spanish-born English composer Roberto Gerhard required that a xylorimba be played by two percussionists simultaneously. 𝄢

RARE PERCUSSION

♯ Bells

The first composer to use bells in a 'serious' context apparently was Georg Melchior Hoffmann in a funeral cantata *Schlage doch* (c.1730), formerly attributed to J. S. Bach. The score calls for *campanelle*, which is translated as '2 Glöckchen' ('little bells'). The opera *Camille* (1791) by Nicolas-Marie Dalayrac requires the ringing of church bells, as does Ignaz Pleyel's *La Révolution du Dix Août* of the following year. Giacomo Meyerbeer's opera *Les Huguenots* (1836) demanded a specially made huge bell, and

Tchaikovsky's *1812* Overture (1880) called for 'all the bells of Moscow'.

♯ Bell Bars

These are literally bars of metal that ring like bells when struck. These are included by the dozen in David Bedford's children's piece *Whitefield Music 1* (1967), along with a dozen milk bottles and four drums. Marrowbones-and-cleaver, once regularly heard at butchers' weddings, can make a similar sound.

♯ Bird Scare

Used in the Symphony No. 1, 'Gothic' (1927), by Havergal Brian. Percussionist James Blades identifies the bird scare as no more than a rattle, an alarm signal familiar in Spain and Latin America as the *matraca* (see page 199) and on football terraces as a noise maker.

♯ Cannon

Tchaikovsky's well-known cannon shots in the *1812* Overture were presaged by those in François-Joseph Gossec's Overture in C, *Le Triomphe de la Republique ou le Corps de Grand Pré*, published in Paris in 1793.

♪ NAUTICAL TUBULAR BELLS – CAPTAIN LINDELL OF SS *STRATHMORE* PHOTOGRAPHED IN **1935**; SEE PAGE **107**.

♯ Chains

Large and small, dragged along the floor and shaken, are requested, respectively, in Arnold Schoenberg's *Gurrelieder* (1901) and Havergal Brian's 'Gothic' Symphony (see Bird scare entry, above).

♯ Cuckoo Clock

Together with an alarm clock bell, this appears in Leroy Anderson's *The Syncopated Clock* (1945). The sound of a cuckoo, played by a toy, flute or recorder, is heard in the 'Toy Symphony' attributed to Joseph Haydn but actually part of a Cassation in G (1756) by Mozart's father, Leopold. Therein are also heard quail, nightingale, toy trumpet and rattle.

♯ Drum Sticks

These play a vital part in the percussion section of course, but they usually have a drum to hit. It is reported that Isaac Albéniz, the Spanish composer, dispensed with the latter accoutrement and instructed that in one of his works the percussionist is to beat the music desk with drum sticks. This recalls Rossini's eccentric instruction to his second violins in the overture to the comic opera *Il Signor Bruschino* (1813) to strike their music stands (or, according to one report, their candle holders) with the wood of their bows.

✀ Dulcitone

A keyboard instrument in which hammers strike a row of tuning forks within the cabinet. The result is not strong in tone, the dulcitone being essentially for domestic enjoyment, but Vincent d'Indy imaginatively suggested its use in his *Song of the Bells* (1883). In most performances, where the bell-like instrument's tone is expected to fill the recital room, the part is taken instead by *glockenspiel*, see page 106.

✀ Sandpaper

As unlikely a musical instrument as one will ever meet, perhaps, but Leroy Anderson in his *Sandpaper Ballet* (1954) required sheets to be rubbed on a hard surface as a rhythmic accompaniment. The effect is not unlike the 'soft-shoe shuffle' once in vogue in music halls.

✀ Saw

Also optimistically called musical saw, this was another favourite music-hall gimmick. The saw was played with a violin bow to create a ghostly wailing sound, to the amazement of the audience. Several composers have scored for it, notably the Japanese Toshiro Mayuzumi in *Tone Pleromas 55* (1955), where it is joined by five saxophones, and in *Mikrokosmos* (1957), where its colleagues are claviolin (an electronic keyboard instrument), guitar, vibraphone, piano and percussion. Darius Milhaud put the saw to more percussive use when he called for it to be hit with a drumstick in his *Cinq Etudes*, Op. 63 (1920), only one of the outrageous effects in a score for piano and orchestra that took polytonality to new extremes with four independent fugues playing simultaneously in different keys. This caused a near-riot at its Paris premiere the following year.

✀ Spoons

Ordinary household ones are rattled together in George Auric's ballet *Les Matelots* (1924). We may again thank music hall, and perhaps also the street musician, for familiarizing us with the rhythmic possibilities inherent in spoons.

✀ Thunder Sheet

A noise-maker par excellence, this is an orchestral instrument borrowed from the theatrical effects department, where several means were employed to imitate meteorological roaring. In some, heavy metal balls were dropped onto leather, in others they were rotated in a barrel or rolled down a wooden ramp. The orchestral version is only slightly less inconvenient: a suspended metal sheet, 3.65m (10 feet) high and 1.2m (4 feet) wide, is attacked with soft headed sticks, its resonance being increased if necessary by its being placed against a bass drum. Today, old fashioned is the organization that fails to use the convenience of pre-recorded real thunder. Richard Strauss, in the days before tape recorders (1915), used a thunder sheet to depict stormy weather in his 'Alpine' Symphony, but John Cage was somewhat more demanding in his *First Construction* (1942): he wanted five thunder sheets of different sizes.

✀ Tumba

A long (1m/3 feet), thin drum, usually found in pairs and played by the hands, the pitch varying

♪ A KEYBOARD-OPERATED *CARILLON*.
THE KEY AND PEDAL MOVEMENTS
ARE CONVEYED BY METAL RODS TO
CLAPPERS WHICH STRIKE THE BELLS
HIGH ABOVE IN THE 'BELL CHAMBER'.

according to the area of the head being hit. Kurt Wege's arrangements of Leroy Anderson's *Jazz Pizzicato* (1949) and *Fiddle-Faddle* (1952) included them and they are common (as conga drums) in Latin American dance bands. To Pakistanis the word *tumba* refers to a long lute.

✀ Typewriter

Perhaps a threatened species in these days of word processors, but still recognizable by its quiet clicking in some offices. When Erik Satie in *Parade* (1917), Ferde Grofé in *Tabloid* (1947), Leroy Anderson in *The Typewriter* (1950) and Rolf Liebermann in *Concert des changes* (before 1964) required typewriters, the machine made a much more piercing sound, such that in Liebermann's work it could be heard equally with the cash registers and calculating machines which are its co-soloists in the score. ⑬

CHAPTER 4

Keyboard Instruments

Keyboard instruments have been in existence since pre-Christian times. They come in all shapes and sizes and produce sound in different ways. Organs, the most ancient keyboard instruments, are wind machines; harp- sichords pluck strings; and pianos hammer. The keyboard instruments found in this section are of the closed case type. Open uncased variants, such as marimbas, vibraphones and xylo- phones, will be found under Percussion. The principal keyboard instruments of the renaissance and baroque were the harpsichord, virginal, spinet and clavichord. Generically, like the piano, all can be classified as chor- dophones of the boarded *zither* family. In the first three (effectively keyboard psalteries) the strings are set into vibra- tion by being plucked mechanically. In the clavichord, they are excited by brass tangents. The layout of strings custom- arily defines the identity of the plucked examples. In a virginal, they run roughly parallel to the keyboard. In a spinet, they run away diagonally to the right. In a harpsichord, they run directly away. Virginals and spinets have single sets (choirs) of strings, and single keyboards (manuals). The harpsi- chord usually has two or three sets, with either one or two keyboards (or manuals).

EARLY KEYBOARDS

♯ *Clavichord*

Chronologically the oldest, and possibly derived from the ancient monochord (a string stretched across a resonator with the vibrating length, or pitch, determined by a movable bridge), the clavichord looks like a simpler form of the rectangular virginal, with the keyboard likewise displaced to the left. In the 15th century it was often known as either *monochordium* or *monacordo*; the earliest use of the term 'clavichord' dates from 1404. Italian examples from the 16th century (with projecting keyboards) were transverse-strung. German instruments from the 17th/18th centuries (with inset keyboards) were oblique-strung (right front to left back). The rear ends of the keys have tangents or blades which strike pairs of metal strings. To the right of the strike-point is the vibrating length (pitch) of the string which crosses a bridge that carries the vibrations to the soundboard. Cloth, or 'listing', damps that part of the strings to the left.

Clavichords may be 'fretted' (each string-pair being struck in succession by differently-placed tangents), or 'unfretted' (in which each string-pair gives only one note). Needing half as many strings again, an unfretted instrument is described by Johann Speth (*Ars magna consoni ed dissoni*, 1693): "each key has its own strings and not some [strings] touched by two, three, and even four keys". Players on unfretted clavichords were able to accommodate pieces in distant tonalities. Fretted instruments were more limiting. The clavichordist has direct control over dynamic loudness, depending (piano-like) on the force of the strike; and over changes in sound through varying pressure on the sustained key - making possible vibrato or *Bebung* effects, and impressions of 'swelling' tone. (*Bebung* is particularly unique – C. P. E. Bach indicated it, and Beethoven may even have tried to simulate it in his late piano sonatas.)

By the late 18th century, the compass of the clavichord was that of the harpsichord and piano (five octaves). Three-and-a-half to four (with the omission of some bottom chromatics - the so-called 'short octave') seems to have been the earlier norm. Originally a learning or practice aid, yet with an unexpectedly intense range of expressive possibilities, the intimate clavichord was the domestic instrument of the German-speaking lands from the 16th century onwards. But it was not until the 18th century, when it was already being challenged by the harpsichord and the piano, that it finally came into its own as a creative and performing tool, "ideal ... for solitary musical self-communion" (Helen Rice Hollis). It was the favourite *Empfindsamkeit* medium of C. P. E. Bach. He praised it in his *Versuch über die wahre Art das Clavier zu spielen* (1754–62): "the clavichord and pianoforte enjoy great advantages over the harpsichord and organ because of the many ways in which their volume can be gradually changed". He even wrote a rondo in farewell to a specially loved example by Gottfried Silbermann (1781).

♯ FAR LEFT: A DETAIL OF A GERMAN CLAVICHORD.
♯ BELOW: A RECREATION OF A CLAVICHORD, BY THE DOLMETSCH WORKSHOP.

❧ Harpsichord

In appearance the harpsichord foreshadows the wing-shaped, wooden-framed grand pianos of the late 18th century. The principal element of the harpsichord's activating mechanism is a slender wooden fork-shaped jack fixed vertically to the back of the key. The jack carries in a pivoted tongue a plectrum of quill; originally this was of crow, raven, turkey or eagle primary wing/tail feathers, later of soft buff leather or plastic. Depressing the key releases a cloth damper from the string, raises the jack and forces the plectrum past the string, plucking it. A release mechanism lets the jack return to rest. Depending on the point at which the string is plucked, and the material of the plectra, different tone qualities can be obtained. The sound lasts while the key is depressed, but decays quickly. In the hands of a good player, sophisticated *legato* (joined) and *staccato* (detached) articulation are possible. Many baroque composers devised ingenious ways of implying sustained sound, not least through ornamentation and trills. Changes of dynamic are impossible, though, unless there are extra jacks, strings or other mechanics. When, on bigger instruments, changes of dynamic are possible, they are by nature terraced rather than graduated: a vivid example of such stratified dynamics, with boldly stepped contrasts of *forte* (loud) and *piano* (soft), is found in Bach's solo Concerto in the Italian Style (1735). The harpsichord's dynamic limitations were eloquently lamented by Couperin in the preface to his first book of *Pièces de clavecin* (1713): "The harpsichord is perfect as to its compass, and brilliant in itself, but as it is impossible to swell or diminish the volume of its sound, I shall always feel grateful to any who, by

the exercise of infinite art supported by fine taste, contrive to render this instrument capable of expression".

❧ Types of harpsichord

First mentioned in Padua in 1397 as a 'clavicymbalum', with the earliest surviving example made in Bologna in 1521, harpsichords have been built and presented in different ways, depending on place and period. Originally they were short and thick-cased, with a single manual; a double-manual is mentioned in 1514. Another two-manual instrument, described as 'a pair of virginals in one coffer with four stops', is listed in Henry VIII's Privy Purse expenses for 1530. Typically, 16th-century Venetian examples, with one (8 foot) or two (8 foot plus 4 foot) choirs, had slender bodies made of cypress wood, with decorated outer cases.

The 16th/17th century Flemish school, centred on the legendary Ruckers family of Antwerp (who also made virginals), favoured thicker, generally painted casework, double choirs, and, by the 1590s, un-coupled double-manuals. Hallmarked by a distinctive soundboard rose, Ruckers' highly-valued harpsichords were resonant, tonally balanced instruments, and especially popular in England and France. A beautifully-crafted, rebuilt and enlarged French version of Ruckers, with an elegantly lacquered or painted soundboard and body, was created at the end of the 17th century by the Blanchet family of Paris. The instruments of the Blanchet dynasty were celebrated; Couperin 'le Grand' owned one of their harpsichords. By the mid-18th century they had been appointed 'facteur des clavessins du Roi', and by 1827 they were making their

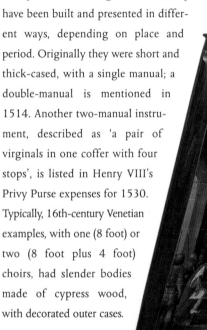

𝄞 A BEAUTIFULLY PAINTED HARPSICHORD OF PROBABLY 16TH CENTURY SOUTH GERMAN OR ITALIAN ORIGIN.

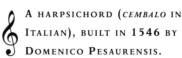

first high-quality upright pianos. German harpsichords of the 18th century, principally from Hamburg, tended to be large and complex, with extra 2 foot (high) and 16 foot (low) registers, occasional pedal keyboards, and even (in one case, a Hass, made in 1740, with five choirs of strings) three manuals. Bach preferred such examples.

The English instruments of the 17th and 18th centuries were undecorated, oak or walnut veneered, and richly powerful with thicker soundboards. The most acclaimed makers of the 'English' type were the Swiss-born Burkat Shudi and the Alsatians Jacob and Abraham Kirkman. Shudi enjoyed exclusive patronage: from his friends Handel, Gainsborough and Reynolds to Haydn, Frederick the Great of Prussia and Maria Theresia of Austria. Among his inventions was the dubiously effective Venetian Swell (1769), designed to vary dynamic volume by the use of louvred wooden shutters (based on the Venetian blind idea). He also incorporated a 'machine stop' for quick changes in registration: a single (foot) pedal overriding individual hand stops and controlling several different registers of strings.

Broadly similar in specification, Kirkman's harpsichords were more numerous than Shudi's and had a virtual monopoly in London. Contrary to European tradition, the keyboards of English double-manual harpsichords were uncoupled in the Flemish style and produced harsh contrasts of timbre. This characteristic has often brought into question the suitability of 'English disposition' instruments to the mainstream continental harpsichord music of the baroque period.

℀ The modern harpsichord

Friedrich Heinrich Himmel is said to have played the harpsichord publicly in Berlin as late as 1805, with the Kirkman workshops making their last model in 1809. Together with the clavichord, the instrument was not to be heard again until Louis Diemer and Arnold Dolmetsch resurrected it

An example of the craftsmanship of Jacob Kirkman, this harpsichord dates from 1756.

in the 1880s. The Parisian piano makers Pleyel and Erard revitalized interest as well, with the former exhibiting an instrument at the 1889 Paris Exposition. So, too, did Chickering in America, and Ibach and Neupert in Germany.

Like the modern piano, the early 20th-century harpsichord was largely a hybrid, bearing only a passing resemblance to its original form. Manufacturers went for size, sustaining power and projection, with more focus and less overtoning. It was usual to fit concert harpsichords with pedals rather than hand-stops to enable a quicker, more dramatically coloured response when changing registers. Treble strings were lengthened, bass ones were shortened and overspun with copper, as in the piano. Then, in 1923, Pleyel introduced a high-tensioned, iron-framed instrument – clearly an all-conquering, sensibility-attacking, jangling anachronism but one that nevertheless found favour with Wanda Landowska and her disciples – and for which Falla and Poulenc were to write their harpsichord concertos. Modern harpsichord making (and the construction kit industry) has largely reverted to period values, continental-style, as have most modern players.

℅ *Virginal*

In a treatise of about 1460 the virginal is identified as "having the [rectangular, box-like] shape of a clavichord and [transverse] metal strings making the sound of a [small] harpsichord". The instrument was intended originally to be either placed on a table or held in the lap. English virginals generally followed Flemish design, with the keyboard either centred, or displaced, like the later 'square piano', to the left (called a 'spinett') or the right (called a 'muselar'). The spinett was bright in sound, the muselar rounded and flute-like. A more elaborate double model by Ruckers featured a small 'child' virginal at octave pitch, interfaced with a 'mother' virginal at unison pitch. They could be played separately or coupled. The origin of the name is unclear. "Like a virgin ... with a sweet and tranquil voice", says one 15th century source. Only "virgins played

BELOW: AN ITALIAN VIRGINAL BY ONOFRIO GUARRACINO, DATED 1668.

on them" says another, 150 years later. Most repesentations show it played by young women (mostly standing, rarely seated). Copied out in 1606–19, the *Fitzwilliam Virginal Book* comprises 297 pieces by all the most eminent composers of the English virginalist school, including Bull, Byrd and Farnaby. *Parthenia or the Maydenhead of the First Musicke that ever was Printed for the Virginals, with works by William Byrd, Dr. John Bull and Orlando Gibbons,* was the first collection of keyboard music to be published in England, in 1613.

ABOVE: A MUSICAL PARTY SHOWING VIRGINALS AND FLUTE. IN ENGLAND FROM THE END OF THE 16TH CENTURY, 'VIRGINAL' WAS LOOSELY USED TO DESCRIBE ANY KIND OF QUILLED, PLUCKED KEYBOARD INSTRUMENT.

Temperaments

The octave is divided into twelve semitones. Depending on register, these vibrate at different frequencies (cycles per second), from slow (bass/low) to rapid (treble/high). Acoustically, modern 'equal temperament' (dividing the octave span uniformly) is impure in tuning (save for the octave interval) but allows free exchange, or modulation, between the major or minor keys (modes) of Western theory. Older 'mean tone temperament' (c. 1500) was purer in interval (notably thirds). In 'equal temperament' the black keys, or enharmonic 'accidentals' of the keyboard (C sharp/D flat, D sharp/E flat, F sharp/G flat, G sharp/A flat and A sharp/B flat) sound the same. But in 'mean tone temperament' there was an audible acoustic/frequency difference between each letter name. Theoretically, the major/minor scale patterns were shared. Practically, pitch was not (at least not without progressively unsatisfactory dissonance). In 'mean tone' tuning 'local' keys around C major were considered acoustically 'good'/possible for modulation, more 'distant' ones 'bad'/impossible, hence the restricted orbit of tonalities and key relationships found in so much Baroque and early Classical repertory. Depending on what key(s) they were playing in, string players could tune correspondingly to the 'mean' tone of the time, making slight but intonationally critical finger adjustments as necessary. Keyboard players were less fortunate, to such an extent that some harpsichords were even constructed with 'divided accidentals' so that each sharp and flat of the scale had its own string and key mechanism, giving seventeen keys to the octave (an unwieldy and expensive luxury).

'Equal temperament' solved the problem by splitting or 'tempering' the difference between sharps and flats, exchanging purity for practicality. Notwithstanding some modern disagreement, it is generally accepted that Bach's *Well Tempered Clavier* (two books, 1722; 1738–42) comprising 48 preludes and fugues, two in each of the major and minor keys, was the first work to comprehensively endorse the principle. Originally proposed in the 16th century, and strongly supported in the 18th by Rameau and C. P. E. Bach, the impurities of 'equal temperament' took time to get accepted. It was not until the mid-19th century that it was finally adopted in England and France. Now it is in general use, except in reconstructive 'period practice' playing where there has been a return to older temperament tunings.

Spinet

The spinet was another form of early domestic harpsichord, replacing the virginal. In French and Italian the term once defined any kind of small single-choir, single keyboard, plucked action instrument. Apart from outward shape, the principal difference between a virginal and a spinet is acoustic. In the former, both ends of the vibrating string length are supported by bridges on the soundboard. In the latter, which resembles a harpsichord, one end is supported by bridges fixed to the solid wrestplank – creating a fuller, firmer tone. German spinets of the 16th-century tended to be rectangular in design. Early 17th-century Italian ones were five or six-sided.

A double-manual spinet of c. 1600 from the famed workshop of Ruckers in Antwerp.

♪ PIANO

Unlike the harpsichord or the clavichord, the piano is an equal temperament instrument in which the strings are struck percussively by rebounding hammers. Capable of graded dynamic contrasts depending on pressure of touch, its importance has been unchallenged for over two hundred years. No other modern acoustic instrument, apart from the organ, has such a wide frequency response from low to high, nor such expressive capacity, dynamic power, or colouristic possibility. Composers have used the piano to suggest a whole symphony orchestra. Arrangers have inventively used it to simulate one – from Czerny and Liszt to Mahler and the Second Viennese School.

♪ A GRAND PIANO OF 1793 BY THE SOUTH GERMAN MAKER SEBASTIAN LENGERER OF KUFSTEIN.

✄ Cristofori's Piano

Beethoven chauvinistically believed the piano to be a German invention, the powerful, all-encompassing post-Congress of Vienna Hammerklavier of his late sonatas. Given the pre-eminence of so many Austrian and German makers, many of them refugees of the Seven Years' War (1756–63), and the hammer action design of Christoph Schröter (without escapement), his presumption can be forgiven. Whatever the evidence for piano prototypes (some going back to the 15th century), it was however not a German but a celebrated Paduan, Bartolomeo Cristofori, keeper of harpsichords and spinets at the court of Ferdinand de'Medici in Florence, who is traditionally credited with having invented the instrument – the first, an *arpicimbalo* (effectively a keyed dulcimer) around 1698–1700. Scipione Maffei went to Florence in 1709, and in his *Giornale dei letterati d'Italia* (1711) he mentions four "cleverly thought-out" Cristofori *gravicembali col piano e forte* ('harpsichords with soft and loud'), comparing their gradation of dynamic volume and power to that of the cello. Cristofori's pianos had paper-coiled, leather-covered hammers, and, innovatively, escapement action, which prevented the hammers rebounding onto the strings after the initial strike.

✄ The Square Piano

In Germany the principle of Cristofori's Italian invention was taken up by the Freiberg organ-builder, Gottfried Silbermann. After some persuasion, J. S. Bach eventually came to admire and play his pianos, making suggestions for their improvement and even selling them. During his visit to the Potsdam court of Frederick the Great in 1747, he endorsed their assets publicly. Like Cristofori's, Silbermann's instruments were in the form of 'wing-shaped' grands. Many German makers, however, opted for the horizontal 'square' (oblong) clavichord-descended type, without escapement. An already sophisticated 'square' piano by Johann Socher, made in 1742, is the earliest surviving example of the type.

✄ Piano Actions:
German/Viennese vs English

During the latter half of the 18th century, two characteristic types of piano action evolved – the lighter 'German' and the heavier 'English' (forerunner of the type familiar today). Based physically and aesthetically on the intimately expressive characteristics of Silbermann's pre-1750 clavichords, so beloved of C. P. E. Bach, 'German' *Prell-mechanik* action (with the hammer facing the player) was famous for its delicate touch and subtlety of nuance. Johann Andreas Silbermann of Strasbourg is credited with its invention, but it was left to his pupil, Johann Andreas Stein of Augsburg, extravagantly admired by Mozart and Beethoven, to perfect its damping and escapement elements, the former

Piano
NAMES
℅

COTTAGE PIANO A small domestic upright marketed by Clementi and others in London early in the 19th century.

FLUGEL German for 'wing'. Both harpsichords and pianos are approximately wing-shaped.

FORTEPIANO An early name meaning 'loud-soft' (see Pianoforte), now reserved for early pianos, almost specifically those lacking full iron frames.

GRAND A horizontal piano, wing-shaped, with strings running diagonally away from the player.

HAMMERFLUGEL German. A wing-shaped instrument (keyboard by inference) in which the strings are struck by hammers.

HAMMERKLAVIER German for 'keyboard with hammers', as opposed to the plucked harpsichord. Beethoven specified a Hammerklavier for his late piano sonatas. In its narrow sense, *Hammerklavier* refers to a 'square' piano with hammers.

IVORIES Slang for piano (1855), referring to the material from which piano keyused to be made.

JOANNA (JOANO) English rhyming slang for 'piano' (1846).

KLAVIER German term for any keyboard instrument, but generally taken to mean 'piano'.

PIANOFORTE Italian for 'soft-loud', to distinguish the piano from the standard harpsichord, upon which graduated harmonics are not possible.

UPRIGHT A vertical piano for domestic use, rectangular in shape, with the strings running diagonally behind the keyboard.

controlled not by foot pedals but knee-levers.

In 1794 Stein's daughter, Nannette, set up business in Vienna with her husband J. A. Streicher: 'German' action became 'Viennese'. From this time until its closure in 1896, the firm of Streicher was the most important quality piano maker in Vienna. Their early instruments were favoured by all the great composers and virtuosos, from Beethoven to Hummel. Other eminent Austrian makers included Walter and Schantz (favoured by Haydn), Graf and (later) Bösendorfer.

℅ The 'English' Piano

Born in Saxony, Johannes Zumpe, who had served his apprenticeship in the workshops of Silbermann and Shudi, was predominantly responsible for the evolution of the 'English' piano during the reign of King George III. His earliest surviving trestle-supported single-action 'square' piano (without escapement) dates from 1766. Resembling a clavichord and largely tuned to an unequal temperament of 17 notes per octave, this had a small soundboard to the right, light hammers and reduced dynamic range. On 2 June 1768 Bach's youngest son, Johann Christian, the 'London' Bach, played a Zumpe instrument in the first solo performance on a piano in England. Zumpe's piano charmed English society. Its action was unsophisticated, and it was cheap to produce. Known on the continent as 'piano anglais', it made its way around the civilized world, reaching even as far as the harems of Ottoman sultans.

℅ Broadwood and the Grand Piano

In 1772 a Dutchman living in London, Americus Backers, helped develop 'English' grand or double-action (with escapement). Robert Stodart and

A SILBERMANN PIANO OF 1746, FROM AN ORIGINAL USED BY J. S. BACH AT THE COURT OF FREDERICK THE GREAT IN POTSDAM.

John Geib (another German) patented forms of it in 1777 and 1786 respectively. And the Scotsman John Broadwood (Shudi's son-in-law) improved its evenness, flexibility and dynamic power. Originally a joiner and cabinet maker, Broadwood was a visionary in piano design. He recognized that the optimum point at which hammer should strike string was critical in determining tone quality. In 1783 he patented foot-pedals; and in his redesigned 'square' pianos he introduced an under-damping mechanism. In 1788 he patented a divided bridge, with bass strings allocated a separate bridge (the long, single bridge of the harpsichord having formerly been customary). In 1818 Beethoven was sent a Broadwood grand (subsequently inherited by Liszt) that had a split damper pedal mechanism independently controlling bass and treble; Chopin played one during his final concerts in London and Manchester thirty years later. The family firm's instruments – according to a factory hand, "3,800 separate pieces of ivory, woods, metals, cloth, felt, leather and vellum, all fashioned and adjusted by hand" – were in wide demand in Victorian England, with an output of 2,500 a year by the 1850s.

SOUND & WORLDS

FRENCH, ENGLISH AND VIENNESE

🎼 A PIANOFORTE OF 1801 MADE BY THE FRENCH FIRM OF ERARD. BY THIS TIME ERARDS INCORPORATED THE ENGLISH ACTION.

Like Chopin, the Alsatian piano and harp maker Sébastien Erard preferred the greater volume and character of 'English' action instruments. He came to London in 1792, after fleeing the French Revolution, and opened a workshop. His first grand, improved 'English' style, appeared in 1796/7. Napoleon later owned one, and the great virtuoso Thalberg played them. Another illustrious French maker was the Austrian-born Ignaz Pleyel, in whose brilliantly lit Parisian concert room, the Salle Pleyel – graced by "a complete aristocracy of birth, wealth, talent and beauty" (Liszt) – all the greatest virtuosos of the Romantic age played. Apprenticed in London to Broadwood, Collard and Clementi, Pleyel's son Camille successfully carried on the family name.

As well as Broadwood, both Erard and Pleyel placed instruments at Chopin's disposal during his final stay in London. And it was on a Pleyel that Chopin completed his *Préludes* in Valdemosa, dedicating them to Camille. Like Field, Kalkbrenner and Gottschalk, he liked Pleyels for their "silvery and somewhat veiled sonority and their easy touch" (Liszt) and because they encouraged him "to find the sounds I want – when I am in good spirits and strong enough. When I am in a bad mood, I play Erard pianos and easily find in them a ready-made sound." Not so the American Edward MacDowell fifty years later. He likened Erard instruments – by then out of touch with progress and substantially more costly than any of their rivals – to be "a combination of wood and glass". Present-day French pianos – such as they are, for there are very few – are still thin-toned, a matter of national taste reflected no less in the crystalline character of Gallic keyboard writing – from Couperin 'le Grand' and Rameau to Ravel.

🎼 A BOSENDORFER COMMISSIONED FOR THE EMPRESS EUGENIE IN 1867. DESIGNED BY AUSTRIAN CRAFTSMAN HANS MAKART, IT HAS BURR, WALNUT AND ROSEWOOD MARQUETRY WITH BRASS INLAYS, AND CAST BRONZE STATUETTES.

❧ 'English' vs 'Viennese'

The different characteristics of 'Viennese' and 'English' pianos were tangible and audible. 'Viennese' action was shallower and easier, 'English' action, more resistant, deeper and harder. It 'pushed' rather than 'bounced'. 'Viennese' instruments (a tenth of the weight of their 20th-century descendents) had the benefit of rapid articulation, utmost

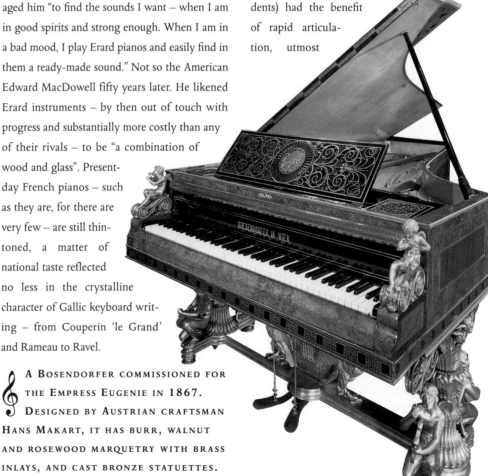

clarity, minimum delay between action and sound, and quick damping. 'English' ones were slower in speech and repetition because it was necessary for keys to return fully to rest before re-activation. In sound 'Viennese' pianos were thinner and more neutral within, though not between, treble, tenor and bass registers. 'English' ones were fuller and more coloured, with the tone more evenly distributed, thereby lending melodies, as Hummel wrote, "a peculiar charm and harmonious sweetness". Each action produced its own type of performer, and even its own type of composer. Mozart and Haydn belonged to Stein and the 'Viennese' school, Clementi and Dussek to Broadwood and the 'English'. Beethoven bridged the two – and dreamt further.

✄ The Upright

The 'square' piano endured in the drawing rooms of the wealthy for much of the 19th century – especially in America. Robert Wornum of London began making examples of vertically strung upright pianos in the 1800s, calling them 'cottage'

Piano Music Firsts
✄

Styles of composition usually associated with the piano fall into three categories:

1. Those taken over from other mediums as the piano became popular; eg, ballade ('narrative song'), barcarolle ('Venetian gondolier song'), polonaise, prelude, scherzo, variations, waltz etc. – omitted here.
2. Those taken over from other instruments but rethought in the light of the piano's capabilities; eg, concerto, sonata.
3. Those taken by and from other instruments but evolved with the piano in mind.

ALBUMBLATT ('album leaf'), originally an intimate short piece for a friend's album. Beethoven's *Für Elise* (1808), may have originated as such. In 1854 Schumann published a collection of twenty *Albumblätter*.

BAGATELLE ('a trifle', something insignificant), a name first used by Couperin (1717) but taken over for far-from-insignificant works by Beethoven from 1801.

BERCEUSE ('lullaby') first used by Chopin (1843–4) and later by Liszt.

CONCERTO The first concertos written specifically for a 'Pian e forte' (pianoforte) were the six of J. C. Bach's Op. 7 set of 1770.

ECLOGUE ('pastoral piece'), a word used by Tomášek from 1807 for 42 piano pieces.

IMPROMPTU (literally an improvisation, but written out). Schubert's two collections (1827) are substantial 'studies' in sonata, rondo, variation, nocturne

and other forms. The title of the first set was at the suggestion of the publisher Haslinger.

LYRIC PIECE ('songful piece'), the title of ten sets (1867–1901) by Grieg.

MORCEAU ('piece'; 'morsel'), equates with *Stück*.

NOCTURNE ('night piece'), a term used by Mozart, Haydn and others for vocal ensemble pieces or serenades ('evening music'). The first three of John Field's Nocturnes for piano were published in 1814; the first three of Chopin's (Op. 9) in 1832.

SONATA Lodovico Giustini wrote 12 Sonatas, Op. 1, in 1732, titling them *Sonate da cimbalo di piano e forte detto volgarmente di martelletti* ('Sonatas for harpsichord with soft and loud, familiarly with little hammers'), to distinguish the intended instrument from the hammerless harpsichord.

SONGS WITHOUT WORDS, the title of eight sets of piano miniatures (1829–45) by Mendelssohn.

STUDY or **ETUDE** Developed from such collections as Bach's *Clavier-Ubung* ('keyboard exercises', 1731–42) and Türk's *Clavierschule* (1789), the first musically self-contained studies/études were by Cramer (1804, 1810) and Clementi (1817–26). Moscheles, Chopin, Liszt, Czerny and Alkan concentrated the style.

STUCK ('piece'), literally a 'piece' of music. *Klavierstücke* means 'pieces for piano'.

pianos. His future designs for small parlour instruments included low 'piccolo' and taller 'cabinet' models. A neat 'portable grand' from 1801, by Hawkins of Philadelphia featured a folding keyboard and boxwood naturals, as well as a revolutionary part-metal frame. Thomas Jefferson owned one. In their most basic form, uprights resembled dark coffins with broken

teeth, and their voice was basic, but they were convenient and popular. All the leading European and American firms built them, with Steinway taking credit, in 1863, for the first identifiably modern prototype. 𝄡

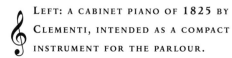

𝄞 LEFT: A CABINET PIANO OF **1825** BY CLEMENTI, INTENDED AS A COMPACT INSTRUMENT FOR THE PARLOUR.

THE MODERN PIANO

The technology of the modern piano was confirmed during the 19th century, with an emphasis on equality of sound, brilliance of execution, projection and staying power. There were two critical innovations: Pierre Erard's 'double-escapement' action, patented in 1821, an advancement "of priceless value for the [rapid] repetition of notes" (Moscheles); and the development of an integral single-piece cast-iron ring frame, to replace the weaker, jointed (metal-braced) wooden ones of former design.

Cast-iron framing was perfected in America - first in 1825 by Alpheus Babcock (who applied it to the 'square'), then in 1843 by Jonas Chickering of Boston (who rendered the same service to the grand). At the 1851 Crystal Palace Exhibition, Chickering's majestic pianos were

Transposing

PIANO

%

Proficient musicians and skilled accompanists can transpose into any key at will. To help those who could not, 19th-century piano makers, taking advantage of equal temperament, designed the transposing piano. In 1808 Broadwood introduced a movable keyboard. Four years later Erard patented a circular, rotating design. There were other methods, too. Most simplified the task but still to the disadvantage of the instrument. Modern electronic keyboards usually come with comprehensive transposition facilities.

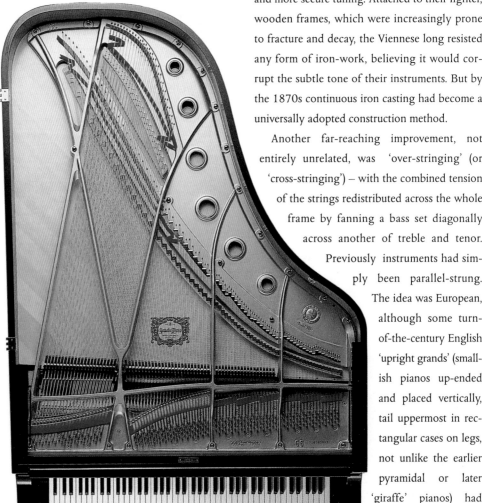

AN OVER-STRUNG YAMAHA GRAND. NOTE THE SOUNDBOARD UNDER THE STRINGS. (ALSO SEE PAGE 127)

sensationally received: "I never thought a piano could possess such qualities", declared Liszt. Heavier and less susceptible to temperature variation, continuous iron-casting allowed for greater stress, thicker strings, more power and loudness,

and more secure tuning. Attached to their lighter, wooden frames, which were increasingly prone to fracture and decay, the Viennese long resisted any form of iron-work, believing it would corrupt the subtle tone of their instruments. But by the 1870s continuous iron casting had become a universally adopted construction method.

Another far-reaching improvement, not entirely unrelated, was 'over-stringing' (or 'cross-stringing') – with the combined tension of the strings redistributed across the whole frame by fanning a bass set diagonally across another of treble and tenor. Previously instruments had simply been parallel-strung. The idea was European, although some turn-of-the-century English 'upright grands' (small-ish pianos up-ended and placed vertically, tail uppermost in rectangular cases on legs, not unlike the earlier pyramidal or later 'giraffe' pianos) had incorporated diagonal bass stringing. It was Babcock, however, who appreciated its value, as did Steinway, whose New York patent (December 1859) for an iron-framed, over-strung, double-escapement grand, with Cristofori ancestry, English facets and Viennese-style touch sensitivity, effectively confirmed the essentials of the piano as we now know it. The exhibition medals that followed triumphantly marked a new supremacy in the field.

℁ *Piano Making*

For practically three centuries pianos have been made by anyone and everyone from master builders to backstreet garret hands. The modern 'iron-age' alone has seen the rise and fall of more than 600 manufacturers in the UK, over 300 in Germany and nearly the same number in the USA – of whom only a few still survive. Around 1910 these countries were producing 75,000, 120,000 and 370,000 examples a year respectively. By 1970 that output had dropped significantly – to just 17,000, 45,000 and 220,000 – in the face of growing competition from the Soviet Union (with 200,000) and Japan (273,000). Ten years later, world production stood at around 800,000, an increase of 45,000. Today, China is making about half-a-million pianos annually; while in South Korea, Young

AN ENGLISH UPRIGHT GRAND OF c. 1810 BY LONDON MAKERS JONES, RICE AND COMPANY.

IMPORTANT
Piano Makers
℁

BECHSTEIN This Berlin company was established in 1853. Hans von Bülow inaugurated their first grand in a concert that included the first performance of Liszt's B minor Sonata (22 January 1857). Schnabel believed that the distinction of a good piano lay in its neutrality of sound. For him Bechsteins met this criterion ideally. Opened in 1901, the Bechstein Hall in London later became the Wigmore Hall.

BLUTHNER Founded, like Bechstein, in 1853, this Leipzig company is noted for its unusual, occasionally controversial, use of aliquot scaling to enrich the upper register (a 'sympathetically vibrating' fourth string added to each trichord treble, patented in 1873). Still largely made by hand, Blüthners have a silvery, romantic tone that arguably projects less well in bigger concert halls.

BOSENDORFER Originally this Austrian company, founded in 1828, only produced Viennese-action grands, but late in the 19th century they began to make English-action concert instruments. Bösendorfer's richly over-toned eight-octave Imperial Grands are among the most aristocratic instruments around, with a limpid clarity of sound and a bass response of profound gravity. Liszt, the great Viennese Romantics, royal patrons, and (in 1936) the BBC all helped establish the instrument's pedigree. Its devotees since have included Alfred Brendel and Oscar Peterson, Andras Schiff and Jools

Holland. Bösendorfers are exclusive: in 1828 only four were made, in 1990 just 600.

STEINWAY The pre-eminent concert piano: powerful, richly characterful, resonant. Founded, like Bechstein and Blüthner, in 1853 (in New York, with a Hamburg branch in 1880), Steinway perfected the modern grand and upright. "A Steinway," Paderewski claimed, "is always singing, no matter who plays it". The company's early marketing initiative was breathtaking. They courted nobility – from the Queen of Spain and the Empress of Russia to Queen Victoria and the Sultan of Turkey, along with a passing clutch of Rothschilds. They won over Liszt and Wagner. And, with Anton Rubinstein they toured their grands across the cities and heartlands of gun-law America, paying him $43,000 in gold for the privilege. Steinway thought big, made big, did big. They have not changed.

YAMAHA Japan's principal piano maker (together with Kawai, founded in 1925). Its first upright appeared in 1900, its first grand fifty years later. Yamaha enjoyed no early accolades, but now, with their reliably robust, bright, American-styled concert grands enjoying the endorsement of legendary pianists like Sviatoslav Richter, and sales flourishing, it is a different story. Constantly innovating and developing, Yamaha are the world leaders in synthesizers and digital electronic pianos.

Chang, a company boasting the largest piano factory in the world, claims a yearly turnover of around 150,000 uprights and grands.

Unlike violins, old pianos are particularly susceptible to damp, temperature variations, central heating, dust in the overspun coils of the strings, in addition to mechanical wear-and-tear and worn-out felts. They either fall apart or their

soundboards (in essence, their hearts and souls) crack open. Some good instruments from before the First World War (especially those built by Steinway) linger on, but generally the best vintage pianos today are German-built from the 1920s and 1930s – when craftsmen in touch with older, traditional skills of instrument-making were still around.

The Performers

JAZZ PIANISTS
※

"Jazz came to America 300 years ago in chains," wrote the band-leader Paul Whiteman in 1926. To George Gershwin, jazz was the whole pent-up energy of the New World, the blood and pulse of slaves and outcasts. During the late 19th century the ivories and ebonies of the piano bridged in a curious way the segregation and split values of American society.

SCOTT JOPLIN, the 'King of Ragtime', son of a slave, the Schubert of the Mississippi nightlands. His celebrated *Maple Leaf Rag* (1899) and *The Entertainer* ('a ragtime two step', 1902) have been favourably compared to the popular dances of Mozart, Chopin and Brahms.

JELLY ROLL MORTON, self-styled 'inventor of jazz' from New Orleans with a weakness for women and diamonds. He was famous for his sense of rhythm and syncopation, and for how he developed the jazz 'break'. He never forgot the Latin/Creole roots of his birth ("if you can't manage to put tinges of Spanish in your tunes, you'll never get the right seasoning for jazz"), nor the fact that his pale skin made him a 'white' black.

DUKE ELLINGTON, Cotton Club pioneer of big band 'jungle' jazz, who claimed: "I don't write jazz, I write Negro music". He was a formidable pianist in his later years.

FATS WALLER, the 'Black Horowitz', wrote around 400 pieces. He made nearly 500 recordings, and cut many piano rolls. Inventive and diverse, he not only composed and played the piano and organ, but sang, was a band-leader and appeared in films. He used his humour to communicate in the most spectacular way. His exuberant pianism, rich in right-hand dazzle and left-hand drive, was a heady mixture of ragtime, barrelhouse, authentic blues, Harlem stride and cabaret.

COUNT BASIE, master of the 'riff', started out in vaudeville and had some informal piano lessons from Fats Waller. The Count Basie Orchestra, formed in 1937, was the leading Big Band of the 'swing' era.

 DUKE ELLINGTON – "BACH AND MYSELF WRITE WITH THE ... PERFORMER IN MIND."

EARL HINES, the so-called 'father of jazz piano', served his apprenticeship in Chicago, and was closely associated with Louis Armstrong – with whom he recorded *Weatherbird* in 1928, perhaps the most celebrated duet in jazz history. Bridging blues, folk, pop, romantic/impressionist art-music and Hollywood, Hines was one of the undisputed kings of his world.

ART TATUM was the highest octane nightclub soloist of his generation, the pianistic phenomenon of the Big Band age. Informed, inventive and imaginative, he gave jazz piano a completely new dimension. His cast-iron technique, and his powers of transcendental improvisation, caused Fats to liken him to God.

THELONIOUS MONK was a pioneering 'bop' pianist in 1940s New York. Master of crushed notes, chord clusters and percussive dissonances, poet of anguish and silence, his lack of early piano training made for a characteristically flat-fingered technique. Since his death, he has acquired a considerable cult following.

DAVE BRUBECK studied with Milhaud, and has been a leading 'white' force in the experimental jazz scene since his West Coast days. "Jazz," he says, "is about the only form of art existing today in which there is freedom of the individual without loss of group contact".

OSCAR PETERSON, a Canadian, made his Carnegie Hall debut in 1949. As a jazz pianist of flawlessly natural technique, and as an informed jazz 'teacher', historian, and media presenter, his reputation worldwide is formidable.

CLASSICAL PIANISTS
※

WOLFGANG AMADEUS MOZART (Austrian) — "It is much easier to play a thing quickly than slowly: in certain passages you can leave out a few notes without anyone noticing it. But is that beautiful? ... [you ought to be able to play a] piece in the time [tempo] in which it ought to be played, and [play] all the notes, appoggiaturas and so forth, exactly as they are written and with the appropiate expression and taste, so that you might suppose that the performer had composed it himself."

LUDWIG VAN BEETHOVEN (German) "Nobody equalled him in the rapidity of his scales, double trills, skips, etc – even Hummel. His bearing while playing was masterfully quiet, noble and beautiful, without the slightest grimace (only bent forward low, as his deafness grew upon him); his fingers were very powerful, not long, and broadened at the tips ... In teaching he laid great stress on a correct position of the fingers (after the school of Emanuel Bach, which he used in teaching me); he could scarcely span a tenth. He made frequent use of the pedals ... [more] than is indicated in his works" – Czerny

FRANZ LISZT (Hungarian) – "The virtuoso is not a mason who, chisel in hand, faithfully and conscientiously whittles stone after the design of an architect ... [Rather] he is called upon to make emotion speak, and weep, and sing, and sigh ... He creates as the composer himself created, for he himself must live the passions he will call to light in all their brilliance."

LOUIS MOREAU GOTTSCHALK ('The First American') "There is an exquisite grace in his manner of phrasing sweet melodies and scattering the light passages from the top of the keyboard" – Berlioz

ANTON RUBINSTEIN (Russian) "For every possible mistake he may have made, he gave, in return, ideas and musical tone pictures that would have made up for a million mistakes" – Rachmaninov

IGNACY JAN PADEREWSKI (Polish) "[The] most legendary pianist after Liszt ... The man had style and a big heart; and he had immense dignity and glamour; and he could produce golden sounds; and he was an unparalleled showman. And so while his competitors were counting his wrong notes, he was counting his dollars" – Harold C. Schonberg

LEOPOLD GODOWSKY (Polish-American) "The superman of piano playing. Nothing like him, as far as I know, is to be found in the history of piano playing since Chopin ... a pianist for pianists" – James Huneker

SERGEI RACHMANINOV (Russian) "By the time [Rachmaninov] has gone through a long work we know all, or nearly all, that it is possible for a piano musically to express ... he concentrates his essences in the chalice of style ... the aristocrat of pianists" – Neville Cardus

ARTUR SCHNABEL (Austrian-American) – "To buy a ticket [to a concert] is no insurance of happiness. The performer only promises to try his best, but he cannot promise to please the listener."

ARTHUR RUBINSTEIN (Polish-American) – "I was chastened [by critics] for my 'severe' interpretations of Chopin. Stubbornly I continued programming Chopin... stubbornly the critics continued to criticise ... Only very much later was the validity of my interpretation granted. Only then was I permitted to have my Chopin and to give him to audiences."

CLAUDIO ARRAU (Chilean) – "I don't believe in an afterlife, so whatever is, is right here and now ... That is why I have stressed the building of one's own structure and one's own vision based on truth, on fidelity to the composer's text. That is my legacy."

VLADIMIR HOROWITZ ('The Last Romantic', Ukrainian-American) – "A pianist is a citizen of the world. And that is the most important thing to be."

CLIFFORD CURZON (British) – "I wonder if many people ... realise the crucial importance of fingering? You've only got ten fingers, and you've got nearly one hundred keys. And it's the arrangement of those ten fingers, and the way each follows the other, that not only allows you to play the right notes, but lets you shape the music, and make it speak."

SVIATOSLAV RICHTER (Russian) "An inspired poet of music and in that is his mesmerising power ... I caught myself thinking that I was witnessing an exceptional phenomenon of the 20th century" – Rosina Lhevinne

DINU LIPATTI (Rumanian) "An artist of divine spirituality" – Poulenc

ALFRED BRENDEL (Austrian) – "Records are a kind of offspring of which one can't, unfortunately, say that one has to nurse them until they grow up and then forget them as soon as possible and let them lead their own lives. They lead their own lives at once, and are scarcely ever grown up! There's always something infantile about a record, at least as far as the artist is concerned. Records are interesting to learn from – but not always to enjoy."

GLENN GOULD (Canadian) – "Music is something that ought to be listened to in private. I do not believe that it should be treated as group therapy or any other kind of communal experience. I think that music ought to lead the listener – and, indeed, the performer – to a state of contemplation, and I don't think it's really possible to attain that condition with 2,999 other souls sitting all around ... I don't much care for piano music."

VLADIMIR ASHKENAZY (Russian-Icelandic) – "The concert pianist must devote all his life and all his time to music. Style, technique, meaning, and interpretation are not accidental qualities that just seem to fall into place at a given time; they are the result of practice and concentration [and] a lot of hard work."

MAURIZIO POLLINI (Italian) "Complete supremacy" – Artur Rubinstein

SVIATOSLAV RICHTER – FORMIDABLY TALENTED RUSSIAN VIRTUOSO OF WIDE REPERTORY.

THE CONCERT GRAND

THEN AND NOW

THE MODERN CONCERT piano is a durable, heavy-weight, high-tensioned, high-performance, scientifically optimized, individually crafted, voiced and regulated machine of nearly 12,000 parts, more than capable of holding its own against an orchestra. Today's grand is a radically different proposition from its 18th-century pro-totype. Its compass is expanded: up to eight octaves (Bösendorfer imperial) compared with Cristofori's four-and-a-half. Its action is heavier and more muscular. Beethoven's and Weber's brilliant octave work and *glissandi*, not to men-tion Liszt's or Brahms's, were envisaged for something much lighter and shallower. Steel and copper strings (thicker, tougher) have replaced brass and wire thread (thiner, brittler).

According to time and place, pitch has changed. Today's concert A (above middle C) is standardized at 440 Hz (cps), as agreed in 1939, and again in 1955. Stein's tuning fork, which Mozart knew, gave a reading of only 421.6 (1780), about the same as Handel's. In London, Broadwood favoured changing pitch according to purpose – from 434 (pianos accompanying voice) to 452.5 (pianos with instruments) or even higher (455.5). Chopin's recital A was fixed at 449. Elsewhere in Europe measurements dif-fered, sometimes radically so. In France in 1859, A was established at 435 (diapason normal); in Dresden it stood at 441; in Liszt's Weimar at 444.7; in Leipzig at 448.7; in Prague at 449.7; in St Petersburg at 451.5; in Berlin at 451.7; in Vienna at 456. Across the Atlantic it was raised further: in 1879 Steinway tuned their A to 457

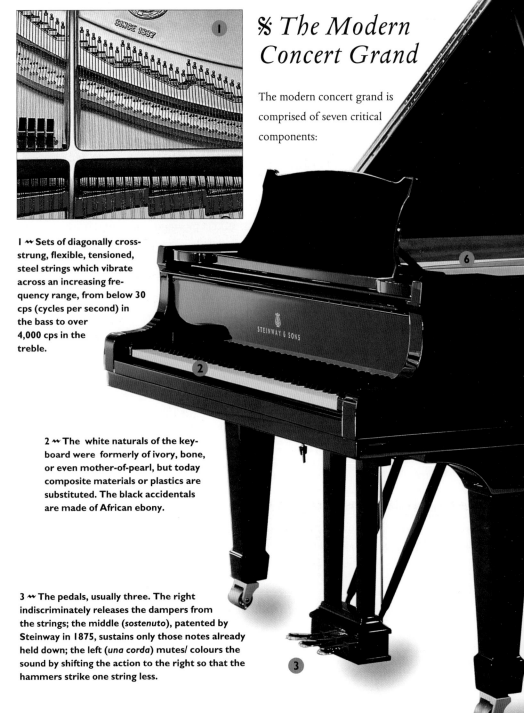

1 ❧ Sets of diagonally cross-strung, flexible, tensioned, steel strings which vibrate across an increasing fre-quency range, from below 30 cps (cycles per second) in the bass to over 4,000 cps in the treble.

2 ❧ The white naturals of the key-board were formerly of ivory, bone, or even mother-of-pearl, but today composite materials or plastics are substituted. The black accidentals are made of African ebony.

3 ❧ The pedals, usually three. The right indiscriminately releases the dampers from the strings; the middle (*sostenuto*), patented by Steinway in 1875, sustains only those notes already held down; the left (*una corda*) mutes/ colours the sound by shifting the action to the right so that the hammers strike one string less.

❧ *The Modern Concert Grand*

The modern concert grand is comprised of seven critical components:

4 ~ A wooden case (ebonized, veneered, lacquered, poly-ure-thaned), and bracings that can have the effect of a secondary soundboard. The lid acts as a directional sound reflector.

Hz – gaining brightness in the process but at the expense of greater stress on the frame. Old instruments cannot withstand such high tensions: period practice performances, therefore, usually revert to lower pitch (pre-1800) tunings, with A averaging around 430 for Classical works and 415 for Baroque repertory.

Modern pedalling possibilities are less varied. A true una corda, for example – striking just one string with a proportionately dramatic change in volume and timbre – can only be managed on old 'English' action instruments. Modifying the sound even further, the *sourdine* or mute-stop (moderator) of 'Viennese' actions – a piece of felt between the strings and hammers, originally activated by hand-stops – is likewise no longer available. Nor, too, is the (dry, soft) lute-stop. Other early colouristic effects – 'Turkish music' ('Janissary'), bassoon and harpsichord stops, for instance – have similarly long since disappeared. Their transmogrifying principle of making the piano what it was not – of contriving or distorting other timbres by making drumsticks, for instance, strike the underbelly of the soundboard, or using foreign materials placed on or between the strings – has not been forgotten, though. 'Playing' the strings rather than the keyboard (Cowell's *The Banshee*, 1925), the 'prepared' piano sounds of Tudor, Crumb or Wolff, the nuts and bolts, screw and rubber prescription of Cage's *Sonatas and Interludes* (1946–8), and the piano 'preparations' of our own day are, in a sense, no different. All are a common denial of what we are aurally conditioned to expect.

The tonal palette of today's piano, as occasionally magnificent as it can frequently be impersonal, is not that of Mozart's or Beethoven's time, nor even of Liszt's wandering years of transcendental execution as Europe's greatest *klaviertiger*. Its focussed, brighter, metallic timbre, its facility to scale massive dynamic ranges and project sound, is a response to modern halls and modern excesses. Its ability to fake a 'singing' *legato* line may be better, but gone is the luminous, crystalline, stringy resonance of its thin-wired, buckskin-hammered ancestors. In the concertos of Mozart, where in the *tuttis* the instrument is expected to have an interactive continuo role, it almost always blends uneasily with the orchestra, no matter how sympathetic the artist. In such situations, only the thinnest, shallowest sounding instruments ever convince - those closest to the intimacy and transparency of the Steins and Streichers of the late 18th century 𝄢.

5 ~ An internal cast-iron frame, bearing the aggregate tension of the strings (16–30 tons), which run from hitch pins (far end) to wrest (tuning) pins (near end).

6 ~ A soundboard, a thin, flexible wooden diaphragm, typically of seasoned Norwegian spruce. This transmits the vibrations of the strings and acts as a powerful resonator. (Also see illustration on page 122)

7 ~ A removable action of infinitely fine adjustment, consisting normally of an 88-note keyboard, felted hammers, felted gravity over-dampers, and a series of intricate operating mechanisms. The same keys equally activate hammers (which induce sound) and dampers (which silence it). To prevent hammers from rebounding back onto strings already struck, an 'escapement' mechanism is used.

ORGAN

"There let the pealing Organ blow, / To the full voic'd Quire below, / In Service high, with Anthem cleer, / As may with sweetness, through mine ear, / Dissolve me into extasies, / And bring all Heav'n before mine eyes." – Milton, *Il Penseroso* (1632)

From the pre-Christian hydraulis (see page 230) and hand-held pagan syrinx or panpipes (originally dried-out plant stalks of varying diameter and length) (see page 190), to the gigantic seven-manual instruments of the New World with the massed force of 25 military bands, the organ has evolved to become the most complex, sonically awesome and technically demanding of all musical instruments. "There's nothing to it," Bach may have said, "you only have to hit the right notes at the right time and the instrument plays itself". Beethoven believed otherwise: "an organist who is master of his intrument [should be placed] at the very head of all virtuosi".

Early History

The organ has a long and ancient history, extending back to the 3rd century BC. Later, it was popular with the Romans: a surviving example from 228 AD has four ranks of thirteen bronze flue pipes (one open, three stopped). It was then forgotten until Byzantium revived interest in it during the 9th and 10th centuries, by which time pneumatic action had virtually replaced water. (Winchester Cathedral supposedly had one with 400 pipes and 26 bellows, calling for two organists at two keyboards of 20 notes each.) The Byzantines regarded the organ as a gilded and silvered instrument of royal gift – Charlemagne was a recipient.

By the 1400s the large organ had become an important feature in churches, with the Rhinelanders calling for two or three manual instruments (among the most mechanically

A POSITIVE ORGAN IS THE CENTREPIECE OF THIS ITALIAN BOOK PAINTING (C. 1350), BY BOETHIUS.

TYPES OF
Organ
%

BARREL ORGAN (Hand organ) An English barrel-and-pin portable instrument with flue pipes and bellows, cranked by a handle and first advertised in London as early as 1772. Some were capable only of mechanical performance, but others included separate keyboards. Barrel organs usually had five stops and up to five interchangeable barrels pegged with tunes of the day, religious and secular. Barrel organs were to be found in many Anglican churches up to the 1950s. They were popular, too, in their street form – though not everyone appreciated them: "In this unmusical country," wrote the Princess Lieven to Metternich in July 1820, "there are dreadful barrel organs which go up and down the streets - there is one playing under my window right now, which is so out of tune that it almost makes me weep ..."

ORGUE DE BARBARIE Neither an organ of the Barbary coast nor a barbaric instrument but a corruption of the name of its late 18th-century Italian adaptor, possibly Barbieri. This instrument consists of a portable case with pipes of metal or wood, or both. A handle turns a barrel and feeds the bellows.

PORTATIVE ORGAN (*Organetto*) A small portable melody instrument of the late Middle Ages. Resting on the left knee, it was played by the right hand, with the left operating the bellows. "So beautiful that even the birds listened to it", it was frequently depicted in contemporary paintings as an instrument of angels.

POSITIVE ORGAN The organ is traditionally associated with size and mighty sound, but there have been plenty of smaller domestic examples. The positive was one such, a small semi-portable medieval chamber organ of reduced compass. It came with flue pipes (usually in two ranks of 4 foot and 2 foot), a single manual and no pedalboard. A smaller table-top model needed an assistant to work the bellows.

REGAL Another portable organ, this one popular in Germany in the 15th-17th centuries. The origin of the name is unclear; perhaps a corruption of 'reed', for the regal was a reed-pipe instrument (in contrast to the positive). Monteverdi used a regal in his opera *L'Orfeo* (1607). The Bible Regal was a very much smaller folding version.

advanced in Europe). The needs of the Italians and French were more modest: one manual, fewer than a dozen stops. (In Italy double manuals, reed stops and swell boxes were not to gain currency until the 18th century.) The English followed suit, though they showed more interest in evolving new flute and reed stops. By the 15th century it was customary for the wind-chests, pipes and operating mechanics of the organ to be enclosed in a fretworked, screened wooden case, with the keyboard(s) and stops centred in front. This case, which possessed important cavity resonances, pro-

tected the fragile mechanism of the instrument, blended the sound and projected it to the listener.

During the 16th and 17th centuries European instrument builders, composers and players increasingly became streamed into national organ schools, each with their own identity and preferences. The French were drawn to bold contrasts and imposing choruses (*plein jeu, grand jeu*), to well-differentiated colours and echoes, to flute mutations (*tièrce*), to reeds with brilliant tops and

robust bottoms. A typical Louis XIV organ of around 1650 was a characterful beast. Equally so were those silvered visions of the 18th century, built by men like Andreas Silbermann (brother of Gottfried) and Clicquot. In post-Reformation England (less single-minded), the influence of the French held sway until the 18th century. The adoption of the pedal-board and the replacement of the Choir by the Swell as principal second manual was not until the 1720s. 𝄢

THE CLASSICAL ORGAN

The Swiss emigré John Snetzler brought notably fine voicing to the Anglican baroque/classical organ, as well as a colourful (and prophetic) resource of European stops, the manual coupler and the tremulant (from *tremolante*, meaning 'with tremolo'). During the 1760s some of his most impressive commissions were undertaken for Buck House, Peterhouse Cambridge and Beverley Minster – a lasting legacy from George III's reign. Throughout the 18th century, continental-style English organs were regularly shipped to the Americas, to the flourishing 'English' schools in New York and Boston.

The Spanish 18th-century organ, originally modelled on the Flemish type, was distinctive for its horizontally projecting reed pipes. It was used for ceremonial occasions. The German chapel organ of Bach's time represented the golden age of the instrument. This technically sophisticated, highly ornate example of the builder's craft was designed to stimulate many kinds of possible registrations and effects, rather like its 17th-century Dutch secular predecessor. Placing a premium on power, albeit sometimes at the expense of finesse, and with makers of the standing of Silbermann and Casparini, the Germans decided the organ of the 18th-century organ.

Compass

Paralleling the clavichord, harpsichord and fortepiano, the compass of the early 18th cen-

THE THREE-MANUAL, 45-STOP
SILBERMANN ORGAN OF 1710–14,
FREIBURG CATHEDRAL (SAXONY).

tury organ was less than it is today. Bach's German instruments, with a pedal-board short of the four highest notes, normally had only a four-octave manual compass (lacking the modern top octave). Handel's English examples, mostly without pedal-board, had a manual compass generally both lower and higher than Bach's.

Pitch, too, was different. Compared with modern concert A = 440 Hz (cps) – or the exceptionally high 506 of the organ of Halberstadt Cathedral, 1495 – Mattheson's in Hamburg (1762) measured 408, with the organ of Trinity College Cambridge lower still at 395 (1759).

Germany, England and France led the organ into the Romantic age, post-Waterloo (1815). Many old instruments were modified and added to as a result of gathering interest in Bach's organ works. Octave couplers, double pedal-boards and solo manuals became standard with larger models. By 1833 mechanical-pneumatic action ('Barker lever') was in use on English examples in England (as well as higher wind pressure and better swell boxes). It was left not to the Germans (they now of decadent effect, coarse sound and 'orchestral' exaggeration – witness their mania for monster music mechanalia) but a Frenchman, Cavaillé-Coll of Paris, to perfect the electric-powered, fully pneumatic tracker action organ of the later 19th century. Through innovative design and mechanical re-thinking, he unleashed unheard of volume and expressivity. He gave the instrument its modern flexibility. He also gave it access to many non-classical French traditions (from Spain and Germany, as well as England), forging on the way an entirely new hybrid. Cavaillé-Coll was the Steinway of the Romantic

organ, and composers from Franck and Widor to Poulenc and Messiaen gloried in the cocktail. Today the vogue is either for building costly new instruments in big concert-halls or for period reconstructions and restorations, with performer-consultants continuing to play their time-honoured role of advising and improving.

% The Cinema or Theatre Organ

This product of the early 1900s was the favourite musical accompaniment/intermission instrument of the picture house and seaside pier. Largely replacing the orchestral group, it produced a warm, excessively syrupy sound – a combination of vox humana and tremulant richly smeared. The 'Mighty Wurlitzer', introduced in 1910, was only one of many examples. Wurlitzer began in the same year as Steinway, 1853, and continue to be in the forefront of electronic organ production for domestic use. Like the German Hupfeld company, they made innumerable mechanical instruments, a number specifically for theatre, cinema or ice rink application (including photoplayers). Elaborately housed and keenly marketed, these were impressive performers with ear-catching mechanics. Contemporary with their theatre organs, the Model 32A Concert Pian-Orchestra, for instance (using pneumatic rolls), boasted an instrumentation of piano, 56 violins, 30 cellos, 30 violas, 26 saxophones, 30 flutes, 30 piccolos, 30 clarinets, 30 oboes, 26 French horns, 26 bass violins, chimes, bass and snare drums, triangle, tambourine, castanets, tremolo, kettledrum and cymbals. The cinema organ, with its whiff of smoky nostalgia and fancy tricks, remains popular with audiences. ♭

THE VETERAN ORGANIST GERALD SHAW PLAYING A FIVE-MANUAL CINEMA ORGAN.

SOUNDING PRINCIPLES

OF THE ORGAN

The organ is activated by pressurized air from a wind-chest, released by valves into sets (stops, registers) of different-sized and tuned pipes. One or more coupled five-octave 61-note normal pitch keyboards (manuals, C to c ''''), together with a 32-note foot pedal board, control the individual opening or shutting of these valves (known as pallets). Different stops can be drawn to sound several ranks of pipes together – thereby selecting, mixing, reducing or strengthening different tone-colours (registration). By depressing the manual or foot keys it is possible to open the valves in several ways.

♯ Types of Action

- Tracker (mechnical) action – wind gathered in the pallets is released to each stop (pipe row) by means of a perforated wooden slider. This directs or diverts (retires) the wind to/from the row.
- Tubular-pneumatic action – pressurized air in a touch-box above the keys flows along tubing to a pneumatic motor, controlling the pipe-chest valves.
- Electro-pneumatic action – considered the best means of controlling very large instruments. In this type the pallet is opened by a magnet.

♫ THE UPPER PART OF THE CONSOLE OF THE ORGAN IN WESTMINSTER ABBEY, LONDON, SHOWING MANUALS (FOUR) AND STOPS.

According to Charles B. Fisk, the American organ-builder, modern tracker action, characterized by its mechanical connections between keys and valves and low wind pressures, "retains a geometry and a tonal ideal already firmly established in the 17th century ... A well-built tracker action affords the player a sense of immediacy (through 'feedback') that is totally unattainable with electro-pneumatic action".

♯ The Pipes: Pitch and Voicing

The separately mounted pipe divisions are normally identified as Great Organ, Choir Organ, Solo Organ, and Pedal Organ, together with a manual Swell Organ (related to the Venetian blind principle of the harpsichord) allowing the volume to be graduated. Occasionally, these specifications can be varied. The 6,655-pipe organ of Norwich Cathedral (1899, rebuilt 1942, originally five manual), for example, includes primary and secondary Greats, an unenclosed Positive and enclosed Swell Choir Organ, Great Reeds and an Echo Organ.

The bodies, or resonators, of pipes come in various forms. Flue pipes are usually of tin, or a tin/lead alloy, or wood, with the air striking the edge of the upper lip. Reed pipes have beating reed tongues (brass) setting an air-column into vibration. In a flue pipe, pitch is determined principally by length (the longer the pipe, the lower the pitch), and tone quality is affected by the size of the flue (or wind passage), foot-hole bore, and positioning of the lip. In a reed pipe, pitch is determined by the length of the air column, and by the length, mass and flexibility of the reed.

Regulating and adjusting the timbre, attack and loudness of pipes is called 'voicing'. In flue pipes this affects the amount of air coming from

the wind passage, in reed pipes the curvature and mass of the reed tongue. Family groups of tone colour, controlled by keyboard console 'stop-knobs', are determined by scaling. This is the relationship between the diameter and length of the pipes. Wide-bore pipes are less overtoned and penetrating than narrow ones, which have a brighter tonal quality (principal tone or diapason). 'Principals' are open flue pipes. 'Flutes', which are wider scaled, are usually stopped at their upper end (which acoustically doubles the length of the body, lowering pitch by an octave). Reed pipes come in three kinds: chorus (trumpet, brass); semi-chorus (non-imitative baroque); and solo/orchestral (imitative of orchestral single/ double reed woodwind). Evocatively descriptive, stop names, largely standardized by the end of the 16th century, refer either to family identities and pipe construction, or the orchestral instruments they imitate.

✄ *Pitch*

The scalic pitch of a rank, or register, of pipes is customarily measured in feet, taken from the speaking length of the fundamental or lowest pitch (a terminology also adopted by harpsichord makers). A unison open flue stop with a speaking length of 8 feet, for instance - sounding the C fundamental two octaves below middle C (the lowest note of the manuals at normal pitch) - is known as an 8-foot stop, or Foundation Stop (Open diapason); 4-foot or 2-foot stops (Octave, Super-Octave Stops) sound the same pitch respectively an octave or two octaves higher. A 16-foot stop (Double Stop) will sound an octave lower. Most modern big organs, such as that of the London Royal Festival Hall's 1951 Harrison & Harrison, extend to 32 feet. However, the organ in Hull City Hall (1950 Compton recon-

𝄞 **BRIGHTLY PAINTED FLUE PIPES OF A FAIRGROUND ORGAN. THE PIPES ARE GRADUATED AS TO SIZE (AND HENCE PITCH).**

struction) goes one better, to a rare 64-foot Gravissima Stop, giving a bottom infra-frequency outside human hearing (five octaves below middle C): the vibratory sensation of such a stop is physical rather than auditory. Mutation Stops are those which sound at a pitch or harmonic other than the fundamental or its octaves. Compound or Mixture Stops are those comprised of two or more ranks of pipes. The organ of Liverpool Cathedral has a ten-rank Mixture ('Grand Chorus'), giving ten pipes for each pitch, or 610 in all for a complete five-octave stop. An Acoustic (Resultant) Bass pedal Stop is one whereby the physiological phenomenon of a differential tone an octave lower than its possible fundamental (the Tartini Tones of the 18th century) is operated. 𝄢

THE ORGAN IN PERFORMANCE

THE ORGAN has been associated with the Church since medieval times, much of its music having been written with either liturgical function, liturgical association or liturgical performance in mind. This is still the case – despite evidence that the orchestral, concerto and recital use of the instrument in the 19th and 20th centuries helped broaden and secularize its image. The fact remains, however, that an organ recital is more likely to take place in a cathedral or church than a concert hall, and that its programme will consist of pieces largely intended for such a spiritual ambience.

✵ Symphonies and Concertos

In sacred music of the Baroque and Classical periods, the organ usually played a continuo role within the ensemble, doubling the bass line and supporting or filling-in the harmonies. It is in such capacity that Bach wrote for it in his *B Minor Mass*, Handel in *Messiah*, Mozart and Haydn in their Latin masses, and Beethoven in the *Missa Solemnis*. Even Brahms, much later (1854–68), thought of it in this way in his Lutheran *German Requiem*. Some of Haydn's masses (for instance, the *Grosse Orgelmesse*, by 1774; the *Nelson*, 1798) give it an *obbligato* function, but its first really spectacular appearance – theatrically confronting orchestra and choir – does not seem to have been until Berlioz's *Te deum* (1849).

Between the period of the 1848 Revolutions and the First World War, eight key late-Romantic symphonies or symphonic-type works by five composers use the organ – either to evoke mood

and association, to command attention, to introduce a sense of (physically-felt) gravitational vibration, or to lend climactic finality to cadential perorations: Liszt's *Faust* Symphony (1854–7); Saint-Saëns' Third ('Organ') Symphony, 1886 – not to be confused with the pioneering unaccompanied organ-symphony tradition of Widor, qv);

THE FOUR-MANUAL, 49-STOP ORGAN IN THE ABBEY OF WEINGARTHEN, BUILT BY GABLER (1737–50).

Mahler's Second ('Resurrection', 1888–94); Richard Strauss's *Also sprach Zarathustra* (1895–6); Scriabin's *Poem of Ecstasy* (1905–8); Mahler's Eighth

Symphony (1906–7); Scriabin's *Prometheus, The Poem of Fire* (1908–10); and Strauss's 'Alpine' Symphony (1911–15).

The earliest organ concertos, a secular product of largely Protestant countries, were by J. S. Bach (unaccompanied, c. 1713–14, arranged from the music of other composers, including Vivaldi) and Handel (eighteen in all, published in London in three sets between 1738 and 1761). Scored for organ (without pedal-boards), strings and reed woodwind, and comprised of a tuneful if complex web of self-borrowings and quotations (notably from Telemann), these were intended originally to be played as interludes between the acts of Handel's odes and oratorios. Other contributions were made by Johann Gottfried Walther, Bach's cousin (1741; plus a number of transcriptions); Michel Corrette (Six Concertos, Op. 26, 1756), who was responsible for bringing the virtuosic Handelian organ style to France; Samuel Wesley (several, the first in 1776, also one on Arne's *Rule Britannia*, and another (in 1800) for solo organ and violin); and Soler, a pupil of Scarlatti (Six Double Concertos for Two Organs). Given the non-portable nature of an installed organ (orchestras had to come to it, and venues were fewer, less varied and, if consecrated, more liturgically restrictive than today), the 19th century witnessed a steep decline of interest in the medium. But the aloof Rheinberger did contribute a couple of concertos, the first in 1884.

The 20th-century concerto remains a selective genre, in spite of the modern phenomenon of the ecclesiastically independent virtuoso concert organist: Hindemith (*Kammermusik No. 7*, 1927; Organ Concerto, 1962); Dupré (First Symphony, 1928; Concerto, 1934); Poulenc (Concerto for Organ, Timpani and Strings, 1938); Petr Eben (1954; 1982); Malcolm Williamson (1961); Anton Heiller (1964; Concerto for Organ, Piano and Chamber Orchestra, 1972); Charles Chaynes (1966); Jacques Charpentier (Concerto for Positive Organ, 1970; Symphony No. 6, 1979); Charles Camilleri (1981). 𝄡

THE
Organ Symphony

Just as the symphony for solo piano was a French invention (Alkan's), so too was the symphony for solo organ. Multi-movemented, exploiting the whole awesome range, power and registration of the French Romantic organ as built and expanded by Cavaillé-Coll, the organ-symphony was the creation of Widor, an organist in the grand manner who ruled the organ-loft of St. Sulpice in Paris from 1870 to 1934. He wrote ten in all (1876–1900), with the Toccata finale of the Fifth enjoying special popularity (not least at weddings). Central to the repertory and unmistakeably Gallic in idiom, Widor's organ-symphonies were to exert a major influence on organ technique. However, it has been said that they were sometimes guilty of favouring the smaller-scale set piece at the expense of larger-scale symphonic thought. Lacking a sonata design, the seven movements of the First, for instance – a neo-Classical Prelude, a Mendelssohnian Allegretto, an Intermezzo, a Romantic Adagio chorale, a triumphal Marche pontificale, a Meditation, and a closing classical Fugue – add up to not so much a symphony as a diversionary suite.

The 19th-century French organ school streamed, on the one hand, from Benoist (who taught Franck and Saint-Saëns) and, on the other, from Lemmens (who taught Widor and Guilmant). It was Widor's Paris Conservatoire pupils – principally Vierne, Dupré and André Fleury, cream of the French Establishment - who carried on his organ-symphony tradition. Vierne succeeded Widor as organist at the Conservatoire, and later became organist of Notre Dame (where he died). His six symphonies (1899–1930) generally adopt a five-movement layout. Like Widor, Dupré (who taught Messiaen) was both organist at St. Sulpice (1934–71) and a professor at the Conservatoire. 'The World awaiting the Saviour', 'Nativity', 'Crucifixion' and 'Resurrection' make up the four scenes of his Symphonie-Passion (1924). The solo Second Symphony (1929) reverts to a Prelude/Intermezzo/Toccata-type pattern. Fleury, organist at Dijon Cathedral from 1949 to 1971, effectively brought the genre to a close with two four-movement organ-symphonies completed after the Second World War (1947; 1949).

𝄞 WIDOR PLAYING THE ORGAN AT ST. SULPICE, WHERE HE WAS ORGANIST FROM 1869 TO 1933.

500 Years

OF GREAT ORGAN COMPOSERS

ANTONIO DE CABEZON (Spanish) was born blind. Organist to the court of Spain, his reputation as master composer and charismatic performer was not just a Spanish phenomenon: through his travels abroad, he impressed and influenced as many foreign musicians as he learnt from. His *tientos* Iberianized the Italian *ricercar* style.

GIROLAMO CAVAZZONI (Italian), associated with Venice and Mantua, represented the high point of the 16th-century Italian organ tradition. He left organ masses, hymns and ricercari, and, together with his father, is credited with having written the earliest *canzoni* (based on French *chansons*).

CLAUDIO MERULO (Italian) was the illustrious organist of the cathedrals of Brescia and Parma, as well as St. Mark's, Venice. He formalized the keyboard toccata (pioneered by Andrea Gabrieli) into a glittering succession of alternating display and fugal sections.

JEHAN TITELOUZE (French), organist at Rouen Cathedral from 1588 to 1633, was the first important French composer for the instrument. His late-Renaissance-styled polyphonic *versets* (lit. 'verses') based on plainchant (published in notation, not tablature, 1623, 1626) were intended to alternate with the choir during services.

JAN PIETERSZOON SWEELINCK (Dutch), organist of the Oude Kerk, Amsterdam for more than forty years and one of the most famous teachers of his time. He laid the foundations for Baroque organ style, absorbing elements from the English, French and Italians. His keyboard output included fugal fantasias, variations and toccatas. His influence on the North German 'Gothic' school was considerable.

St. Thomas's, Leipzig, a church synonymous with the name of its most famous cantor, J. S. Bach.

GIROLAMO FRESCOBALDI (Italian) dazzled the courts of Italy, from Ferrara (where he came personally under the influence of Gesualdo, Prince of Venosa) to Mantua and Florence. When he gave his first concert as organist of St Peter's, Rome, it is said that 30,000 people came to hear him. Bach learnt well from his scholarship and art.

SAMUEL SCHEIDT (German), a pupil of Sweelinck, closely linked with the Halle court. He established an Italianate line of German organ writing (chorale variations, fugues, fantasias, magnificats) that led to Bach.

JOHANN JACOB FROBERGER (German), organist to the Viennese court, summed-up the South German style of the Baroque. His discerningly cosmopolitan make-up provocatively acknowledged Italian and French influences (he had been a pupil of Frescobaldi, and was a friend of the French clavecinist Chambonnières).

DIETRICH BUXTEHUDE (Danish/German) Among the guiding stars of the North German school, including the Praetorius family, Buxtehude was the most famous. Organist of the Marienkirche in Lübeck, most of his instrumental music was for organ and included chorale settings and toccatas. Bach as a young man journeyed 200 miles on foot, from Arnstadt to Lübeck, to hear him play.

JUAN BAUTISTA JOSE CABANILLES (Spanish), organist at Valencia Cathedral. His grandly inventive music represented the Baroque culmination of the Iberian tradition founded by Cabezon. "The world will go to ruins before another Cabanilles will arise", lamented one of his pupils.

ANDRE RAISON (French) was one of several major French Baroque organists – together with Clérambault (his pupil, later organist at St Sulpice), Couperin 'le Grand' (organist of St Gervais and organiste du Roi), Daquin (of *Le coucou* fame, organist of Notre Dame), Gigault, Lebègue (*organiste du Roi*), and Marchand (organist of the Cordeliers). Raison's two published collections of organ music, including five masses, are interesting for their notes on performance and for their carefully indicated registrations.

JOHANN PACHELBEL (German) – of *Canon* popularity – epitomized the more easy-going, intimate, uncomplicated surroundings and expectations of the Central German (Thuringian/North Bavarian) school. For a time assistant organist at St Stephen's Cathedral in Vienna, he taught Bach's elder brother. His copious organ music included all the expected genres of the period (chorales, toccatas, preludes, *chaconnes*, *ricercari* and fantasias) but also nearly 100 Magnificat fugues.

JOHANN SEBASTIAN BACH (German) - gatherer of the past, inspirer of the future, a colossus astride history and civilization - was Kantor of St Thomas's, Leipzig. "Lamented Bach!" wrote Telemann, "Your touch upon the organ's keys/Long since has earned you company among the great,/And what your quill upon the music-sheet has writ/Has filled hearts with delight, though some did envy seize". His organ works endure supreme and glorious, as rich in Baroque device as Romantic intensity – though one of them, the popular Toccata and Fugue in D minor, has recently been shown to be not by him.

GEORG FRIDERIC HANDEL (German) was an organist from his youth, enjoying an early appointment at the Calvinist Cathedral in Halle, but apart from his eighteen organ concertos he wrote no other music for the instrument. "I would uncover my head, and kneel down at his tomb," declared Beethoven.

SAMUEL WESLEY (English), a devout admirer of Bach and Handel, was regarded as the greatest English organist of his day, a position inherited by his natural son, Samuel Sebastian Wesley, Anglican organist variously of Hereford, Winchester and Gloucester Cathedrals. Apart from concertos, the bulk of Samuel's organ music took the form of voluntaries for use in church services.

FELIX MENDELSSOHN (German) "There is one god (Bach) and Mendelssohn is his prophet" (Berlioz). Mendelssohn was a key player in the 19th-century Bach Revival movement, and also helped rekindle interest in the organ, stemming its post-Bach decline.

FRANZ LISZT (Hungarian) – Grand Ducal Director of Music Extraordinary to the Weimar court from 1848, champion of

Wagner, Berlioz and Verdi, and defender of the 'New German school' – may have been largely responsible for single-handedly creating modern pianism, but he was also an ambitiously inventive composer for the organ (1850–85), at one stage even planning to write a symphonic poem for the instrument (based on a poem by Herder). His oratorios and settings for the Catholic Church feature it to grand effect.

CESAR FRANCK (Belgian/French), organist of Ste Clothilde and professor of organ at the Paris Conservatoire, was the teacher of d'Indy (founder of the 'New German'-style Schola Cantorum in 1894), Duparc, Chausson, Guilmant and Dukas. He established the Romantic organ school in France (1858–90) at a time when the French organ tradition was particularly impoverished.

ANTON BRUCKNER (Austrian), for a time organist of Linz Cathedral, was celebrated as one of the great organ virtuosos of his day: in 1871, together with Saint-Saëns and others, he helped to inaugurate the large Willis organ of the new Royal Albert Hall in London. But although he wrote for it extensively in his masses, *Te deum* and sacred settings, he left nothing of significance otherwise.

JOHANNES BRAHMS (German), the master classicist of the Romantic age, movingly resurrected the spirit and style of Bach in a set of late Chorale Preludes for organ, published only after his death.

CAMILLE SAINT-SAENS (French), organist of the Madeleine and the teacher of Fauré, was precociously gifted and generously admired – as composer, virtuoso pianist, educator, champion of the Baroque, inquiring ethnomusicologist, poet, critic, Establishment sage. Liszt thought him the greatest organist in the world. Others found him shallow. Initially progressive, latterly conservative, he produced a quantity of organ music from 1886 (the year of his 'Organ' Symphony, No. 3, and *The Carnival of Animals*) to 1919.

ALEXANDRE GUILMANT (French) was organist of the Trinité in Paris, and professor at both the Schola Cantorum and the Conservatoire. His eight sonatas (1874–1906)

are as significant to the French Romantic Cavaillé-Coll organ tradition as the organ-symphonies of Widor and Vierne (qv).

CHARLES-MARIE WIDOR (French), organist of St. Sulpice for over 60 years, dominated Parisian musical life from before Ravel to beyond Fauré. His legacy was the unaccompanied organ-symphony (qv), an original genre taken up by some of his students.

CHARLES TOURNEMIRE (French) studied with Widor and succeeded Franck as organist of Ste. Clothilde. His masterpiece was the *L'orgue mystique* (1932) – 51 organ masses based on plainsong melodies appropiate to different Sundays of the liturgical calendar.

MAX REGER (German) closed the German Romantic organ tradition. Steeped in the magnitude, formal intricacy and polyphony of Bach, Beethoven and Brahms, filtered through the innovation of Liszt, his imposing body of organ music (1898–1913) included chorale fantasias, chorale preludes, fugues, variations, toccatas, sonatas, written-out 'improvisations' and sundry other inventions – all of them characterized by detailed craftsmanship and fastidious attention to detail.

OLIVIER MESSIAEN (French), a pupil of Dupré and Dukas and the teacher of Boulez and Stockhausen, was organist of the Trinité and professor at the Paris Conservatoire from 1941 to 1978. Uniquely personal in sound, rhythmic complexity, source material and religious symbolism, his organ music (1927–86) is profoundly mystical, an extraordinary coming together of the meditative and the ecstatic, of time released and time contained, of centuries-old French organ style absorbed, transcended and reborn.

CHARLES CAMILLERI (Maltese) combines Messiaen's Gallic mysticism with independently imagined rhythms and rituals of a completely different kind - orientally valued, African rooted, New Orleans shadowed. Inspired by the writings of the Jesuit scientist Teilhard de Chardin, his emotionally charged five-movement *Missa Mundi* (1972) towers among the great organ statements of the 20th century.

MISCELLANEOUS KEYBOARDS

✵ Accordion / Concertina

The 20th-century piano accordion (a 'developed mouth organ') is an air-vacuum or pressure-operated instrument, with freely beating metal reeds - in other words, a portable reed organ. The instrument consists of a pair of rectangular headboards joined by bellows. Power is supplied to the bellows by alternately pushing out (expiration) and then drawing in (inspiration) each end. The right hand plays a piano-style treble keyboard (originally buttons), while the left controls the bellow action and rows of studs governing bass notes and chords. In the hands of a virtuoso player, the accordion can be a dazzling tour-de-force. Roy Harris wrote a concerto for the instrument, and accordion orchestras are common.

The concertina, which was invented seven years after the accordion, in 1829 in England, is smaller and has two studded keyboards, one for each hexagonal casing. On an English concertina the pitches remain constant on extension and compression of the bellows. On German examples, they change. The concertina is considered artistically superior to the accordion, and is more difficult to play. Its greatest early popularizer was the Italian Giulio Regondi, who left concertos, chamber music and many solo pieces. Tchaikovsky used a quartet of concertinas in his Second Orchestral Suite (1883).

With their strong sound and carrying-power, the accordion and concertina have both been widely used in the performance of traditional and open-air music, particularly as an accompaniment to dancing.

✵ Barrel Piano (Street piano)

An upright piano, often without keyboard, operated by a pinned wooden cylinder situated at the bottom of the instrument. The pins of the cylinder, usually configuring several tunes, selectively activated lever arms connected to the hammer mechanism. Popular from the 1850s onwards, frequently with the addition of other instrumental effects, barrel pianos were usually either hand-cranked or spring-wound. Later models were electrically motorized.

✵ Clavicytherium

An upright wing-shaped harpsichord with vertical soundboard, in use until the 18th century. The Royal College of Music in London has a playable example dating from the late 15th century, believed to be the oldest surviving stringed keyboard of any kind.

✵ Claviorganum

A versatile instrument dating from the 16th century, combining a single manual harpsichord (or virginal) with a small organ. Either could be played separately or coupled.

✵ Echiquier (Eschaquier d'Angleterre)

An elusive keyboard instrument of the 14th century onwards, contemporary with the harpsichord and clavichord and often wrongly mistaken for them. Associated with dancing, it was presumably a loud instrument. John I of Aragon (1387) referred to it as "similar to the organ but sounding with strings". Various theories have been pro-

𝄞 THE PIANO-ACCORDION HAS A SMALL KEYBOARD OF UP TO THREE-AND-A-HALF OCTAVES.

Sostenente
PIANO
॰

Many mechanical attempts, damper pedal apart, have been made to deny the piano its natural attack-decay-release sound character, and to turn it instead into a singing, sustaining hybrid. An early fore-runner from the end of the 16th century was the *Clavecin a archet* – a bowed harpsichord with pedalled and cranked rotating rosined wooden wheels functioning as circular bows on the strings.

Following the hurdy-gurdy principle, the harmonichord (1808) favoured a pedalled revolving leather cylinder which came into contact with the strings. Weber wrote an Adagio and Rondo for it. Other initiatives included compressed air (an Aeolian harp with keyboard); rapid hammer repetition (the double-keyboard piano tremelophone, 1842, with one manual controlling the repetition notes); and the piano scande, 1853 (with the hammered string setting free-reeds into vibration).

However, the first convincing *sostenente* instrument, in which the sound can be indefinitely sustained, as on an organ, was not produced until the 1960s when the electric piano made its first appearance.

posed as to what it was: a clavichord with hammer action; an upright harpsichord; an early prototype of a *clavicymbalum*, originating from or associated with England. In a treatise of c.1440, Henri Arnault de Zwolle possibly refers to such an instrument, drawing attention to a mechanism like piano escapement. Nothing has survived.

A LONDON BARREL-PIANO, POPULARLY CALLED A BARREL ORGAN. ITALIAN WORKERS CALLED SUCH INSTRUMENTS 'PIANO-ORGANS'.

✄ Harmonium

A compressed, foot-treadled air reed organ pioneered by Kratzenstein of Copenhagen and Grenie of Paris (patented by Alexandre Debain in 1842). Debain designed wind channels of different size and pressure, which bore on the individual tone-colours of the reeds. Harmon-iums have 'slow speech' (agile music is ineffective), and their sound does not carry well. But they have had their admirers – from Berlioz and Richard Strauss to the Indian outposts of the old British Empire. Dvořák wrote a charming set of *Bagatelles* for harmonium, two violins and cello (1878); and Tchaikovsky stipulates one (not an organ, the usual substitution) for the close of his 'Manfred' Symphony (1885). "The most sensitively and intimately expressive of all instruments," Percy Grainger fervently believed (1929): "… It is unique as a refining musical influence, for it tempts the player to tonal subtleties of gradation as does no other instrument" – sentiments worthy to place beside Mattheson's and C.P.E Bach's endorsement of the clavichord.

✄ Harpsichord-Piano

Combining the plucking jacks of the harpsichord with the hammer action of the piano, these were a late 18th-century fashion, developed in Vienna by Stein and in Paris by Erard.

✄ Melodeon

A suction air reed organ, first manufactured commercially in 1854 by Mason & Hamlin of Boston Massachusetts. Easier to control than the harmonium, though less varied in tone-colour or expression, this was a useful domestic substitute for pipe organ practice. In America the melodeon was known as a 'cabinet organ'; in England as an 'American organ'.

A 'NEW ENGLISH HARMONIUM' OF 1859. THE INSTRUMENT IS 'BLOWN' BY LEFT AND RIGHT FOOT APPLYING PRESSURE ALTERNATELY.

✄ Pedal Piano

A piano fitted with an organ-like pedalboard enabling the bass line to be played with the feet. A 19th-century invention, related functionally to the pedal harpsichord, pedal clavichord and (later) pedal melodeon, it was a useful practice instrument. Mendelssohn and Liszt owned pedal pianos, and Schumann (1845) and Alkan (c. 1869) wrote for it.

✄ Piano Organ

A piano with two or three ranks of pipes, popular with American theatres and funeral parlours up to 1930.

✄ Portable Piano

An "expanding and collapsing piano for gentlemen's yachts, the saloons of steam ships, ladies' cabins etc., only 13 and-a-half inches [34cm] from front to back when collapsed" was shown at the Great Exhibition of 1851. In 1883 a folding harmonium was advertised ' … being only two feet wide and six inches deep [60 x 15cm]'. Neither fashion caught on.

✄ Reed Organ

The generic label for any keyboard instrument whose sound is generated by metal reed tongues of fixed pitch set in motion by air under compression or suction. Reed organs vary from single to two (or even three) manuals. Air is blown by either foot treadles or motorized electric power. Octave couplers and tremulant devices are usual.

During the 19th century reed organs were as popular domestically as the piano, and were often used in smaller churches in the absence of fixed pipe organs – their modernized, electronic descedents still are. Historically, the technology of the reed organ has its roots in the Chinese *sheng*, or free-reed mouth organ (see page 193). A simplified form of this instrument became popular all over Europe in the later 18th century, and it is said that the acoustician, inventor and theorist Abbe Vogler (teacher of Weber and Meyerbeer) had encountered an original example in Russia.

℈ *Tastiera per luce*

Invented in 1895 by an Englishman, Wallace Rimington, the 'colour keyboard' or 'colour organ' found lasting fame in the treble stave allocated to it by Scriabin in his *Prometheus, The Poem of Fire* (1908–10). Scriabin adapted Rimington's principle, using a twelve-note keyboard to control the opening and closing of apertures of illuminated tinted glass light intended to bathe the performance in a spectrum of colours according to his own specific key/colour associations (red for C major, bright blue for F sharp, and so on).

Among the many other attempts to wed colour to music and vice versa, typical is Alexander Laszló's *Farblichtklavier* (colour-light keyboard), pictured on page 142. Laszló's piano compositions are adorned in the score with an additional colour notation which indicates the lights (singly or in combination) which are to glow at given points in the music. He introduced his invention to an audience in 1925 at the German Music Art Festival in Kiel. In addition to Rimington's and Laszló's inventions, several others have been demonstrated, among them later colour organs, in 1912 and 1919, Colour Projector (1921), Clavilux (1922), Musichrome (1932) and Light Console (1934). 𝄡

Pneumatic Fantasy

℈

COIN PIANO (Nickleodeon) A pneumatically-operated automatic piano triggered by a coin that sets off a mechanical linkage responsible for activating the performing mechanism. Popular in America from before the Great War to Prohibition (1920), coin pianos were considered ideal for relaxed background listening. They flourished everywhere – but, at 25 or 50 cents a two-minute tune, made their best income out of 'sporting house' or brothel money. Speakeasies, too, offered good pickings.

ORCHESTRION A general term describing large self-contained early 20th century pneumatically operated automatic instruments that imitated the sounds of an orchestra. They came in many shapes and sizes (some with keyboards, some without), and used perforated paper-rolls. They enjoyed a vogue in not only (pre-Prohibition) America – where Wurlitzers could come with price tags up to $10,000) but also Europe and England. With origins going back to the Viennese Panharmonican and Orpheusharmonican of Beethoven's time (designed by Maelzel, patentee of the metronome), there were orchestrions to suit any occasion – from playing the classics (the Hupfeld Pan Orchestra), to the latest dance craze and jazz (Hupfeld's Symphony Jazz [with saxophone and lotus flute pipes], the Losche Jazz Band Piano).

PHONOLISZT-VIOLINA Commercialized in 1908 by Hupfeld and later popular In cinemas, this was a pneumatic roll-playing automatic piano with violin (or violins) attached, activated by a circular horsehair bow. *Vibrato, glissandi* and muting (*sordino*) were all possible. Efrem Zimbalist called the invention "the eighth wonder and marvel of our time".

PHOTO-PLAYER THEATRE ORGAN An extraordinary altar-piece of the American silent cinema from about 1910 to 1928. Generically, a mechanical keyboard orchestrion or orchestra piano, it took the form of an ornately fanciful twenty-foot wide pneumatic roll-playing automatic orchestra, with a central piano console (complete with pedals, buttons and other controls) framed by cabinets containing various effects. Around 10,000 instruments were manufactured, of which no more than a few dozen survive today. One variant was called a Pipe-organ Orchestra, capable, according to the maker's publicity, of rendering "the tender, true tones of a violin, the brisk notes of a xylophone, the gay click of the castanets, the silver rattle of the tambourine, and the syncopated beats of the drum. He is master of every situation. He is the living interpreter of every shade of emotion registered by the silent players ..."

PIANOLA The basic principle of this self-playing automatic piano was pneumatic leverage to activate the hammers, triggered by a paper-roll of varyingly placed and lengthened perforations corresponding with the pitches and rhythmic durations of a given piece of music. There were two basic types of system. The external, pushed up to a grand or upright piano and aligned, had levered 'fingers' which lay over the keys of the instrument. In its original foot-treadled (pumped) form, 1896, this was known as a Piano Player (popularly Pianola). In its later electrically-motorized cabinet form (c. 1904), equipped with felted wooden 'fingers' and pedal-activating mechanism, it was called a Vorsetzer. The internal (popularized c. 1900), built into the case of the instrument and physically connected with the hammer action, was known as an 'inner player' or Player Piano. The medium was developed further with the appearance of the Reproducing Piano (1904). Patented in Germany, this was an 'expression' instrument, purporting to convey through its mechanics and the digitalized marginelia of its rolls, an artist's tempo, pedalling, touch, phrasing, etc. The big three reproducing pianos were (in Germany) Welte (1905) and (in America) Duo-Art and Ampico (both launched in 1913). Fierce rivals, none of their systems was compatible.

CHAPTER 5

Electronic Instruments

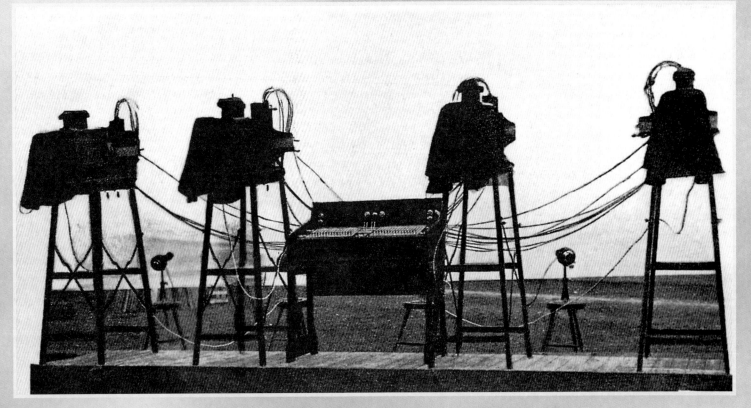

The invention and development of electronically generated music has depended on several disparate factors: a number of scientific inventions, on acoustical research into how sounds are generated and their fundamental characteristics and on the strong desire of some pioneering composers to explore sounds not made by conventional instruments. The first attempt to power musical instruments with electricity was made in 1762 by the Bohemian, Prokop Divis. His *Denis d'or* was described as an 'orchestrion' because it could imitate most string and wind sounds. It was keyboard-

operated. There were similar experiments throughout the 18th and 19th centuries. The development of greatest significance in the evolution of electronic instruments was Alexander Graham Bell's invention of the telephone in 1876. This demonstrated that sound could be converted to electric signals and vice versa. Emile Berliner, in 1877, developed a telephone receiver and, ten years later, a disc recording machine he called 'gramophone'. The latter helped to amend the weaknesses in Thomas Edison's 'talking machine' of 1877, a 'phonograph' for recording and reproducing sound. In 1898 a Danish scientist, Valdemar Poulsen, invented the 'telegraphone', the first magnetic recording machine. Its use of piano wire on which to record proved problematical; a satisfactory result was achieved only when magnetic tape was introduced in 1935. This remained the basis of recording until the present, when digital recording onto hard disc looks set to replace it.

Electronics vs. Music

These inventions, made at a time of exciting discoveries in every scientific and mechanical field, were not obviously connected with music. Indeed, orchestral and operatic music might seem to be the antithesis of electronic music. Yet, from the second half of the 19th century, composers such as Wagner, Richard Strauss, Mahler, Debussy, Scriabin and Schoenberg were all searching for new sonorities. Theodore Boehm and Adolphe Sax had made woodwind and brass instruments more chromatically flexible, louder and more reliable. Soon, the search for different sonorities that led Wagner to use a new tuba, and Strauss to write for the heckelphone, would encourage others to explore the possibilities of musical sounds produced by means other than existing instruments.

The Search for New Music

As important as the development of new instruments and electrical machines was the exploration of sound itself. In 1863 Hermann von Helmholtz published his seminal study on this subject, *Die Lehre von den Tonempfindungen als physiologische Grundlage für die Theorie der Musik* (translated by A. J. Ellis in 1875 as *On the Sensations of Tone as a Physiological Basis for the Theory of Music*). Helmholtz demonstrated

that the sound produced by any instrument can be divided into several parts. Most important for the timbre, or nature, of the sound is the 'formant', a term for how a sound is characterized by the shape, dimension and material of an instrument. Also important for the timbre is the 'onset', 'attack' or first impact of a note, for this contains its character. After the 'onset', notes of all instruments are remarkably similar, as can now be demonstrated on tape by removing the 'onset' and playing the remaining sound. It is the combination of overtones (vibrations additional to the basic note) that give the 'onset' its identity. Thus, Helmholtz not only isolated the elements that constitute the timbre of a note, but postulated the possibility of creating a note without overtones – in effect, a 'pure' note. For this, an electric machine was needed.

Dispassionate scientific investigation and a passionate desire to write music for the new industrial age of the early 20th century were in equal measure responsible for bringing all these elements together to produce the first experiments with electrically generated sound.

LEFT: LASZLO'S *FARBLICHTKLAVIER* – SEE PAGE 141. BELOW: POULSEN'S 'TELEGRAPHONE'.

First Generation

One of the earliest instruments to put Helmholtz's discoveries into practice was 'Sounding Staves', patented in 1896 by the American, Dr. Thaddeus Cahill. Designed to be a synthetic orchestra of 'pure' sounds operated by a single player, it could regulate the number of upper harmonics contained in a pitch, thus achieving a new timbral control of notes. Its chief novelties were the range of sounds it could achieve and its capacity to change sounds derived from traditional instruments. Cahill's machine was called variously a *Dynamophone* or a *Telharmonium*, with Cahill preferring the latter. The aim of this invention, according to Cahill, was 'to generate music electrically with tones of good quality and great power and with perfect musical expression, and to distribute music electrically generated by what we may term "original electrical generation" from a central point to translating instruments located at different points'. The prototype was built in 1900 in Washington, but the first full-sized version was not completed until 1906 in New York. Unfortunately for Cahill, his invention was ahead of its time and his instruments were eventually sold as scrap, although many later developments were based on them.

In 1906 another American, Lee De Forest, invented a vacuum tube (also called a thermionic valve or triode tube) which could control electrical current precisely and could be used to generate, amplify, modulate and detect electrical current. It greatly improved the amplification of sound on the gramophone and radio, as well as generating audio signals in tube oscillators. This was but the beginnings of what De Forest eventually perfected in 1915 as the oscillator, which still forms the basis of electronically generated sound. The oscillator made it possible to generate accurately pitched sounds from electrical signals and paved the way for the invention of further electronic musical instruments.

INSTRUMENTS OF FUTURISM

THE MOST SYSTEMATIC experimentation with new instruments and novel sounds in the years either side of the First World War occurred in Italy, under the influence of Futurism. The credo of Futurism was made known to the world in 1909 by the Italian poet Filippo Marinetti, in his *Foundation and Manifesto of Futurism*, in which he celebrated the energy of contemporary industrial life and its machines. The search for a new kind of music was soon underway. In 1911 the musician Francesco Pratella published *The Technical Manifesto of Futurist Music*, in which he argued for the use of microtones and sounds to replace

music by "venal flatterers of the public's base taste", by which he primarily meant Puccini and his very successful verismo operas.

Ironically, it was not the composer Pratella but the painter Luigi Russolo who had the most impact on Futurism's musical thinking and thereby on the development of electronic musical instruments. In 1916 he enshrined his ideas in another Futurist manifesto, *L'arte de rumori*, in which he criticized traditional theories of harmony and advocated a new music that would use different sounds, collected from everyday life (the musical equivalent of *objet trouvé*). Russolo

THE FUTURISTS IN 1912: (LEFT TO RIGHT) RUSSOLO, CARLO CARRE, MARINETTI, UMBERTO BOCCIONI AND GINO SEVERINI.

had been pursuing these ideals since 1913, in which year he produced, together with Ugo Piatti, the first of his *Intonarumori*.

Each of the *Intonarumori* consisted of a brightly coloured box from which at the front projected a horn, like an early gramophone, and at the back a handle which the player turned to produce the noise. Inside the box of most of the

Russolo's Inventions

INTONARUMORI

A group of machines/instruments designed by Russolo and Ugo Piatti in Milan between 1913 and 1921 to produce various noises. (The word intonarumori means 'noise intoners'.) Russolo divided the groups of noises into six categories:

Rumbles	Whistles	Whispers	Screeches	NOISES OBTAINED	VOICES OF ANIMALS
Roars	Hisses	Murmurs	Creaks	BY PERCUSSION	AND MEN
Explosions	Snorts	Mumbles	Rustles	ON:	Shouts
Crashes		Grumbles	Buzzes	metal	Screams
Splashes		Gurgles	Crackles	wood	Groans
Booms			Scrapes	skin	Shrieks
				stone	Howls
				terracotta	Laughs
					Wheezes
					Sobs

ARCO ENARMONICO

A special bow for stringed instruments devised by Russolo in Milan in 1925. It was made of a rod wound round with wire so that it had a slightly ridged surface. The stringed instrument was bowed in the normal way, but the sound it produced was different: coarse *legato* and rapid repetitions could be achieved. The sounds resembled the rumbles and whispers of Russolo's *Intonarumori*. A reconstruction of the bow was made in Venice in 1977.

PIANO ENARMONICO

A keyboard instrument developed by Russolo in the Thirties in which each piano key makes a moving driving-belt come into contact with a long coiled spring mounted on a resonance box. The principle on which it operates is similar to that of a hurdy-gurdy (see page 194).

Intonarumori was a wheel, made either of wood or metal, which rotated against a gut or metal string. The tension of the string could be altered by a lever to give different pitches, including microtones. At one end of the string and attached to the horn was a stretched skin (like that of a drum), whose vibration, along with the string, made the required noise. Various modifications were made to this design, depending on the noise desired.

Russolo's vocabulary of new sounds included noises from objects and machines, and also from nature and humans. In 1914 he devised a graphic form of notating these, entitled *Enharmonic Notation for the Futurist Intonarumori*, in which a horizontal line denotes the duration of a sound. This notation was later adopted by Cage and Stockhausen.

Russolo's first concerts on his noise machines took place in Milan in 1913 and caused an uproar. Subsequent performances were held in Genoa and London, but it was in 1920s Paris, the pre-eminent centre for experimentation, that these machines aroused the most sympathetic interest, attracting the attention of Stravinsky, Ravel, Milhaud and, most significantly, Edgard Varèse.

Russolo and Marinetti, though not Pratella, remained faithful to Futurist ideals. As late as 1933, when the white-heat of the early polemics had cooled and the political situation in Italy was increasingly unfavourable to experimental art, Russolo and Marinetti were working with a Futurist Radiophonic Theatre in which tiny sounds, inaudible to the human ear, could be amplified and used in musical compositions.

EDGAR VARESE WAS ONE OF THE FIRST MAJOR COMPOSERS TO ENTHU-SIASTICALLY EMBRACE THE POSSIBILITIES OF ELECTRONIC MUSIC.

IMPORTANT
Electronic Instruments

%

THEREMIN In 1920 the Russian scientist Lev Theremin invented a *thérémin* (as it is best known in its French form), consisting of an oscillator controlled by movement of the hands. The closer the operating hand approaches the antenna (which sticks vertically out of the instrument) the higher the pitch climbs, while the other hand controls the volume by its proximity to a metal loop. The *thérémin* gained some fame through the performances of a few virtuosi who could demonstrate its highly expressive, almost vocal, qualities, but never became widely used because of the great difficulty of playing it. Some attempts are being made to revive interest in it. Perhaps its most famous orchestral use was in Varèse's *Ecuatorial*, which originally called for two *thérémins*. At the work's premiere in 1934, the volume of the two *thérémins* proved so difficult to control that Varèse replaced them with two *ondes martenots* (see below). In 1926 Theremin invented an electric harmonium capable of dividing the octave into 1200 pitches, a refinement far too subtle for the human ear to detect.

ONDES MARTENOT Probably the most successful post-Cahill electronic musical instrument, the *ondes martenot* was patented in 1922 by the Frenchman Maurice Martenot and produced by him in 1928. It has oscillating valves similar to those of the *thérémin*, but pitch can be controlled more easily: players move their fingers along a wire stretched in front of a five-octave keyboard. Timbral and tonal changes are effected by means of buttons and keys. Like the *thérémin*, the *ondes martenot* is capable of a moving, disembodied vocal-like timbre and of achieving great volume, audible above even a large orchestra. Messiaen used it particularly effectively in his *Trois Petites Liturgies de la Présence Divine* (1944) and *Turgangalîla Symphony* (1946–8). Other composers to have used the instrument include Honegger, Jolivet and Boulez.

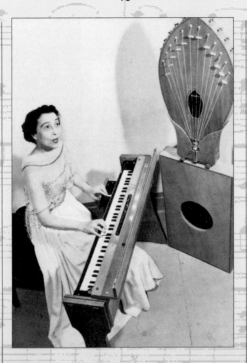

ABOVE: *ONDES MARTENOT* PLAYED BY GINETTE MARTENOT, THE SISTER OF THE INSTRUMENT'S INVENTOR.

HAMMOND ORGAN Invented in 1935 by the American Laurens Hammond, who also invented the *solovox*, chord organ and *novachord*, this was intended to replace the pipe organ for pseudo-ecclesiastical and domestic uses. The Hammond organ resembled it in having two manuals and a pedal board, but the sound was produced by electrical means similar to the *ondes martenot*. In the 1960s Stockhausen became interested in its potential and released it from its intended original purpose, notably in *Mikrophonie II* (1965). It has also been widely used in jazz and pop music.

TRAUTONIUM This instrument, invented by the German Friedrich Trautwein in 1930, proved popular at the time with some German composers, not least because of its ability to obtain varieties of tone-colour and, with relative ease, accurate pitches. Richard Strauss and Hindemith both experimented with it.

COMPOSERS OF ELECTRONIC MUSIC USED FILTER MACHINES TO CREATE THEIR COMPOSITIONS.

MUSIQUE CONCRETE

IT IS ONE of the strange ironies of the evolution of electronic music and instruments that the founder of *musique concrète*, Pierre Schaeffer, did not know of Russolo's experiments with noise machines. Initially, Schaeffer used 78 rpm records and relatively unsophisticated mechanical means to produce his new music. From the 1950s onwards he used the magnetic tape recorder which, although invented in 1935, was not widely available until after the Second World War. This proved an indispensable part of the new developments, because it could store and retrieve sounds and compositions, and because eventually it could be used to alter sounds.

Schaeffer was a radio technician by training, not a musician. In 1948, while working for French Radio, he developed a means of using several tape recorders to extract sounds from pre-existing recordings. What he could do with the sounds was relatively limited: the techniques available enabled him only to exclude some parts of the sounds, play them backwards ('tape reversal') or combine different sounds ('collage'). Even so, he managed to achieve a wider range of sounds than Russolo, employing means that were simpler to use but much more sophisticated in their results.

The distinctive feature of *musique concrète* is that the original sounds, from which the final compositions were made, were pre-existing and non-electronically generated. The term 'concrète' was used to denote both that the sounds from which the pieces were derived were from concrete (ie, 'tangible') natural sources, and that the pieces were composed 'concretely' onto the tapes rather than abstractly in the head of the composer using notation as a guide to subsequent performance.

Schaeffer, like Russolo, utilized sounds from everyday life, and began making compositions with objects such as clashing saucepan lids. From the outset, though, *musique concrète* also encompassed pre-existing musical sounds as sources. Schaeffer was also attracted to the multiple sounds obtainable from the piano other than by playing the keyboard. On 5 October 1948 he broadcast a 'concert of noises' in which five works were 'played'. These included two 'études' derived from piano sounds (for whom the pianist was Boulez), and *Etude aux casseroles*, which used sounds taken from, among other sources, spin-

♪ *MUSIQUE CONCRETE* MARKED A TURNING AWAY FROM ELECTRICAL MEANS OF COMPOSITION (HERE A TRAUTONIUM).

ning saucepan lids, boats and human voices.

In 1949 Schaeffer was joined by Pierre Henry. Two years later French Radio rewarded the efforts of the two men by constructing a special studio which included tape recorders, sound filters and many other means for creating and manipulating sounds. In the pioneering work completed here, Schaeffer and Henry were considerably aided by their technical assistant, Jacques Poullin.

MAJOR COMPOSERS OF
Musique Concrète
❧

PIERRE SCHAEFFER was the founder of *musique concrète* at the station of French Radio. His *Etude aux chemins de fer* (Study for Railroad Trains) (1948) was the first 'concrete' composition. He composed less frequently after the early 1950s and spent more time training and advising other composers in his studio.

PIERRE HENRY was one of the most prolific composers of *musique concrète*. He worked at the studio of French Radio until 1958 after which he set up his own studio, Studio Apsome, with the choreographer Maurice Béjart. His *Symphonie pour homme seul* (1949–50) (written jointly with Schaeffer) was based principally on 'human' noises, such as breathing, whistling, talking and laughing, together with some transformed orchestral sounds and effects such as 'footsteps'. The piece was so evocative that it was later used as a ballet. In 1955 Henry and Schaeffer worked on the first *musique-concrète* opera, *Orphée 53*. Two other works by Henry are among the best-known *musique-concrète* works: *Le voyage* (1961–62) and *Variations pour une porte et un soupir* (Variations for a door and a sigh) (1963).

LUCIANO BERIO was one of the many young composers to work with Schaeffer in Paris. Among his most celebrated *musique-concrète* pieces was *Thema* (1958), subtitled *Omaggio à Joyce*. The sound source was his then-wife, the singer Cathy Berberian, reading part of Molly's soliloquy from James Joyce's *Ulysses*. After almost two minutes the voice is dissolved into a series of ono-matopoeic fragmentations of the text. The 'oo' in a word such as 'blooming' is enormously extended to suggest its meaning, as is the 'ss' in 'hiss'. The result is an evocative and suggestive interpretation of the original text, achieved solely by manipulating the sound of the original reading.

STEVE REICH (shown below in rehearsal) Many of Reich's minimalist compositions owe much to electronic effects, particularly tape loops. The idea for his *concrète* piece *Come Out* (1966) came from the events associated with a riot in Harlem in 1964 in which a young African-American, Daniel Hamm, was arrested for murder. Hamm was beaten by the police and in order to gain hospitalization had to "... open the bruise up and let the bruise blood come out to show them". Reich repeats this phrase three times before selecting the last five words for continuous repetition on tape loops of different lengths, each repetition getting the voice further and further 'out of phase' with itself until it became unrecognizable. The work was recorded on two channels so needs two speakers for performance.

Paris was not the only city to set up a studio dedicated to electronic music. In New York, Vladimir Ussachevsky and Otto Luening founded a studio at Columbia University in 1951. Among the first compositions to come out of this studio were *Transposition and Reverberation* (1952), a collaborative effort, and Ussachevsky's *Sonic Contours* (1952). Both works used piano sounds as their basis, showing that, unlike the French, the Americans preferred using pre-existing 'musical' sounds rather than 'natural', 'everyday' sounds.

Musique concrète had to be painstakingly assembled by splicing together many bits of tape, so much of the music seemed to be full of rather angular and sudden changes of sound and dynamics. In time, however, greater sophistication led to improvements in the ability to transform sounds and to achieve a wider range of different effects. French *musique concrète* is often suggestively sombre and dark, reflecting a French aesthetic more than an inevitable electronic aesthetic. Later American composers discovered lighter textures and even humour. The growth in sounds and suggestive effects, as well as the fact that most of the early studios were connected with radio stations, inevitably led to these early *concrète* experiments finding their way into radio effects and, eventually, films.

Musique concrète was at first used to define music whose sound sources were natural. The new technology (and some of the old) could also generate its own sounds, and quite rapidly composers such as Stockhausen and Xenakis started using a mixture of electronically generated sounds as well as natural and musical noises. At first, electronically generated music and *musique concrète* appeared as opposites, but over the years they have merged and composers happily use either or both sources. The heyday of purely *musique concrète* lasted from the late 1940s until the end of the 1950s. During this time the French studio attracted many leading composers, from young neophytes such as Boulez, Stockhausen and Messiaen, to established figures like Milhaud.

❧ *Experimentation: Cologne*

Slightly later than Schaeffer's experiments in Paris, Herbert Eimert founded a studio in Cologne (at Westdeutscher Rundfunk) dedicated to experimenting with electronically generated rather than 'natural' or 'instrumental' sounds. He was soon joined by Stockhausen and together they embarked on the creation of what they termed 'Elektronische Musik'. Their starting point was an instrument called the 'melochord', devised by Werner Meyer-Eppler and Robert Beyer in Cologne in 1950. This produced sounds by means of oscillators and other purely electronic means. What particularly attracted Stockhausen was the complete control he would have over sounds. Musical experiments since the late 1940s had been trying to extend the serialization of twelve tones (begun by Schoenberg in the 1920s and subsequently by Webern) to include rhythms, durations and so on, as Messiaen had done in his pioneering *Modes de valeurs et d'intensités* (1949). In performance much of the precision that had been intended by the composer was lost in the license that a performer was obliged or felt able to take. The prospect of the composer being able to control a piece from its inception to its final production was particularly alluring.

Stockhausen's first attempts – his two *Studien* – showed the way, but his most outstanding early work, the magnificent *Gesang der Jünglinge* (1955–6), represents the kind of compromise between *concrète* and purely electronic sounds that would become increasingly evident in the works of many other composers. In the *Gesang* a boy's voice singing the Benedicite is processed and mixed with electronic sounds. Originally 'performances' of this work were to be played on

𝄞 BY THE MID 1950S STOCKHAUSEN WAS THE ACKNOWLEDGED LEADER OF THE AVANT-GARDE.

FIVE PIONEERS OF *Electronic composition* ❧

EDGARD VARESE was an influential avant-garde composer. He used two *thérémins* in his *Ecuatorial* and wrote two mainly electronic pieces: *Good Friday Procession in Verges* (1955–6) and *Poème Electronique* (1957–8).

KARLHEINZ STOCKHAUSEN has been one of the pioneers of using purely electronic, as well as *concrète,* sounds. His *Gesang der Jünglinge* set a new standard for electronic music, as did his later *Kontakte.* He pioneered using electronically prepared tapes in live performances.

JOHN CAGE was one of the most innovative experimenters with a wide range of computer-generated sounds. Following his experiments with non-music *concrète* sounds, in 1951 he wrote *Imaginary landscape 4* for 12 radios and 24 operators. He pioneered, with the pianist David Tudor, live electronic music with his *Music for Amplified Toy Pianos,* and *Cartridge Music* (both 1960).

IANNIS XENAKIS assisted le Corbusier in the design of the Philips exhibit in Brussels in 1958 at which Varèse's *Poeme Electronique* was performed. Fascinated by computers, he has devised a special kind of music based on the notion that, depending on chance, music will eventually conclude itself, using computers to help calculate this. Among his most ambitious pieces is *Hibiki-Hana-Ma* (1970), written for 12 tapes sounding from 800 speakers.

MILTON BABBITT is one of the most important American composers to have used electronic means for composing. Included among his major works are *Composition for Synthesizer* (1970), *Philomel* (1964) for soprano, recorded soprano and synthesizer, and *Phenomena* (1974) for soprano and tape.

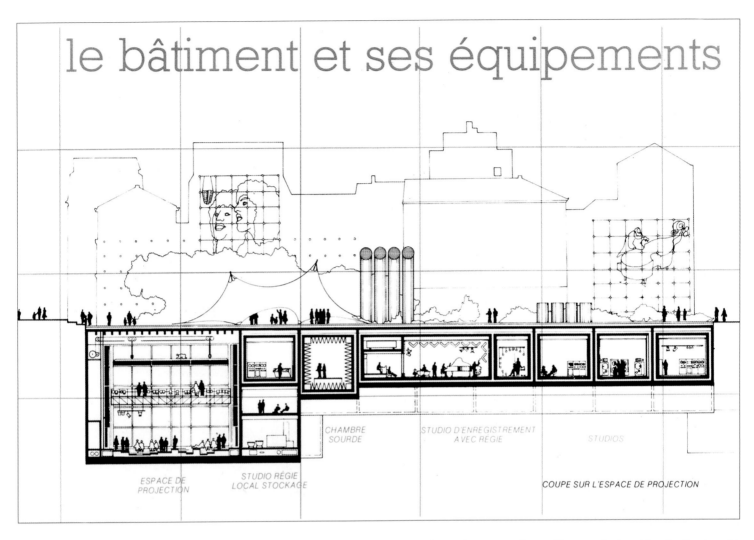

le bâtiment et ses équipements

CHAMBRE SOURDE
STUDIO D'ENREGISTREMENT AVEC RÉGIE
STUDIOS
ESPACE DE PROJECTION
STUDIO RÉGIE LOCAL STOCKAGE
COUPE SUR L'ESPACE DE PROJECTION

 A PLAN OF IRCAM, THE PARIS STUDIO DEDICATED TO THE DEVELOPMENT OF ELECTRONIC/COMPUTER MUSIC.

five speakers spaced around a concert hall, but this number was eventually reduced to four. At the same time, electronic devices began to be imitated by Stockhausen in purely instrumental works, such as *Klavierstück IX*, whose opening repeated chords and subsequent fragmentation mimic first reverberation and later the interplay of upper harmonics.

One of the great difficulties of early electronic music was that the composition of works took an inordinately long time, because the machines were not originally intended for the composition of music. Stockhausen's *Gesang der Jünglinge* took a year and a half to prepare. His

next major electronic piece, *Kontakte*, took two years. It was the synthesizer that eventually took the painstaking construction out of electronic composition and opened the way for both more flexible studio compositions and live 'real-time' interaction between computers and live musicians and their instruments.

✻ *Experimentation: Brussels And New York*

Meanwhile, composers elsewhere continued to experiment with the technology at their disposal. One of the most astonishing pieces of early electronic composition was the *Poème Electronique*, written by the 70-year-old Edgard Varèse for the Philips Pavilion at the 1958 Brussels World Fair.

The pavilion was designed by the Greek architect and composer Iannis Xenakis and the French architect Le Corbusier. Varèse's music, projected from 350 loudspeakers, was accompanied by lighting effects and slide projections. The sounds, a mixture of *concrète* and electronically produced, were recorded on three-channel tape with two of the channels being reserved for reverberation and stereo effects.

The wide divide between the conflicting aims of Paris and Cologne in the 1950s led some composers to work elsewhere, though at first their choice was limited due to the scarcity of electronic studios. This situation began to change in the late 1950s with studios in New York, at Columbia University (1951), the Electronic Studio in Tokyo at Japanese Radio (1953), the Studio de Musique Electronique in Brussels

(1958), and, perhaps as significant as any, the Studio di Fonologia at Italian Radio in Milan (1958). Not only did Italian composers such as Maderna and Berio work in Milan, but so did one of the most imaginative and innovative composers to experiment with electronic music, John Cage.

Cage had already experimented with electronically processed sounds, in his series of *Imaginary Landscapes* (1:1939, 2:1942, 3:1942). In the first he had used early experimental test records of pure sound played on variable speed turntables; and in the second he had added to the five percussionists an amplified coil of wire. In the third the six percussionists are also required to operate an audio frequency oscillator, an electric buzzer, recordings of different frequencies and an electronically amplified marimbula. The arrival of the tape recorder and more modern technology prompted Cage to compose *Williams Mix* and *Imaginary Landscape 5* (New York, 1952), and *Fontana Mix* (Milan 1958). Each of these pieces is a collage of different sounds. *Fontana Mix* moves away from the determinacy of the Cologne and Paris schools by giving minimal directions to the performer and allowing the prepared tape to be played with or without other accompanying music.

JOHN CAGE. HIS ACCEPTANCE OF THE ROLE OF CHANCE IN MUSIC BROADENED COMPOSITIONAL HORIZONS.

FOUR FAMOUS
Electronic Studios

COLUMBIA-PRINCETON ELECTRONIC MUSIC CENTER established in New York in 1951 by Ussachevsky and Luening. The Mark II RCA Music Synthesizer constructed by Belar and Olsen was transferred to the Center. This was the most advanced machine of its time and for a while gave the Center's resident composers an advantage in working with purely electronically generated sounds.

STUDIO FÜR ELEKTRONISCHE MUSIK, COLOGNE Established 1951 by Eimert. The first studio designed to produce music entirely by electronic means, it possessed the familiar devices of the *concrète* studio (variable speed tape recorders, filter, reverberating devices for creating echo effects, amplifiers, etc.) as well as oscillators and noise generators. Among the first works composed at the studio were Stockhausen's *Study I* (1953) and *Study II* (1954), as well as the pioneering synthesis of *concrète* and electronic, *Gesang der Jünglinge* (1956).

STUDIO DI FONOLOGIA, MILAN Established in 1953, this was one of the most productive early studios. From the beginning both *concrète* and electronic compositions were encouraged. Berio's *Thema: Omaggio à Joyce* (1958) is an example of the former, and Pousseur's *Scambi* (1957), which used only 'white noise' as its source, an example of the latter. Nono and Maderna also worked at the studio. Cage wrote his *Fontana Mix* there.

INSTITUT DE RECHERCHE ET DE COORDINATION ACOUSTIC/MUSIQUE (IRCAM) Established in Paris in 1976, since when it has aimed to be the most sophisticated and extensive studio for the production of electronic music in the world. Under the general direction of Boulez and paid for by the French government, it was designed for creating music and for research into acoustics and the psychology of how sounds are perceived. Emphasis is also placed on using the equipment as active participants in live music, especially transforming 'live sounds'. The studio is thus as much dedicated to *musique concrète* as to electronically generated music, though the distinction between these has become blurred if not extinct since the arrival of digital technology. In addition to Boulez, who used the IRCAM facilities for his work *Répons*, a wide range of composers have been invited to use the studio, from Berio, Trevor Wishart, Harrison Birtwistle. Jonathan Harvey and George Benjamin to the jazz composer George Lewis.

♪ SYNTHESIZERS

THE EARLIEST ELECTRONIC instruments, such as Russolo's *Intonarumori*, were unwieldy and capable of producing relatively few sounds. In the late 1950s and early 1960s composers and technicians were increasingly looking at ways of producing machines that were relatively simple to operate and offering a wider range of sounds. What composers wanted, and what eventually emerged in the shape of the synthesizer, was a single, easily operated machine capable of integrating the various means by which electronic sounds could be processed and generated.

The arrival of the synthesizer revolutionized electronic music making. It was both considerably cheaper than the elaborate machines produced hitherto and a time saver. Previously,

♪ BABBITT WITH THE **RCA Mk II** SYN-THESIZER WHICH, IN HIS WORDS, WAS 'NO MORE INHUMAN THAN THE PIANO'.

each sound had had to be recorded onto tape, then each piece of tape cut to exactly the right length to give the sound its required duration. The synthesizer changed this.

✄ How the Synthesizer Works

Every synthesizer possesses a number of components, each of which has a specific function. The synthesizer's principal functions are to generate sounds and to process these sounds to suit the composer. Some of the components that fulfil these two requirements can be linked in a process known as 'patching'.

A synthesizer makes sounds, called audio signals, by means of an oscillator. This was specifically designed to produce pitches, called sine waves, that have no overtones. Normally, a note will travel through the ether like a wave. The notes generated by a synthesizer's sine wave produce a simple curve without 'overtones' or 'harmonics'. The pitch of a note can be altered by means of 'control voltages', which affect the power supply and thus move the pitch up or down. The sound-generating part of the synthesizer can produce a wide range of harmonics and create the sound known as 'white noise'.

There are many ways of processing the sounds on a synthesizer. The most basic one is to make the sound audible, which is done by an amplifier and through several monitoring speakers. Sometimes composers want to create the effect of a sound moving through space, in which case a 'spatial locator' is used to stagger the sound so that it reaches each speaker in turn rather than simultaneously. Sounds can also be combined to make a complex, or filtered so that some elements are removed or altered; a 'ring modulator' will achieve the former, a filter the latter. An artificial echo effect can be created by means of a 'reverberator'. 'Envelope generators' enable control of the attack and lengthen or shorten the decay of a sound.

The most significant control on a synthesizer is the keyboard (or keyboards), which looks like an ordinary piano keyboard but rarely behaves in the same way. The pitch of the keyboard can be altered, so that although each note is separated from its neighbour by a semitone, its pitch may not correspond to its equivalent key on a piano keyboard. The keyboard also controls the length of a note as well as its pitch. In some examples the keyboard is touch-sensitive so that several functions can be performed by the same key, depending on the way it is depressed or released.

🎼 THE YAMAHA VL7, ONE OF THE NEW GENERATION OF PORTABLE SYNTHESIZERS FOR COMMERCIAL USE.

✄ *Types of Synthesizer*

The first synthesizer was the RCA Mark II, developed at the Sarnoff Research Centre in New Jersey in 1955 and later housed at the Columbia-Princeton Electronic Studio (see page 151). Compared with what had gone before, it was much reduced in size due to the replacement of valves by transistors, although still quite bulky by later standards. The Mark II gave composers a marvellous new range of timbres and greatly increased their control over the sounds. This was of particular interest to those composers, such as Milton Babbitt, who wanted to extend the serialization of their music to include all elements, not just pitches or rhythms. The new synthesizer allowed the composer unprecedented control

𝄞 JEAN-MICHEL JARRE, ONE OF THE FIRST COMPOSERS OF 'POPULAR' ELECTRONIC MUSIC.

and eliminated the distorting effect a live performance could have.

The RCA Mark II was superseded by smaller, more versatile machines. The two most important designers of the first commercially available synthesizers, which appeared in the mid-1960s, were Robert Moog and Donald Buchla. Moog's invention of a voltage-control amplifier meant that sounds could be controlled by voltages, relieving the composer of the chore of having to 'tune' each of his notes by hand before obtaining the right pitch or volume. The synthesizer performed the task automatically, and more quickly and accurately.

✄ *Portables*

The attempt to combine live performance with a pre-prepared tape is not new. Varèse, for instance, in his *Déserts* (1954), alternated passages for chamber ensemble with purely electronic sounds. Typically, Varèse contrasted the timbres of the live instruments with the electronic ones. Later composers tried to combine and fuse the two sounds. Berio, for instance, in his *Différences* (1959), combined a live chamber group and recordings of the same instruments electronically processed.

However, the introduction of portable synthesizers has enabled electronics to take an active part in live performance, to generate sounds and combine them with those of other instruments. Paolo Ketoff designed and produced his Synket in Rome in 1964. Smaller and more portable than the Moog synthesizer, it was limited in having only three wave-selecting generators and one 'white noise' generator. The Synket also had limited 'patching' facilities – though for the most part the machine was hard-wired (ie, the wiring was predetermined and fixed in the machine and several outputs could not be combined) and three touch-sensitive two-octave keyboards. The first composer to use a Synket was the American John Eaton, in 1965, almost simultaneously with the first live performances using a Moog synthesizer.

♪ ROBERT MOOG, PIONEER OF THE
COMMERCIAL SYNTHESIZER, DEMON-
STRATING A HYBRID ASSEMBLED FROM
THE 900 SERIES AND VARIOUS DEVICES.

Ketoff built seven later Synkets, each a modification of the prototype.

Many other portable synthesizers have been
made since the Synket. Chief among their users
from the late 1960s have been rock bands keen
on loud amplification and on generating the
many special effects that processed sounds can
achieve. Among these groups have been USA,
The Mothers of Invention and The Grateful
Dead. The event that probably drew most attention to the new technology in the world of
popular music was the record *Switched on Bach*,
performed on a Moog synthesizer by Walter
(later Wendy) Carlos in 1968.

The introduction of digital technology has
allowed a further reduction in size. The use of
microprocessing enabled the inventors of the
Synclavier to make a small portable synthesizer of
considerable flexibility. The first model appeared
commercially in 1976 and was superseded in
1980 by the Synclavier II. Both were conceived
and manufactured at Dartmouth College, New
Hampshire and White River Junction, Vermont in
New England, USA, by Sydney Alonso, Cameron
Jones and Jon Appleton. The Synclavier was followed by several rivals, such as the PPG Wave
Computer, the DMX-1000, the AlphaSyntauri
and the Soundchaser. But none has the versatility
of the two massive, extensively computerized,
non-commercial systems – the SSSP at the
University of Toronto and the 4X, later the 16X
and now being replaced with new defence-indus-
try supported technology, at IRCAM in Paris.

EARLY
Synthesizers
✀

**RCA ELECTRONIC MUSIC
SYNTHESIZER MARK I (1951–2):** Mark
II (1958) Compared with Moog's inventions these two RCA machines would not
be categorized as synthesizers today but
rather as programmable electronic
machines. Very large and bulky, and taking
a great deal of time to use for composition,
they were programmed by punching holes
in a long strip of paper rather like a piano
roll. The machine could never be used in a
live, or 'real-time', performance because a
slight delay occurred before the relay of
the composer's role. The RCA machines
were, however, very versatile and enabled
the composer to programme and connect
almost anything. Their range of sounds
and effects could not possibly be matched
by the smaller machines introduced later.

MOOG SYNTHESIZER Robert Moog
developed the first commercial synthesizer
in 1964 and in it initiated many features that
have since become standard. His synthesizer digitally controlled the voltage – one
volt per octave, which became the standard
for synthesizers. In 1970 Moog developed
the Minimoog, a fully portable monophonic
instrument primarily designed for use by
rock bands. A number of successors to the
Moog synthesizer have developed, providing different features and attributes. These
include the Polymoog, invented by David
Luce, 1976–1980; the Opus 3, which was a
string synthesizer with organ and brass sections; and the guitar-like Liberation.

BYRD-DURRELL SYNTHESIZER Used
by the first American rock band to
employ electronics extensively in their
music: USA, founded in 1967 by Joseph
Byrd. Custom built, the synthesizer had
ring modulators and echo units controlled by foot pedals.

Important Hybrid Synthesizers

AND SYSTEMS

※

GROOVE – Generated Real-Time Operations on Voltage-Controlled Equipment. Developed by Max Matthews at Bell Telephone Laboratories in 1970.

MUSYS – completed in 1970 by David Cockerell, Peter Grogono and Peter Zinovieff in London.

PDP 15/40 (computer) with **EMS 1** (synthesizing programme) – developed in Stockholm at the Elektronmusikstudion in the early 1970s. It remained in use and operational into the early 1980s when it was dismantled.

SYNCLAVIER – developed at Dartmouth College, New Hampshire, USA and at White River Junction in 1975. It was the first digital synthesizer and was designed to be an up-market, compact system.

FAIRLIGHT CMI – first manufactured in 1979 in Australia. It possessed two six-octave keyboards, an interactive graphics unit and an alphanumeric keyboard.

DMX-1000 – Digital Music Systems, first appeared in the USA in 1979. Connected to a control computer, such as a **PDP 11**, it was a programmable computer.

4X – Similar to the **DMX 1000** in that it is controlled by a **PDP 11** computer, it succeeded early 4A, 4B and 4C models. Notable for its extensive digital signalling processing, it was the first synthesizer used at **IRCAM**.

SSSP – Structured Sound Synthesis Project, initiated by the University of Toronto, Ontario in 1977 but discontinued in 1983 through lack of funding.

MIDI – Musical Instrument Digital Interface. The first version (Version 1.0) was produced in 1983, and was almost immediately incorporated by most synthesizer manufacturers as an invaluable component.

CASIO VL-1 – the first miniature all-digital synthesizer aimed at the domestic rather than the professional or institutional market. It appeared in 1981.

DX – this series of compact, portable synthesizers, incorporating the MIDI system, began appearing in 1983. In 1985 the DX7 Mark II was launched with increased timbral potential.

FOUNDED BY TWO STUDENTS OF IMPROVISED MUSIC, GERMAN ROCK GROUP KRAFTWERK USE SYNTHESIZERS, TAPE RECORDERS AND COMPUTERS TO CREATE THEIR MINIMALIST COMPOSITIONS. ACCORDING TO KRAFTWERK CO-FOUNDER RALF HUTTER, "TECHNOLOGY AND EMOTION CAN JOIN HANDS".

COMPUTER MUSIC

THE COMPUTER, ONE of the most remarkable inventions of the 20th century, has had an important effect on the development of music. The rapid advance of computers in the 1990s has produced programmes for writing music down. The traditional method, with pen and paper, was a skill requiring a long time to both learn and execute. Now there are a number of computer programmes that can, for example, replace writing out music for orchestral symphonies or songs with piano accompaniment, with quasi-printed copies; notable is the Sibelius 7. The invention of the synthesizer has also made it possible to link a computer to a keyboard and convert what is played into written symbols. This is achieved by an interface between the keyboard and a computer, the most celebrated being the MIDI (Musical Instrument Digital Interface) (1983).

More radical are the programmes that enable relatively untrained musicians to 'compose'. On electronic keyboards, for instance, a player need play only a simple single melody to be provided with rhythm backing and simple harmonization, each of which has been pre-programmed into the instrument. Such programming has been vastly extended recently, allowing composers to interact with the material to a much greater degree. Musical sounds can now be simulated with greater accuracy and combined to create even orchestral effects by the scientific sampling of the ingredients of complexes of sounds. The effect of this process has been felt in a wide spectrum of applications, from film composers trying out their full orchestral scores in

THE INCREASING COMPLEXITY OF HIS MUSICAL IDEAS LED XENAKIS TO USE A COMPUTER TO HELP ORGANIZE THEM.

their studios (thus saving enormous amounts of time and money in making alterations to scores while live musicians wait to play new material) to large computerized church organs that can simulate the sounds of organs from a wide range of ages, builders and countries.

Computers can be used to help composers select their notes. Some aspects of musical composition have become possible only through the use of computers. Highly complex rhythms and com-

binations of rhythms can be realized exactly through computerization, as can genuinely random choice. A computer can also transform given sounds in a programmed way, as did Henze in his massive work, *Tristan* (1974).

Computers have also been used to 'compose' music. This has been done by programming the computer with a selection of data and criteria for its choices. In the 1950s at Harvard University, F. B. Brooks produced some computer-generated hymn-tunes, and in 1956 Lejaren Hiller and Leonard Isaacson managed to get a computer to write a string quartet, which they called *Illiac Suite*. Each of the movements of this suite were intended to mimic the style of a variety of composers, ranging from Bach to Bartók. Perhaps with more originality and ingenuity, Xenakis composed his *ST/4* (1956–62) for string quartet with the help of calculations made on a computer. Xenakis has described the music resulting from his computer-programmed works as 'stochastic music'.

Getting a computer to make the sophisticated choices needed for composing requires a great deal of painstaking analysis of musical models, as well as intricate scientific know-how to perfect the inputs that create the sounds. The limited amount of music composed by computer probably reflects the time and energy this involves. However, the monumental researches of IRCAM and the imaginative use composers have made of pre-performance preparations and 'real-time' interactions suggest that it is only a matter of time before computers became an even-more active ingredient in the composition of music.

CHAPTER 6

Ensembles

What constitutes an ensemble? It may seem obvious: a musician alone, and the work performed, is called 'solo', yet there is an exception: 18th-century composers wrote 'solos' for one instrument accompanied by at least one other! Thereafter, common sense prevails as we chase numbers: duo, trio, quartet, quintet, sextet, septet, octet, nonet and dectet or decimette. More, and it becomes ensemble (though fewer than eleven might still be called that, or group, or chamber orchestra, so vague is the terminology).

Informally, a 'band' might number from, say, four musicians upwards. Older terms are coming back into vogue – 'Academy' (orchestra), 'Consort' (a group of instruments strictly of the same family; a mixture was a 'broken consort') 'Camerata' (chamber ensemble) and similar names in different languages.

Instrumental groups may be constituted in countless ways. Lyres, lutes and percussion were at the centre of the earliest labour dispute when Aristos (lead lute?) called a strike in Rome about 309 BC because his brothers were missing meal breaks. From AD 1571 to 1642 an ensemble of shawms, recorders, sackbuts and strings gathered in the turret of London's Royal Exchange to play, free, to the populace. No charge was made for the cornett and trombone music sounding from German church towers from the 16th century, the Stadtpfeifer (town pipers) being paid from the rates. Seemingly free, too, were tea-shop trios (usually piano, violin, cello) and café orchestras (violin led) that used to exist in the Western world, though customers paid indirectly.

A charming 18th-century convention, notably in Austria, was the open-air serenade played by wind groups in the streets at evening. These played *Feldparthien* (field works), a term taken from their instruments' earlier military use. In 1755 Moscow heard the first horn band: 37 hunting horns, each player blowing only one note. Extensions followed: groups of up to 60 players; and the radical decision to allow players the luxury of two, or even three, notes. Horn bands spread throughout Europe but are now heard only in enthusiasts' enclaves in Russia.

Early jazz bands consisted of whatever instruments were available, but usually present were piano, banjo, trumpet or cornet, clarinet, trombone and drums. Not all of them played all the time: part of their attraction was the contrasting sounds and moods of solo 'breaks'.

Jazz began before World War I. The Original Dixieland Jazz Band (1916) in New Orleans and Joe 'King' Oliver's Creole Jazz Band (1922) in Chicago, respectively black and white since segregation was practised then, were the first prominent groups to appear. This 'New Orleans Style' became popular all over the States, and early jazz under the catch-all title 'traditional' enjoyed a great resurgence in the 1950s and 1960s as a reaction to the desiccated, esoteric

A CHRONOLOGY OF FAMOUS
Jazz Bands
& THEIR LEADERS

All of the following bands are American except for those of British musicians Chris Barber and John Dankworth.

ORIGINAL DIXIELAND JAZZ BAND Formed 1916: cornet, trombone, clarinet, piano, drums.

BENNIE MOTEN, piano: Trio, 1918; and Kansas City Orchestra, 1923.

DUKE (EDWARD KENNEDY) ELLINGTON, piano: Band, 1921; and His Famous Orchestra, 1927.

(JOE) 'KING' OLIVER, cornet: Creole Jazz Band, 1922; and Dixie Syncopators, 1925.

PAUL WHITEMAN, viola and leader: Orchestra, 1924.

LOUIS ARMSTRONG, trumpet, formed several bands: Hot Five, 1925; Hot Seven, 1927; Savoy Ballroom Five, 1928; Orchestra, 1928?; All-Stars, 1947. He played and sang with many other groups.

'JELLY ROLL' MORTON (Ferdinand Joseph Le Menthe), piano: Red Hot Peppers, 1926.

JIMMY DORSEY, alto sax and clarinet, and Tommy Dorsey, trombone and trumpet, formed the Dorsey Brothers Orchestra, 1928. Tommy formed the Clambake Seven, 1935, to record 'traditional' jazz.

BENNY GOODMAN, clarinet: Band, 1934; re-formed 1940.

'COUNT' (WILLIAM) BASIE, piano: Barons of Rhythm, 1935; Count Basie Orchestra, 1936.

WOODY (WOODROW) HERMAN, clarinet, sax and vocal: Orchestra, 1936; re-formed 1947.

GLENN MILLER, trombone: Orchestra, 1937.

STAN KENTON (Stanley Newcomb), piano and leader: Orchestra, 1940.

DAVE BRUBECK, piano: Octet, 1946; Trio, 1949; Quintet, 1951.

CHRIS BARBER, trombone: Jazz Band, 1949, to play 'traditional' jazz.

JOHN(NY) DANKWORTH, alto sax and clarinet: Seven, 1950; Orchestra, 1953; Quintet, 1982.

MODERN JAZZ QUARTET, 1951: Milt Jackson, vibes; John Lewis, piano; Percy Heath, bass; Kenny Clarke, drums.

sound of 'modern' jazz. By playing in clubs and dance halls, jazz bands earned their keep but had to bear in mind the requirements of dancers to such an extent that the dividing line between jazz and dance music became blurred.

In the late 1930s the Big Band era arrived with Count Basie, the Dorsey Brothers and Glenn Miller – part dance music, part jazz, part progressive, part orchestral. The constitution of these bands ranged from a full orchestra, with brass or strings or reeds predominating, to a group of blown instruments alone, but a strong percussion element, the rhythm section, was always present. So-called 'modern' jazz emerged in the late 1940s, a sophisticated art, modern chamber music if you will, with limpid textures and progressive approach that acquired cult following. The cool sounds of acoustic guitar, or vibes or flute or alto sax, indeed any instrument or combination, typified the modern jazz idiom.

A constant quest for the new in a bid to attract listeners has led to some strange and not necessarily musically fruitful partnerships, with uncomfortable mixes of jazz and non-Western instruments, and electronic devices with or without 'live' players.

CHAMBER ENSEMBLES

VIOL CONSORTS, so common in the 16th and 17th centuries, died out early in the 18th century as the violin family took over and wind instruments grew in popularity. Ensemble music was now increasingly linked to the harpsichord, which was employed in three distinct roles: as the leading instrument, in equal partnership with another soloist, or acting as continuo to one or more principal players.

In the wind department the bassoon, surprisingly, was first to be given an important place. In 1621 Dario Castello published a set of *Sonate concertante* in which a treble instrument (?violin) shares responsibilities with bassoon. Trumpet came next, with two sonatas published in 1638 in an instruction book by Girolamo Fantini. An

instruction book (authorship unknown) appeared in 1700 for the oboe; then at last came the first solos for the instrument that was to prove the most popular ensemble workhorse of the 18th century, the flute. Michel de la Barre composed his sonatas for flute and continuo in 1702, but he was so unsure that the flute would become popular that he made them equally suitable for violin. Similarly, William Babell's sonatas (c. 1720) for oboe or violin.

By the mid-18th century wind serenades including oboes, horns, bassoons and even clarinets were common, mainly for open-air use. Indoors, the harpsichord was declining in favour of the fortepiano, and this more powerful instrument formed the kernel of a whole series of genres. In

violin sonatas and so-called piano trios (violin, cello, piano) it took the lion's share of musical material since strings were regarded merely as accompanists, only gradually emerging as contenders in their own right. Piano quartets and quintets also appeared, some with wind instruments, but works for four or five were more regularly written for an 'unbroken' group of strings.

Whereas wind serenades had featured instruments in pairs (two each of oboes, bassoons, horns, for example), a later development tended to use them singly in quintets for flute, oboe, clarinet, bassoon and horn. This combination also appeared occasionally against orchestra in the *Symphonie concertante*, invented in France about 1770.

At one time, orchestral and chamber music had merged (there were 'orchestral trios' and 'orchestral quartets' at Mannheim, playable by small groups or by string orchestras), but by 1800 there was a clear distinction. Beethoven's early string quartets are no more successful when played on full string band than is his Second Symphony in his own arrangement for piano trio. As the 19th century progressed chamber music grew in duration and stature: Dvořák's early string quartets are as long as his symphonies, while Brahms's carefully written piano trios and piano quartets have great depth and intensity of thought.

There was a move towards freedom of instru-

THE ALLEGRI STRING QUARTET IN 1964, WITH CO-FOUNDER ELI GOREN AND PETER THOMAS (VIOLINS), PATRICK IRELAND (VIOLA) AND WILLIAM PLEETH (CELLO).

A RECITAL OF 1760, WITH OBOE, VIOLIN, HORN AND CELLO. NO WORK REQUIRING THIS PRECISE MIX IS KNOWN.

mental deployment, too. Almost any instrument might join the standard string quartet to oblige and honour a famous soloist, and larger groups were catered for as required. Variety was the order of the day. With fewer nobles extending patronage, and financial considerations placing limits on the size of instrumental groups, early 20th-century composers would write to order for any ensemble that happened to be available. This is evident in Prokofiev's 'Overture on Hebrew Themes' (1919) for clarinet, string quartet and piano (he orchestrated it in 1934), and Stravinsky's *Pastorale* (1934) for violin, oboe, English horn, clarinet and bassoon. These odd 'convenience' ensembles, however, hardly equalled the strange combinations of earlier centuries, each, it must be imagined, gathered for special circumstances. Telemann wrote quartets for four violins alone and another for trumpet, two oboes and continuo, but few bettered Johann Ernst Galliard, a German resident in England, who in 1745 produced a sonata for 24 bassoons and four double bassoons.

Chamber Ensembles
TYPES, COMPONENTS AND FAMOUS EXPONENTS

FLUTE DUET	(two flutes)	W. F. Bach
FLUTE SONATA	(flute, harpsichord, continuo)	C. P. E. Bach, J. S. Bach, Handel
VIOLIN SONATA:		
TYPE I	(violin, harpsichord, continuo)	Bach, Handel
TYPE II	(keyboard, violin)	Boccherini, Mozart
TYPE III	(violin, piano)	Bartók, Beethoven, Brahms, Grieg, Mendelssohn
CELLO SONATA	(cello, piano)	Beethoven; Brahms
FLUTE TRIO	(flute, violin, continuo)	C. P. E. Bach, J. C. Bach
OBOE TRIO	(2 oboes, bass)	Handel
HORN TRIO	(horn, violin, cello)	Brahms
STRING TRIO	(2 violins, cello)	J. C. Bach, Boccherini
PIANO TRIO	(keyboard, violin, cello)	Beethoven, Boccherini, Brahms, Dvořák, Haydn, Mendelssohn, Mozart, Schubert, Schumann
FLUTE QUARTET	(flute, violin, viola, cello)	J. C. Bach
OBOE QUARTET	(oboe, violin, viola, cello)	Boccherini, Mozart
PIANO QUARTET	(piano, violin, viola, cello)	Brahms, Schumann
STRING QUARTET I	(2 violins, viola, cello)	Bartók, Beethoven, Boccherini, Brahms, Cambini, Dvořák, Haydn, Mendelssohn, Mozart, Schubert, Shostakovich
STRING QUARTET II	(2 violins, cello, double bass)	Rossini
WIND QUINTET:		
TYPE I	(2 clarinets, 2 horns, bassoon)	J. C. Bach
TYPE II	(flute, oboe, clarinet, horn, bassoon)	Cambini, Danzi, Hindemith, Nielsen, Reicha
STRING QUINTET:		
TYPE I	(2 violins, 2 violas, cello)	Boccherini, Brahms, Bruckner, Dvořák, Mendelssohn, Mozart
TYPE II	(2 violins, viola, 2 cellos)	Boccherini, Borodin, Schubert
PIANO QUINTET:		
TYPE I	(piano, 2 violins, viola, cello)	Berwald, Boccherini, Brahms, Dvořák, Schumann
TYPE II	(piano, violin, viola, cello, bass)	Schubert
PIANO AND WIND QUINTET	(piano, oboe, clarinet, horn, bassoon)	Beethoven, Mozart
WIND SEXTET	(various combinations)	Beethoven, Haydn, Mozart,
STRING SEXTET	(2 violins, 2 violas, 2 cellos)	Boccherini, Brahms, Pleyel, Dvořák, Tchaikovsky
MIXED SEXTET		Beethoven, Boccherini
WIND SEPTET		Janáček
MIXED SEPTET	(clarinet, bassoon, horn, violin, viola, cellos, bass)	Berwald
WIND OCTET		Beethoven, Hummel, Krommer
MIXED OCTET		Boccherini, Schubert
STRING OCTET		Mendelssohn, Spohr
WIND NONET		Krommer
WIND DECTET		Krommer, Spohr

THE EARLY ORCHESTRA

THE RISE OF THE ORCHESTRA has been closely tied to developments in the world of opera. Even the name 'orchestra' originated in the opera house. It dates from Ancient Greece, when theatrical productions often involved music in some form, and the word *orkhéstra* denoted the space in front of the stage used by the singing and dancing chorus. The first operas were intended to imitate that early Greek style of theatre, so it seemed quite natural to Renaissance musicians to apply the name 'orchestra' to the ensemble that now occupied the space once used by the chorus.

As the popularity of opera grew during the 17th century, composers realized that instruments needed to do more than simply accompany the singing and that they should express the thoughts and emotions of the characters. So instruments used for opera performances became the first to be sorted into groups with distinct roles – in other words, an orchestra. In Monteverdi's *Orfeo* (1607), the first real opera, one group of instruments stands out, the strings, including the newly invented violin which was capable of a more powerful sound than its predecessors, the viols. Violins soon came to be accepted as effective concert instruments, and by

SINGERS AND INSTRUMENTALISTS GATHERED ROUND A HARPSICHORD DURING A CANTATA REHEARSAL, 1775.

the mid-1600s Monteverdi's use of an orchestra comprising strings and harp was regarded as a benchmark. Equally influential was the court of Louis XIV in France, particularly with the appointment in 1653 of Jean-Baptiste Lully as composer-in-chief. The court's influence throughout Europe was considerable. With Louis' 24 'Violons' or 'Grande Bande' at his disposal, as well as the oboes and bassoons of the

THE MAKE-UP OF
Early Orchestral Forces

FOR MONTEVERDI'S *ORFEO*
When Monteverdi scored his opera he was very specific about the instruments he required, unusually so for the time. His large orchestra of 1607 was made up as follows: 4 violins, 4 violas, 2 cellos, 2 double basses, 3 viols, 2 flutes, 4 trumpets and 2 cornetts, 4 trombones, 6 keyboards and 6 plucked strings and drums (?).

THE '24 VIOLONS DU ROI'
The band of 24 strings in the court of Louis XIV of France was more typical of the day. When used by Lully for his operas it was often supplemented by instruments from the king's 12 *Grandes Hautbois* and other miscellaneous instruments as necessary. A typical example from the 1670s would be: 6 violins, 12 violas, 6 cellos, 2 flutes, 2 oboes, 1 bassoon, 2 trumpets, 1 drum, 1 keyboard.

AMATEUR BAROQUE ORCHESTRA
During the Baroque period it was just as common to hear a group of amateur players gathered together to form an informal orchestra as it was to hear one in an opera house. In 1770 the music historian Charles Burney recorded the make-up of a typical Italian amateur orchestra as follows:

"There were 12 or 14 performers: several good violins; two German [transverse] flutes, a violoncello and a small double bass."

FOR HANDEL'S OPERAS
Handel moved to London around 1710, and by the late 1720s was promoting opera performances at the King's Theatre, London, towards the end of what had been a very successful career as an opera composer in England. At that time an orchestra for his operas probably took the following form, with one of the earliest uses of the French horn in England: 22 violins, 2 violas, 3 cellos, 2 double basses, 2 flutes, 2 oboes, 3 bassoons, 2 horns, 2 keyboards, 1 plucked string.

MANNHEIM COURT ORCHESTRA
The famous orchestra at Mannheim exerted considerable influence in establishing the standard Classical orchestra. In the 1770s the orchestra there consisted of the following: 20 violins, 4 violas, 4 cellos, 4 double basses 3 flutes, 3 oboes, 3 clarinets, 4 bassoons, 4 horns, 2 trumpets, 1 timpani, 1 keyboard.

♪ AN OPERATIC SCENE OF THE 1760s THOUGHT TO BE FROM A 'TURKISH' OPERA BY GLUCK.

12 *Grandes Hautbois*, Lully was able to establish the first real orchestral ensembles.

By the late 17th century, almost all the instruments now associated with the orchestra were available for use, but the strings retained their prominence. The melody and bass line of a piece of music were still the most important, and these were taken by the upper and lower strings while the middle parts were filled by 'continuo' instruments. The continuo remained important throughout the first half of the 18th century, and even in the early 19th century a keyboard was often found holding the harmony of orchestral music together. In Mozart's piano concertos, for example, the composer expected the pianist to play a continuo during the *tutti* sections as well as the solo parts.

During the 1700s writers like Quantz and Rousseau expressed differing views on the proper make-up of an orchestra. Strings and continuo, plus woodwinds and sometimes brass, was a generally accepted formula, but difficulties of travel and communication meant that ensembles were rarely consistent except in the most basic outline. Gradually, as international communication improved, the qualities of those orchestras benefitting from better organization came to be appreciated more widely. One of the most influential of these orchestras was that of Duke Carl Theodor at Mannheim. It was established in the 1740s by his *Kapellmeister*, Johann Stamitz, who was encouraged to engage musicians from all over Europe. As the skills of performing and composing often went hand-in-hand at this time, many of the players in the Mannheim orchestra were also accomplished composers. Among the advancements made at Mannheim were an attention to musical phrasing, the idea of uniform bowing for each string section and the techniques of *crescendo* and *diminuendo*, and the famous 'Mannheim rocket' of ascending *tutti* crotchets. The Mannheim orchestra also pioneered the replacement of improvised continuo with written-out parts. ♭

THE MODERN ORCHESTRA

Brian's 'GOTHIC' SYMPHONY

✄

At a time when composers were leaving behind the mighty orchestras demanded by some late-Romantic scores, and the Depression was causing the depletion of musical forces everywhere, Havergal Brian produced the first of his output of 32 symphonies, the Symphony No. 1, written between 1919 and 1927. This 90-minute work is constructed in two parts, with each part composed of three movements. The *Te Deum* setting that constitutes Part Two requires forces of unparalleled scale. These are listed below and include those instruments doubled by existing players:

- 2 piccolos, 6 flutes, alto flute, 6 oboes, oboe d'amore, bass oboe, 2 cor anglais
- 2 E flat and 5 B flat clarinets, 2 basset horns, 2 bass clarinets, pedal clarinet
- 3 bassoons, 2 contrabassoons, 8 horns, 2 E flat cornets, 8 trumpets, bass trumpet
- 3 tenor trombones, 1 bass trombone, 2 contrabass trombones, 2 euphoniums, 2 tubas
- 2 sets of timpani, 2 harps, organ, celesta
- Other percussion, including: glockenspiel, xylophone, 2 bass drums, 6 large pairs of cymbals, tubular bells, bird scare, thunder machine
- Strings
- Soprano, alto, tenor and bass soloists, 2 large choruses, children's chorus
- Plus 4 brass bands each comprising 2 horns, 2 trumpets, 2 tenor trombones, 2 tubas and a set of timpani.

DURING THE 19th century the orchestra underwent astonishing growth. Particularly influential in this were the revolutionary changes that the woodwind and brass families underwent during the 1800s (as discussed in pages 18 to 45). In the later symphonies of Mozart and Haydn clarinets had become an integral part of the woodwind section, and now other instruments began to be added. These included the piccolo, trombone and contrabassoon in symphonies by Beethoven, and the cor anglais and bass clarinet in music by Berlioz and Meyerbeer respectively. However, it was Richard Wagner, more than any other 19th-century composer, who changed the constitution of the orchestra. Not content with merely accepting what was available to him, he wrote for vastly extended forces and was even prone to inventing new instruments when the particular sound he wanted was not immediately achievable. In writing for such large orchestras,

Wagner set the pace for late-Romantic composers like Strauss and Schoenberg, who, at least until World War I, behaved as if they thought the orchestra would continue to develop in size.

By the 1920s this extravagance had lost favour. Composers began to experiment with smaller ensembles, some even making a deliberate return to the modestly proportioned orchestras of earlier generations (Prokofiev, for example, in his 'Classical' Symphony of 1917). In a situation remarkably similar to what had occurred in opera's infancy, composers were now prepared to score works according to what was available to them, or to use existing forces in new and interesting ways. Stravinsky, for example, in his *Symphony of Psalms* (1930) used an orchestra without any violins or violas. The percussion section, in particular, grew in size and importance as composers experimented with increasingly complex rhythms.

Generally speaking, today's orchestra corresponds in size to that of the late 19th century. It is big enough to cope with most of the larger late-Classical and Romantic works and flexible enough to present authentically-scored performances of music by Mozart or Schubert. Other than strings, the usual constituents of a modern orchestra are three flutes (one doubling piccolo), three oboes (one doubling cor anglais), three clarinets (one doubling bass clarinet), three bassoons (one doubling contrabassoon), four horns, three trumpets, three trombones and a tuba. Also common are two harps in addition to a set of timpani and a range of other percussion. Among other 'instruments' occasionally added to the 20th-century orchestra have been typewriters, anvils, chains, wine glasses, the wind machine (often used to represent the breathing scored in the 'birth to death' journey of Tippett's Fourth Symphony, 1977), and the electronic *ondes*

martenot, whose unearthly sound makes a remarkable addition to the orchestra in Messiaen's *Turangalîla-symphonie* (1948).

Where economic or other factors have forced limitations on orchestral size, some musicians have established permanent groups of leaner proportions that are particularly suited to a great deal of music written since World War I. Among many such ensembles, two of particular note are the Basle and Zürich Chamber Orchestras, established by Paul Sacher in the years between the two world wars and responsible for commissioning music from some of the century's leading composers, including Bartók, Berio, Henze, Stravinsky and Tippett. Also notable is the Orpheus Chamber Orchestra which, though apparently unusual in performing without a conductor, reminds us that the conductor in the form now familiar to us did not appear until the early 19th century. (Many orchestral musicians aver

♪ **ABOVE: GEORG SOLTI AND MURRAY PERAHIA REHEARSE WITH THE ENGLISH CHAMBER ORCHESTRA IN 1986. BELOW LEFT: GUSTAV MAHLER CONDUCTING THE LARGE FORCES OF THE VIENNA PHILHARMONIC.**

that conductors are, at best, a mixed blessing!)

While the modern orchestra's principal purpose remains to perform concerts, many groups also recognize their importance as a community resource. Increasingly, the job of an orchestra is to take the music to the people, rather than simply expecting the people to come to the music. This often takes the form of music workshops or small-scale performances in local community venues and schools. Increasingly, an orchestra's outreach programme is now seen as a core part of its artistic activity. It is a far cry from the early days of the orchestra when access to its performances was largely restricted to a privileged few. ♭

WRITING FOR THE ORCHESTRA

THE ORCHESTRA'S CAPACITY to produce an homogenous sound in performance can be explained by the complex balancing act that lies at the heart of successful composition. As the orchestra developed from its early days of purely strings, or strings doubled by woodwind, composers were often highly circumspect when it came to adding new instruments. Only those instruments thought suitable for orchestral performance were included, and then only in appropriate quantities. The composer's skill has always been as much concerned with achieving the correct instrumental balance for the desired effect as it has been with simply getting the notes right.

The standard modern orchestra mixes everything in moderation, according to the relative strengths of the instrumental 'voices' at its disposal. The result is a natural homogeneity that gives the composer a head start. The real skill of writing for orchestra, or 'orchestration' as the discipline is usually called, is in moulding the constituent parts of the ensemble in such a way as to produce constantly varied and interesting results, without losing essential elements of the music in a mêlée.

To a greater or lesser extent composers have always been interested in the sound effect of individual instruments. However, it is only quite recently that the art of blending and balancing those instruments has received serious consideration. Trumpets have always had an association with the battlefield and horns with hunting, while in early opera the double bass was commonly

♭ IGOR STRAVINSKY, ONE OF THE
20TH-CENTURY'S MOST IMAGINATIVE
ORCHESTRATORS.

 BENJAMIN BRITTEN (LEFT), MASTER OF ORCHESTRATION, SITS IN AT A REHEARSAL IN 1976.

reserved for storm or earthquake scenes. Towards the end of the 18th century, however, the first masters of orchestration emerged. Chief among them was Mozart. In his symphonies and piano concertos he developed dialogues between the sections of the orchestra, including the soloist in the concertos, resulting in constantly shifting instrumental colour that was previously unknown.

For all the myriad directives laid down in text books, not least Berlioz's *Treatise on Instrumentation and Orchestration* (1843), the basic skills required have not changed. Essentially orchestration is about understanding the sound of individual instruments, their place in the grand scheme of the orchestra, and how successfully or otherwise they might be paired with other instruments. Even in the 1770s, for instance, it was understood that an ensemble of strings, woodwind and horns would, in the normal course of events, not present any serious deficiencies in balance. However, to add trumpeters to it, who at that stage habitually occupied the upper reaches of their compass, might upset the status quo. So trumpeters lost their high florid parts, and found themselves restricted to more mundane material in the lower registers.

Not surprisingly, the strength of the body of strings in an early orchestra did not approach that in a modern ensemble, and woodwind instruments have since developed greater power, too. Today the appreciation of how instruments may be mixed is far in advance of what it was in these early ensembles. Extremes of register are known to sit quite happily together in the right context. A low flute passage, for example, might be particularly affecting, but it would also be drowned out easily unless employed at a quiet moment. Likewise a high, piercing trumpet part will readily dominate strings and woodwind.

For all their skill in shaping the sound of the orchestra, composers have from time to time asked the impossible of their players, often without shame. On being told that his Violin Concerto would need a player with six fingers, Schoenberg is reputed to have replied, "I can wait!" Usually, though, asking a great deal of performers is a natural result of experimentation with musical form. Certainly, without occasionally stretching the capabilities of an instrument or the technique of a player, few advancements would be made.

In the final analysis, though, only so much about orchestration can be learned from a secondary source. The best way to acquire the skill, as composers have found since time immemorial, is to listen with a critical ear. This will always be the best tutor. 𝄢

Orchestration
A MUSICAL GUIDE
℀

Benjamin Britten is counted among the best orchestrators of the 20th century. Few pieces, by him or anyone else, introduce the art of orchestration better than his *Young Person's Guide*. Subtitled 'Variations and Fugue on a Theme by Purcell', the piece was written for a documentary film of 1946 called *The Instruments of the Orchestra*. The skill of the music, as with any great work, must really be heard to be appreciated, but a schematic plan can perhaps demonstrate the simple ingenuity of Britten's introduction to the orchestra and its myriad colours.

PART ONE – THEME
Played section by section: woodwind, brass, strings, percussion

PART TWO – VARIATIONS
Instruments present variations on the theme in an array of different groupings, including:
➵ flutes and harp, with *tremolo* strings.
➵ bassoons with *sforzando* string chords.
➵ *staccato* wind and brass chords, moving from the top of the range to the bottom.
➵ tam-tam and harp, over shimmering strings.
➵ side-drum and trumpets in a *galop*.
➵ strings and percussion, notably timpani and xylophone, but also castanets and whip.

PART THREE – FUGUE
Each section joins in the fugue, starting with the highest instrument and working to the lowest, where appropriate, in the following order: woodwind, strings, harp, brass and percussion.

THE MAESTRO IN THE MAKING

THE SIGHT OF SOMEONE directing a group of musicians by waving a small wooden stick evolved around 200 years ago. The origins of the modern conductor's baton, though, were reported as early as the 11th century. An Italian monk wrote: "A master stood in the midst of the choir holding a shepherd's crook, his symbol of authority, in his left hand. With his right he made decisive gestures, so that all sang with one mouth".

By the 16th century, this symbol of authority had developed into the smaller precentor's staff, now held vertically in the right hand and used to keep or beat the time. Palestrina is said to have directed the Vatican choir in the 1550s with a "kingly, golden rod". Time beating, as the name implies, could also be audible. In 1753, the then director of the Paris Opéra was described as a "wood-chopper" for the way he struck a desk with a wooden mallet. The French composer Lully died from blood-poisoning in 1687 after hitting his foot with the metal ferrule on the end of a vast conducting pole.

As purely instrumental music evolved, time-beating became less necessary. During the 18th century, orchestras were small and easily directed from the keyboard or the violin, hence the term leader or concertmaster for the principal violinist. Larger-scale performances continued to need time beaters, though, and in 1762 C. P. E. Bach, son of the great J.S., wrote: "Performers will find in the simultaneous motion of both hands an inescapable, visual portrayal of the beat."

It was the rise of the classical orchestra, with its additional instruments, that brought the need for a totally independent musical director. At the turn of the 19th century, there was an unsatisfactory dual direction for orchestral concerts.

KAPELLMEISTER FRANZ RICHTER KEEPING TIME WITH A ROLL OF MUSIC PAPER.

A so-called conductor sat at a piano and played along from the full score. The *tempi* were given by the leader using his bow, with only the first violin part in front of him.

In this period, many different objects were tried to keep time, from rolls of paper to wooden tubes. The German violinist and composer, Louis Spohr, is credited with having introduced the small wooden baton. In London in 1820, he was supposed to lead a concert of his own music. As usual, the conductor sat at the piano. "Fortunately," Spohr reported, "he readily agreed to surrender the full score to me. I took a position at a separate music desk and drew my directing baton from my pocket. I soon found that I could not only give the *tempi* in a decisive manner, but also ensure the players a confidence they had not known before. Inspired by the results, they immediately expressed their unanimous assent to this new way of conducting."

During the 19th century, the finest conductors were also the finest composers. Mendelssohn was praised for the elegance of his gestures and his fast *tempi*. When the performance was going well, he would put down his baton and stop beating time altogether. Continuous and disciplined gestures were advocated by Berlioz, who wrote the first treatise of conducting, still a bible of commonsense. By all accounts, his performances were exciting but relatively straightforward.

There was also the intensely emotional approach of Beethoven. One pupil wrote: "Our master was ceaselessly occupied by manifold gesticulations to indicate the expression in his own works. Everything about him was active, not a bit of his body idle." Another reported "little breaks in the tempo" with no less than seven tempo changes in a short passage from the Larghetto of his Second Symphony. Liszt and his son-in-law Wagner developed more flexible approaches to

FAMOUS
Symphony Orchestras

BERLIN PHILHARMONIC ORCHESTRA 1882
Present: Claudio Abbado.
Previous incl. Hans von Bülow, Artur Nikisch, Wilhelm Furtwängler, Herbert von Karajan.

BOSTON SYMPHONY ORCHESTRA 1881
Present: Seiji Ozawa.
Previous incl. Georg Henschel, Arthur Nikisch, Karl Muck, Pierre Monteux, Serge Koussevitzky, Charles Munch.

CHICAGO SYMPHONY ORCHESTRA 1891
Present: Daniel Barenboim.
Previous incl. Theodore Thomas, Frederick Stock, Fritz Reiner, Sir Georg Solti.

CLEVELAND ORCHESTRA 1918
Present: Christoph von Dohnanyi.
Previous incl. Nikolai Sokoloff, Artur Rodzinski, George Szell, Lorin Maazel.

CONCERTGEBOUW ORCHESTRA 1888
(Amsterdam)
Present: Riccardo Chailly.
Previous incl. Willem Mengelberg, Pierre Monteux, Eduard van Beinum, Bernard Haitink.

DRESDEN STAATSKAPELLE 1735
Present: Hans Vonk.
Previous incl. Carl Maria von Weber, Richard Wagner, Richard Strauss, Karl Böhm, Rudolf Kempe.

LEIPZIG GEWANDHAUS ORCHESTRA 1743
Present: Kurt Masur.
Previous incl. J. S. Bach, Felix Mendelssohn, Arthur Nikisch, Wilhelm Furtwängler, Bruno Walter.

LONDON PHILHARMONIC ORCHESTRA 1932
Guest conductors. Previous incl. Sir Thomas Beecham, Sir Adrian Boult, Bernard Haitink, Klaus Tennstedt.

LONDON SYMPHONY ORCHESTRA 1904
Present: Sir Colin Davis.
Previous incl. Sir Edward Elgar, Arthur Nikisch, Hans Richter, Felix Weingartner, Pierre Monteux, André Previn, Michael Tilson Thomas.

NEW YORK PHILHARMONIC ORCHESTRA 1928
Present: Kurt Masur.
Previous incl. Gustav Mahler, Arturo Toscanini, Sir John Barbirolli, Dmitri Mitropoulos, Leonard Bernstein, Pierre Boulez.

PHILHARMONIA ORCHESTRA 1945 (LONDON)
Present: Christoph von Dohnanyi.
Previous incl. Otto Klemperer, Riccardo Muti, Giuseppe Sinopoli.

PHILADELPHIA ORCHESTRA 1900
Present: Wolfgang Sawallisch.
Previous incl. Leopold Stokowski, Eugene Ormandy, Riccardo Muti.

VIENNA PHILHARMONIC ORCHESTRA 1842
Guest conductors. Previous incl. Otto Nicolai, Hans Richter, Gustav Mahler, Felix Weingartner, Wilhelm Furtwängler, Clemens Krauss, Herbert von Karajan, Lorin Maazel, Zubin Mehta, Carlos Kleiber.

HERBERT VON KARAJAN, REVERED PRINCIPAL CONDUCTOR OF THE BERLIN PHILHARMONIC FROM 1954 UNTIL HIS DEATH IN 1989.

interpretation. Liszt is even said to have aped physical reports of Beethoven's conducting, "crouching down" for *pianissimo* and "rising up as out of a trap door" in a *crescendo*.

In the 1870s, Wagner's opera house at Bayreuth became the training ground for the first group of purely professional conductors. Hans Richter in Vienna and Hans von Bülow in Berlin further developed the flexible style, adapting their basic tempi to the character of an individual musical phrase. Richter's successor in Vienna, Gustav Mahler, more revered as a conductor than a composer in his lifetime, was described as "quicksilver" in his approach to tempo.

Listening now to recordings made in the early 1900s, such as those with the Berlin Philharmonic under their mesmeric conductor Artur Nikisch, it is a sense of *accelerando* in passages of *crescendo* that is most disconcerting. Today, we have retained the idea of quiet music slowing down, but the thought of exciting music becoming faster, often to a degree where the orchestra cannot play the notes, seems anathema to the listener of today.

Yet many of the greatest conductors of this century have displayed something of this volatile approach to interpretation. Wilhelm Furtwängler took over from Nikisch in Berlin in the 1920s. Whereas Nikisch was noted for his clarity of gesture, Furtwängler was notoriously difficult for orchestras to follow. His interpretations of the classics now seem somewhat mannered, yet there was a visionary sense of architecture in almost everything he conducted.

Arturo Toscanini was much more literal in his approach to a score. Famed in his youth for 'cleaning up' the overly Romantic tradition in Italian opera, he did the same for the great orchestral repertoire during the 1940s and early-1950s in New York. Performing under Toscanini involved a great fear factor, and his tongue could

THE CONDUCTING STYLE OF ARTURO TOSCANINI – INSPIRATION THROUGH CLARITY AND INTENSITY.

be vitriolic. Most players, though, forgave him for the clarity and intensity of his music-making.

Sir Thomas Beecham, on the other hand, was loved by orchestras for his geniality and famous wit. Noted for his Haydn and Mozart performances, Beecham's urbane approach was not ideally suited to Brahms or Beethoven, but many lesser composers sparkled under his direction.

Bruno Walter was a warm-hearted disciple of Mahler. In the half-century from 1910 to 1960 when the Mahler Symphonies were rarely performed, Walter kept his master's performance traditions alive, pushing onwards where many others now hold back.

SOME NOTABLE
Conductors
%

FELIX MENDELSSOHN, GERMAN
One of the first great conductor/composers. Leipzig Gewandhaus Orchestra, 1835–47.

HANS VON BÜLOW, GERMAN
Munich Opera, 1864–69; Meiningen Orchestra, 1880–85; Berlin Philharmonic, 1887–92. Premiered Wagner's *Die Meistersinger* and *Tristan und Isolde*, and Brahms' Fourth Symphony.

HANS RICHTER, AUSTRO-HUNGARIAN
Hungarian Opera, Budapest, 1871–75; Bayreuth Festival, 1876–1912; Vienna Philharmonic, 1893–1900; Hallé Orchestra 1897–1911. Premiered Wagner's *Ring*, Brahms' Second and Third Symphonies, Elgar's First and Bruckner's Fourth Symphonies.

ARTUR NIKISCH, AUSTRO-HUNGARIAN
Boston Symphony, 1889–93; Hungarian Opera, Budapest, 1893–95; Leipzig Gewandhaus, 1895–1922; Berlin Philharmonic, 1895–1922; Hamburg Philharmonic, 1897–1922; London Symphony, 1905–13.

GUSTAV MAHLER, AUSTRO-HUNGARIAN
Hungarian Opera, Budapest, 1888–91; Hamburg Opera, 1891–97; Vienna Opera, 1897–1907; Vienna Philharmonic, 1898–1901; Metropolitan Opera, New York, 1908–9; New York Philharmonic, 1909–11. Premiered eight of his own symphonies.

ARTURO TOSCANINI, ITALIAN
La Scala Opera, Milan, 1898–1908 and 1921–29; Metropolitan Opera, New York, 1908–15; New York Philharmonic, 1920–26; NBC Symphony, 1937–54. Premiered Puccini's *Turandot*.

BRUNO WALTER, GERMAN
Munich Opera, 1911–22; Berlin Opera, 1925–29; Leipzig Gewandhaus, 1929–33; Vienna Opera, 1936–38; New York Philharmonic, 1947–49. Premiered Mahler's Ninth Symphony and *Das Lied von der Erde*.

SIR THOMAS BEECHAM, BRITISH
Founder/Conductor, Beecham Symphony Orchestra, 1909–12; London Philharmonic, 1932–39; Royal Philharmonic, 1946–61. Premiered major works of Delius.

OTTO KLEMPERER, AUSTRO-HUNGARIAN
Operas in Prague, Hamburg, Strasbourg, Cologne, Wiesbaden, Berlin 1908–31; Los Angeles Philharmonic, 1933–39; Budapest Opera 1947–50; Philharmonia Orchestra, London, 1951–72.

WILHELM FURTWANGLER, GERMAN
Mannheim Opera, 1915–20; Leipzig Gewandhaus, 1922–28; Berlin Philharmonic, 1922–45 and 1952–54.

ERICH KLEIBER, GERMAN
Berlin State Opera, 1923–34; New York Philharmonic, 1930–2; Teatro Colon, Buenos Aires, 1939–48; Havana Philharmonic, 1943–48; Covent Garden, 1950–3; East Berlin Opera, 1951–55. Premiered Berg's *Wozzeck*. Kleiber's son, Carlos, is among the world's foremost conducting talents.

SIR GEORG SOLTI, HUNGARIAN
Munich Opera, 1946–52; Frankfurt Opera, 1952–61; Covent Garden Opera, 1961–71; London Philharmonic, 1979–83; Chicago Symphony, 1969–91.

CARLO MARIA GIULINI, ITALIAN
La Scala, Milan, 1953–56; Vienna Symphony, 1973–78; Los Angeles Philharmonic, 1978–84.

SIR COLIN DAVIS, BRITISH
Sadler's Wells Opera, 1961–65; BBC Symphony, 1967–71; Covent Garden Opera, 1971–86; Bavarian Radio Symphony, 1987–91; London Symphony, 1995–.

NIKOLAUS HARNONCOURT, GERMAN
Founder/Director, Concentus Musicus Wien, 1953; Guest, Chamber Orchestra of Europe; Vienna Philharmonic; Concertgebouw, Amsterdam etc.

FRANS BRUGGEN, DUTCH
Founder/Conductor, Orchestra of the Eighteenth Century 1981; Stavanger Symphony, Norway from 1991.

DANIEL BARENBOIM, ISRAELI
Orchestre de Paris, 1975–89; Bastille Opera, Paris 1987-89; Chicago Symphony, 1991–.

SIR SIMON RATTLE, BRITISH
City of Birmingham Symphony, 1980–98.

In his old age in the 1960s, Otto Klemperer was greatly praised for his holding back of basic *tempi*. Klemperer's final, monumental recordings of Beethoven remain a yardstick for many. Others warm to Toscanini, Furtwängler or lusher textures under Herbert von Karajan. Understandably, many would opt for the warm yet lean approach to Beethoven from Erich Kleiber.

Contemporary conductors of the core classical repertoire have been influenced by the movement towards authenticity. The doyens of this approach, Nikolaus Harnoncourt and Frans Brüggen, remain influenced by the time-honoured aural traditions. Meanwhile, mainstream, senior conductors like Carlo Maria Giulini and Sir Colin Davis have followed the visionary path taken by Furtwängler, while Sir Georg Solti remains more literal, after the style of Toscanini. Of younger maestros, Daniel Barenboim is certainly a visionary, while Sir Simon Rattle seems to combine authenticity with elements of both traditional styles. And, perhaps, that can be seen as the truest interpretative approach for our age. B

the Authentic Revival

WHY, IT IS OFTEN asked, did 18th-century composers feel the need, and were able, to produce such prodigious quantities of new music? Instrumental works were published by the half-dozen and the dozen, opera composers were despised if they produced less than two major works per year, and whole cycles of cantatas were written every year for special dates in the calendar.

The reason for this prodigious output was that audiences constantly demanded the 'new'. Today's was acceptable, last week's tolerable; last year's already gathering dust in the basement. Composers kept up with the demand simply because they had to; if they failed, there were plenty of others seeking secure court appointments, ready to take their place.

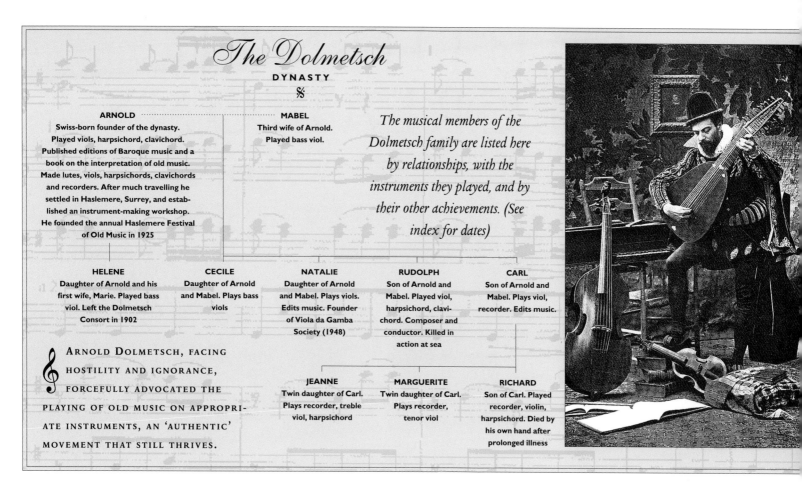

The Dolmetsch
DYNASTY
℀

ARNOLD
Swiss-born founder of the dynasty. Played viols, harpsichord, clavichord. Published editions of Baroque music and a book on the interpretation of old music. Made lutes, viols, harpsichords, clavichords and recorders. After much travelling he settled in Haslemere, Surrey, and established an instrument-making workshop. He founded the annual Haslemere Festival of Old Music in 1925

MABEL
Third wife of Arnold. Played bass viol.

The musical members of the Dolmetsch family are listed here by relationships, with the instruments they played, and by their other achievements. (See index for dates)

HELENE
Daughter of Arnold and his first wife, Marie. Played bass viol. Left the Dolmetsch Consort in 1902

CECILE
Daughter of Arnold and Mabel. Plays bass viols

NATALIE
Daughter of Arnold and Mabel. Plays viols. Edits music. Founder of Viola da Gamba Society (1948)

RUDOLPH
Son of Arnold and Mabel. Played viol, harpsichord, clavichord. Composer and conductor. Killed in action at sea

CARL
Son of Arnold and Mabel. Plays viol, recorder. Edits music.

𝄞 ARNOLD DOLMETSCH, FACING HOSTILITY AND IGNORANCE, FORCEFULLY ADVOCATED THE PLAYING OF OLD MUSIC ON APPROPRIATE INSTRUMENTS, AN 'AUTHENTIC' MOVEMENT THAT STILL THRIVES.

JEANNE
Twin daughter of Carl. Plays recorder, treble viol, harpsichord

MARGUERITE
Twin daughter of Carl. Plays recorder, tenor viol

RICHARD
Son of Carl. Played recorder, violin, harpsichord. Died by his own hand after prolonged illness

FORTUNATELY, NOT EVERYONE felt the same. Some saw value in preserving old music. The first to do so was a group of professionals and amateurs who met in London from 1726 "to restore ancient church music". This group was at first allied to the Academy of Ancient Music, founded somewhere between 1710 and 1732. The aim of both organizations was resurrection, not re-creation.

Johann Sebastian Bach was indirectly responsible for the next wave of interest in old music. His *St Matthew Passion* was considered unperformable in 1819. Ten years later the 20-year-old Mendelssohn was studying the score and forming a determination to change this opinion. But who would be interested in a huge unknown choral work by a long-dead organist? Certainly, the Berlin Singakademie, founded in 1791 to perform old music, had shown interest, but it took the drive and enthusiasm of young Mendelssohn to galvanize them into bringing the *St Matthew Passion* to performance, in 1829.

Again, the aim was to resurrect the music, not to re-create a performance Bach would have recognized. In 1829, the Romantic period was well underway and performances of any music had to suit the modern taste. For all his skill, Mendelssohn's performance exhibited Romantic excesses that would have dumbfounded Bach. Nevertheless, it excited a popular interest in the composer which has not abated and which gradually widened to embrace old music in general. Germany's re-discovery of Bach spread to England where other societies had sprung up to advance 'antient' music in the wake of the Academy of Ancient Music. William Sterndale Bennett, himself a famous composer, founded the Bach Society in London in 1849, thereby ensuring that Bach's music would never again be as neglected as it was during the composer's lifetime.

The 'authentic' performance of old music made slow headway against the strong tide of gigantism and homogenized textures in vogue during the late 19th century, and such performances as there were had to be made under the generally unfavourable conditions then prevailing. Bach's and Handel's choral music was grossly inflated by the gargantuan forces that were the order of the day. Even Mozart had stooped to 'improve' Handel's *Acis and Galatea*, *Messiah* and *Alexander's Feast* by adding or revising instrumental parts, but the Victorians went much further. England's burgeoning choral societies needed to be balanced by large orchestral forces: tripling or quadrupling woodwind and brass, adding instruments (clarinets, trombones, tubas, etc.) that were not envisaged by the composers, and considerably increasing the number of strings. Consequently, Bach's and Handel's music became unrecognizable and in many cases impossibly stodgy. One man spoke out against this deplorable tendency: Arnold Dolmetsch. Futhermore, he said that the Romantic style had no place in the performance of early music.

AUTHENTIC RECREATIONS

ANOTHER GREAT CHAMPION of authentic instruments was the Polish-born virtuoso harpsichordist Wanda Landowska. In her position as a distinguished artist and noted authority on old keyboard music, she wielded considerable influence at a time when the pianoforte was regarded as the supreme keyboard instrument. Manuel de Falla and Francis Poulenc were among those who wrote works for her. Ripples of her remarkable advocacy endure still. Few have argued the case for authentic instruments better:

"To understand and interpret old music we must know thoroughly how to use the instruments of the period. How often a piece which has sounded hitherto grey and monotonous becomes clear and full of point when it is played on the instrument for which it was written. We get back again not only the appropriate colour but the right tempo and true character – in fact, its whole construction."

A counter argument runs as follows: if Bach were alive today he would be writing for modern instruments. The point is that he is not alive, and that living composers are writing perfectly well for modern instruments. Even if it were possible, no one would suggest playing their avant-garde works on sackbuts and spinet.

Landowska was among the first to encourage instrument makers like Dolmetsch to do their research and build instruments according to old principles and designs and with the materials that would have been available at the time. Plastic, for example, never had a place in the Dolmetsch workshop.

To perform old music one needs to be able to

locate and purchase instruments of the approximate date of the works to be played. Ideally, these instruments have to be in perfect working order. Some wind instruments have survived in playing condition, but time, misuse, careless storage and other factors have combined to reduce most to a state where they have to be restored by a specialist or, all too often, discarded altogether. In some cases, however, even instruments that can not be played or restored still provide valuable information about materials and construction methods. What wood was used? How was it worked? What kind of glue or cement was required to best join the parts? Was any filling agent used and, if so, did it affect the sound? How were brass instruments shaped?

WANDA LANDOWSKA. HER DETERMINATION TO REINSTATE THE HARPSICHORD AS THE PROPER INSTRUMENT FOR EARLY KEYBOARD MUSIC LED TO ITS TOTAL ACCEPTANCE TODAY.

What were woodwind reeds made of? What kind of cotton, string, cord or other medium was used to bind together the dividing parts of wind instruments and to make them airtight? How were the skins of drums prepared and what kind of cord or rope was used in tensioning?

Many of these questions were answered by painstaking experimentation and research in the Dolmetsch workshop and by other instrument makers subsequently, but decades later, questions remain. It has been suggested only recently that

Old and New Instruments
COMPARED
※

FLUTE The pre-Boehm flute had a softer, more seductive tone than the modern instrument, more akin to a recorder's.

OBOE Compared with a modern oboe, 18th-century models had a more rustic, bell-like quality, with a richer low register. They were also louder but less smooth because of the short-scrape reeds which strengthened the tone.

CLARINET Before Mozart, clarinets were strident and close in tone to the trumpet if played loudly. Modern clarinets in A and B flat have a smooth, fluent quality, quite different from the early instruments pitched in C, D and G.

BASSOON The tone of the Baroque bassoon was somewhat muffled, a characteristic that would remain until the instrument's refinement in the 19th century.

HORN Before various devices such as hand-stopping and valves made the horn more tonally flexible, its narrow bore gave a raw sound; French hunting horns, for example, possessed a rasping quality even in a low pitch such as *C basso*. So limited were the notes available in the lower part of the harmonic series that composers sought the increased number available higher up, which helped to make the horn particularly prominent when crooked in *G, A, B flat* and *C alto*. A modern valve horn has a reliable range throughout the keys.

TRUMPET The early unvalved trumpet tended to sound brighter and clearer than its modern counterpart but shared the horn's limitations.

TROMBONE Of all the instruments, the trombone's tone has changed least over the years. Early narrow-bore instruments sounded slightly more 'open'.

TIMPANI Tight animal skins and harder sticks gave the early timpani a much sharper, more definite pitch than is achievable with today's plastic skins.

VIOLIN A shorter neck, gut strings and slacker bow hairs contribute to the early violin's soft tone, relatively weak compared with recent powerful instruments.

VIOLA Like the violin, the viola has become stronger in tone, the better to play more demanding roles.

CELLO Gut strings and a different bowing technique made the early cello less powerful and lighter-toned than the modern instrument.

DOUBLE BASS Shaped like a viol, the modern double bass shows its heritage. Apart from an overall strengthening of tone, the sound has not greatly changed. The once-common C string has largely disappeared.

---

it was the cement filler used by Stradivari that gave his violins their distinctive tonal beauty. A previous theory concerned the property of the water in the Cremona area which, it was argued, had acted favourably upon the wood from which the violins were made. The truth might yet turn out to be something entirely different, or it might never become known. With their computers, vast experience and up-to-date working techniques, modern violin makers produce excellent instruments, but none that can match the magical tone of a 300-year-old Stradivari. 𝄡

THE DOLMETSCH WORKSHOP, FOUNDED IN HASLEMERE IN 1920 AND STILL PRODUCING ACCURATE REPLICAS OF PERIOD INSTRUMENTS.

𝄞 CONTINUO

This is the subject of much discussion and misunderstanding, even in 'authentic' circles. The continuo (properly 'basso continuo') is a musical device introduced around 1600. Its role changed a century or so later (although there is much overlap), and in its modified form it extended into Beethoven's era and beyond. Literally, 'basso continuo' means that a bass instrument, or instruments, should provide continuity. This would entail filling in vertical harmonies implied but not actually written out by a composer in a musical score; or, in early song, providing continuity between words, phrases and verses. This latter,

so-called horizontal form may be thought of as the informal strumming of a lute player or guitarist as he sings a song or narrates a poetic story, thus providing a connecting thread between words. Such an artist would doubtless use his instrument to stress a mood of a song and perhaps give imitative effects: rainfall, birdsong, weeping, a horseride and so on.

Elaborate horizontal continuo of this kind was suitable for domestic and recital purposes, but not in church where the rules were stricter. Viadana's vocal works, *Cento concerti ecclesiastici* (1602) required a continuous organ line to play

the lowest note of the harmony and harmonies above it, whether the singers were singing or pausing, but extemporization was forbidden. The harmonic sense of the music must not be violated, lest the singers become disorientated. A few years before the appearance of Viadana's works, the continuo principle was used in accompanied

𝄞 ROY GOODMAN AND THE HANOVER BAND. THIS METHOD OF CONDUCTING FROM THE HARPSICHORD, AND THE ORCHESTRAL LAYOUT, FAITHFULLY REPLICATE 18TH-CENTURY PRACTICE.

recitatives in early opera and oratorio. Just before the actor/singer embarked on his recitative, the continuo's decisive chord would give the signal to begin and also the note he should attain. This use lasted until at least Rossini's day, in the latter half of the 19th century.

Usually it was left to the continuo player to supply what was necessary to ensure good ensemble and to keep the musicians in tune. In a score, his role was often indicated by a series of numbers to show the degrees of the scale required to create the correct harmonies (hence 'figured bass', an alternative name for continuo), but he was given some freedom as to what he actually played: ornaments, echoing phrases, roulades, and so on, to fill in where he considered it right and proper to do so. This is where the skill of the expert continuo player came into play, since it is easy to over-elaborate and draw unwarranted attention to the continuo part. Every player developed his own style despite many scholarly treatises laying down ground rules. Some players would merely repeat every bass note in the score (a boring procedure too often encountered in today's 'authentic' performances), others would make far too much of it and clog up the textures with every imaginable ornamental device, and even a few new melodies or counter-subjects of their own. The best players would play discreetly, adding chords at decisive moments, providing rapid connective tissue against long notes in the melody, spurring along the rhythm if it should slacken, and exercising severe restraint in delicate Adagios (the harpsichordist, for example, might use the lute stop) while marking the rhythm in dance-like Andantes.

Early in the 18th century, continuo was also employed in chamber works. In this role it would contribute more generously than was considered proper in orchestral music and, sometimes, as in a flute sonata, would include harpsichord, cello, double bass and, perhaps, a lute in order to give a strong bass balance against the high solo voice.

The 1740s saw a move to abolish continuo. The concerto and the new symphony were cur-

SIENA CATHEDRAL. SUCH AN INTERIOR CAN PROVIDE A THRILLING RESONANT EFFECT FOR CONTINUO INSTRUMENTS.

rently for small forces: a four-part string ensemble (plus soloist), the string ensemble often lacking viola. Continuo helped to fill in the gap between violin and cello parts. In Mannheim, Johann Stamitz was leading an expert orchestra which grew to include violas as well as woodwind and brass, and sometimes timpani. These extra voices provided the in-filling. Elsewhere, despite a parallel increase in size, orchestras continued to employ continuo, partly because of habit, partly because composers wrote their music expecting it to be present. Until the 1770s they regarded orchestral music as unthinkable without continuo. By about 1800, however, three things had conspired to make the continuo superfluous: larger orchestras which left no harmonic gaps, fully written-out keyboard parts in chamber music, and the increasing use of non-playing conductors to maintain ensemble discipline; see Spohr's experience, page 168. Continuo survived in some areas for years, but its eventual redundancy was assured.

Continuo INSTRUMENTS

It is usually advisable to employ more than one of the following, in almost any permutation, to provide a firm foundation to the upper parts, although discretion is required in light-textured music.

BASSOON, in orchestra and opera; also in chamber works and concertos where the upper voices are woodwind.

CELLO, playing the same notes as the harpsichord's lowest stave, and often seated behind the harpsichord and reading over his or her shoulder.

DOUBLE BASS, which increasingly assumed the role of the violone (below) from about 1740.

GUITAR, interchangeable with lute, depending upon availability.

HARPSICHORD, in most contexts and inescapably in orchestras up to c. 1770, and providing harmonic accompaniment to recitative passages in opera to c. 1850.

LUTE (archlute, theorbo, chitarrone, etc) in most contexts before c. 1730, particularly in expressive slow movements where its tone, softer than a harpsichord's, contributed to the effect.

ORGAN, in sacred music; also in secular works before c. 1730.

REGAL, a small chamber organ used in intimate music-making.

TROMBONE, in church music and also in some secular situations up to c. 1700.

VIOLONE, as for cello and to give extra strength to the bass line.

AUTHENTIC & RECORDINGS

THE DOLMETSCH FAMILY made the first attempt to resurrect the actual sounds of old music in a series of interesting recordings on old, reconditioned and specially-built period instruments. Their viols and lutes, playing music by unknowns such as Marin Marais, sounded alien to ears brought up on music of the 1920s and 1930s; furthermore, some performances were a little shaky. Other groups took up the idea but most were short-lived due to lack of public interest. One of the contentions in Arnold Dolmetsch's writings was that dotted rhythms in Baroque music should be double-dotted. This enlivens the rhythm and has since been adopted by most 'authentic' artists.

In 1933 an Australian, Louise Dyer, opened a publishing house in Paris devoted to rare, old music, Éditions de l'Oiseau-Lyre. (Later the firm moved to London, where it continues to make recordings.) The company's recordings of early music were made by groups playing on modern instruments. Their example of abandoning old instruments was, with very few exceptions, followed for the next 30 years by other organizations keen to explore old music. Various 'histo-ries of music' appeared in both book and recorded form. Deutsche Grammophon's Archiv label, launched in 1952, endeavoured to explore this history in great depth. The musicians who contributed to this enterprise were expert in the performance of old music, but they could not make up for the absence of genuine old instruments.

THE ENGLISH CONCERT, FOUNDED TO RECREATE THE PERFORMING TRADITIONS OF 18TH-CENTURY ORCHESTRAL MUSIC.

PHILIP PICKETT AND THE NEW LONDON CONSORT GIVE AUTHENTIC PERFORMANCES OF MUSIC FROM THE MIDDLE AGES TO THE EARLY 18TH CENTURY.

A fresh attempt to re-create the real sound of period performance was made in about 1960 by the Telemann Society. They recorded Handel's *Royal Fireworks Music* on valveless trumpets and horns, short-scrape reed oboes, bassoons, serpent and drums, all drawn from the Casadesus Collection, Boston, Massachusetts. The one drawback of this valiant effort was the lack of rehearsal evident in the result. Later, Collegium Aureum began performing on old instruments, but with modern techniques of bowing and *vibrato*.

Everything seemed to come together with the formation in 1970 of the Academy of Ancient Music. There were problems at first due to the players' unfamiliarity with their instruments, but the sound of lean-toned violins, played with virtually no *vibrato* so that stopped strings gave the same ringing tone as open ones, the rustic sound of woodwind, valveless trumpets and horns making their full noble impact, and period timpani played with hard sticks, was a revelation to most listeners. Since then many period groups have appeared, the concentration of effort being centred on England and Germany. France (with Les Musiciens du Louvre under Marc Minkowski) and the United States (Handel and Haydn Society with Christopher Hogwood) are set to catch up. 𝄢

A CHRONOLOGY OF
Modern Period Groups
※

1953 ～ VIENNA CONCENTUS MUSICUS
Founded by Nikolaus Harnoncourt to perform on authentic instruments. After four years of research, they gave their first concerts (1957), and recorded Bach's 'Brandenburg' Concertos on original instruments for the first time. Their repertoire extends back to Monteverdi. With the Leonhardt Consort, the VCM recorded all of Bach's cantatas. Harnoncourt, not limited to pure 'authenticity', also conducts, among others, the Chamber Orchestra of Europe and the Royal Concertgebouw, Amsterdam.

1955 ～ TELEMANN SOCIETY
Founded in New York by Richard Schultz to research and perform 17th- and 18th-century music on original instruments.

1955 ～ LEONHARDT CONSORT
Founded by Dutch harpsichordist Gustav Leonhardt. See Vienna Concentus Musicus.

1964 ～ COLLEGIUM AUREUM
A German group founded by the leader Franzjosef Maier to perform on old instruments but in modern style. In 1976, made the first recording of a Beethoven symphony on original instruments (No. 3, 'Eroica').

1970 ～ ACADEMY OF ANCIENT MUSIC
Named after the early 18th-century organization (see page 173); it was founded in London by harpsichordist Christopher Hogwood. Performs choral, chamber and orchestral music, has recorded all Mozart's and Beethoven's symphonies, and plans to do the same for Haydn.

1973 ～ ENGLISH CONCERT
Formed in London by harpsichordist Trevor Pinnock as a rival organization to the AAM, covering a similar field but often achieving different results.

1973 ～ L'ESTRO ARMONICO
Founded in London by Derek Solomons to promote Vivaldi (from whose Op. 3 Concertos it took its name). Since 1980 the orchestra has performed entirely on authentic instruments.

1978 ～ LONDON CLASSICAL PLAYERS
Formed by Roger Norrington. Believing 'authenticity' should not be restricted, the LCP repertoire extends from Haydn to Brahms in both orchestral and choral fields.

1980 ～ HANOVER BAND
Takes its name from the Royal House of Hanover, Britain's monarchs between 1714 and 1830, which is the period of the Band's focus. Caroline Brown founded the orchestra; violinist and harpsichordist Roy Goodman is its present leader. It has also been led by Anthony Halstead and Monica Huggett. Its complete Haydn symphony series was abandoned half-way through.

1980 ～ MUSICA ANTIQUA KOLN
Formed by Reinhard Goebel, who concentrates on music of the Bach period.

1985 ～ CONCERTO KOLN
Plays unconducted as a true chamber-orchestral group concentrating on rare Baroque and Classical works, many of which have been recorded.

1986 ～ ORCHESTRA OF THE AGE OF ENLIGHTENMENT
Despite its name, its repertoire extends from Baroque (eg, Bach; Rameau) to early Romantic (eg, Crusell; Mendelssohn). There is no permanent conductor; guests have included Sigiswald Kuijken, Gustav Leonhardt and Sir Charles Mackerras.

1988 ～ LA STAGIONE
An authentic group formed in Frankfurt from members of the Camerata Köln to focus on Baroque operas and oratorios. Also plays instrumental works.

1990 ～ CONCERTO COPENHAGEN
At the time of writing Denmark's only period group. Formed by Andrew Manze to play rare orchestral and choral works, it is supported by the Danish Music Council.

1991 ～ TAFELMUSIK
Takes its name from Telemann's three collections of orchestral and instrumental works (1733). Formed in Ontario, Canada. Director: Jeanne Lamon, violin; conductor: Bruno Weil.

AUTHENTICITY IN PRACTICE

allegro in common time overlooks the fact that no two *allegros* are the same. Slow movements should never drag: most *andantes* are akin to dances. *Vivace*, taken today to mean somewhat faster than *allegro*, meant a tempo akin to *moderato* in the 18th century. All repeats should be observed. Phrasing should be carefully obeyed: if four quavers are tied in pairs they should not be played as if tied in four; and if violins phrase in one way, echoing oboes should, it goes without saying, adopt the same phrasing.

Woodwind should be allowed clear tonal differentiation between instruments. Trumpets and horns, once played respectively by soldiers and huntsmen, should sound out strongly. Timpani should be heard clearly as two (or more) distinct tones, with firm and definite voices. Continuo should be used according to historical practice. Ornamentation, sometimes carelessly notated by composers, should be interpreted according to the conventions of the time, and may be added judiciously at points appropriate to historical authenticity.

Many of the above rules apply equally to instruments and voices. This is frequently overlooked even by specialists in period singing. Few sounds are more disruptive in a carefully prepared period performance than the entry of a vocal soloist singing with heavy 19th-century operatic *vibrato*. 𝄡

℘ **AUGSBURG MUSICIANS OF C. 1520; FROM LEFT TO RIGHT: BOWED LUTE, PLUCKED LUTE, SHAWMS, SACKBUT, SHAWM, BAGPIPES AND SNARE DRUM.**

HAVING CLEANSED the scores to discover what the composer wrote, the authenticist has to research performing practices, conventions and unwritten rules to find out what the composer heard. Instruments have to be assembled and tuned, and musicians schooled in the ways of old. Rehearsals must remove any remaining bad habits of performance and solve problems of intonation between one instrument and another. Seating arrangements must be authentic yet ensure that the audience is not presented with unbalanced sound; and in a recording session the microphones have to be positioned to reflect this authentic seating in the listener's sitting room.

Dolmetsch and others have given valuable clues as to how old music should sound. J. J. Quantz, Frederick the Great's flautist, Bach's son Carl Philipp Emanuel, and Mozart's father Leopold left textbooks on performance conventions of their own day, and there are other useful sources concerning authentic playing. A consensus of these sources should ensure performances have the following qualities:

Vibrato should be used only on long notes where expressive playing is called for. Phrasing should be light and lively. Rhythms should be springy in fast movements and appropriate to the mood of slow ones. *Tempi* should suit the character of the music: a similar pace chosen for every

Orchestral Layout

AUTHENTIC VERSUS TRADITIONAL

⁂

A typical 'authentic' layout of about 1790

In this layout all the players can see the leader seated at the harpsichord. It is probable that a second bassoonist and a cellist would be seated to the side of the harpsichordist and reading over his shoulder. These would be relics from earlier continuo practice. The harpsichordist's task at this date would be to keep the ensemble together, since the harmonic gaps that an earlier continuo would have been expected to fill are now being filled by composers. Therefore, the lid was probably down. In many situations the harpsichordist and first violinist would share responsibility for orchestral discipline in performance. Divided violins were able to exploit the antiphonal effects of the score. Trumpets and timpani, raised high at the back, would have been heard clearly throughout the auditorium.

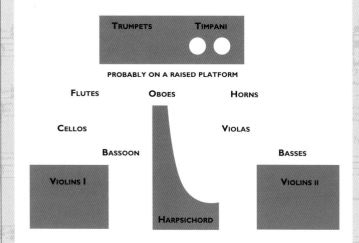

A typical 19th and early 20th century layout for a work of c.1790

With this layout, horns, trumpets, timpani and woodwind are hidden from view and their voices are therefore muffled by the army of strings in front of them. Violins, all grouped to the conductor's left so that their fingerboards face the audience (thereby further maximizing their sound at the additional expense of the wind), are unable to convey the antiphonal interplay the composer intended. The conductor on his rostrum has his back to the audience. The visual appeal of the conductor's arm movements and the actions of the violins and double basses detract from the rest of the orchestra, for it is well-known that the sight of an instrument being played intensifies the sound for most people – and the wind cannot be seen. All is geared in favour of the string sound which, being so rich from over 60 players, outbalances that from the six woodwind and 4–6 brass.

In this situation, too, the conductor would instruct the timpanist to 'keep it down'. With the string sound predominating, the audience would register only half of what the composer had written, and that half would be bloated.

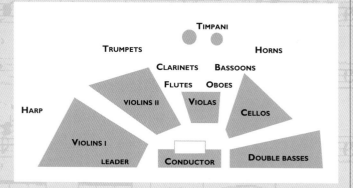

CHAPTER 8

Non-Western and Obsolete Instruments

We saw in the Introduction how instruments were discovered accidentally and haphazardly. Some developed rapidly and their use spread widely among primitive peoples; others evolved slowly as if awaiting later technological developments, new materials and advanced workmanship. The main beneficiary of the sophisticated mechanical devices that have made advances in instrument-making possible has been Western music, though some other cultures have pursued their own developments to often extraordinarily elaborate lengths. Consider, for instance, the complicated stringed instruments of India compared with the basic examples of Tibet.

In less-developed cultures, musical instruments have evolved only modestly from basic designs thousands of years old. They did not need to change: they fulfilled the requirements asked of them, and more pressing needs were found for the often meagre resources available to early man; changing perfectly adequate instruments just for the sake of it was not a priority. Development was not important; diversity was.

'Blow', 'scrape', 'pluck' and 'bang', the four original methods of producing sound from instruments, continue to hold good, but designs are constantly changing in literally hundreds of ways. While a drum, for instance, still retains the original components of membrane and resonating body, different designs have multiplied so vastly that their number is no longer quantifiable. And what applies to 'bang' applies equally to 'blow', 'scrape' and 'pluck'. Only a small fraction of the different types that belong in each of these categories can be dealt with here, but that fraction is large enough, one hopes, to indicate the amazing diversity of instruments to be found in Africa, the Middle East, the Orient and Asia.

Also included here are some ancient instruments that have been obsolete for so long that, by existing in a different era, they have become just as 'foreign' to us as those instruments from non-Western cultures. This seems doubly appropriate if one considers that religious considerations of great antiquity often play a more fundamental role in non-Western than in Western musical activity. As Longfellow wrote:

"These are ancient ethnic revels/of a faith long since forsaken."

The standard Western grouping into woodwind, brass, strings and percussion cannot cope with every possible type of instrument, so in this section of the book we have used less formal divisions. That said, even 'blow', 'scrape', 'pluck' and 'bang' cannot account for every example! We will begin this survey by looking at blown instruments.

Although dates are given where known (or surmised from available evidence), it is not possible to attempt a chronology. Musical archaeology has not progressed far enough for even guesses to be advisable in most cases, but it is safe to assume that many of these instruments are older than existing evidence leads us to believe. Alphabetical ordering, then, has been chosen instead of anything more scientific.

PRIMITIVE MAN IMPROVISED HIS INSTRUMENTS FROM WHATEVER MATERIALS WERE TO HAND. BY DRILLING A MOUTH HOLE IN A DISCARDED ANIMAL HORN A USEFUL SIGNALLING INSTRUMENT WAS CREATED (FAR LEFT). THE HUNTER'S BOW (TOP) WOULD PRODUCE A NATURAL 'TWANG' WHICH WAS AMPLIFIED WHEN A GOURD WAS ATTACHED TO THE WILLOW WOOD. MODIFIED GOURDS (MIDDLE) WERE USED AS DRUMS AND RATTLES. A FEW STRIPS OF THIN METAL FASTENED TO A SUPPORTING BOARD WILL VIBRATE WHEN DEPRESSED AND RELEASED BY FINGERS AND THUMBS. THIS IS THE 'THUMB PIANO' (LEFT).

A NOTE ON
Spelling
℅

Ethnic instruments often betray the sounds they make in their names, for it is natural, not only in primitive societies, to identify objects by their characteristics. Researchers in the field would ask players and makers what their instruments were called and then faithfully copy down a representation of the words they heard. A German researcher would render the English 'V' sound as 'W', for instance, and when the word eventually appeared in a scholarly paper and was translated, the 'W' would be retained.

Moreover, had the researcher asked the same question of a player of a similar instrument in the next village, he might have been given a different pronunciation, or a different word entirely. All of the following have a bearing upon the problems of naming non-Western instruments –
1, local accents
2, tribal conventions
3, differing uses of similar instruments
4, local modifications to instruments
5, difficulties experienced in obtaining authoritative information from natives
6, vagueness surrounding transliteration.

These problems are compounded when instruments cross language frontiers. (See *davul* in the section on Banged Instruments for an example of how a name may change from country to country, page 218.)

The spellings used are necessarily approximate but it is hoped that, when read together with the descriptions, they are accurate enough to enable reliable identification to be made.

BLOWN INSTRUMENTS

THE PRINCIPLE ADOPTED by the player of a 'blown' instrument is simple: air is forced down a tube. However, unless some way is found of modifying that passage of air, all that will emerge at the far end is air, its sound perhaps slightly changed by the hollowness of the tube. Various means of making that modification have evolved.

AN *ALPHORN* (OR *ALPENHORN*), TYPI-CAL OF THE TYPE USED IN EUROPEAN MOUNTAIN REGIONS FOR SIGNALLING.

In the recorder and flute the air strikes a sharp edge which makes it vibrate, while in other instruments (eg, clarinet and oboe respectively) one or two reeds in the mouthpiece vibrate and impart that vibration to the air. Alternatively, the player's lips create the vibration, as in the trumpet and horn, where specially shaped mouthpieces assist in controlling the vibration.

Once the column of air is set in vibration, a note will be produced. This note may be altered by perforations along the length of the tube which are opened or closed selectively by fingers, or by keys or valves operated by the fingers. The timbre of the note may be changed according to whether the tube is cylindrical or conical. In most cases the air is directed along the tube straight from the mouth; an exception is the bagpipe family, in which a reservoir of air in a bag is introduced into the pipe by pressure, the reservoir being replenished as necessary by the player's breath through another pipe. Another exception is when the air in a flexible reservoir is driven past tuned valves by the pressure of the hands, as in a concertina or bible organ. In these cases the air is replenished through inlet valves. In larger organs, bellows, either manually or mechanically driven, supply the air. Other exceptions will be noted as they arise.

✸ Alphorn

Most famous for its signalling role among the peaks of the Alps, the first reference to an *alphorn* dates from the 15th century, though the instru-

ment is certainly much older, probably prehistoric. A hollow tree trunk once provided the basic material, and wood remains its source of construction. The player stands at one end, the instrument stretching away in front of him, its upturned far end resting on the ground or on a stand. The sound, resembling that of a cow in agony, echoes over great distances. Some alphorns are so long that the time it takes for the sound to emerge can be measured. Peter Wutherich, a resident of Idaho, built an *alphorn* in 1984. It is 24m (78.7 feet) long; its sound travels that distance in 73.01 milliseconds.

✸ Anata

Two possibilities, both Peruvian. The *anata* is a primitive wooden flute with a mouthpiece; the name also refers to a species of panpipe with half-a-dozen canes.

✸ Aulos

This double-reed instrument may still be heard in Mediterranean folk gatherings, its piercing tone dominating the ensemble. It dates from the ancient Greeks. The Romans called it *tibia*. It is no accident that their word for the instrument means both 'flute' and 'shin-bone' – the latter often provided the material for the former. The lung pressure

A WOODEN FLUTE OF PERU, THE *ANATA*, EMBELLISHED WITH GOLD ORNAMENTATION.

COMPONENTS OF THE
Bagpipe
𝄋

THE BAG: The skin of a lamb or goat, sealed airtight. This acts as an air reservoir. The player squeezes the bag (under the arm, between the knees, between arm and chest, etc) to feed a continuous supply of air to the chanter and drones.

THE BLOWPIPE/BELLOWS: The blowpipe is a reeded, sometimes double-reeded, pipe through which the player blows air into the bag via a non-return valve. Some designs use a bellows depressed by hand or knees to supply the air.

THE CHANTER: A pipe with fingerholes (and, very occasionally, keys) which the player uses to produce the melody. Some designs have a double chanter, either in one block or separately: the second may be either a second melody pipe or a drone. Chanters usually terminate in a small bell, but animal horns of various sizes have been encountered.

THE DRONES: Reed pipes exiting the bag and usually sounding continuously while the instrument is being played. Three drones are common, two and one less so. Some designs dispense with a drone altogether, in which case the instrument is little more than a reed pipe with a bag which provides a continuous flow of air .

required to make the aulos sound is phenomenal; players once bandaged their cheeks to prevent them from splitting. Perhaps to allow more air to escape, two- and three-pipe *auloi* developed, affording the melody pipe a drone accompaniment. Greek virtuoso *aulos* players were extravagantly feted as they travelled from town to town bedecked in jewels and clothes of amazing colours and quality. Crowds gathered to hear them, and the players would, for a handsome fee, condescend to give lessons to the better-off.

𝄋 *Bagpipe*

The bagpipe was invented, probably by a shepherd with spare animal skins and bones to hand, somewhere in the East, c. 5000 BC. Reports that it arose in China cannot be substantiated. An area covering India and extending westwards to Syria is likely, the most probable location being Sumeria, where at this time many basic devices, including wheeled vehicles and the plough, were invented.

AN ADAPTATION OF THE ANCIENT BAGPIPE-MAKER'S ART: A SCOTTISH BAGPIPE WITH MOUTHPIECE, CHANTER AND THREE DRONES.

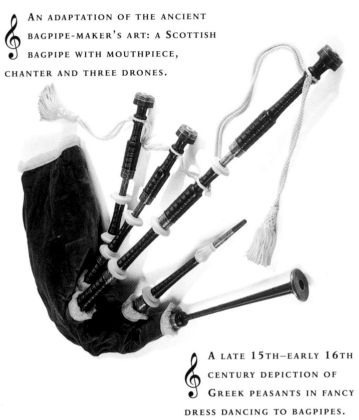

A LATE 15TH–EARLY 16TH CENTURY DEPICTION OF GREEK PEASANTS IN FANCY DRESS DANCING TO BAGPIPES.

In the early Christian era the bagpipe spread eastwards as a folk instrument, into India and west and north into eastern Europe. By the Middle Ages it was well established throughout this area and even into western parts of Europe.

European courts accepted the bagpipe as a 'respectable' instrument in the 17th century, at the same time as countless different designs of bagpipe were evolving in folk circles. By the 18th century, though, the bagpipe was in decline everywhere except in the Balkans and the extreme west and north of Europe.

The Americas, Australia, Africa and the East beyond India have no traceable bagpipe culture apart from local groups of enthusiasts. Even in India, if bagpipes are heard today they have usually been made to Scottish designs.

Bagpipes

COUNTRY BY COUNTRY

※

In the following geographical plan we begin in the Middle East, as did the bagpipe, and move gradually westwards. The similarities in names reveal interesting connections between instruments, and suggest lines of evolution not otherwise obvious. All these bagpipes are mouth-blown, except where bellows are mentioned.

IRAQ: *zummara bi-soan*, a short blowpipe with a large goatskin bag, two parallel chanters in a block with separate bells, but no drones.

PAKISTAN: *bin*, a gourd bag, two parallel pipes, one a chanter, the other a drone, played by snake-charmers. *Mashq*, a simple blowpipe-to-bag-to-chanter and a single drone. Similar instruments are found in northern India (*moshug*) and Hindustan (*masak*).

BELORUSSIA: *duda*, various simple forms of the Czech *dudy*.

ROMANIA: *cimpoi*, similar to the Hungarian *duda* but made in five different designs.

BULGARIA: *gaida* or *gayda*, a generic term for 'bagpipe', found in Macedonia, the former Yugoslavia and Greece, where the commonest bagpipe (*tsambouna*) has a single chanter and single drone. *Dzhura*, a high-pitched instrument in eastern Bulgaria; its low-pitched counterpart is called *kaba*.

SLOVAKIA: *gajdy* and *gajde*, a small version of the Bohemian *dudy*.

SERBIA AND FORMER YUGOSLAVIA: *gajde*, a bellows-blown low-pitched bagpipe with an oval chanter containing two channels. There is a large, upturned wooden bell. The Albanian *gajde* is similar. *Dude*, bellows- or mouth-blown, with a triple chanter.

POLAND: the *koza*, distinct from the Ukrainian *koza*, has a three-channel chanter, one being a drone, and two additional drones. The chanter has no bell. *Koziot*, like the Czech *dudy*, was originally mouth-blown when introduced in the 14th century but now has bellows. There is a single chanter and a single drone. The *koziot* is often played at wedding ceremonies.

GREECE: *askaulos*, an ancient Greek generic name for the bagpipe. Today it is called *zampouna* (*tsambouna* in the Greek islands): a droneless bagpipe whose double chanter terminates in a small, sharply-upturned bell. Far to the west, in the Balearic Islands, Greek influence is felt in the *zampona*, a shepherd pipe in which the two drones can be silenced.

HUNGARY: *duda*, with a double chanter in one rectangular block of wood.

BOHEMIA/CZECHOSLOVAKIA: *dudy*, a bellows-blown but originally (14th century) mouth-blown, instrument with curved chanter and a curved single drone, each terminating in a large bell. The outlet to the chanter may be carved in the shape of a goat's head. Similar instruments are found in Belorussia and, called *hoza*, in the Ukraine, while in Germany *dudy* refers to a small pipe.

GERMANY: *Sachpfîfe, Blâterfife*, are ancient generic terms of today's *Schäferpfeife* ('shepherd pipe') and *Platterspiel* ('bladder-play'), and *Dudelsack* is derived from Balkan names. The *Hümmelchen*, a small pipe, has long since vanished, and the *Bock* is now obsolete. Introduced before 1600, the *Bock* had an elongated chanter that terminated in a large horn curving out at right-angles.

ITALY: in Ancient Rome *tibia* was both shin-bone and flute; *utarius* was a person who carried water, often in an animal skin, and the *tibia utricularis* was the 'flute-skin', or 'pipe-bag'. By the 16th century the name had become *zampogna*, from the Greek, and had come to refer to two different instruments. The first type has two separate chanters and is played mainly by street musicians for dancing. The other is itself two instruments, the second (*piffaro*) being mouth-blown by a separate player. This is the instrument associated with pastoral scenes of the Nativity. *Cornamusa*, a Sicilian name for the *zampogna*. *Piva*, a small bagpipe of northern Italy. *Sordellina*, an elaborate Neapolitan *zampogna* introduced about 1500.

FRANCE: *cornamuse*, a generic name for bagpipe. *Cabrette*, a name for the *cornamuse* in south and central France. It was favoured at court during the 17th and early 18th centuries. *Musette*, a bellows-blown bagpipe in use by the 17th century. *Biniou*, a peasant instrument of Brittany used in conjunction with a bass instrument, the *bombarde*.

FLANDERS: *muse-en-sac*, a bagpipe with one chanter and three drones, familiar from the 14th century to c. 1900.

ENGLAND: Northumbrian small pipes, dating from the late 17th century. An indoor instrument with an intimate sound, like a nasal oboe. It has a unique feature in that the chanter end is blocked to allow *staccato* playing.

SCOTLAND: three distinct types existed. The small-pipe was sometimes bellows-blown; the obsolete lowland pipe was played by a seated player; and the Highland pipe is the elaborately tasselled, tartan-bagged ceremonial instrument familiar today. The last mentioned has one chanter, two tenor drones and a bass drone.

IRELAND: union pipe, bellows-blown, played indoors for dancing or pure entertainment by a seated player. Its name may be derived from Gaelic *uilleann* ('elbow'), since the bellows are activated under the arm. It has been known since at least c. 1600.

WALES: *pibau cod*. No example is known. It was probably mouth-blown and it had a double chanter with two bells separated at the end. Introduced in the 12th century, it fell out of use by the 18th.

SPAIN: *gaita gallega*, a small bagpipe with single chanter and one long drone, found in north-west Spain. The name means 'Galician flute'. *Gaita* is a generic name for folk flute or oboe in the Iberian peninsula. A typical Spanish bagpipe would resemble the Scottish Highland pipe but with one drone.

❧ Bass Horn

Louis Frichot, a French refugee to London from the Revolution of 1789, wisely decided that the serpent needed improvement. When he developed his instrument in the 1790s he called it 'English horn' to acknowledge his debt to his adopted country while causing confusion with the totally unrelated cor anglais. Now referred to, if at all, as 'bass horn', Frichot's instrument is a long copper tube doubled into the shape of a narrow 'V', and with a long crook leading to the mouthpiece. Its tone was best suited to outdoor and military bands, but by about 1835 it had been superseded by the *ophicleide* (see below).

♪ THE ROMAN *CORNU* (LATIN FOR HORN). ITS REPORTED *SOTTO VOCE* TONE SUGGESTS IT WAS USED IN NUMBERS AS A PROCESSIONAL INSTRUMENT.

❧ Black Pudding

With typical forthrightness, British North Country players of the serpent thus described their instruments. The leather covering of the serpent is likely to be dark brown than black in colour, but the overall impression of the instrument suggests the sinuous shape of the 'blood sausage' whose skin is black (see page 192)

❧ Bladder-pipe

Using an animal bladder as an air reserve, the bladder-pipe is a primitive bagpipe, usually with just two pipes emerging, one to the mouth, the other carrying a raucous melody to the outside world.

❧ Buccina

Dating from Roman times, this trumpet possessed a tuning slide and is thus an ancestor of the slide trumpet.

❧ Chacocra

At least 2000 years old, the *chacocra* was a brass trumpet used in Jewish religious ceremonies.

❧ Chalumeau

A French word meaning a bagpipe chanter (sounding pipe) with two reeds. The Nuremberg instrument-maker Denner applied the word to an instrument he was improving about 1700, thinking that it equated with shawm (English), *salmoe* (Italian) and *Schalmei* (German), an ancient instrument probably of Far Eastern origin. At the same time as carrying out these improvements, Denner was working on developing a hybrid instrument, a *chalumeau* plus-recorder. This became the clarinet. The *chalumeau* has a deeper, more throaty sound than the clarinet. The lower range of the clarinet is still called the '*chalumeau* register'.

❧ Clarin

The inhabitants of Chile's Atacamá desert blow this long, straight trumpet like a flute: out at one side. Its primary use appears to be for signalling.

❧ Cornet

A 19th-century brass instrument allied to the trumpet but now restricted mainly to brass and military bands. Not to be confused with cornett.

❧ Cornett

A medieval instrument of wood or ivory with a pure, high tone suitable for church music or open-air serenades. In 1728 Roger North described its voice as eunuch-like. The cornett is usually gracefully curved, with an octagonal cross-section and finger holes; straight versions also existed. The Germans called it *Zink* (= the smallest tine of a stag's antlers), and to the French it was *cornet à bouquin* ('goat cornet').

❧ Cornu

A long brass instrument shaped like a letter 'G', its crossbar extended to rest on the player's shoulder. The *cornu* originated in Tuscany (then Etruria), five centuries before Christ, and the Romans gave it a threatening dragon's mouth bell. The Roman poet Quintus Horatius Flaccus was impressed by its voice, which he described as "a menacing murmur".

♯ Crumhorn

A two-reed wooden instrument which enlivened the Middle Ages with its warm, mid-range voice, not heard since the 17th century except in modern 'authentic' bands. Its name, related to 'crumpled' or crooked, refers to its shape, which resembles a hockey stick with fingerholes.

♯ Jonkametótzi

A reed pipe from Peru, played cross-ways like a flute but lacking fingerholes. Instead, to control the note, a finger is inserted in the end.

♯ Karnyx

As the Iron-Age Celts closed for battle their enemies would have been cowed by the 2m (6.5 feet) long *karnyx*, a metal trumpet with a carved animal-horn bell that rose high above the player's head. If the battle were with the Danes, one might imagine the frightful din as *karnyx* player met *lur* player (see below), each inciting his fighting men with raucous bellows.

♯ Lichiguayo

An end-blown flute of Chile, 500 or more years old. A 'V'-shaped notch is cut at the upper end to facilitate sound production. Being of considerable length, its tone is low and seductive.

♯ Lituus

A Roman name for a pre-Roman bronze instrument shaped like a letter 'J'. Its straight conical pipe ended in a sharply-bent animal horn, and its use was probably mainly military.

♯ Lur

Thought of primarily as Danish, these large bronze trumpets were once widespread throughout Bronze Age northern Europe, where they had several uses: in battle, as a processional instrument and, in pairs, at religious festivals. In shape they resembled mammoth tusks. As noise makers they were effective; as musical instruments, mere curiosities.

♩ A MODERN *OCARINA* IN A DESIGN STANDARDIZED IN ITALY ABOUT 1860. THIS ELABORATE EXAMPLE IS MADE OF TERRACOTTA.

♯ Ocarina

Upper Egypt enjoyed the pure liquid tones of the *ocarina* 5000 years ago, when they were made of baked earth. Shaped like an elongated egg with a blowing-hole and fingerholes, they may still be bought today if one accepts plastic as a suitable substitute for mud. The name means 'little goose' in Italian. Modern examples are considerably slimmer than their predecessors. The voice is particularly attractive in that, unlike most wind instruments, the *ocarina* produces no overtones. This acoustic phenomenon is due to the globe-like shape of the instrument which allows the air within to vibrate as a whole when set in motion by blowing.

♩ MOST OF THE *OPHICLEIDE*'S HISTORY, OF ABOUT A CENTURY FROM 1821, UNFOLDED IN FRANCE, ITS COUNTRY OF ORIGIN.

♯ Ophicleide

This translates from the Greek as 'keyed serpent'. The instrument belies the antiquity its name suggests. Early in the 19th century efforts were made to improve the serpent (see bass horn, above); the best way was to replace it, which is what the Frenchman Halary did in 1821. As the bass voice of the cornet family the *ophicleide* was itself replaced by the bass tuba in orchestras. One Thomas Macbean Glen of Edinburgh invented a wooden version about 1850. He called it *serpentkleide*.

♯ Palawta

A six-hole flute of the Philippines, with slight variations in design between islands but wide differences in name. It is played cross-ways, as is the modern Western flute.

Panpipes
A PARALLEL EVOLUTION

It seems possible that panpipes evolved twice, independently. They were known in China (*p'ai-siao*) by 500 BC and in ancient Greece (*syrinx*) 1000 years earlier, where they were said to have been played to the water nymph Syrinx by Pan (hence their name). (Egyptian examples date from at least 330 BC.) From China panpipes spread throughout the Pacific and into South America, where they are known by various names:

CHILE (PRE-COLUMBIAN): *Laka*

PERU: *Anata; jonkari; urusa*

ARGENTINA, BOLIVIA, PARAGUAY, PERU: *Siku*, which, lacking a full chromatic range, require the melody to be divided between several players, giving a jerky stereo effect. Pipes may exceed 2m (6.5 feet) in length; they slant away from the player and rest on the ground.

From Greece, panpipes spread into the Balkans. Gheorghe Zamfir, the Romanian panpipes virtuoso, maintains that panpipes are the oldest of all musical instruments. He has composed a Concerto and a Rhapsody for them, and performances by him and his compatriots have widely popularized their virtuosic use in Romanian folk music. But they are to be heard at their most evocative in South American folk ensembles, where their haunting tones, together with the stomach-thumping rhythm of the *bomba* (large drum), seem to capture the atmosphere of high remote plains and snow-capped peaks.

℅ Panpipes

Panpipes consist of a collection of pipes, graded in length and bound together side-by-side in a curved or straight pattern. The player blows across the top of each pipe in turn by moving his head or the pipes. The lower ends of the pipes are blocked. Panpipes are used for festive entertainments and dancing. Also see panel (left).

℅ Pinkillo

The European recorder, being relatively easy to play, has given rise to local varieties. One, the *pinkillo* of Chile, is a small reed pipe with a mouthpiece; another, in Peru, is somewhat larger but bears the same name. Both produce clear tones, not unlike the familiar recorder family.

℅ Putu or Pututu

Natural horns of great antiquity, played by the indigenous Indians of the Atacamá desert region of Chile. These horns, together with native trumpets and percussion, accompany ancient ritual songs sung in the pre-Columbian *kunza* language.

℅ Quena

One of the most ancient of all flutes, the *quena* of Bolivia is an end-blown instrument made of bone, clay, reed or metal. In appearance and tone production it resembles the European recorder.

℅ Recorder

We cannot know what the earliest recorders were called because nothing is known of the language spoken by the Middle Eastern peoples of the

A WELL-ORGANIZED (NOTE MICROPHONE!) STREET MUSICIAN WITH A SPECIES OF PANPIPES AND DRUM.

Upper Palaeolithic era, up to 27,000 years ago, who played the instrument, and even they may not have been the first. They constructed their end-blown instruments of reed, wood or bone, and a characteristic feature was, and remains today, the shape of the mouthpiece. This gave rise to the more recent Italian and German terms, *flauto a becco* and *Schnabelflöte* respectively, both meaning 'beak-flute'. Its pure tone attracted the French description *recordour,* bird-song imitation, from which our name derives. The recorder family is populous (see panel) as well as ancient in origin.

℅ Shahnai

Common as an out-door instrument in North India (related instruments with similar names are found in Persia, Bangladesh and neighbouring areas), the *shahnai* is a two-reed oboe or shawm (the latter word derived from *shahnai*) with an extremely piercing sound. It is straight, with a small flared bell. Rather larger bells are found in the closely-related southern Indian *nagasvaram*.

✵ Shakuhachi

A Chinese bamboo flute, adopted by the Japanese, which may vary greatly in length. Its woody voice is capable of much variety and it can arouse emotional responses in the listener when played by an expert.

✵ Shofar

A ram's-horn trumpet bent into a 'J'-shape by the application of heat, sometimes equipped with a shaped end to act as a mouthpiece, and bearing sacred and/or secular inscriptions. Its main use is in Jewish religious ceremonies. The simple construction of the instrument limits it to very few notes, but these echo impressively within the synagogue to add solemnity to the occasion. It was probably *shofarot* (the correct plural) which sent Jericho's walls crashing down.

✵ Tiama

A long, low-pitched flute of Peru, made from bone, wood or reed.

 A BASIC IMPALA-HORN TRUMPET FROM WHICH THE JEWISH LITURGICAL *SHOFAR* DEVELOPED (SEE TEXT).

✵ Trumpet

Widespread as an ethnic instrument. The term trumpet, used loosely, covers anything from the conch shell and *didgeridoo* to the modern valve instrument. Furthermore, large trumpets and small horns were virtually identical in the Middle Ages, and even into Baroque times. The principal difference between horn and trumpet during the developing years was that the trumpet was basically cylindrical until the abrupt flaring of the bell, while the horn was gently conical throughout its length until reaching the area of the, often larger, bell. This tended to give the horn a less piercing tone, though one may cite many exceptions in nomenclature, construction and sound production.

In pre-Roman days, simple straight tube-like trumpets were common throughout Africa and the East. They were used in hunting and battle but were unsuitable for indoor use. The situation changed by the Baroque period, when trumpeters and their drumming companions, from whom they were virtually inseparable, were honoured with special positions on platforms raised above the rest of the ensemble.

 INDIAN SILVER TRUMPET, OR *KARNA*, WHICH IS FOUND IN VARIABLE LENGTHS UP TO ABOUT 1.3 METRES (4 FEET).

WIND ODDITIES

※ Apunga

Medieval European armies tried to strike terror into the hearts of their enemies by the use of *apungas*. These were elephant tusks, blown through the clipped sharp ends to imitate the bellow of the real animal. Often elaborately carved, these ivory instruments were highly valued both on and off the battlefield and became known as *oliphants*.

※ Bag-hornpipe

A hybrid bagpipe, in that it lacks drones but compensates by having a double chanter terminating in a double cowhorn bell. The bag may be of kidskin. Bag-hornpipes are of unknown antiquity. Their distribution may be ascertained by reference to their differing nomenclature: *askomandoura* (Crete); *chiboni* (Caucasus); *gudastviri* (Georgia); *parkapzuk* (Armenia); *sabouna* (Aegean Islands); *shabr* (Volga basin); *tulum* (Turkey); *zukra* (North Africa).

※ Bible Organ

A small domestic reed organ whose appearance accounts for its name. When standing on a table, it resembles a large family bible. When opened, as one would a large book, one side presents a keyboard, the other a set of bellows. The player operates the keyboard with one hand and the bellows with the other.

※ Bottle

While panpipes are carefully constructed to produce correct pitches when the openings are blown, bottles come ready-made, awaiting only fine-tuning. Musicians have employed every type of bottle as novel sound producers, from demijohn to aspirin bottle size, the notes being modified if required by adding liquid to the instrument. At a famous Hoffnung Music Festival Concert on 13 November 1956, tuned bottles supplied the coda to the *andante* of Haydn's 'Surprise' Symphony, No. 94 in G, thereby

enhancing the surprise. Jazz artists have blown bottles; they have also hit them (gently) and slapped their tops with the flat of the hand to produce a rhythmic bass. Kuniharu Akiyama included bottles in his *Arcana 19* (1962), and the *bouteillophone*, consisting of water-tuned bottles suspended from a frame and struck by xylophone beaters, have been used in Satie's *Parade* (1916) and Bo Nilsson's *Reaktionen* (1978). The effect can be delightful if not overdone.

A bottle organ built in Germany in 1798 is

preserved in Liverpool City Museum. Sound is produced via a keyboard which directs air across the mouth of each of 106 bottles. Red wax in the bottles ensures correct tuning.

※ Didgeridoo

The best-known name for an indigenous prehistoric Australian instrument invented by nature. Nature simply awaited the drop of a dead tree branch, then introduced termites to hollow it out. An Aborigine would happen along, shake out the detritus, and blow down the end with a rhythmic humming interspersed with tongue and lip movements. Sometimes he might add further rhythm by striking the wood with a stick or metal object, such as a ring. The sound is unmistakable: a weird drone wafting endlessly across the plain like the subdued grumbling of an animal.

※ Mirliton

An oddity certainly, but a familiar one. The *kazoo* is a *mirliton*, the principle of humming against a membrane being common to all types. Children

𝄞 AN 18TH-CENTURY SERPENT MADE BY AN ANONYMOUS PARISIAN COMPANY. LATER MODELS REPLACED DIRECT FINGERING WITH KEYS.

make *mirlitons* by applying a sheet of paper to a comb and humming against it. In Africa the principle is even more basic: a horn-shaped *mirliton* with a membrane made of spiderweb. Jazz musicians occasionally employ a *kazoo*.

❦ *Roekua*

An *ocarina*-like folk-instrument of the Peruvian rain forests. Unlike its European counterpart, which is ceramic, the Peruvian 'little goose' is made of beeswax.

❦ *Serpent*

A late 16th-century French invention, the serpent truly justifies its name, being a long wooden tube, fashioned in two halves stuck together in the shape of a double-S. It was originally used in church but soon found a place in military and open-air bands. Handel required it in both the *Water Music* (1717) and the *Musick for the Royal Fireworks* (1749). Berlioz, Mendelssohn and even Wagner tolerated its unpredictable tones before the *ophicleide* and tuba presented themselves as replacements.

Blown Instruments
OCCASIONALLY HEARD IN CONCERT

ALPHORN Leopold Mozart called thia instrument *corno pastoriccio* when he wrote a concerto for it in the 1750s. More recently, the Hungarian composer Ferenc Farkas wrote a *Petite Suite Alpestre* (1976) and a *Concertino Rustico* (1977) for *alphorn*, and a recent symphony by Hans Stadlmair features the instrument.

BAGPIPE Leopold Mozart wrote a divertimento for bagpipe and hurdy-gurdy titled *Die Bauern Hochzeit* ('The Peasant Wedding', c. 1756), which was laid out in such a manner that one player might play both parts, pauses in the solo parts enabling a quick change between instruments.

CHALUMEAU, OR SALMO Vivaldi's Concerto RV558 includes two *salmoè*, and Johann Christoph Graupner wrote several works including *chalumeaux*.

DIDGERIDOO The Australian composer George Dreyfus wrote a Sextet in 1971 for *didgeridoo* and wind quintet.

KAZOO In 1972 David Bedford wrote *With 100 Kazoos* for audience participation. Tchaikovsky's *Nutcracker* (1892) includes a 'Dance of the Mirlitons', an alternative name

for the *kazoo*, but this is usually translated as 'Reed-pipe Dance' and played on flutes.

LUR The Icelandic composer Jón Leifs included a *lur* in his 'Saga' Symphony (1943)

PANPIPES Georg Philipp Telemann wrote a tiny *Flauto Pastorale* for *syrinx* (the Greek name for panpipes) and included it in his *Der Getreue Music-Meister* (1721).

RECORDER For long displaced by the flute, the recorder was revived by Arnold Dolmetsch in about 1912 and now features regularly in concerts of Baroque music. In the early 18th century, *flauto* almost invariably meant 'recorder'. Works for the instrument this century include Hindemith's Trio for three recorders (1932), and another (1955) by Henk Badings.

SHAKUHACHI The Japanese composer Minoru Miki wrote a *Sonnet* for three *shakuhachis* (1962), as well as several other works for this and other native Japanese instruments.

ABOVE: A *KAZOO*, A TOY INSTRUMENT MADE OF TINPLATE AND SOMETIMES FOUND IN CHRISTMAS CRACKERS.

❦ *Sheng*

Dating from at least 2500 years ago, this ancient Chinese instrument is a true mouth-organ. Its sound is that of a high-pitched reed organ, but its appearance is startling. The player fills a gourd with air which is directed in turn up 17 vertical bamboo pipes, the melody being produced by covering the relevant fingerholes while one or more pipes produce drones.

❦ *Trutruka*

A vegetable-stem trumpet 2m (6.5 feet) long with an animal horn stuck out at right-angles at the end. This gawky instrument is found in Chile and Argentina. 𝄢

TOP LEFT: THE *SHENG*'S SOUND RESEMBLES THAT OF A CONSORT OF LOW-PITCHED OBOES.

SCRAPED INSTRUMENTS

IN THE VIOLIN family, drawing a resined bow across a string with the right hand causes the string to vibrate, the note produced being related to the length of the string. To produce a higher note, the string is 'stopped', either by a finger placed on the string with a force sufficient to press it against the fingerboard, or some mechanical device which achieves the same objective.

The method of holding the violin has undergone many changes. It may be rested against the

The Bow

EVIDENCE OF BOWS IS SCANTY BEFORE **1000 AD** BUT THEY WERE DOUBTLESS IN USE MUCH EARLIER. THE TWO BASIC TYPES BOTH FEATURE A CURVED STICK WITH HORSEHAIR FIXED AT BOTH ENDS.

CONVEX BOWS These existed exclusively until about 1750. Some examples were strongly arched; others, for recital use, were gracefully curved and almost parallel with the hair. The hair itself was slacker than is the case with modern bows.

CONCAVE BOWS With the Tourte bow, made by the Tourte family between 1770 and 1835 in Paris, the concave bow superseded its venerable ancestor and has been prevalent ever since. Its hair is tensioned by a screw mechanism.

the Old way of Playing the Fiddle.

the new way!!

♭ 18TH CENTURY VS 1830 METHODS OF VIOLIN PLAYING, SHOWING ALSO CONVEX AND CONCAVE BOWS.

chest or shoulder, or under the chin with the tailpiece resting on either side. With the invention of the chin rest, claimed by the composer Louis Spohr as his invention of about 1822, the under-the-chin position became standard, though non-Western fiddlers still practice various methods.

Depending upon the strength and speed of attack of bow on string, considerable variation may be obtained in the character of the note produced. Furthermore, in the case of 'stopped' strings, modifications in expressive quality, mellowness and projection may be introduced by the application of *vibrato* by the left hand. This entails a shaking of the 'stopping' finger which alternately slightly increases and decreases the length of the string left to vibrate. Again, *vibrato*

may be applied in varying degrees depending upon the quality of effect required. Nowadays string players use *vibrato* constantly. When in solo performance the added carrying power this lends to the tone is hardly necessary except when 'extra' expression is required on longer notes. In sonatas for stringed instrument and piano some listeners cannot reconcile the vibrated string notes with unvibrated piano notes. However, in a string orchestra the massed *vibrato* makes for warmth and richness of sound. Before the mid-18th century string tone was largely unmodified by *vibrato*, an effect modern players emulate when playing in

THE NORWEGIAN HARDANGER FIDDLE – SEE PANEL (RIGHT) AND ENTRY ON PAGE **196**.

'period' style. *Portamento*, achieved by moving the finger smoothly along the string between notes during a bow stroke, was common until the 1930s but is now discredited.

Another effect produces 'harmonics', a disembodied sound achieved by lightly resting the stopping finger on the string rather than pressing down. Further effects have been called for, among them *martellato*, or hammering with the bow, which produces a violent and sudden attack.

In non-Western instruments all these devices are common, plus a host of others. Any movement that applies friction between materials qualifies as 'scrape'. Man's ingenuity dictates that any device designed for one purpose might be put to another. Therefore, a 'scraped' instrument, having an inviting taut string, will inevitably be plucked. Given certain conditions, most of the stringed instruments included here should have found themselves in the 'plucked' section. 𝄡

Scraped Instruments
OCCASIONALLY HEARD IN CONCERT
℘

BARYTON In addition to Joseph Haydn's 125 baryton trios, 12 *divertimenti*, two concertos and 24 duos for the instrument may be added Johann Georg Krause's nine partitas in 1703. The 20th century saw a modest increase in the instrument's use, mainly for the resurrection of Haydn's trios, but Ferenc Farkas, the Hungarian composer, provided a *Concerto all'Antica* for it in 1955; see page 84.

HARDANGER FIDDLE This Norwegian folk instrument has attracted the attention of several of its native composers. Eivind Groven's *Fjelltonar* (1938) is for Hardanger fiddle and chamber orchestra, and in his *Margit Hjukse* (1964) the instrument is joined by a chorus. Nils Geirr Tveitt has composed two concertos for Hardanger fiddle (in 1956 and 1965).

HURDY-GURDY In 1972 the Swedish composer Sven-Erik Emanuel Johanson wrote a concerto for hurdy-gurdy and orchestra.

KIT Although the diminutive *kit* is totally unsuitable for concert use, the Italian-born French composer Antoine-Louis Clapisson nonetheless included a gavotte for one in his opera *Les trois Nicolas* (1858).

MUSICAL GLASSES Mozart's Quintet in C minor, K617 (1791) is scored for musical glasses, flute, oboe, viola and cello. The *armonica* called for by Saint-Saëns in his 'Carnival of the Animals' to represent bubbles rising in an aquarium was probably the glass armonica, but its place is often taken by mouth-organ – giving a totally different effect.

TROMBA MARINA The strangely offensive voice of the *tromba marina* has attracted few composers. J.-B. Lully included it in the ballet music he wrote for Cavalli's *Serse* in 1660, and Alessandro Scarlatti used it in the introduction to Act Four of his opera *Il Mitridate Eupatore* (1707).

VIOLA D'AMORE This honey-toned instrument has attracted many composers. The most productive was Vivaldi, who provided it with seven concertos. In one, RV 548 in D minor, he makes a uniquely seductive effect by sharing the viola d'amore's solo with a lute and directing that the whole of the accompanying string orchestra should play muted.

HAYDN'S BARYTON. IN THE BARYTON A HOLE IN THE BACK OF THE FINGERBOARD ALLOWS ACCESS TO THE LEFT THUMB TO PLUCK THE SYMPATHETIC STRINGS.

✹ Chainuri

A small, long-necked lute played cello-fashion with a deeply curved bow, familiar in Georgian folk music.

✹ Er-hu

Variously described as a violin or a bowed lute, this Chinese instrument cleverly prevents the player from misplacing his bow. The two strings of the *er-hu* pass between the bow and the hair. The sound produced by the resonance of the snakeskin-covered body is insubstantial and intolerably scratchy to Western ears.

✹ Fidhla

This bowed *zither* found in Iceland possesses a body in the shape of an elongated triangle. Two, or sometimes three, strings run the length of the body and are raised high so that the left hand may stop them from below. References to the *fidhla* date from the 18th century; it is possible the instrument may have originated before that.

✹ Fiedel

First heard in Europe during the 9th century after its introduction from the East, the *fiedel*, *fidel* or *fidula* is the basis of the whole modern viol and violin families, yet it is also related to the lute and was probably itself derived from that huge family. Early users of the instrument supported it vertically on the knee and bowed cross-ways. Some time during the Renaissance players adopted an alternative position, tucking the base of the instrument under the chin. The *fiedel* was used as an accom-

paniment to dancing. It possessed a weak tone and it took centuries of development, culminating in the Cremonese violin makers, before the instrument could be made to sound anything remotely approaching melodious.

✹ Friction Block

In Papua New Guinea and many other areas, rasps are made from solid or hollow ridged wooden blocks which are scraped vigorously with a stick or stone. The most basic examples are found in Aboriginal Australia, where a ridged stick is scraped by another.

✹ Glass Armonica – see panel

✹ Gusle or Gussli

Names for the violin found in the former Yugoslavia, these also refer to the folk fiddle. This primitive fiddle is made in one piece and played with a simple bow. Balkan culture is rich in epic stories of heroes and romantic events, often of considerable duration, and even today folk singers will relate them to willing listeners while accompanying themselves on the *gusle*.

✹ Hardanger Fiddle

Named after the Norwegian district in which it originated in the 16th century, the Hardanger fiddle at first sported six strings. Developed from the viola d'amore and folk fiddles, it now has four strings which cross a flattened bridge. This facilitates multiple stopping (the artificial shortening of more than one string simultaneously

A PRIMITIVE *FIEDEL* WITH SINGLE STRING AND CONVEX BOW. THE DECORATIVE HEAD OF THE INSTRUMENT OFTEN TOOK AN ANIMAL FORM.

with the fingers of the left hand), thus making harmonized melodies possible. Players exploit this facility and, by adding plentiful embellishments, produce a richly varied accompaniment to dancing. The tone is further enriched by four or five sympathetic strings.

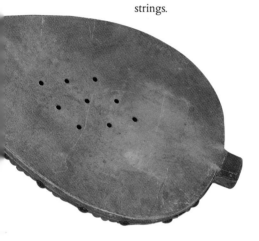

⸿ Hiiukannel

An Estonian bowed *zither* of square outline, with four strings. The player holds the instrument on his knees and bows obliquely downwards.

⸿ Hu-ch'in

(Sometimes transliterated from the Chinese as *gu-ch'in*) The word *hu-ch'in* is also taken to mean any of the bowed lutes found in China, including the two-string bamboo *ching-hu*. That these instruments did not originate in that country is implied by the meaining of *hu-ch'in*: 'instruments played by barbarians'. Like the closely-related *er-hu* (above), the *hu-ch'in*'s two strings are threaded through the hair of the bamboo bow. The instrument's body resonator is a small cylindrical box and is usually covered in snakeskin.

Glass Armonica

⸿

Unlike bottles which are blown (see Blown Instruments), the glass armonica, or musical glasses, are sounded by rubbing wet fingertips round the rims of tumblers. First, the glasses have to be charged with water to 'tune' them to the correct pitches; then they are placed in a frame, conveniently positioned for the player to create a melody. As early as 1743 an Irishman named Richard Pockrich played such an instrument in London; 16 years later he died in a fire which, it is said, involved his glass-and-water instrument! Christoph Willibald von Gluck performed a concerto in London in 1746, using '26 drinking glasses tuned with spring water', but Benjamin Franklin, encountering the instrument on a visit to London, decided that it needed improvement.

He regularized the technique and construction of the glass armonica. His instrument, completed in 1761, consisted of a rectangular box half-filled with water. Running inside the box and fitting closely one into the other, but not touching, were a series of shallow glass plates mounted centrally on a horizontal rod. A pedal-operated handle turned the plates in the trough of water, keeping their edges moist, and the player applied his fingertips to each in turn, or to several if chords were required.

Described as extremely ethereal, the sound of the musical glasses created a craze in the late 18th century. Anton Mesmer, who gave the world the term 'mesmerism', used it as an aid to hypnotism, and Franz Xaver Joseph Peter Schnyder von Wartensee put its soothing tones to use in 1830 in a kind of chamber tone poem, *The Angry Man Calmed by Music*, the man's irascible role being taken by a piano. Sadly, the calming effect upon the angry man and upon listeners was not paralleled in performers. Nervous trouble developed either due to the extremely lively upper harmonics of the instrument which, over a period, would seriously affect the hearing, or the contact of water-sensitized fingertips on the revolving glass. In some towns the instrument was banned from performance.

It should be noted that references to 'musical glasses' in various forms date from some 500 years before Pockrich's experiments, but in all these early forms the glasses were struck rather than rubbed.

BRUNO HOFFMANN, THE GERMAN PLAYER WHO REVIVED THE ART OF GLASS ARMONICA PLAYING IN THE 1930s.

✀ Hurdy-gurdy

Probably originating in the inventive East, the hurdy-gurdy was brought to Europe some time before the 9th century. For such an antique instrument, and one regarded as suitable only for peasant entertainment, the hurdy-gurdy is surprisingly sophisticated in construction. The body resembles a thick and chunky violin with strings running longitudinally. Under the strings a resined wheel acts as a circular bow which is turned by a handle at the lower end of the instrument. A keyboard mechanism stops the strings, while others, being in permanent contact with the wheel, sound a continuous drone. As well as melody and drone, the hurdy-gurdy can produce rhythmic effects and in the hands of an expert, can sound like several instruments playing together. The drone, however, can sound tiring, which is probably why, after initial popularity during the Middle Ages, it became despised as being suitable only for wandering musicians. The hurdy-gurdy's status rose for a time during the 18th century when both Charles Baton and Leopold Mozart composed for it. The French composer Nicolas Chédeville actually arranged Vivaldi's 'The Four Seasons' for hurdy-gurdy, violin, flute and continuo.

✀ Kamancha

Also known as *kamanga* and similar names, the spike fiddle is widespread from Algeria to the Black Sea, though local varieties differ in detail. Built upon a 'spike', a wooden rod that supports the instrument at the lower end then runs through the body and out at the top to serve as a pegboard, the resonating body may be of any shape from square to round. Some models utilize a gourd. Strings may number six or more, and single-string versions are known. The Iranian *kemanja* sometimes has sympathetic strings. Usually the method of sound production is by bowing with a horsehair bow, but plucked versions also exist.

✀ Klompviool

Literally 'wooden-shoe fiddle', or clog fiddle, this is exactly that in old Holland: a rough and ready fiddle fashioned out of a clog with virtually no fingerboard, the body contiguous with the peg box. A soundboard is nailed to the rim of the clog. Models exist with four strings. Used at informal gatherings, such as tavern dances, the *Klompviool* is not noted for its power or beauty of tone.

✀ Kucho

An ancient three-stringed fiddle of Okinawa which has recently enjoyed a revival of interest after several decades of obscurity.

✀ Masenqo

A one-stringed bowed lute from Ethiopia. Basically a spike fiddle in shape (see *kamancha*, above), it has a diamond-shaped body through the larger axis of which passes the spike, and a high bridge. The string is stopped from the side by a finger or thumb of the left hand.

℅ Matraca

A rattle of Spanish origin much used there and in Brazil and Chile as an accompaniment to dancing and other festivities. It is included in Scraped Instruments because, like the familiar football rattle, its wooden tongues are scraped over a wooden or metal cog as the instrument is whirled by hand.

℅ Nikelharpa

A Swedish instrument dating from the 15th century, the *nikelharpa* ('keyed harp') is not a harp at all but an elongated violin with a system of finger-operated keys to stop the seven strings. Unlike the hurdy-gurdy, which also has a key mechanism, the *nikelharpa* is bowed like a violin.

℅ Pi-wang

A Tibetan fiddle whose alternative name, *hor-chin*, reveals its relationship to the Chinese *hu-chin* (above). Both display a distinguishing feature of Far Eastern fiddles: that the bow hair is threaded between the strings, which might number anything from two to four. The *pi-wang* is classed as a long-necked bowed lute. Its bow is sharply convex. The player holds the small cylindrical body against his stomach and bows with an underhand grip. Used as an accompaniment to singing, the tone is sharp and piercing. Some examples boast a carved animal head surmounting the pegbox.

℅ Rabel

A Chilean violin of rather small size, though much broader in the body than a *kit* (see page 85). Its three strings are played with a substan-

tially convex bow, and its sound holes resemble the necks of two graceful facing swans.

℅ Rebab

Probably originating in North Africa, this basic design is found throughout the Arabic countries and northwards into the Balkans. An elongated body, sometimes pear-shaped, sometimes waisted, bears several strings, up to five in number, and one foot of the bridge extends right through to the back of the body to act as a soundpost.

In Malaysia instruments called *rebab tiga tali* (with three strings) and *rebab dua tali* (two strings) are, like the Middle Eastern *rebab*, spike fiddles. The soundbox of the former is shaped rather like a bellows standing on the sharper end; rising from it is an ornate, long, round-sectioned

RESOURCES ARE OFTEN LIMITED FOR LUXURIES LIKE MUSIC IN ARABIAN SOCIETIES. THESE HOME-MADE SPIKE FIDDLES ARE A TYPE OF *REBAB*.

fingerboard terminating in a carved crown of native design. The lower end of the spike serves as a foot when the instrument is played. An animal skin soundboard and a shallow convex bow strung with coconut fibre complete the ensemble of the genuine instrument, but modern materials are used increasingly because of their easy availability and greater resistance to wear. The three-stringed instrument attracts veneration due to its alleged magical qualities and high status as an accompaniment to dance dramas. The humbler, and much less elaborate, two-stringed version was used, with other instruments, to accompany lengthy narrations from the *Mahabharata*.

✵ Sarinda

This Indian bowed lute is stubby and compact in shape and may be decorated with elaborate designs. Its round body is deeply channelled on either side of the sound box to allow access for the bow. There are seven or more strings, and some examples have a range of sympathetic strings.

𝄞 A BENGALI *SARINDA*. INSTRUMENTS OF SIMILAR NAME BUT VARYING IN DETAILS OF CONSTRUCTION AND TUNING ARE FOUND IN INDIA, AFGHANISTAN AND IRAN.

✵ Saw bip and Saw mai pai

The *saw mai pai* is a folk-fiddle of Laos, made out of a coconut shell to which a fingerboard and two strings are attached. Even more basic is the *saw bip* of the same area. An empty metal can serves as an amplifier for a strung stick, the lower end of which is placed inside through the lid opening and bowed with a carved wooden bow held underhand. Presumably these folk fiddles can be of any shape: beggars can't be choosers.

✵ Skrypka

A generic term for a fiddle of the Balkans and southern Russia. In detail, these fiddles vary greatly from area to area.

✵ Suka

A Polish violin well-distributed during the 19th century but now largely superseded by various types of fiddle. The *suka* resembled a small violin but with only three strings, these stopped by the fingernails, and it was played vertically like a tiny cello. One foot of the bridge was lengthened to rest inside against the back of the instrument's body.

✵ Tontorentzi

In Peru, only women play the *tontorentzi*, which consists of a simple bow with a single string. One end of the bow is held between the teeth, the mouth cavity acting as a resonator, while the string is rubbed with palm leaf fibre. A smaller version, the *piom pirintzi* (qv), may be played by either sex.

✵ Wang-pi

A Tibetan lute with a long fingerboard surmounted by a peg box bearing an animal-head carving. The bow is made from a yak's tail through which run the two-to-four strings.

✵ Yü

An ancient rhythm instrument of China consisting of a wooden block carved in the shape of a tiger but with transverse ridges along its back. These are scraped bamboo sticks, shredded and tied in a bundle to make a sharp, fluttering sound.

The Violin

IN INDIA

✵

Apart from the bowed lute, such as the *sarangi*, India was not well appointed with bowed stringed instruments until the violin was introduced in about 1800. This was adopted fairly rapidly after its entrance in the south of the sub-Continent. The instrument was also adapted to suit Indian taste, its tuning and playing position differing substantially from European convention: the g d a e tuning was converted to a system based on fourths and fifths, and the instrument was played in a sitting position, wedged between ankle and chin, thus relieving the left arm of the weight.

The violin's popularity in India was given added impetus when Yehudi Menuhin became interested in Indian music and played a series of recitals with sitarist Ravi Shankar, see page 210.

A remarkable recent instrument, called the double violin, has been introduced. It is electronically amplified and consists of two parallel fingerboards, each with five strings. The range of expression is astonishing; even more so is its compass, extending from the highest note attainable on a normal violin to the lowest note of the double bass.

✵ Zlobcoki

A slim, three/four string Polish fiddle carved out of a single piece of wood. Often still used at folk gatherings, it has a light, pleasant tone; the four-stringed version is tuned as the Western fiddle. 𝄢

SCRAPED ODDITIES

❦ Charrango

One of the most basic instruments of Chile, used for dancing or light entertainment, the *charrango* (not to be confused with the plucked *charango*, which comes from the same general geographical area) comprises a wooden platform to which one or more wires are nailed or stapled. These are induced to sound rhythmically when rubbed by metal rings.

❦ Kemae

In Peru music may be made by taking an empty turtle shell and scraping its surface with a stick. This is the *kemae*, a rhythm instrument whose technique and tone are reflected in the skiffle washboards popular in Western music in the 1950s.

❦ Morin Khuur

A Mongolian spike fiddle, known as the 'horse-head fiddle', this has deep symbolism with the folklore of the area. The first *morin khuur* was said to have been made out of the remains of a horse famous in mythology. The horse motif extends from the carved horse head at the top of the pegbox, through the two horsehair strings (one thick, the other thin), to the arched horse hair bow. Only men are allowed to play the *morin khuur*; they do so seated or by adopting a squatting position and bowing the instrument like a cello.

❦ Nail Violin

The 18th-century German violinist Johann Wilde habitually hung his bow on a nail in a rafter at his home in St Petersburg. Noticing the pure note created as the bow contacted the nail, he experimented by creating a semi-circular block of wood adorned with nails, or rather staples, driven in to depths which gave the notes required. The result may be played with one or two ordinary violin bows. Later models even gave the nail violin sympathetic strings, but popularity for the instrument remains limited.

ABOVE: A HERDSMAN OF THE GOBI DESERT IN TRADITIONAL DRESS PLAYS A *MORIN KHUUR*, OR HORSE-HEAD FIDDLE.

RIGHT: A *TROMBA MARINA*. THIS EXAMPLE HAS AN ADDITIONAL, SHORTER, STRING FOR VARIETY.

❦ Piom Pirintzi

A Peruvian, when not playing panpipes, might apply a small bow to his mouth and rub it with a palm leaf. The mouth cavity provides both resonance and 'melody', and ambitious Peruvians have been known to play the first bow with a second.

❦ Tromba Marina

A truly strange instrument, whose name, 'marine trumpet', has nothing to do with either the sea or a trumpet. Rising to over 220cm (7.2 feet) in height, roughly triangular in cross-section, and tapering from about 17cm (6.7 inches) at the base to 5cm (2 inches) at the top, the *tromba marina* possesses but one string which is stopped and bowed like a simple cello. The bridge near the lower end is attached by only one foot. The other is left free to vibrate against the table as the string is bowed. The resulting sound is incredibly harsh. Despite this, music was written for it, possibly out of sympathy, before the instrument lost all credibility about 1750, after some 90 years of existence.

PLUCKED & INSTRUMENTS

STRINGS MAY be plucked by a variety of materials to produce a sharp but often rapidly decaying note. In the violin family the usual method is to pluck the string with the fingertip. In other instruments a plectrum may be used. This may be made of tortoiseshell, metal, wood or plastic. The plucking action in a harpsichord is achieved by a quill rising in response to the pressing of a key, plucking the string as it passes, then, in a configuration resembling a vertically elongated letter D, bypassing the string on its downward path before coming to rest.

Plucked stringed instruments are of extreme antiquity. Early in their history they divided into three families: lutes, harps and lyres. All three underwent diversification, but by far the most productive family was the lutes, which have

LEFT: THE CELEBRATED INDIAN SITARIST RAVI SHANKAR (SEE PAGE 210).
ABOVE: A JAPANESE *BIWA*, 1898, A TYPE OF PLUCKED LUTE; SEE PAGES 208–9.

Plucked Instruments

OCCASIONALLY HEARD IN CONCERT

BALALAIKA The Russian composer Yuri Shushakov wrote a Balalaika Concerto (c. 1955) but representation of the instrument in concert and opera is most often made by imitation, as in Balakirev's Overture No. 1 on Russian Themes (1858, revised 1881).

BANJO Ernst Křenek's 'Little' Symphony, Op. 58 (1928) employs two banjos.

DOMBRA Nicolai Pavlovich Budashkin composed a concerto for Russian *dombra* in 1940.

GUSLI Rimsky-Korsakov required a plucked *gusli* to sound in his opera *Sadko* (1896), but the part is often taken instead by *pizzicato* strings.

GUITAR Famous guitar concertos have been written by Joaquín Rodrigo (in 1939), Mario Castelnuovo-Tedesco in the same year, André Previn (1971) and many others, and there is a Serenade (1955) by Malcolm Arnold. Boccherini transcribed six of his piano quintets for guitar, two violins, viola and cello in 1798–9 for the benefit of the guitar-playing Marquis de Benevente, and an early version (c. 1841) of Robert Schumann's Fourth Symphony includes one guitar in the slow movement.

JEW'S HARP Johann Heinrich Hörmann was apparently the first to welcome the Jew's harp into the recital room when he presented his Partita in C in about 1750. The instrument is accompanied by two recorders, four violins (two muted and two played *pizzicato*, to allow the strange visitor to be heard) and continuo. Around 1770 Johann Georg Albrechtsberger, later to be one of Beethoven's teachers, composed three concertos for what he termed *trombula* or *crembalum*. One of the works, for

trombula, harpsichord, violin, viola and cello, has been performed and recorded with a trumpet substituting for the *trombula*, a wildly anachronistic course since a trumpet of 1771 could not play the chromatic part Albrechtsberger wrote for the *trombula*. Furthermore, balance problems were acute. Light dawned when it was discovered that *trombula* and *crembalum* both referred to types of instrument in which several Jew's harps were attached to a frame.

KANTELE The Finnish composer Pehr Henrik Nordgren wrote a concerto, Op. 14, for clarinet, *kantele* and other Finnish folk instruments in 1970.

KITHARA Harry Partch composed his *Two Settings for Finnegan's Wake* (1944) for voice, flute and *kithara*.

MANDOLIN For an 'ethnic', and specifically Italian, instrument, the mandolin has been used widely by composers in many contexts and genres. Among the earliest, probably during the 1730s, were a solo concerto by Vivaldi (RV425) and another for two mandolins (RV532). After A. M. Bononcini used a mandolin in his opera *La conquista delle Spagne* (1707), the instrument travelled to England for Michael Arne's *Almena* (1764) and then to Germany three years later for J. G. Naumann's opera *L'Achille in Sciro*. Other operas have included it, among them Mozart's *Don Giovanni* (1787), Verdi's *Otello* (1887) and Pfitzner's *Palestrina* (1915). Mahler called for it in his Seventh and Eighth

Symphonies (1905; 1906). In the Seventh, together with guitar, it helps to create the nocturnal atmosphere of the fourth movement. In *Das Lied von der Erde* (1909), Mahler drew on its frail timbre for the unworldly landscape of the long final movement, 'Der Abschied'. Karl Amadeus Hartmann also required the mandolin in his Symphony No. 6 (1953).

OUD John Haywood recently collaborated with the Iraqi composer Salman Shukur on a concerto for *oud* and orchestra.

QANUN Muhammed Rifaat Garrana, the Egyptian composer, wrote a concerto for this instrument in 1967.

SANSA See Plucked Oddities, page 213. George Crumb, the American experimental composer, called for a *sansa* in his *Night of the Four Moons* (1966).

SITAR Ravi Shankar has written two concertos for *sitar*.

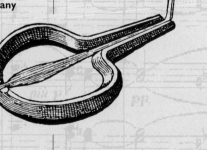

TOP: THE *BANJO*, POPULAR IN EARLY JAZZ, MUSIC HALLS AND, SOMETIMES, THE SYMPHONY.
BELOW: THE SUPREMELY PORTABLE AND EASILY PLAYED JEW'S HARP, THE ORIGIN OF WHOSE NAME REMAINS OBSCURE.

spread worldwide and given rise to innumerable varieties. Lyres have been dying out since about the 17th century, but harps are still current and very popular in both 'art' and folk music. The sound of a plucked string holds an abiding fascination for man. But, as will be seen, strings are not the only material which may be plucked in order to produce music.

℀ Baglama

A pear-shaped Turkish lute, found in various sizes in Turkey and played with a plectrum.

℀ Balalaika

A development of the lute (see *dombra*, below), the *balalaika* was known in Europe by the 17th century, when it appeared in several forms. It is now regarded as the national instrument of Russia, where the *balalaika* family underwent change during the modernization and regularization that took place in that country towards the end of the 19th century. The instrument's body shape was standardized to the familiar triangular form with three strings. The number of sizes in which the family now comes is six: *piccolo, primo, secunda, viola, bass* and *contrabass.*

℀ Banjo

Sir Hans Sloane encountered a small lute in Jamaica and depicted it in a book written in 1688. He called the instrument *strum-strum*, a name lacking in imagination but indicative of what it sounded like. The *strum-strum* developed into the *banjo*, a name possibly derived from Spanish *bandore* via the French 18th-century *banza*. It became popular in the southern states of America (where it was called *banzer*), and later found a place in early jazz recordings because its piercing tone was easy to record and recognize. The body is round, with a skin resonator, and there are usually five strings. Hybrid *ukelele-banjos* of similar shape also exist; one example is mentioned below.

℀ Banjulele

A hydrid instrument of *banjo* and *ukelele*, invented by Albin and Kelvin Keech in 1925/6.

℀ Birimbao

A Jew's harp with a metal tongue in a pear-shaped metal frame, native to Cuba, Argentina, Brazil and other South American countries. In some of these countries the *birimbao* is known as the *trompa* or *trompe*. In Europe the Jew's harp is sometimes referred to as the 'Jew's trump' and this influence may be responsible for this alternative name. The name *birimbao* is doubtless of onomatopoeic origin.

℀ Charango

There were no stringed instruments in South America before the time of Christopher Columbus. The Spaniards brought their guitars with them and these were enthusiastically copied by the natives. The Bolivian *Quechua* Indians, for instance, created the *charango* at first from the shell of a small ground-burrowing armadillo. The drying shell of the animal was formed into a figure-of-eight shape, given a fingerboard and five double strings, and played like a guitar. So rapid was the spread of popularity of the *charango*, not only in Bolivia but in Peru, northern Argentina and other countries, that the armadillo was threatened with extinction until its hunting was banned by government. The subsequent change to wood as the principal material has brought dramatic variations in the size of the *charango*: some bodies are the size of a man's hand; others might be larger than that of a guitar. The name *charango* is said to be a corruption of the native term for armadillo: *quirkincho*.

𝄞 A RUSSIAN NAVY BAND PICTURED IN 1915. ALL SIZES OF *BALALAIKA* ARE SHOWN, THE LARGEST, SOMETIMES CALLED *DOMRA*, TAKING ITS NAME FROM AN EARLIER INSTRUMENT, THE *DOMBRA*, SEE PAGE 205.

℘ Crwth

A lyre-derived instrument originating in the western British Isles in the first century BC and surviving in Wales until the early 1800s. Its Celtic name was *cruit* or *crot*, the English name *crowd* or *crowth*. From c. 1300 the *crwth* was given a fingerboard and was bowed.

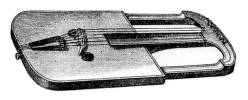

℘ A WELSH *CRWTH*, WHICH SHOWS ELEMENTS OF BOTH THE VIOLIN AND THE LYRE.

℘ Dactylomonocordo

Meaning 'finger-one-string', this instrument was invented by a Neapolitan called Guida in about 1877, probably as an aid for music pupils.

℘ Dan Doc Huyen

This Vietnamese one-string *zither* is a rectangular box, slightly tapered and about one metre long. Near the left-hand end rises a stem with a gourd resonator from which runs a string which passes through the soundboard to a peg inside the box. The player carries a sliver of bamboo with which he plucks the string, meanwhile controlling the note with the outer edge of the other hand. The string tension is changed by pressing on the upright stem.

℘ Dan Tranh

A Vietnamese board *zither* with movable bridges and 16 steel strings, related to the Japanese *koto*.

℘ Dombra

This two-stringed lute may well have been the instrument from which the Russian *balalaika* derived. It is found in various forms in Kazakhstan, Kirghistan, Turkmenistan and Mongolia.

℘ Gottuvadyam

A south Indian modification of the *vina* (below), with a bowl and gourd upon which the instrument rests. The player plucks the strings and stops them with a wooden cylinder held in the left hand.

℘ Gurumi

A lute which was depicted on Ancient Egyptian tomb paintings and is still to be found, virtually unchanged, in Egypt today. It consists of a simple elongated body pierced by a fingerboard. The strings are not tuned by pegs but are bound by leather straps where the pegbox would have been.

℘ Gusli or Gussly

Confusion with the *gusle* or *gussli* in the section on Scraped Instruments (see page 196) is understandable, because the Slav word *gosl*, meaning strings, gave rise to both instruments. However, the presence of strings in both is their only point of similarity. The north-west Russian *gusli* is a large horizontal psaltery with up to 36 finger-plucked strings. It was familiar in Russia in the 18th century when Vasily Fyodorovich Trutovsky entertained the Russian aristocracy with his collection of folk tunes and original works on a *gusli*.

Jew's Harp
THE NAME
℘

Because of its supposedly humble origins, this instrument was said to be associated with beggars, who in turn were often regarded as Jewish immigrants reduced to being street musicians. There is no firm evidence for this, or for the name being a corruption of 'jaw's harp'; a possible derivation is from the Northern English name *jewjaw*, an onomatopoeia.

In Europe one encounters other names. *Munngiga* (Sweden) and *Maulgeige* (Germany) both mean 'mouth fiddle', the German *Maultrommel* means 'mouth drum', and early names suggest a connection with the trumpet: *trump*; *tromba*. This connection has been retained in many non-European names for the instrument.

℘ Jew's Harp

As a small pocket instrument, cheap to buy and rewarding to play, the Jew's harp has been popular for centuries and over a wide area. The familiar instrument comprises a metal flagon- or pear-shaped body and a central tongue plucked with the finger. When put to the mouth the instrument's weak tone is amplified by the mouth cavity and the note is modified as the lips move. Varieties are widespread in the Pacific region, India, Asia and Europe, some dating from 2000 years ago, or even more in Egypt. They might be made of metal, wood (bamboo and palm are found), bone or ivory. The European metal model has been exported to many peoples, including the North American Indians, who made copies locally.

✵ Kerar

An Ethiopian bowl lyre, in which a circular bowl made from tortoise shell or some cooking utensil supports the two arms which in turn support the yoke to which the strings are attached. Often heavily decorated, the *kerar* is used by tribal doctors to drive out the evil spirits of a sick person using music, incantations and the supposed magical powers of the decorations which may include mirrors and charms.

✵ Kinnor

Pictorial representations of King David playing a 'harp' actually show a *kinnor*, a type of lyre.

✵ Kithara

An ancient Greek lyre made of a wooden resonator and, usually, seven strings which were tuned by adjusting their tension rather than their length. From its Middle Eastern origins, the *kithara* became immensely popular in Greece, where both Apollo and Orpheus are said to have

✵ Kantele

A Finnish psaltery reputed to be 2000 years old. In its early form the *kantele* consisted of a horizontal board up to 80cm (31 inches) long, a maximum of 40cm (16 inches) wide tapering to about 10cm (4 inches), and with up to ten metal or gut strings running along its length. Their tuning pegs lie below the wider end, which is usually angled to accommodate the different lengths of the strings. Hitherto characterized by a weak voice and limited range, the instrument has latterly undergone conversion into a concert instrument thanks to a number of improvements during the 20th century, including an increase in the number of strings. The Finnish composer Martti Pokela has helped preserve the *kantele* tradition at the Sibelius Academy and has composed several works for the instrument.

♪ ABOVE: GREEK TERRACOTTA STATUETTES FROM THE 3RD CENTURY AD. THE MAIDEN ON THE LEFT PLAYS A *KITHARA* (LYRE) TO THE ACCOMPANIMENT OF A SLENDER LUTE.

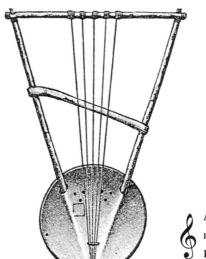

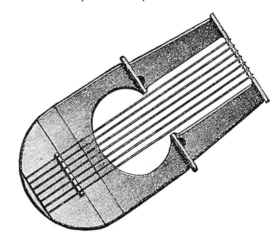

♪ A PRIMITIVE LYRE (LEFT) FROM ETHIOPIA COMPARED TO A MORE DEVELOPED TYPE FROM GREECE. IT IS EASY TO IMAGINE HOW THE FORMER DERIVED FROM THE SKULL AND HORNS OF AN ANIMAL.

played it, and where it served as accompaniment to epic songs of mythical adventures, and eventually this popularity travelled with it to Rome. Mark Anthony so admired the playing of Anaxemor that he put a military guard at his disposal and awarded him the rights to levy tribute on four Roman cities. Two *kithara* players visiting Rome so impressed the normally parsimonious Emperor Vespasian that he paid them 200 000 *sesterces*, and Nero awarded the *kithara* player Menecrates with a palace and a fortune. Although itself a lyre, the *kithara* developed a separate existence, so that writers refer to it as 'supplanting the lyre' in popularity. The word *kithara* is influential. It is almost certainly the root of both *guitar* and *zither*, and may have influenced *sitar* (see page 211).

℘ Konting

A five-stringed lute of the *Mandinka* people of the Gambia. It is a diminutive instrument, oval-bodied and with an animal-skin membrane.

℘ Kora

An instrument of West African origin, most commonly found in the Gambia. Its hybrid design is reflected in the description 'harp lute'. A large leather-covered gourd resonator is pierced by a long neck which supports 21 strings. These, divided 10-11, run down in two courses to a flat horizontal bridge protruding from the gourd towards the player, always male, who plucks the strings with his fingers. Two wooden dowel handles emerge from the gourd upwards at an angle and close to the strings. In performance the *kora* has a wide range of sounds. Not only are melody and accompaniment combinations possible but the player will sometimes flick his fingers against the handles to produce a percussive rhythm. This is further enhanced when a colleague strikes the rear of the gourd with a stick. Particularly charming aspects of the *kora* are the attachment of jingles to the bridge, and a hole in the gourd to accept monetary contributions.

THIS **1898** REPRESENTATION OF A *KOTO* PLAYER CONVEYS THE ATMOSPHERE OF A MORE LEISURELY AGE IN JAPANESE COURTS. TO PLAY *KOTO* WITH DELICACY WAS THE AIM OF MANY A YOUNG WOMAN OF GOOD BIRTH.

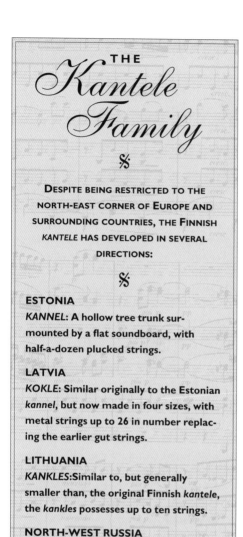

THE Kantele Family

℘

DESPITE BEING RESTRICTED TO THE NORTH-EAST CORNER OF EUROPE AND SURROUNDING COUNTRIES, THE FINNISH *KANTELE* HAS DEVELOPED IN SEVERAL DIRECTIONS:

℘

ESTONIA
KANNEL: A hollow tree trunk surmounted by a flat soundboard, with half-a-dozen plucked strings.

LATVIA
KOKLE: Similar originally to the Estonian *kannel*, but now made in four sizes, with metal strings up to 26 in number replacing the earlier gut strings.

LITHUANIA
KANKLES: Similar to, but generally smaller than, the original Finnish *kantele*, the *kankles* possesses up to ten strings.

NORTH-WEST RUSSIA
GUSLI: Early *guslis* in north west Russia had up to 14 strings; later versions are more developed. See *gusli*.

℘ Koto

Originally from China, where a similar instrument called *cheng* still exists, the *koto* is now regarded as specifically Japanese. It was introduced to Japan in the 8th century AD and has remained basically unchanged ever since. It is a 2m (6.5 feet) long wooden *zither*, placed horizontally in front of the player who plays the 13 silk strings (though nylon is increasingly used) with fingertips or plectra. Each string has a dedicated bridge which is movable for tuning. Related varieties of the *koto* are still found in China, and in Korea.

Lute, Lyre and Harp
ESSENTIAL DIFFERENCES

LUTE In its basic form the lute consists of a sound table, usually of wood. This comprises the fingerboard (with or without frets) and the upper face of the resonating body. Strings run parallel to the sound table; they are attached by tuning pegs at the upper end, run across a bridge on the resonating body and are then attached at the lower end. The resonating body may be of virtually any shape and is, of course, hollow, sometimes with holes or slots in the upper face. Lutes may be plucked (like the *banjo*) or bowed (like the violin).

LYRE Instead of running parallel with a fingerboard, the lyre's strings are attached to a yoke which is held away from the sound table by two struts, making, with the table, four sides of a square, or, in some models, an 'H' shape. Thus, the strings run freely through the air between the yoke and the sound table. This table, as in the lute, is a resonating box which may be of any shape and may be pierced by a soundhole. Bowed lyres are rare. See also *kithara*.

HARP Non-Western and ancient harps fall into three categories:

ARCH HARP (or bow harp): the earliest and most primitive type, is a gracefully curved wooden bow to which strings are attached twice at different points along its length. A resonator is usually attached to, or is part of, the bow.

ANGLE HARP: possibly a slightly later design than the arch harp but certainly of pre-Christian date, the angle harp is an 'L'-shaped structure, across the angle of which runs a number of strings. A resonator may form either arm of the 'L'-shaped body.

FRAME HARP: first depicted in the 8th century AD, the frame harp is a structure in the shape of a 'V' with a closed top and is therefore more robust in construction than the other types. Strings run from one side of the 'V' (which also houses the resonator) to the enclosing bar at the top. It is from this design that the modern harp developed. Harps are always plucked; the structure of all three types would make bowing impracticable.

These brief harp descriptions are amplified on pages 72–3.

AN ANCIENT EGYPTIAN BOW HARP COMPLETE WITH BOWL RESONATOR WHICH SUPPORTS THE CARVED HEAD OF A NOBLE FIGURE.

Lute

From its prehistoric origins somewhere in the Middle East, the plucked lute has undergone vast diversification, too vast in fact for more than a sample to be discussed here. Its wide distribution, too, defeats detailed examination in a general book, but if we endeavour to follow its names along geographical lines it may help to illustrate its spread.

A representation on a Mesopotamian seal of about 2000 BC may show a long-necked lute; more decisive of its early existence are Egyptian paintings of about a thousand years later, by when the lute was well established throughout the Middle East. The Egyptian pictograph, a circle from which rose a vertical line cut by two short horizontal lines, represents the non-vowel sound *n-f-r* and is a certain illustration of a stringed instrument. Later Egyptian words included *a'guz* (cf. Yugoslav *gusle*), while the Arabian word *al'ud* ('flexible stick') gave rise to *outi* and *laghoute* (Greece), *liuto* and *lutina* (Italy), *laud* (Spain), *luth* (France); *Laute* (Germany) and *lute* (England). Arab-Moroccan *gunibri* and Sudanese *gunbri* are clearly related, and the Arab *kobus* and *qabus* probably gave rise to *gambus* and *kabosa*, found in both North Africa and Asia, the *kobza* of Romania and the *qupuz* of eastern Europe. The North African *quitara* led to the

Italian *chitarra* and *chitarrone* and thence to *cistre* (France), *Cithrinchen* and *Erzcistre* (Germany), *cittern* (Europe), *cithare, citole* and *cither* (England) and guitar. Local names also arose: *tanpur, tanbur* and *dambura* are found in Afghanistan, Turkey, Pakistan, and may be the root of Indian *tambura* and Georgian *panturi*, while Italian *bandola, mandola, mandolin, mandora*, etc probably became *pandora* and *pandurina* in the rest of Europe, the *pandurion* in Greece, and *Mandürchen* in Germany. In India the *mayuri* and *tayus* both mean 'peacock' (Sanskrit and Hindustani respectively) which suggests the shape of the instrument. Further east, China developed its own words for different lute-type instruments: *pi'pa, san hsien, shuang ch'in, su hu,* etc; and in Japan are found *chicuzen,*

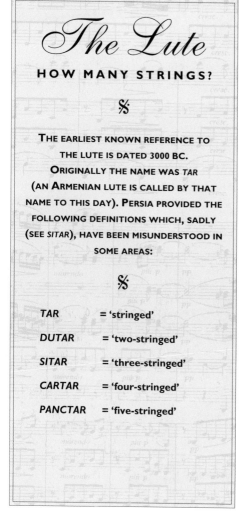

The Lute

HOW MANY STRINGS?

THE EARLIEST KNOWN REFERENCE TO THE LUTE IS DATED 3000 BC. ORIGINALLY THE NAME WAS *TAR* (AN ARMENIAN LUTE IS CALLED BY THAT NAME TO THIS DAY). PERSIA PROVIDED THE FOLLOWING DEFINITIONS WHICH, SADLY (SEE *SITAR*), HAVE BEEN MISUNDERSTOOD IN SOME AREAS:

TAR	= 'stringed'
DUTAR	= 'two-stringed'
SITAR	= 'three-stringed'
CARTAR	= 'four-stringed'
PANCTAR	= 'five-stringed'

gekkin, genkwan, ku, satsuma and *shamisen.*

The body of the European lute resembles a pear cut in half, its rounded back made up of ribs of wood. The soundboard bears a 'rose', a soundhole under the courses of paired strings. The fretted fingerboard terminates in a pegboard angled downwards almost at right-angles. Largely superseded in the 19th century by the guitar, the lute has undergone a strong revival in the 20th century in the hands of such artists as Julian Bream and the revived interest in early music in general.

A LATE EXAMPLE OF A LYRE IN A ROMANTIC EARLY 19TH CENTURY DOMESTIC SETTING. BY THEN, THE LYRE WAS AN ANACHRONISTIC CURIOSITY.

Musical Bow

A simple instrument of Papua New Guinea, some 30cm (12 inches) long, comprising a vegetable fibre attached either at both ends of a bow or at one end and hooked round a notch to provide two playing strings. The instrument's weak tone reduces its suitability for musical uses other than private amusement.

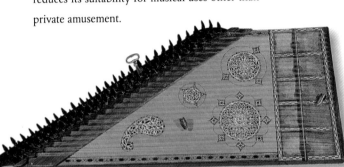

A TYPE OF PSALTERY FROM DAMASCUS, THE *QANUN* BEARS ONE OF MANY DIFFERENT NAMES FOR SIMILAR INSTRUMENTS IN OTHER AREAS.

Nanga

A *trough zither* of Tanzania. *Trough zithers* are made of a piece of wood hollowed out longitudinally with strings attached at each end, wound round slits in the wood. The hollow trough acts as a resonator when the strings are plucked.

Oud

An Arabic lute of five strings, without frets. The name may be the (French-influenced) version of Arabic *al'ud* ('flexible stick'), from which 'lute' was derived.

AN *OUD*. THIS EXAMPLE IS A 'SHORT LUTE', IN CONTRAST TO THE 'LONG LUTE', THE TURKISH *COLASCIONE*, PICTURED ON PAGE 208.

Psaltery

A dulcimer-type instrument of considerable antiquity, being a flat box with plucked strings. The word 'psaltery' may be from the Greek *psaltein* (to pluck), or from the instrument's role in accompanying the psalms.

Qanun

An Arab instrument found in Egypt and many points east, the *qanun* is a psaltery. The strings, which may number up to 100, are played with plectra. Said to have been invented during the tenth century, it spread across the Mediterranean and has enjoyed sporadic popularity in Middle Eastern countries ever since. For two centuries, starting in the 13th century, the *qanum* was played with its back against the player's chest instead of, as before and since, being placed across the player's knees.

Robab

A six-stringed long lute of Afghanistan.

Saz

A slender Turkish lute of varying size and ornate appearance.
The parts of

Ravi Shankar

Western awareness of Indian music was awoken for the first time in the 1950s due to the tireless championship of Ravi Shankar. It continues largely by later artists following his example. Shankar was born in Uttar Pradesh in 1920 and first came to Europe and the United States on tour in 1956–7. He gave three sell-out performances at the Edinburgh Festival in 1963. Western musicians quickly discovered the value of Indian music through Shankar's performances, Yehudi Menuhin becoming involved enough to travel to India and to record duets with Shankar in classic 'East-meets-West' programmes. In the popular scene, too, there were experiments with Eastern philosophies and Indian music, most notably by The Beatles, under the influence of George Harrison, in 'Within You Without You' from their album *Sergeant Pepper's Lonely Hearts Club Band*. Harrison appeared with Shankar at the Woodstock Festival in August 1969.

Shankar began as a musician and dancer under the guidance of his elder brother Uday. Later, a more formal musical education was secured with Ustad Allauddin Khan and Ali Akbar Khan, after which he quickly rose to become the foremost *sitar* virtuoso.
Critics have found his later performances to be too stylized and virtuosic to be true to the Indian tradition, but he remains an important influence on Western musicians and the public. He has also composed several film scores, ballet music including *Discovery of India* (1944) and *Samanya Kshati* (after Rabindranath Tagore's poem, 1961) and two concertos for sitar (1971; 1976). He has recorded these concertos and made many recordings of *ragas*.

the *saz* are connected with Islamic religious symbolism: the body of the instrument represents Ali, the fourth caliph of Islam, the neck is his sword, and when twelve strings are present they are the twelve prayer leaders of Islam. *Saz* is also the generic Turkish word for musical instrument, but in Russia and the former Yugoslavia the word specifies the long-necked lute.

✱ Sitar

Together with the double drum, the *tabla*, the *sitar* is regarded in the West as the quintessence of Indian music. It retains elements of both lute and *zither* design but has reached a stage of high sophistication. A thick fingerboard terminates at the lower end in a bulbous body. At the upper end a resonator gourd of almost equal size balances the instrument while lending it an ungainly appearance when played. Of the seven strings, two are drones; there are a further 12 or more sympathetic strings running inside the neck, and there are metal frets. The origin of the *sitar* is obscure, and further obscured by the name, which means 'three-stringed'. If the instrument derives from the Persian *setar* (also meaning 'three-stringed') it has evolved quite dramatically, for the *setar* was, confusingly, a four-stringed lute of slender construction with a small wooden resonating body and a thin neck.

✱ Tambura

An Indian lute with four unstopped metal strings. The open strings are plucked to provide a drone accompaniment.

✱ Vambi

A primitive arch harp consisting of a resonator of wood and animal skin from which run four strings to tuning pegs on a gently-curving stem. This is one of hundreds of varieties of arch harp found around the world; its use is limited to the *Bateke* tribe of Central Africa.

✱ Vanniyayar

(Also *muhonyu, quongon,* etc) A Siberian Jew's harp which, unlike others of this description, does not rely upon the mouth cavity to provide resonance. Instead, the bulb-shaped end, which terminates and joins two parallel metal bars, is held while a metal tongue lying between them is activated by the finger. The sound produced is a loose, high-pitched rattle rich in overtones. Players, usually female, are adept at producing a range of tones.

✱ Vaz

An Afghan arch harp comprising a bow set like a letter 'U' in a firm, flat base. The four strings are plucked with the fingertips.

✱ Vicitra Vina

A large Hindustani *zither* of substantial construction. One end of the table bears a bowl, the other

A NORTH INDIAN *BIN*, TECHNICALLY A *STICK ZITHER* WITH TWO HUGE GOURD RESONATORS.

a heavily-made pegbox, and the whole is supported on two huge gourd resonators. The plucked strings are stopped with an egg-shaped glass globe in the left hand.

✱ Vina

A long-necked lute of southern India with a large body and a gourd resonator of equal size attached behind the pegboard. There are seven strings, three of which are drones.

✱ Zither

The term *zither* defines a stringed instrument distinct from lute, lyre and harp in that any resonating device may be detached from the *zither* without making it unplayable. A *zither* in its basic form, therefore, consists of a stick with strings running parallel with it, and frets to raise

ANTON KARAS WITH HIS *ZITHER*. HE PROVIDED THE SOUNDTRACK MUSIC TO THE FILM *THE THIRD MAN*.

the strings away from the stick and to provide 'stopping' points for the fingers of the player. This type is called a *stick zither*. The strings may be plucked or struck; in some rare examples they are bowed. Frets in the form of raised blocks of wood may number as few as three or more than a dozen.

The south Indian *vina* is classed as a lute because the lower resonator has over the centuries become an integral part of the isntrument and cannot be removed. In northern India an equivalent instruments, the *bin* (the two words are clearly related) is a *zither* because the gourd resonators, usually two but sometimes three in number, may be detached. This removal will, of course, affect the strength and quality of the instrument's tone but the *bin* will remain playable.

In the *tube zither*, fibres from the wooden tubular body are detached and raised on shallow bridges to form strings. These are common in Madagascar but probably originated in South-East Asia. When several *tube zithers* are bound side-by-side a *raft zither* is created, a form popular in several areas of Africa. (For the *trough zither*, see *nanga*, above.) A *board zither* comprises a rectangular board, which may include a box or gourd resonator, carrying a number of strings end-to-end. Bridges raise the strings off the face of the board. This type of design shades off into the psaltery family, where the box may vary from the rectangular; see *qanum*, page 210.

More advanced are the so-called *long zithers*, such as the *koto* (above), the Burmese *mi gyuan* (ingeniously constructed to resemble a crocodile with an arched back), and the European *zithers* which have become popular in Austrian, French, German and the folk cultures of other nations. Strictly speaking, harpsichord, spinet and virginals are sophisticated examples of *zither* in which the strings are plucked mechanically rather than by the fingers. Struck *zithers*, such as the dulcimer, are dealt with under Banged Instruments. The Aeolian harp is also a type of *zither* (see page 228).

METHODS OF
Plucking

There are two methods of plucking a stringed instrument: by the fingers or with a plectrum (plural: plectra) attached to or held by the fingers.

FINGER Some instruments, such as the harp, are plucked by the fingertips since they need a delicate, sensitive touch, although on occasion these call for a sharper, more incisive sound. For some compositions the harp strings are 'stroked' by the flesh of the fingertips to make a ghostly *glissando* effect.

FINGERNAILS In Eastern countries, and indeed elsewhere, musicians will sometimes let their fingernails grow extremely long and tough, the better to sound plucked instruments. In certain circumstances, on instruments with wound wire strings, composers will ask for a grating *glissando*, achieved when the string is scratched longitudinally by the fingernails.

PLECTRUM The Romans called this playing technique *plectrum*, which was also one of their words for lyre; the method of playing thus transferred to the instrument itself. Plectra may be made from virtually any hard but slightly yielding material. Wood, bone, reed, ivory and tortoiseshell were common, and the quill of a feather continued to be used for many years as the plucking component of the harpsichord. Modern harpsichord plectra of plastic are still

called quills. In the Middle Ages plectra were called *penna*, a word which relates to 'pen', also made from quills. Large birds also provided plectra from their beaks and talons.

A plectrum in the shape of a flat egg with a sharply pointed end is used by banjo and ukulele players, and other shapes, elongated but with an easily-held widening are found. Mandolin players used to use pointed plectra of overall thin design which protruded beyond the backs of the fingers, but most are held between thumb and forefinger. Japanese *shamisen* players use plectra some 25cm (10 inches) long, widened at the playing end and narrowing to form a handle held in the palm of the hand. (The illustration of a 19th-century *shamisen* player below shows the abnormally large plectrum.)

Other types fit over the finger and thumb, effectively lengthening and strengthening both for prolonged playing of wire-strung instruments. Players of psalteries and horizontal *zithers* will use thimble-type or ring plectra which fit over the end of the finger and thumb or slide to between the first and second joint, with extensions beyond the ends of the digits.

PLUCKED ODDITIES

✶ Ektara

Used as an accompaniment to singing, the *ektara* of Bangladesh consists of a gourd or small drum to which is fastened the two split sides of a bamboo stem. A string runs from the centre of the drum to the dividing node of the bamboo and is plucked with the fingers. A lower note may be obtained when the end of the bamboo is pressed to relax the string. The *ektara* also rejoices in alternative names: *gopijantra* and *gupijantra*. A similar Indian instrument is called *gopiyantra*.

✶ Ground Harp

In central Africa the natives will tie a string to a flexible stem either growing or planted in the ground. The other end is led down to a soundboard fixed over a small pit with a weight or a system of pegs. The string, under tension from the stem, is then plucked with the fingers and resonates dully in the pit. Some tribes prefer to hit the string with sticks and/or play upon the soundboard with beaters. There is only slight musical value in the result; mainly the instrument gives delight to children. In Bangladesh a portable version is called *ananda lahari*.

✶ Kalumbu Bow

A *zither* of central Africa which goes under many different names, indicating its extreme antiquity. It originated as a hunter's bow to which was affixed a resonator (gourd or cooking pot) and a single string to be plucked by a finger. Really sophisticated models attached a second string, but some Africans drew music from smaller models of it by attaching a cord and whirling it round their heads. This had the effect of raising the player's reputation because he was then capable of creating mysterious sounds out of the air. Compare *bull-roarer*, page 228.

✶ Khamak

A small wooden cylinder, about 17cm (6.7 inches) in diameter, is held under the left arm of a Bangladeshi musician, who holds a string in his left hand. This string passes through the open end of the cylinder and is flexed with the fingers. The right hand strums the string with a plectrum. This variety of string drum is also called *gubgubi*. A similar instrument in India is also called *khamak*.

✶ Sansa

Also called *kaffir piano, likembe, mbira, zeze, thumb piano*, etc, the *sansa* is named after the Congolese tribe among whom it was first discovered by Western explorers. The instrument probably arose several centuries before the 16th, the date of the earliest extant examples. The *sansa* resembles a flat wooden box (which might be of almost any size) from one side of which emerge a series of metal plates at a shallow angle. These plates are sprung down and released by the fingers and thumbs of the player to produce a liquid, twanging sound. 𝄢

IN ANCIENT GREECE, POETRY AND SONG WERE USUALLY INSEPARABLE. HERE, SAPPHO AND ALCAEUS PERFORM TO THEIR OWN ACCOMPANIMENT OF LYRES.

213

BANGED & INSTRUMENTS

THIS IS THE SIMPLEST and most primitive way to sound an instrument. Infants do not need to be taught how to do it. The instrument is, quite simply, hit by another object. Drums and gongs of almost every type may be attacked by any means, ranging from the lightest tap of a fingernail to a blow with a heavy object that would kill a man.

A drum, singular, comprises two components, a body and a head. The body may be of virtually any hollow shape which contains air, and the head may be made from a large variety of materials. When the head is hit, it vibrates: this in turn induces vibration in the air which is amplified by the body. Some drums have two 'heads', one at each end of the body; others have one head, the other end being either open or enclosed by an extension of the body. A few drums do not have a hollow body: they resound when their solid material is struck.

In instruments which are sounded by hitting (and drums are by no means the only ones), the basic idea is the same: to strike the instrument – with stick, hand, fist, whip, or whatever 'beater' is chosen – with the intention of making it resound. The sounds produced are of unimaginable variety; see Gong, page 219.

The range and variety of 'banged' instruments is so vast that only a selection may be mentioned here. Africa alone would yield enough types to fill this entire book. Indeed, Africa may be called the 'Drum Continent', because nowhere else in the world has a greater range or number of drums. Africa was the continent which saw the emergence of man and probably the beginning of music itself. It is almost certain that the first musical instrument was a drum, and from that beginning arose a whole galaxy of struck instruments. Together with drums, wind and stringed instruments are common in Africa, and all have been used for similar purposes, though variations exist in different cultural areas. Drums predominate in the following activities:

℘ Dance

Tribal rites, births, marriages, and other events of a joyful nature are almost unthinkable without the sound of instruments, and since the native African appreciates rhythm above all other musical utterances, drums are their favourite instruments.

℘ Speech

Human speech, itself basically rhythmic among most of the 1000 or so languages found in Africa, is imitated in music. The best examples are the various types of so-called 'message drums' or 'talking drums' that carry brief messages through forests and for long distances across the plains.

 YORUBA COURT DRUMMERS OF SOUTH-WEST NIGERIA, IN TRADITIONAL FORMAL DRESS.

❧ War

Inter-tribal conflicts were, and still are, accompanied by preliminary bouts of drumming to stir up loyal emotions. Drum rhythms become insistent during the battles themselves to instil excitement and passion in the warriors and terror in their enemies.

❧ Ceremony

Whether this is the installation of a new chief, the arrival of important visitors, or the funeral rites of an elder, drums will accompany it. They may be joined by joyful or doleful horn and trumpet sounds and the chanting or wailing of the tribe.

❧ Talking drums, African style

African languages operate on two levels: rhythmic speech and tonal inflexion. Combined, these may be interpreted by differently-pitched drums or single log drums capable of producing more than one pitch, any ambiguities becoming clear by intelligent appreciation of the context. Message drums are used for short messages. They may warn of danger, though the nature of the danger may not be obvious. They may call the tribe home for some important meeting, or they may signal success in a hunt. Not many syllables are needed, then, for simple messages such as 'Look out!', 'Come home', or 'I have killed'. The continuous rattle of 'talking' drums which so unnerves explorers are not extended messages but the same message repeated over and over.

ZOLTAN KODALY, WHOSE *HARY JANOS* SUITE MAKES PROMINENT USE OF *CIMBALOM*, WITH HIS SECOND WIFE SAVOLTA AND A PUPIL IN 1960.

Banged Instruments
OCCASIONALLY HEARD IN CONCERT
❧

ANVIL The sharp incisive sound of hammer on anvil is required, of course, in Verdi's 'Anvil' Chorus from *Il Trovatore* (1853), in Wagner's *Siegfried* (1876) and in Jón Leif's 'Saga' Symphony (1943); other composers have called for it, none more so than Wagner, who required 18 in *Das Rheingold* (1869).

BELLS These have featured in countless works since the 18th century, but Tchaikovsky outdid every other composer by requesting that "all the bells of Moscow" be rung during his *1812* Overture (1880). More conventionally, composers have called for tubular bells to provide such effects; their low, baleful tolling at the end of Shostakovich's Symphony No. 11 (1957) provides a good example of their effectiveness.

BONGOS The French-born American Edgard Varèse was among many composers who have required the sound of bongos: his *Ionisation* (1931) includes them in the complement of 13 percussion instruments.

BRAKE DRUM John Cage and others have sought the ringing tones of a struck suspended car brake drum in their works. His

First Construction (in Metal) (1939) includes them along with cowbells, sleighbells, gongs and anvils.

CIMBALOM The most famous example of the use of a *cimbalom* in the orchestra is in Kodály's *Hary Janos* Suite (1927).

GONG Gongs have been used in the orchestra since Gossec's *Funeral Music* (1791). The orchestral *tam-tam*, too, features regularly in scores. The gong has, however, occasionally been given an unusual role, for example when it is played by a violin bow – in Penderecki's *Dimensions der Zeit und der Stille* ('Dimensions of Time and Silence', 1960) – or made to produce a *glissando* by being lowered into a tub of water (in works by Lou Harrison and John Cage).

SHIELD In his 'Saga' Symphony of 1943, the Icelandic composer Jón Leifs included several ancient instruments including struck shields.

TABOR A long, narrow drum of high pitch, used in Bizet's *L'Arlesienne* Suite (1873) and Copland's *El Salon Mexico* (1933) and *Appalachian Spring* (1945)

❧ Adapu

A rectangular frame drum from Sumeria, some 7000 years old.

❧ Ala Bohemica

A 14th-century psaltery of Bohemia: the name means 'Bohemian wing'. The flat wing-shaped table has two soundholes. At one end of the table stands a half-moon wooden block through which strings pass, to be secured at the far end. The strings are played with small beaters.

❧ Alal

A Sumerian frame drum, larger than the *adapu*.

❧ Anvil

The blacksmith's anvil produces a loud metallic clang when struck and has done so ever since metal was first worked in a forge. Occasionally, this sound is requested by composers to produce a particularly harsh percussive effect.

❧ Atumpan

Large conical drums of Ghana, sometimes carried on the shoulder of one man while another strikes it with sticks; at other times the player hangs it round his neck on a cord and plays it himself. On the Ivory Coast the instruments are called *atungblan*: they are played in pairs and used for signalling and as talking drums.

❧ Balag

A perhaps slightly inaccurate rendering of the Sumerian generic word for 'drum'.

❧ Baz

A name still used for the Arab small kettledrum and probably identical with the word known by the Ancient Egyptians of the Middle Kingdom, c. 2100 to 1600 BC.

❧ Bell

A familiar instrument, in which a metal bowl is either inverted and suspended to swing so that the clapper inside strikes the inner surface, or is held still and struck upon the outside by strikers. In Ghana, conical bells are held aloft and struck with sticks; another design has a boat-shaped bell held in the hand and struck with an iron rod. The closing or opening of the hand controls the amount and quality of tone required.

MODERN AFRICAN DRUMMERS. THE LONG, SINGLE-HEADED BARREL DRUMS PRODUCE A VARIETY OF TONES DEPENDING UPON THE STRENGTH OF THE FINGER STRIKES AND THEIR POSITIONS ON THE SKINS.

❧ Bendir

A round frame drum, about 50cm (20 inches) in diameter, of western North Africa, in which one or two snares (wires) pass under the single head. These give the tone added bite and carrying power.

❧ Bombo

A large barrel drum, about 60cm (24 inches) in diameter, with two goatskin heads, found in military and folk bands of Chile, Argentina and other South American countries. The player may strike the frame as well as the head.

❧ Bongo

Vellum-headed drums familiar in Latin American dance music. Descended from pre-Columbian models, these small, basin-shaped drums are often joined in pairs. They are held on the knees and played with the fingers. Their pitch is high and penetrating.

❧ Boobams

Recent North American development of the *bongo*: a series of chromatically-tuned drums with resonators (of bamboo, hence the name) of varying length.

❧ Brake Drum

Literally a car part, suspended and hit to produce a resonant, bell-like tone.

❧ Cai Bong

An hourglass drum of Vietnam but with only one head, played with the hands.

✻ Caja

A South American frame drum with two heads and snares, frequently found in Argentina, Bolivia, Chile, Colombia and Paraguay. It may reach 50cm (20 inches) in diameter. The body is of wood, sometimes of tin, and the skins are fastened by crossed cords. The word *caja* is also known in Cuba where it signifies the lead instrument of a percussion group.

✻ Changgo

A wooden hourglass drum with heads of about 40cm (16 inches) in diameter and played horizontally. The head on the left is of cowhide and played by hand, that on the right is of horsehide and played with a bamboo striker.

✻ Chang-ku

A Chinese drum in which the two heads extend beyond the diameter of the body and cords run between the heads. These cords, in 'W' pattern, are tightened and relaxed by metal rings to tune the drum.

✻ Ch'uk

A wooden box of approximately rectangular shape with a hole in the top lid. Korean musicians thrust a stick through the hole and strike the floor of the box in a rhythmic pattern.

♪ TOP: EGYPTIAN CLAPPERS OF THE 18TH DYNASTY (1600-1400 BC). RIGHT: TIBETAN MONKS CHANTING TO THE RHYTHM OF THE *ROL-MO*, METAL CYMBALS WHOSE LARGE CENTRAL BOSSES CONTRIBUTE TO THEIR LOUD TONE.

✻ Cimbalom

A Hungarian struck dulcimer, a horizontal rectangular or trapeziform box of strings, originally an early folk instrument but since improved (during the 1860s) to bring it up to recital standard, with dampers and a wide chromatic range.

✻ Clappers

The Egyptians of c. 1460 BC fashioned wood or ivory into representations of human forearms and hands, then clapped them together during musical entertainments. Similar effects are obtained in the Balkans, the Middle East and Asia, where the objects might vary from spoons to brooms, one hit against the other. Australian Aborigines dance to the rhythm of clashing sticks.

✻ Clay Drum

A Mexican design of the Middle Ages. It comprised two small goblet drums joined by a long hollow clay tube which was bent into a 'U'-shape to bring the two heads into a horizontal line about 60cm (24 inches) apart. One head with an animal skin was beaten by the hands while the other was left open, its tube containing water whose volume could be varied for tuning purposes.

✻ Cymbals

Bronze and other metals are used in non-Western cymbals: two circular plates are clashed together to mark the rhythm. Their distribution is virtually world-wide.

℀ Dai co

In Vietnam this means 'big drum', a large barrel drum with two heads, beaten with sticks.

℀ Da'ira

A tambourine of Mozambique, used to accompany singing. A similar word, *daira*, refers to a Georgian tambourine which may have bells, metal discs and coins round the inside edge.

℀ Da-daiko

A large Japanese barrel drum with two heads each 1.2m (4 feet) in diameter. The instrument is mounted on a heavy wooden frame and played with beaters. The body is 1.5m (5 feet) deep.

℀ Damaran

Paired drums of India, specifically for use in processions and ceremonies. They are conical in shape and hung either side of an ox. The mounted player strikes one drum with a straight stick; the other stick is curved.

℀ Davul

A Near- and Middle-Eastern cylinder drum with two heads, tough laces tensioning the animal-skin heads in a zigzag design. Used in ceremonies and for *al fresco* dancing, the davul of Turkey (*dola* in Kurdish areas) is slung from the shoulder so that both heads may be played, the thicker head uppermost with the heavy beater (*tokmak*), the thinner with a light stick (*cubuk* or *subuk*). Originating in India or Asia about 700 BC, the *davul* now has related instruments in Iran (*dohol*), Armenia (*dool*), Greece (*daouli*) and Albania (*daule*), and is known in Arabia as the 'Turkish drum' (*tabl turki*). The Afghan *dhol* is similar but barrel-shaped and is probably akin to the earliest types since it also survives in India.

℀ Dogdog

A Javanese conical drum with one head.

℀ Doira

A frame drum, sometimes with jingles (thus, a tambourine), played only by women in Afghanistan, Turkey and Iran.

℀ Donno

An hourglass drum (qv) of the *Ashanti* of Ghana.

℀ Drumgong

A Chinese kettledrum dating from the 4th cen-

♪ INDIAN DRUMS AND GONGS BEING PLAYED BY VIRTUOSO UDAY SHANKAR IN 1950.

tury BC. It is made entirely of bronze, even the single head being of thin bronze, and may be of great size. The head is struck by a heavy beater while the body is played with a bamboo stick to produce a thin, sharp sound.

℀ Dulcimer

A kind of psaltery (see Plucked Instruments) in which the strings are struck with beaters. However, such is the confusion of terms that it is possible to encounter plucked dulcimers and struck psalteries. The terms might thus be regarded as interchangeable.

℀ Fontomfrom

A Ghanaian large drum, similar to the *atumpan*. In common with many non-Western instruments, the name is probably onomatopoeic in origin.

℀ Gamelan

The most important indigenous music of Indonesia, and one of the most eerily evocative to Western ears. Associated today primarily with Bali and Java, *gamelan* orchestras (see panel featuring *gamelan* instruments) seem to have had their origin in a bronze culture that spread from the Asian mainland, not in the form of musical instruments but as weapons of war. Javanese gongsmiths, learning from bronze artifacts left by Asian conquerors, were probably masters of their trade well before the Christian era, and primitive *gamelan* ensembles existed then. Sophistication and evolution then took place and today's *gamelan* ensembles consist of highly organized and superbly disciplined groups of players.

This gong-chime culture developed first in Java, where *gamelan* orchestras were playing by

the 16th century. Balinese *gamelan* ensembles came slightly later and have grown much more diversified in their structure. In addition, west Java and central Java each has its own separate developments. In addition to struck instruments, *gamelan* ensembles can include the *suling*, a long end-blown flute with up to six finger holes; the *rebab*, a local variety of spike fiddle; and singers, either singly or in chorus.

𝄋 Ganang

A pair of Vietnamese two-headed drums capable of a wide variety of tone: a stick is used upon one head while the hand beats the other.

𝄋 Ghirbal

A frame drum of Arabia with snares under the single head.

𝄋 Ghomma

A South African instrument of the Cape Malays: a drum with one head, held under the left arm and played with both palms as an accompaniment to song.

 A *GAMELAN* ENSEMBLE, WITH GONG CHIMES, *KENDANG* (CYLINDER DRUM) AND *CHENGCHENG* (CYMBALS) PROMINENT.

𝄋 Gong

Orchestral gongs (*tam-tams*) evolved from types which take the form of disc-shaped metal plates and are struck centrally or towards the outer edge with beaters of any material (from metal to sponge). Some Eastern gongs have raised central bosses, others have rims. Large gongs are suspended in a frame; this may be of any design because the tone of the gong does not depend upon the frame's shape, see page 218. Gong chimes consist of several tuned gongs set in a stand or framework support that gives the player access to each. See *Gamelan*. The *gong ageng* is a large resonant Balinese gong suspended in a frame. The Japanese *goong* measures in excess of a metre in diameter.

𝄋 Gourds

Many uses are found for gourds in percussion. In Ghana are floated on water and struck with the palm of the hand or sticks, the water providing resonance. Gourds also provide the bodies of drums and may be filled with pellets to make rattles.

Gamelan
INSTRUMENTS
𝄋

SINGLE GONGS:
AGENG, a low-pitch gong up to 1m (40 inches) in diameter.
SUWUKAN, a high-pitched gong.

GONG CHIMES (MULTIPLE GONGS):
BONANG BARUNG, 12 centrally-bossed gongs set horizontally in a double line upon a wooden stand.
KENGONG, a range of large gongs, each resting on its own square resonator.
REYONG, resembling an elongated hourglass drum, played horizontally with hands upon each end.

METALLOPHONES:
SARON, a horizontal wooden table supporting up to seven bronze bars hit with a wooden beater.
SLENTEM, similar to the *saron*; played with circular beaters. Cylindrical resonators lie below the bars.
GENDER, a larger form of *slentem*, with 14 bronze bars over bamboo resonators.
GANGSA, Balinese, similar to the *gender* and played with wooden hammers.

DRUM:
KENDANG, a two-headed cylinder drum played horizontally with the hands.

XYLOPHONES:
ANGKLUNG, hollow bamboo tubes, tuned and set in a frame at an angle. The word *angklang* also refers to types of rattle made from bamboo.
GAMBANG, in which wooden keys rest upon an ornate wooden structure.

CYMBALS:
CHENGCHENG, similar to Western cymbals and made in various sizes.

ZITHER:
GUNTANG, a *tube zither* with one or two strings run lengthways over a hollowed-out log with a slit in its upper face. The strings are struck with a short wooden beater.

Types of Drum

The accepted descriptions of drum types clearly indicate their general shape. These descriptions apply equally to non-Western and to orchestral drums.

BARREL DRUM, convex-sided, the body deeper than the diameter of the skin. One or two heads.

CONICAL, its top wider than the base. A double-conical drum resembles two conical drums head to head, with the upper head of a diameter less than that of the waist – a variation of the convex barrel drum.

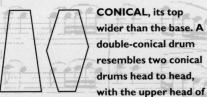

CYLINDER DRUM, straight-sided, the body of any depth equal to or greater than the diameter of the head. One or two heads.

FRAME DRUM, consisting of a frame of wood or other material, round or square, the diameter of the skin greater than the depth of the body. One or two heads. As with most drums, the design is prehistoric. In Arab countries the generic name for frame drum is *daff, duff, dof,* or something similar. Some Middle Eastern frame drums are adorned with metal jingles round the rim, as in the Western tambourine.

GOBLET DRUM, small, single-headed, with a body tapering to a rounded base, often with a supporting foot.

HOURGLASS DRUM, as if two goblet drums were joined at their bases; therefore, two heads. Some are larger than this description suggests. In India, the hourglass drum has existed for at least 2000 years and survives still. Cords run between the heads and the player exerts pressure on the cords to tighten the skins and thus raise the pitch. In this way, an infinite variety of notes is obtainable within the range of the instrument, and drummers can make the drums 'speak' in a startlingly realistic way. Hourglass drums are also found in Africa.

KETTLEDRUM, bowl-shaped, similar to a goblet drum but larger and more variable in shape.

SLIT-DRUM, primarily an African instrument with a strong tone which may be heard over great distances and is therefore useful as a message drum. Some models are of enormous length, being made from a fallen tree trunk, hollowed out and with slits in the upper surface which vary in size and shape. Edges of the slit form tongues of wood which are beaten with sticks or clubs for dancing or to produce the rhythmic accents of speech for messages. There is no skin membrane.

🎼 MANY AFRICAN DRUMS DEVIATE IN DETAIL BECAUSE, LIKE THOSE PICTURED, THEY ARE 'HOME-MADE'.

Gyamadudu

A cylinder drum of Ghana with two heads. Its name probably derives from its characteristic bass sound, with its slightly muffled initial attack.

Handle Drum

A species of African hourglass drum with two heads and a handle carved out from the central body to facilitate manipulation. The presence of the handle precludes the use of tuning ropes. Alternatively, a handle drum may refer to an instrument known from Siberia, through Alaska and into American Indian territory. It is a round frame drum with a handle protruding from it at a tangent. Such a drum is used almost exclusively for religious purposes.

Harp

Not usually thought of as a 'banged' instrument, the harp is sometimes called upon to accompany itself with a rhythmic line. In Africa, and inevitably elsewhere, for the temptation must be irresistible, harpists might well add rhythm by playing a tattoo upon the soundboard with their fingers, an intriguing effect caught in Carlos Salzedo's *Chanson de la nuit* (1924) for harp solo.

Hiuen-ku

Huge drum of the Chinese Chou dynasty (1122 BC), used in ceremonial events at the Imperial court.

Hoe

A simple instrument found in Ghana, consisting of two hoe blades bound together and struck with a metal ring.

Horns

In Ghana and other African countries, animal horns are struck with a stick to produce a noise like dull-sounding bells.

Horseshoes

An instrument invented by the 18th-century composer John Davy at his blacksmith uncle's workshop. He arranged horseshoes in a given order to produce a melody as they were hit. It is not known whether Davy employed such an instrument in one of his operas.

Idu-man

Paired kettledrums of large and small size, found in Tibet.

A JAPANESE DRUMMER IN TRADI-TIONAL COSTUME. NOTE THE ANGLED STAND ON WHICH THE DRUM RESTS.

Isigubu

Possibly modelled upon European military drums, the *isigubu* was adopted by the Zulus, who modified it with tuning cords attached to the two heads. Playing may be with sticks or hands.

Ka'eke'eke

Any hard surface is suitable to make these Hawaiian stamping sticks resound. They are hollowed-out bamboo pipes, usually in sets of four with unequal lengths bound together in pairs, which resonate when 'stamped' vertically on a stone or log. For rhythmic use only.

Kempul

A Javanese gong some 50cm (20") in diameter.

Khong Mon

A large 'U'-shaped frame, along the inner curve of which are set a series of gongs used in Thai ensembles.

Khong Wong Yai

Gongs of Thailand, ranged in a circular rack and struck to make a melody.

Koboro

An Ethiopian two-headed drum, sharply angled towards its lower end so that it resembles a kettledrum in appearance. The lower head, therefore, is of much smaller diameter than the upper.

Ko-daiko

A large (76cm/30in diameter) Japanese barrel drum with two heads. When used in processions, it is suspended from a pole carried by two men, the player walking alongside striking the instrument with sticks.

Ko-tsuzumi

An hourglass drum of Japan, used in *Noh* plays. Cords join the heads and a tuning strap at the central point between the heads. The player holds the instrument against his right shoulder.

Mpingtintoa

An onomatopoeic name for a single-headed gourd drum of Ghana.

❧ Mrdangam

A two-headed drum played by both hands horizontally while resting in the player's lap. The word comes from Sanskrit for 'clay-body' (*mrd-anga*), which tells us the material from which the barrel-shaped body is made. The clay, however, is not visible for it is completely coated with cane in a criss-cross pattern. Found in Bangladesh, India and Vietnam, the *mrdangam* probably originated in India.

In an article written in the 1950s, Krishna Chaitanya, an authority on Indian drums, gave an alternative description of the *mrdangam*. He wrote "[It] is hollowed out of a block of wood. A flour paste applied to the left membrane lowers the tone to a full, bass sound while a mixture of manganese dust, iron filings and other substances applied to the right side yields a characteristic resonant tone."

❧ Musical Bow

The bushmen of southern Africa play a hunting bow, one end of which is placed in or near the mouth which acts as a resonator. The string is then struck with a small stick or the fingers while the note is altered by the fingers of the hand holding the bow.

❧ Naqqara

Kettledrums of different sizes found in Arab countries. The name gave rise to the European medieval *nakers* (see page 91).

❧ Ngoma

A large drum, about one metre in diameter, either suspended from a frame or stood on the ground. It has one head and is struck with wooden sticks by women. At South African native ceremonies and important festivals it forms the bass of a drum trio, the tenor drum (*thungwa*) being similar in shape, design and beaters, the alto drum (*murumba*) being small enough to hold between the knees (or stood on the ground on its sturdy single foot) and beaten with the hands.

❧ Nihbash

A domestic pestle and mortar taken from Jordanian kitchens to make a semi-musical rhythm.

❧ Ntenga

A set of tuned drums of Uganda. Each has two heads, the lower one being of much smaller diameter than the upper. With entirely different pitches from each head, and in the usual ensemble of 15 drums, the variety of tone is considerable.

❧ O-daiko

A double-headed 'great drum' of Japanese percussion ensembles, the *o-daiko* barrel drum can measure 2m (6.5 feet) in diameter and weigh over 300kg (660 pounds). It is usually sited permanently on a wooden wagon and requires the services of two drummers, one at each head, who strike the skins with heavy clubs. Forming the rhythmic foundation of the ensemble, the fearsome sound of the *o-daiko* is often accompanied by the warlike shouts of the players

❧ Paakuru

A Maori mouth resonator, consisting of a stick about 40cm (16 inches) long and 1cm thick, shaped like a bow. With one end between the teeth and the other held between two fingers, the player would attack the *paakuru* with a stick and alter the resonance by moving his lips.

❧ Pantaleon

A dulcimer with 185 strings, invented by the German composer from whom it took its name: Pantaleon Hebenstreit. He called it *cimbal*, but Louis XIV insisted in 1705 that the device should carry its inventor's name. In essence, a dulcimer is a horizontal box of strings, these being struck by hand-held beaters. Its popularity survives in the Hungarian *cimbalom*, but in the 18th century it ran somewhat out of control, for in 1767 a pantaleon was made that was no less than 3.35m (11 feet) long, with 276 strings.

♪ A BUSHMAN OF SOUTHERN AFRICA PLAYING A MUSICAL BOW – THE STRIKING ACTION OF THE RIGHT-HAND FINGERS IS AKIN TO PLUCKING.

𝄞 A SENEGALESE DRUMMER PICTURED IN 1958 PLAYING A BARREL DRUM BY HAND AND STICK.

⅜ Pit Xylophone

A Ghanaian instrument consisting of up to 17 wooden keys arranged on a wooden frame, then placed over a resonating pit dug in the earth.

⅜ Pit Zither

Occasionally encountered in African communities, the *pit zither* is simply a string or wire held taut by two sticks driven into the ground at the

𝄞 AN ESKIMO WITH A *QILAIN*, A SINGLE-HEADED FRAME DRUM OF THE TYPE FOUND THROUGHOUT THE ARCTIC ESKIMO COMMUNITIES.

ends of a pit. The player hits the wire with sticks to accompany himself in song.

⅜ P'yonjong

A Korean bell-chime in which a wooden frame supports a series of 16 tuned bronze bells struck with a cow-horn mallet.

⅜ Qilain

A frame drum of the Eskimo peoples, with a head made of seal skin or the lining of a bear's stomach. The *qilain* differs from other frame drums in being struck with a bone beater only on the rim. The membrane provides resonance as an accompaniment to the Eskimos' most important musical activity: singing, as a social and ceremonial adjunct, often with communities performing against each other in contests.

Beaters
⅜

FINGERNAIL For a light touch.

FINGERS Capable of playing fast intricate rhythms.

HANDS The flat of the hand or the heal, thumbs or knuckles, or the fists, may all be used in certain circumstances.

RUBBER Used by West Indian drummers on their steel drums.

LEATHER THONGS For a dull, indefinite attack.

BRUSHES Dance bands often employ the swishing sound of brushes on drum skins.

RODS Wooden rods, for a light but incisive touch.

DRUMSTICKS May be of any size depending upon what drum is being used and the type of sound required. Their heads may be made of anything from the softness of sponge to the hardness of wood; each, of course, producing a different effect. In shape they may range from short to long, straight to sharply curved, and even double-curved. Some short sticks are double-headed, as in Irish folk bands.

BIRCH TWIGS: For the occasional orchestral requirement; they produce a sound rather more incisive than brushes.

BEATERS A word used for any striker, but normally reserved for heavy clubs such as those used in Japanese drumming.

METAL BEATER Used on orchestral tubular bells, and on some instruments of non-Western origin. For instance, metal rings are used on types of fixed bells and on the body of *didjeridoos* while the player is blowing.

❇ Reyong

A Balinese gong-chime, with several gongs ranged in a straight line in a wooden frame and struck by up to four players with hard beaters.

❇ Ringing Stones

Ch'ing. A Chinese instrument dating from the Chou dynasty (up to 221 BC) consisting of an ornate frame upon which hang tuned slabs of stone with were struck by small mallets. In shape the stones recall the side view of a tiger's head.

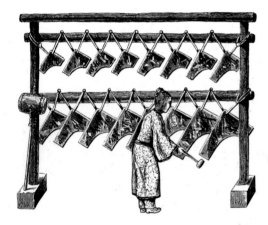

THE CHINESE *CH'ING*, THE ANCESTOR OF MODERN TUBULAR BELLS. ON THIS EXAMPLE A SMALL BARREL DRUM IS ATTACHED TO THE LEFT-HAND UPRIGHT.

Another example of ringing stones is the *p'yon'-gyong*. Like the linguistically almost identical Korean metal *p'yonjong*, this comprises a wooden framework supporting 16 struck 'bells', but in this case the bells are made of tuned stones rectangular in shape.

❇ Rooria

A Maori Jew's harp made from vegetable fibres up to 10cm (4 inches) long. One end is held between the teeth. Adept practitioners have a way of conversing with one another using their voices and the varying tones of the *rooria.*

❇ Saron

A Javanese trough metallophone. The trough is a long wooden construction upon which is set the *saron.* Like xylophones, metallophones have a system of bars or keys, but of metal, which, when struck in the right order, produce a melody. In the *saron,* the keys are thick and resonate with a deep, rich sound in the trough.

❇ Shield

An unlikely choice as a music-maker, but people from Asia to Africa place them with their convex surfaces to the ground and hit them with beaters, thereby resonating the air trapped underneath.

❇ Shime-daiko

A Japanese barrel drum of small size which serves as much as a physical work-out as an instrument. Its body is hollowed out from a log and the two heads are tensioned by two men who sit facing each other on the floor, the drum held between their bare feet. Great effort is required to tighten the ropes with hands and hammers, the drummers often sweating profusely even before the drums are ready for playing.

❇ Stamping Stick

A hollow drumstick produces resonance. This idea was put to use by primitive peoples, who would beat the stick on the ground or a rock to make a rhythmic accompaniment for dancing. The *ka'eke'eke,* above, is a slightly more sophisticated version of stamping stick.

❇ Steel Drum

In Trinidad, where oil drums were plentiful, workers would cut them in half, divide the head into several tuned sections by cutting and welding, and beat the head with rubber beaters. Steel drum bands make a most acceptable sound, both rhythmically and melodically, and a recording exists of a complete performance of Mozart's *Eine kleine Nachtmusik* played entirely on steel drums.

❇ Stone Star

African tribes enjoy the sound of the stone star. It consists of a circle of stones set in the ground. In the middle sits the player, who strikes the stones, each of which has its own note, with a stone held in each hand.

❇ Sunuj

Arabian finger cymbals, used by dancers. The plates are very small. One, attached to a middle finger, is struck by its fellow on the thumb to make a delicate, high-pitched sound as an accompaniment to dancing and singing.

❇ Tabla

An Indian double drum, used as rhythmic accompaniment in *ragas* and often played alone. The skill of an expert *tabla* player is such that the instrument seems to talk. The upper of the two drums is called the *tabla;* the lower is the *bayan.* The player sits cross-legged with the drums held in the angles of his knees and plays the drums with his hands, using fingertips, flat hands, heels of the hands and sometimes even knuckles and fingernails to produce varied sounds. The tone and pitch varies

𝄞 THE SKILL AND RHYTHMIC SPIRIT WITH WHICH STEEL DRUMMERS PLAY THEIR INSTRUMENTS HAVE MADE THEIR MUSIC POPULAR WORLD-WIDE.

according to whether the strikes occur on the centre of the head or towards the outer edge.

℅ Tabor

A generic word for 'drum', but more specifically a small cylinder drum slung by a cord round the neck of a pipe and tabor player, who would strike the drum with a stick in one hand while fingering a pipe with the other. *Tabor* also means a long narrow drum, with or without snares, sometimes used in the orchestra.

℅ Tijeras

Bolivian natives used to dance to the rhythm of the *tijeras*: a pair of scissors struck with a hard object to make a sharp sound.

℅ Twenesin

Signal drums of the *Ashanti* peoples, Ghana.

℅ Yamstick

One needs to stand well clear of a *yamstick* player at an Aboriginal totemic corroboree in Australia, for the 'instrument' is merely a stick which is used to beat out the time for the wild dancers, and any object, vegetable, mineral or animal, might serve as a 'drum'.

℅ Zarb

A single-headed goblet drum of the Middle Eastern regions, Iran and the Persian Gulf predominantly but also found in Turkey. It is held under the left arm and played with the fingers of the right hand. A great variety of tones is obtained, depending upon the strength of strikes

AND OTHER STRUCK MATERIALS

℅

SKIN Originally animal skin, dried and stretched taut over a frame.

BARK Tree-bark, suitable for large drums; in some cases the bark was strong enough to support stamping feet.

PLASTIC Modern materials are routinely used in today's drums, being less ecologically unfriendly, stronger, more reliable and cheaper than animal skins.

STRING In the so-called string-drum, a taut string is hit by a stick. In the piano, strings are struck by felt-covered hammers.

WOOD In the slit drum, tongues of wood or the edges of the slits, are struck with beaters. Bamboo strips, cut to tuned lengths are played like a xylophone.

METAL Many non-Western instruments bear metal plates which are struck. Horseshoes are also used. The Trinidad steel drum (see page 224) is made from oil drums cut to size and modified. Anvils are struck with a metal hammer.

VELLUM Used in some smaller drums.

STONE Some rocks resonate when struck.

and the area of head upon which they are made. Several names attach to the instrument, including *darabukka*, but the Turkish word *dombak* or *tombok* eloquently illustrates the tonal variety of the instrument, from the deep and resonant *tom* to the much shallower, sharper, *bok*.

℅ Zirbaghali

A single-headed goblet drum of Afghanistan, played with the fingers.

THE
Mexican Connection

In his *Xochipilli-Macuilxochitl* ('An Imagined Aztec Music', 1940) the Mexican composer Carlos Chávez assembled a wind group (piccolo, two flutes, E flat clarinet, trombone) and six percussionists to play instruments originating from the time before Columbus. The percussionists' roles were divided as follows:

1. **SMALL** *TEPONAXTLI*
    OMICHICAHUAZLTI

2. **LARGE** *TEPONAXTLI*
    SMALL COPPER RATTLES

3. **SMALL AND MEDIUM INDIAN DRUMS**
    CLAY RATTLE

4. **SMALL** *HUEHUETL*
    SMOOTH RATTLE

5. **MEDIUM** *HUEHUETL*
    CLAY RATTLE

6. **LARGE** *HUEHUETL*
    OMICHICAHUAXTLI

The copper and clay rattles are self-descriptive; a 'smooth rattle' equates with the sound of maracas, a rhythmic swishing of small beans or pebbles in an egg-shaped pod on a stick. The other instruments call for explanation.

ABOVE: A SOUTH AMERICAN NATIVE PLAYING A GOURD MARIMBA.
BELOW: DESCENDANTS OF DANCING AZTECS PICTURED IN 1721, TWO CENTURIES AFTER CORTÉS CONQUERED THEIR LAND AND TWO CENTURIES BEFORE CHÁVEZ ATTEMPTED TO RECONSTRUCT THEIR MUSIC.

GLOSSARY

HUEHUETL A cylinder drum some 90cm (3 feet) tall, standing upon three stout legs contiguous with the body. During construction, the interior is charged with live coals and the animal skin (jaguar or deer) fitted, the heat from the coals drying the skin to a high tension. The outer surface of a *huehuetl* is carved with representations of bird-gods and scenes of war, ritual and revenge.

INDIAN DRUMS These are goblet hand drums of the *bongo* (see page 216) variety.

OMICHICAHUAXTLI A scraper made of bone or wood with notches along one face that are rubbed rhythmically with another bone or stick.

TEPONAXTLI. A two-keyed slit drum (the Mayas called it *tunkul*, and it was known as *tun* in El Salvador). A tree log about one metre long is hollowed, laid horizontally, and an 'H'-shaped slit is cut in the upper surface, the bar of the 'H' at right-angles to the grain of the wood. This gives two keys or tongues of wood which are tuned to give notes a major second or a minor third apart when struck with mallets. Early explorers reported that the 'doleful' boom of the '*teponaxtli*' carried over great distances

All these Aztec instruments found uses in both dance and sacred situations, and Chávez conveyed this in his short composition. However, requirements for its performance are such that normally constituted orchestras cannot mount it without the assistance of museums or collectors.

BANGED ODDITIES

𝄢 Chinzumana

A xylophone of Mozambique of complicated design. It forms the lowest-sounding in a group of xylophones, its four slats providing a resonant drone. The wooden slats have to be fire-hardened before fitting. Each has a tuned resonator of wild orange shell, with a hole in the side for a membrane which produces a grating sound. This sound is modified by a wooden pipe leading out from the membrane.

𝄢 Clapper (or Monkey) Drum

A small double-headed drum from the body of which protrudes a handle. Attached to the body are two short cords, each with a bead, button, pebble or nut secured at the end. When the instrument is twisted rapidly by the handle, the loose objects on cords strike the heads of the drum. The instrument was used by organ-grinders' monkeys to attract crowds; similar versions are found in cultures as remote from Western cities as India, Tibet and Vietnam, which suggests that the *monkey drum*, like its player, originated in the Far East.

𝄢 Ingpongpo

This *Bantu* drum has a 'head' but no body. A dried animal skin is either manually held off the ground or suspended from poles or tree branches while it is beaten with a stick. The noise, similar to beating a carpet, is useful only as a dancing rhythm or for calling home a foraging party.

𝄢 Intambula

In Swaziland, south-west Africa, this instrument consists of a clay pot and an animal skin that has been shaved and moistened. These two components are not attached, and in performance the skin is held tightly in place over the pot by helpers while the player hits it with a stick.

𝄢 Lithophone

The word means 'stone-sound'. Lithophones take different forms. A standing rock may resound when struck, and in some areas a rock suspended from a rope serves as a bell. Ranges of stones, either suspended or resting upon a frame or the ground (see *Stone star*) are found from China to England; their music resembles that of a series of bells or a xylophone.

𝄢 Ma-ch'un

An hourglass drum of Tibet, its body being two human skulls joined at the crowns and shaped to take playing skins.

𝄢 Pahuu

The only *Maori* 'drum' was merely a plank of wood up to 9m (30 feet) in length that was suspended from a wooden framework or between two trees. It was a signalling instrument to be beaten by a watchman at times of danger, and it is reported to have been audible up to 20 kilometres (12 miles) away. In some models, a hole was pierced at a central point, possibly to give added resonance. 𝄡

𝄞 THE MONKEY DRUM IS VERY EASILY SOUNDED (BY TWISTING THE HANDLE) AND EQUALLY USEFUL AS A TOY OR NOISE-MAKER AT FAIRGROUNDS.

MISCELLANEOUS TYPES

SOME INSTRUMENTS SIMPLY do not fit comfortably into any of the categories that we have covered so far in this section. Instead, they exist close to one or more of the standard types, having been invented or discovered under unusual conditions.

Aeolian Harp

An instrument of beautiful tone that requires no intervention from humanity to make it sound. There are several different versions, but the most familiar consists of a rectangular frame across which several strings are stretched. All are tuned identically. The instrument is then stood where Aeolus, the wind god, can get at it: a breeze

vibrates the strings and a soft hum fills the area. As the wind increases in strength overtones begin to be drawn from the strings to produce a ghostly, disembodied sound, and if the wind strength or direction change the notes alter in subtle ways. One may imagine the ancients, hearing wind in the reed beds, experimenting with simple constructions of reeds and wooden frames in an attempt to bring the eerie sounds into their domestic environment.

Prehistoric models have been found, and King David is supposed to have owned an Aeolian harp. Much more recently, in the 19th century, experimenters tried to control the instrument by tuning the strings to a scale and constructing a keyboard which operated shutters that would open to allow the wind to reach selected strings. This seems to be unwarranted interference with a charmingly self-sufficient instrument.

Bull-roarer

A basic instrument of peoples the world over, but normally associated today with the Aboriginal tribes of northern Australia. It requires little skill and no musical knowledge to make a bull-roarer. A flat piece of wood a minimum of 15cm (6 inches) in length (the maximum length depends upon practicalities, as will be seen) is smoothed,

AN AEOLIAN HARP OF ABOUT 1870, MORE SOPHISTICATED IN DESIGN THAN THE EARLIEST EXAMPLES, WHICH WERE PROBABLY CREATED ACCIDENTALLY BY NATURE.

the edges bevelled and curved, then tapered in both planes at each end. Serrations are added to one long edge. A hole is drilled near one end to take a strong cord. Those bull-roarer makers of artistic bent may feel inclined to carve designs on the flat surfaces. The bull-roarer is also found among Eskimo peoples, where it is fashioned out of bone (fish, seal or bear) or driftwood.

To play the bull-roarer, the cord is gripped at the loose end and the player finds a convenient space. He then whirls it round his head to produce a loud fluttering roar. *Hummer-buzzer, swish, thunderstick* and *bummer* are some of the names the instrument has attracted. The ancients used this mysterious 'sound from nowhere' to scare away women not entitled to attend ceremonies, to stampede cattle and to draw down magic powers from the skies. It is the voice of dead ancestors, they thought. It may also have been used as a weapon, particularly if made from a material other than wood. Stone, bone and iron have all been used. Perhaps, during some forgotten battle, warriors were reduced to hurling flat wooden boards at their enemy and noticed, as the weapons fell, they spun in the air and produced a deep roar. By pitching a short lath into the air, this strange may be demonstrated. That may have spurred the more imaginative among them to make purpose-built roarers.

To add ethnic verisimilitude to his ballet *Corroboree* (1946), the Australian composer John Antill added a bull-roarer to the orchestra. The American Henry Cowell scored his *Ensemble* (1924) for the possibly unique combination of two violins, viola, two cellos and three thundersticks.

✂ *Chinese Pavilion*

An inappropriately exotic name for the bell-tree or 'jingling johnny', which is said to have originated as a visible symbol in Turkish military bands as they accompanied their armies to war. Therefore, its alternative name, Turkish crescent, is more appropriate. It consists of a long vertical pole hung with button bells and small cup bells fixed to crescent-shaped cross pieces placed like ladder-rungs. Other decorations, such as plumes, horse tails and patriotic and Islamic emblems

also adorned the instrument. On the march, it rose proud of the soldiers' heads and the carrier would shake it, twist it and bounce it at his feet to accentuate the rhythm of the march.

These military bands included triangles and bass drums since at least the 16th century and

ARM POWER WAS NEEDED FOR THE CHINESE PAVILION BEFORE THE INTRODUCTION OF A HANDLE AND RATCHET DEVICE TO SHAKE THE BELLS.

their sound struck terror into the populations being invaded by the Turks. Mozart, in his opera *Die Entführung aus dem Serail* (1782), Haydn in his Symphony No. 100, 'Military' (1794), and Beethoven in his Symphony No. 9, 'Choral' (1823), are said to have intended the Turkish crescent to be used, but that part is almost invariably taken by triangle, the real thing hardly to be expected as part of a modern orchestra's equipment. Berlioz called for four of them (*pavillon chinois*) in his *Symphonie funèbre et triomphale* (1840).

cheap one, the *hydraulis* nevertheless attracted some worthies, and three centuries after it was invented a model so fascinated Emperor Nero that it distracted him from more important matters – such as how to meet an imminent attack from the Gauls. His military staff were instead regaled with a detailed description of the workings of Nero's new *hydraulis*.

Koororohuu

A simple child's toy of the New Zealand Maori. A disc-shaped piece of thin wood or other suitable material is threaded with string through two holes near the centre. By swinging the toy with a circular motion to 'wind it up', then pulling the two ends of the string, a whirring noise is created. Evidence suggests that such toys are by no means restricted to New Zealand.

Handbells

Today we take this term to mean bells which have been graded in size and pitch and played by a 'circle' or 'choir' of players, each responsible for two or four bells. In ancient China, perhaps as much as two millennia before Christ, small bells existed, but there is no evidence that 'circles' of players were organized. Rather, the bells would have been attached to a frame for striking by one or two players. (This use is mentioned under Banged Instruments; it may have contributed to the evolution of the Far Eastern *gamelan* ensembles, see page 219.)

Handbells today are usually shaken by a handle (though occasionally they are lightly struck) and therefore are a species of rattle which, instead of having many loose objects inside, has one captive clapper that swings against the inside of the body when the bell is shaken. Well disciplined circles of players, their bells resting on a covered table before them when not in use, can perform arrangements of most music with considerable skill. It has been essentially an English art since the 17th century but groups of handbell ringers are now active in other countries, particularly in North America.

THE CHINESE ART OF HANDBELL RINGING HAS LARGELY DIED OUT. THIS ILLUSTRATION OF A GROUP OF CEREMONIAL PLAYERS DATES FROM 1846.

Hydraulis

In Greek, *hydro* + *aulos* = water-pipe, though it is really a water-organ. Its invention can be put at 246 BC, when Ctesibius, an Alexandrian engineer who achieved fame for his inventions of the crossbow and the pneumatic catapult, constructed this complicated musical instrument. He took a water tank, a cistern, an air chest, bellows and a set of pipes and arranged them in such a way that a keyboard could produce a tune. A submerged bell in the water tank contained both air and water, the air being supplied by the bellows. A balance was struck between pressure and weight to ensure a steady supply of air to the air chest and thence to the pipes.

Hardly a portable instrument, or a

Lyra Organizzata

This seems to have been an Italian invention of the 1780s or earlier. It was a hurdy-gurdy to which had been added a system of pipes, and the keys of the hurdy-gurdy also controlled the airflow to the pipes.

Like the hurdy-gurdy, a handle turned the circular bow under the strings and the player's left hand operated the keys. It is not easy to imagine the sound such a hybrid instrument produced, but when the King of Naples ordered some concertos for two *lyrae organizzate* from Joseph Haydn in 1786,

AN EGYPTIAN *SISTRUM* FROM THE 8TH CENTURY BC. THIS TYPE OF RATTLE EXISTED IN MANY DIFFERENT DESIGNS, OFTEN WITH A FIGURINE ON THE FRAME.

The common football rattle is a ratchet device in which wooden tongues are sprung and released by a cogwheel as the rattle is whirled. The tongues in older examples are sometimes of metal, for such rattles were used as bird scares and as warnings of flood, attack, or fire: their voice had to be heard over wide areas. William Walton called for a wooden rattle, or ratchet, in his *Façade* Suite (1926), and the toy version was used in Leopold Mozart's *Cassatio* in G (1765), parts of which have been popularized as the 'Toy Symphony'.

✄ *Wind-chimes*

Like the Aeolian harp, wind-chimes are played by the wind. They consist of bells of various sizes which are hung outside or in a window from a frame by cords of different lengths, and allowed to make contact with each other as they swing in the breeze. A charming instrument of no musical value, its gentle sounds are said to calm even the most frayed of nerves. 𝄡

he instructed that the composer should regard the instrument as sounding like an oboe, but with extremely limited tonal possibilities. As well as Haydn, Ignaz Pleyel, a Haydn pupil, and Joseph Sterkel wrote for the instrument, but their works are lost. Pleyel, much given to rearranging his own music, possibly recycled his for other instruments; Sterkel may have done the same for his instrument, the piano.

✄ *Rattle*

A rattle is a percussion instrument which is not always 'banged', so could not find a place in the appropriate section above. Any device with hard, loose components, either within a closed vessel or attached outside a frame of some kind, may be regarded as a rattle. The hard pellets might be beads, beans, pebbles, stones, seeds (whole dried seed pods sometimes serve), or buttons. The vessel might be of wood, ceramic, basketwork,

🎼 A NIGERIAN PLAQUE DATING PROBA-
BLY FROM THE LATE 17TH CENTURY
SHOWING A CHIEF WITH AN ATTEN-
DANT HOLDING A CALABASH RATTLE.

metal, gourd, plastic or any other hard substance. The egg-shaped *maracas* familiar in Latin American bands are of prehistoric origin and wide distribution, and they may be 'banged' on occasion. In his 'Jeremiah' Symphony, (1942) for instance, Leonard Bernstein has them banged against a drum. Dance band percussionists will hit them into the palm of the hand to emphasize a rhythm. In so-called 'external' rattles, the pebbles, teeth, bells, or whatever, are attached to a frame which might take the form of a rigid wooden or metal structure of virtually any shape, or a strap to be shaken rhythmically. The ancient Egyptian *sistrum* consisted of a frame of metal with a handle; within the frame were several cross-pieces along which slid metal disc jingles which struck the frame as the *sistrum* was shaken.

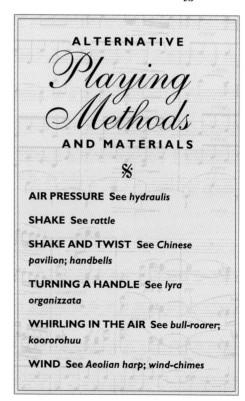

ALTERNATIVE

Playing Methods

AND MATERIALS

✄

AIR PRESSURE See *hydraulis*

SHAKE See *rattle*

SHAKE AND TWIST See *Chinese pavilion; handbells*

TURNING A HANDLE See *lyra organizzata*

WHIRLING IN THE AIR See *bull-roarer; koororohuu*

WIND See *Aeolian harp; wind-chimes*

SCALES, PITCHES & NOTATION

CLEFS

The treble clef, or G clef, is indicated by an ornate letter G, the point of which, now disappeared, used to rest on the line representing G, the second line up.

The tenor clef, or C clef, is indicated by a vestigial letter C, the left-facing arrow head lying on the line representing C.

The bass clef, or F clef, is indicated by all that remains of a cursive F, the two horizontal bars, now reduced to dots, lying either side of the line representing F.

TABLE OF PITCHES

In order to indicate the pitches of notes in print without resorting to music type, a number of alphabetic systems have been invented. The most widely used is based on upper and lower case letters in conjunction with apostrophes to show which pitch is meant. Thus, lower case *c* with one apostrophe (*c'*) identifies middle C, *E flat'* is the flattened note below the fourth line under the bass clef, *d'''* lies above the second line over the treble clef, and so on.

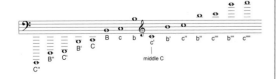

Extreme ranges of orchestral instruments

WOODWIND

piccolo   flute   oboe

clarinet in B flat   clarinet in A   bassoon

BRASS

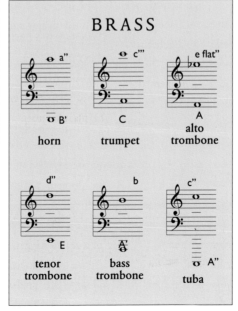

horn   trumpet   alto trombone

tenor trombone   bass trombone   tuba

PERCUSSION

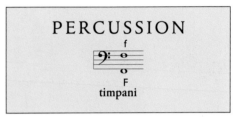

timpani

STRINGS

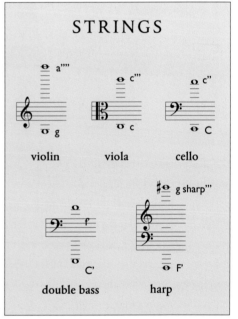

violin   viola   cello

double bass   harp

KEYBOARD

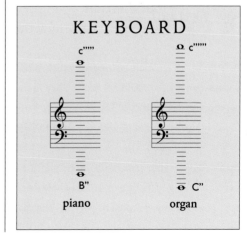

piano   organ

Key Signatures

To indicate the key of a work the composer places a 'key signature' at the beginning of the music. The 'sharp' and 'flat' signs show the notes to be appropriately modified for that key and apply until cancelled with 'natural' signs or the piece ends.

natural ♮   sharp ♯   flat ♭

Open keys:
C major A minor (no sharps or flats)

Sharp keys:
G major E minor (sharpened F)

D major B minor (sharpened F and C)

A major F sharp minor (sharpened F, C and G)

E major C sharp minor (sharpened F, C, G and D)

B major G sharp minor (sharpened F, C, G, D and A)

F sharp major D sharp minor (sharpened F, C, G, D, A and E)

C sharp major A sharp minor (sharpened F, C, G, D, A, E and B)

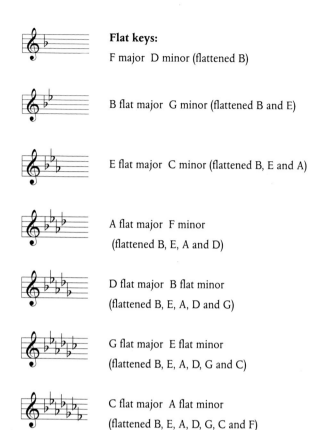

Flat keys:
F major D minor (flattened B)

B flat major G minor (flattened B and E)

E flat major C minor (flattened B, E and A)

A flat major F minor
(flattened B, E, A and D)

D flat major B flat minor
(flattened B, E, A, D and G)

G flat major E flat minor
(flattened B, E, A, D, G and C)

C flat major A flat minor
(flattened B, E, A, D, G, C and F)

Abbreviations

Composers in a hurry (and few were not) employed a kind of musical shorthand that could be read by their copyists, who then wrote out the composer's requirements in full. A few of these abbreviations are shown here, together with the 'plain language' version:

Written

To be played

INDEX

Page numbers in **bold** refer to major references; those in *italics* to illustrations.

A

Abbado, Claudio (1933-), 179
Abel, C F (1723-87), 29, 50
Academy of Ancient Music
    (18th C), 173
Academy of Ancient Music
    (20th C), 179
accordion, *138*, 138
Adam de la Hale (c.1250-c.1288?),
    17
adapu, 216
Aeolian harp, 139, *228*, 228, 231
Afghanistan, 200*ff*
Africa, 15, 192-231 *passim*
ageng, 219
Agricola, M (1486-1556), 20, 49,
    62, 73
Aguardo, D (1784-1849), 82
a'guz, 208
Akiyama, K (1929-), 192
ala Bohemica, 216
alal, 216
Alaska, 220
Albania, 187, 218
Albéniz, I (1860-1909), 110
Albrechtsberger, J (1736-1809),
    68, 203
Alcaeus (611-c580 BC), 213
Algeria, 198
Ali, 211
Alkan, C-V (1813-88), 121, 135,
    140
Allegri String Quartet, *160*
Almenräder, C (1786-1843), 30
Alonso, Sydney, (fl.1970s-80s) 155
Alpha Syntauri, 155
Alphorn; Alpenhorn, *184*, 184, 193
al'ud, 208, 210
Amadinda Percussion Group, 105
Amat, J C (c.1572-1642), 79
America, Latin, 216, 231
    South, 190, 204, 216
American Catgut Society, 86
American Indians, 205, 220
Ampico, 141
Amsterdam (Royal)
    Concertgebouw Orch, 169,
    171, 179
ananda lahari, 213
anata, *184*, 184, 190
Anaxemor (1st C BC), 207
Anderson, Leroy (1908-75), 110*f*
angklung, 219
Antheil, George (1900-59), 89
Antill, John (1904-86), 228
anvil, 215, 216
Apollo, 206
Appleton, Jon (1939-), 155
apunga, 191
Arabia, 91, 199*ff*

Archipoeta (c.1130-1165+), 17
arco enarmonico, 145
Argentina, 190*ff*
Argyle and Sutherland
    Highlanders, *97*
Aristos (3rd C BC), 159
Aristoxenus (fl.375-360 BC), 14
Armenia, 192, 209, 218
Armstrong, Louis (1900-71), 41,
    71, 124, 159
Arne, M (c.1741-86), 203
Arne, T (1710-78), 135
Arnold, Malcolm (1921-), 78, 80,
    81, 203
arpeggione, 86
arpicimbalo, 118
Arrau, Claudio (1903-91), 125
Ashkenazy, Vladimir (1937-), 125
askaulos, 187
askomandoura, 192
Atacamá Desert, 188, 190
Attaignant, P (c.1494-c1552), 21
atumpan, 216
atungblan, 216
Auer, Leopold (1845-1930), 55
aulos, 13, 22, 184, *185*
Auric, George (1899-1983), 111
Australia, 196*ff*
Austria, 159
Ayres, Ray , *107*
Aztec, *226*, 226

B

Babbitt, Milton (1916-), 149, *152*,
    154
Babcock, Alpheus, 122
Babell, W (c1690-1723), 160
Babylon, 76, 90
Bach, C P E (1714-88), 75, 113,
    117, 118, 125, 140, 161,
    168, 180
Bach, J C (1735-81), 27, 50, 119,
    121, 161
Bach, J S (1685-1750), 21, 23, 42,
    61, 65, 118, 119, 128, 131,
    136, 137, 173
    as conductor, 169
    bass viol sonatas, 50
    Brandenburg Concerti, 36, 38,
        39, 50, 59, 86
    Cantatas, 30, 86, 179
    Cello Solo Suites, 66, 67, 86
    Christmas Oratorio, 93
    Es ist genug, 53
    Flute Sonatas, 161
    Italian Concerto, 114,
    Klavier-Ubung, 121,
    Mass in B minor, 134
    Oboe Concerto, 25
    Organ works, 135
    St John Passion, 84

    St Matthew Passion, 23, 173
    Violin Sonatas, 161
    Well-tempered Clavier, 117
Bach, W F (1710-84), 161
Backers, Americus, 119
Badings, Henk (1907-87), 193
bag-hornpipe, 192
baglama, 204
bagpipes, 15, *128*, *180*, 185-7, *186*,
    193,
balag, 216
Balakirev, Mily (1837-1910), 203
balalaika, 203, *204*, 204
Balearic Islands, 187
Bali, 218, 224
Balkans, 27, 100, 190*ff*
bandola, 209
bandore, 204
Bangladesh, 190, 213, 222
banjo, 83, *203*, 203, 204
banjulele, 204
banza, banzer, 204
Barber, Chris (1930-), 159
Barbieri, 129
Barbirolli, Sir John (1899-1970),
    45, 45, 169
Barenboim, Daniel (1942 -), *67*,
    169, 171
Barre, M (1675-1743), 21, 160
barrel organ, 129, *139*
barrel piano, 138
Bartók, Béla (1881-1945), 31, 57,
    59, 61, 89, 93, 161
baryton, **84**, *84*, *195*, 195
Basle Chamber Orch, 165
Bashmet, Yuri (1953-), 61
Basie, Count (1904-84), 124, 159
bass drum, *97, 98*, 100, 100*ff*, *101*,
    102
bass horn, 188
basso continuo - see continuo
bassoon, 18, *30*, 30*f*, 175, 177
Baton, C (?-1754 +), 198
Bavarian Radio Sym Orch, 171
bayan, 91, 224
Bayreuth, 170, 171
baz, 216
BBC Sym Orch, 171
Beatles, The, 210
Beatriz, Countess of Dia
    (fl.1160-?1200), 17
Bechet, Sidney (1897-1959), *28*, 33
Bechstein, 123
Bedford, David (1937-), 110, 193
Beecham, Sir Thomas
    (1879-1961), 42, 169, 170
Beecham Sym Orch, 171
Beethoven, Ludwig van
    (1770-1827), 102, 103,
    118-128 *passim*
    as conductor, 168*f*
    Battle Symphony, 99, 101
    Chamber works, 21, 36, 63, 65,

    66, 71, 86, 160*f*
    concertos, 53, 65
    Missa Solemnis, 134
    Piano Sonatas, 118
    Prometheus, 75
    Ruins of Athens, 101
    Symphonies, 19, 25, 43, 59, 65,
        93, 101, 160, 168, 179, 229
Beiderbecke, Bix (1903-31), 41
Beinum, Eduard van (1901-59),
    169
Béjart, Maurice (1927-), 148
Belar, Herbert, 151
Bell, A G (1847-1922), 142
Bell Telephone Labs, 156
bell bars, 110
bells, 13, 107, *110*, 110, 215, 224,
    230, 230
bendir, 216
Benevente, Marquis de, 203
Benjamin, George (1960-), 151
Bennett, W S (1816-75), 173
Benoist, F (1794-1878), 135
Berberian, Cathy, (1925-83), 148
Berg, A (1885-1935), 42, 53, 171
Berio, Luciano (1925-), 21, 25,
    148, 151, 154
Berkeley, Lennox (1903-89), 81
Berlin Opera, 171
Berlin Phil Orch, 92, 169, 170
Berlin Singakademie, 173
Berliner, Emile (1851-1929), 142
Berlioz, LH (1803-69), 25, 29, 38,
    41, 47, 59, 69, 75, 78, *95*,
    95, 102, 103, 104, 125,
    134, 137, 140, 167,
    168, 193, 229
Bermudo, Juan (c.1510-c.1565), 79
Bernart de Ventadorn (1125-95),
    17
Bernstein, Leonard (1918-90),
    169, 231
Bertoli, G A (fl.c.1639-43), 30
Berwald, F A (1796-1868), 161
Betts, J (1755-1823), 63
Beyer, Robert (1901-), 149
Biber, H (1644-1704), 52
Bible, 14, 72, 76
bible organ, 192
Big Bands, 159
bin, 187, *211*
biniou, 187
bird lure, 13
bird scare, 110
birimbao, 204
Birtwistle, Sir Harrison (1934-), 32
biwa, *202*
Bizet, G (1838-75), 32, 104, 215
black pudding, 188
Black Sea, 198
bladder-pipe, 188
Blades, James (1901-), *98*, 105,
    110

Blanchet family, 114
Blâterfife, 187
Blinder, Naoum (fl.1930s), 57
Blondel de Nesle (c.1155/60 - ?),
    17
Blühmel, F (fl.c.1818), 37, 40, 44
Blüthner, 123
Boccherini, L (1743-1805), 63, 65,
    66, 66, **161**, 203
Boccioni, U (1882-1916), *144*
Bochsa, R-N-C (1789-1856), 73
bock, 187
Boehm, T (1793-1881), 19, *20*,
    22*ff*, 143
Boethius, Anicus (c480-c524), 128
Bohemia, 187, 216
Böhm, Karl (1894-1981), 169
Boieldieu, F (1775-1834), 75
Bolivia, 190*ff*
bomba, 190
bombarde, 187
bombo, 216
bonang barung, 219
Bononcini, A M (1677-1726),
    203
boo(bam), 216
Borisovsky, Vadim, 61
Borodin, A (1833-87), 161
Bösendorfer, 119, 123, 126
Boston Sym Orch, 70, 169, 171
Bottesini, G (1821-89), 70
bottle, 192
Boulez, Pierre (1925-), 21, 105,
    146-8 *passim*, 151, 169
Boult, Sir Adrian (1889-1983),
    169
Bourgeois, Derek (1941-), 44
bouteillephone, 192
bow, *194*, 194
    cello, 54-5, 54*f*, 63
    hunter's, *9*, 10, 11, *183*, 213
    mouth, 11, 13
    viola, *54*
    violin, *51*, 54
Brahms, J (1833-97), 55, 94, 126,
    179
    Chamber works, 29, 61, 66,
        160, 161
    Concertos, 36, 53, 65
    German Requiem, 134
    Organ works, 137
    Paganini Variations, 55
    Symphonies, 66, 171
Brain, Aubrey (1893-1955), 37
Brain, Dennis (1921-57), 37
brake drum, 215, 216
Brazil, 199, 204
Bream, Julian (1933-), *78*, 78, 81,
    209
Brendel, Alfred (1931-), 123, 135
Brian, Havergal (1876-1972), 6,
    110, **164**